# Nixon's Economy

# Nixon's Economy

## Booms, Busts, Dollars, and Votes

Allen J. Matusow

University Press of Kansas

© 1998 by the University Press of Kansas
All rights reserved

Published by the University Press of Kansas (Lawrence, Kansas 66049), which
was organized by the Kansas Board of Regents and is operated and funded by
Emporia State University, Fort Hays State University, Kansas State University,
Pittsburg State University, the University of Kansas, and Wichita State
University

Library of Congress Cataloging-in-Publication Data
Matusow, Allen J.
    Nixon's economy : booms, busts, dollars, and votes / Allen J.
Matusow.
        p.   cm.
    Includes index.
    ISBN 0-7006-0888-5 (alk. paper)
        1. Nixon, Richard M. (Richard Milhous), 1913-    .  2. United States —
    Economic policy — 1961–1971.   3. United States — Economic policy —
    1971–1981.   I. Title.
    HC106.6.M383    1998
    338.973′009′047 — dc21                                                    97-49995

British Library Cataloguing in Publication Data is available.

Printed in the United States of America

10   9   8   7   6   5   4   3   2

The paper used in this publication meets the minimum requirements of the
American National Standard for Permanence of Paper for Printed Library
Materials Z39.48-1984.

*To my children: Eric, Adam, Cathy, and Joe*

# CONTENTS

# ACKNOWLEDGMENTS

The papers at the Nixon Presidential Materials Project at the National Archives provided a rich source for recreating this history. The papers of all modern presidents provide a full picture of the flow of ideas, suggestions, and information into the Oval Office. But the evidence of the president's response is seldom direct. At the outset of this presidency, Nixon, through Haldeman, instituted procedures designed to assure that notes would be taken at the meetings he attended. In addition, Ehrlichman and Haldeman took handwritten notes of their conversations with Nixon, and Haldeman kept a diary of their daily encounters. As the White House tapes gradually come to light, historians of the Nixon administration will even eavesdrop on the living past. Because of this record, knowledge of how economic policy was made and how it was implemented in this presidency may be greater than in any other, past or future. The resulting case study reveals above all how a president obsessed by politics managed the nation's economy to win the race he lived to run.

I want to thank two archivists whose departure from the Nixon Project at the National Archives has been a serious loss to scholars — Joan Howard and Scott Parham. Thanks, too, to my intrepid typist, Connie Coleman; to my graduate assistant, Susan Hannsen; to Barbara Matusow, Peter Mieszkowski, and Alan Grob for reading a draft of the manuscript; and to Judith Brown, Dean of Humanities at Rice University, for her support. Above all, I am grateful to my wife for her patience and to my children, whose adventures provided me welcome diversion during the preparation of this book.

# ABBREVIATIONS

## Text

| | |
|---|---|
| AFL-CIO | American Federation of Labor and Congress of Industrial Organizations |
| BLS | Bureau of Labor Statistics |
| CEA | Council of Economic Advisers |
| CIEP | Council for International Economic Policy |
| COLC | Cost of Living Council |
| CPI | Consumer Price Index |
| EEC | European Economic Community |
| FEO | Federal Energy Office |
| FOMC | Federal Open Market Committee |
| FY | fiscal year, e.g., FY 73 |
| GM | General Motors |
| GNP | gross national product |
| NAACP | National Association for the Advancement of Colored People |
| NEP | New Economic Policy |
| NLF | National Liberation Front (Viet Cong government in South Vietnam) |
| OMB | Office of Management and Budget |
| U.N. | United Nations |
| VAT | Value-Added Tax |
| VFW | Veterans of Foreign Wars |

## Notes

| | |
|---|---|
| Ag | Agriculture |
| BE | Business and Economic |
| CEA | Council of Economic Advisers |
| CF | Confidential Files |
| Chron | Chronological |
| COLC | Cost of Living Council |

| | |
|---|---|
| Cong Rec | Congressional Record |
| DOD | Department of Defense |
| DOE | Department of Energy |
| DOL | Department of Labor |
| E-Notes | Handwritten notes of John D. Ehrlichman |
| EPO | Energy Policy Office |
| FEA | Federal Energy Administration |
| FEO | Federal Energy Office |
| FG | Federal Government |
| FI | Finance |
| FOMC | Federal Open Market Committee |
| H-Notes | Handwritten notes of H. R. Haldeman |
| NA | National Archives |
| NPMP | Nixon Papers and Materials Project |
| OMB | Office of Management and Budget |
| POF | President's Office Files |
| Pub Paps | Public Papers of the Presidents; Richard Nixon |
| RG | Record Group |
| SMOF | Staff Members and Office Files |
| SP | Speech |
| TA | Trade |
| UT | Utilities |
| WHCF | White House Central Files |
| WHSF | White House Special Files |

# INTRODUCTION

"He is like a race horse specially trained to run a particular race and no good for pulling wagons," John Ehrlichman once said of Richard Nixon. "He's for running the race to be President, and that's what he lived for."[1] This partial truth provides the clue for understanding an otherwise enigmatic presidency. During the two decades before Nixon took office, he was perhaps the most scrutinized man in public life. Friend and foe alike believed that they knew him. He was a Republican partisan, a staunch anticommunist, an opponent of an expansive welfare state, and he doubtless always would be. As president, Nixon was none of these things, or at least not often and not consistently. Disdainful of routine administration and unfettered by the past, Nixon considered himself a bold strategic thinker capable of altering history. His overriding purpose as president was to achieve a realignment of political parties in the United States, the first such realignment, if it happened, since the Great Depression. In his conduct of domestic policy and management of the U.S. economy, politics provided whatever consistency there was and dissolved the apparent contradictions.

The Democrats, still the majority party, had made possible the project of realignment by coming apart during the 1960s on issues of war, race, and culture. George Wallace taught Nixon how he might pick up the pieces by exploiting the racial fears and cultural resentments of white southerners and northern blue-collar workers. Nixon's intention was to unite Wallace-leaning Democrats with conservative Republicans to create, not a new Republican majority, but something he called simply the New Majority — or sometimes the Silent Majority. In some moods he even contemplated the formation of a new party altogether. During one White House conversation, summarized by H. R. Haldeman in his diary, Nixon emphasized the "need to build our own new coalition based on Silent Majority, blue-collar Catholic, Poles, Italians, Irish. No promise with Jews and Negroes. Appeal not hard right-wing, Bircher, or anti-Communist."[2] He neglected to men-

---

[1] Ehrlichman interview in Kenneth W. Thompson, ed., *The Nixon Presidency* (1987), 139.
[2] *The Haldeman Diaries* (CD-ROM), Jan. 8, 1970.

tion the white South, which was a given. Stitching together constituencies so diverse would not be easy, but because Nixon was a political technician to whom ideologies and beliefs meant little, he was well-suited to the task.

If Nixon lacked convictions, he did have a fair stock of inclinations and prejudices relevant to the politics he would practice as president. Liberals who characterized him as the servant of corporate interests did not understand the man. "Nothing's smaller than a big businessman," he once said to Haldeman.[3] Nixon needed corporate support, of course, and was prepared to seek it, but the care and feeding of corporations was not among his highest priorities, and corporations did not fare particularly well during his presidency. "My source of strength," he once said, "was more Main Street than Wall Street."[4] The real hero of his political economy rather resembled his father, Frank Nixon, who had overcome hard times to enjoy modest success as the proprietor of a gas station–grocery store in East Whittier, California.[5] When Richard Nixon privately disdained international bankers or denounced Jewish-owned grocery chains, he was his father's son.

If Nixon disliked businessmen, he hated members of the Eastern seaboard elite. As a senior in law school at Duke in 1937, Nixon had visited New York City to seek a job in a prestigious law firm, only to suffer bitter rejection. Years of living on the fringes of the elite only deepened his estrangement. In the president's demonology, Ivy League professors, publishers of the major dailies, big-name columnists and commentators, New York bankers, and upper-class socialites who gave parties in Georgetown — the nation's leadership class — had betrayed their responsibilities during the sixties. They had succumbed to anti-Americanism and had failed the test of Vietnam. They had pampered the spoiled children who were paralyzing the universities and made excuses for the black rioters in the ghetto. During one White House meeting Nixon delivered a remarkable soliloquy — dutifully noted by Haldeman — offering his version of the class struggle:

> In this period of our history, the leaders and the educated class are decadent. Whenever you ask for patriotic support, they all run away: the college types, the professors, the elite, etc. So he con-

---

[3] H. R. Haldeman, Notes of Conversations with the President, Mar. 14, 1969, Haldeman: SMOF, NA (hereafter referred to as H-Notes).

[4] Nixon quoted in Herbert S. Parmet, *Richard Nixon and His America*, 2d rev. ed. (1984), 138.

[5] Roger Morris, *Richard Milhous Nixon* (1990), 52, 71–72, 77–79, 137–138.

cludes the more a person is educated, he becomes brighter in the head and weaker in the spine. When you have to call on the nation to be strong—on such things as drugs, crime, defense . . . the educated people and the leader class no longer have any character and you can't count on them. We can only turn for support to the noneducated people.[6]

Nixon went on to say that the people with character were the labor leaders. "They're short-sighted, partisan, hate Nixon personally," he said. But they had guts. He meant especially George Meany, the Irish-Catholic ex-plumber and president of the AFL-CIO labor federation whose financial and organizational support of Hubert Humphrey in the 1968 election nearly cost Nixon the presidency. But Meany's attachment to the Democratic party had grown weaker as it drifted toward the left through the 1960s. An old-fashioned patriot who backed the war in Vietnam, Meany was both a defender of the welfare state and a cultural conservative. "When I was a plumber, it never occoid to me to have niggers in the union," Meany said—at least as Nixon quoted him with obvious relish in a White House conversation.[7] Meany loomed as the pivotal figure in Nixon's scheme for realignment. If he could secure an alliance with Meany and lock up labor, the New Majority would be his. Nixon courted no businessman, or even all of them together, as assiduously as he courted the crusty Democrat who headed organized labor.

Nixon's domestic policies were a corollary of the politics of realignment. To construct his New Majority and win big in 1972, he aimed to occupy the center, defined not as some fixed point on the ideological spectrum but by the prevailing mood of the two-thirds of the country he called the "constituency of uneducated people."[8] That meant appealing above all to blue-collar Democrats in political transition, still appreciative of benevolent government but conservative on the so-called Social Issue— race, crime, radical youth, cultural change. Nixon wooed this constituency, as the Democrats could not, by denouncing drugs, pornography, campus violence, and ghetto rioters. Playing the race card, he temporarily slowed down school desegregation in the South and opposed busing with all the

---

[6] *Haldeman Diaries*, July 21, 1971.

[7] J. D. Ehrlichman, Notes of Conversations with the President, Dec. 23, 1969, Ehrlichman: SMOF, NA (hereafter referred to as E-Notes).

[8] *Haldeman Diaries*, July 21, 1971.

fervor of George Wallace himself. For Catholics, he threw in opposition to abortion and support for parochial schools.

On issues of welfare and quality of life, Nixon strived to seem unlike the gray Republican nay-sayers of so many defeats in days past, but rather the enlightened centrist — a conservative man of liberal views, not too liberal and not too conservative — judiciously expanding the reach of government to benefit his constituents and solve the nation's problems. "Very few initiatives will be truly in the center," Ehrlichman wrote Nixon, summarizing the strategy. "They will fall on one side or the other. Our domestic policy job . . . [is] to insure some balance. As we can, consistent with the Social Issue concept, we will try to co-opt the opposition's issues . . . if the political cost is not too great."[9] Balance was everything. Nixon vastly expanded aid to the states for worthy social purposes but attempted to collapse this aid into block grants to strengthen state and local governments. He sponsored important environmental legislation but not at the expense of jobs. He proposed welfare reform to provide a guaranteed income for the poor who worked but required work of poor recipients who did not. To help low-income families, he expanded the food-stamp program and proposed national health insurance. To help workers, he sponsored legislation to upgrade safety in the workplace. To help both working-class and middle-income voters, he presided over a vast expansion of the social security system. The zigs and zags of policy gave the appearance of ideological confusion. Politics provided the coherence, and because politics was the point, Nixon cared more about the symbolism of his program — how it played in Peoria — than in actually passing it.

Economic policy, which is the subject of this book, was at the outset hardly one of Nixon's main concerns. Like any president, he considered prosperity a prerequisite of success and knew that unemployment lost incumbents votes, even elections. If the good times of the sixties had kept on rolling, as he early assumed they would, Nixon would have gladly delegated supervision of the economy to a subordinate strong enough to manage it and wise enough not to pester him with issues he found both boring and baffling. When the economy faltered toward the end of 1969, the subject became not economics but political economy, and Nixon had no choice but to pay attention. Soon Nixon was confronting recession, inflation, record-high interest rates, credit crunches, stock market collapse, loss of

---

[9] Ehrlichman for President, Oct. 21, 1970, President's Handwriting file, POF.

dominance in the global economy, and the fall of the dollar. Because of the stakes, Nixon found himself spending more time on the economy than any other domestic issue.[10] Somehow he had to make the economy hum by 1972 or face likely defeat in his quest for reelection. To the extent possible, he would pursue prosperity by means consistent with fashioning a New Majority. If he had to, Nixon was prepared to sacrifice good relations with George Meany to escape the quagmire of economic troubles in which he had become ensnared.

Desperate to stop the economy from wrecking his presidency, Nixon appointed as his secretary of the treasury in February 1971 a Texas Democrat and his co-conspirator in the plot to build the New Majority, John Connally. Nixon was not one of the luckier presidents, but in August of that year, just in time, Connally assembled an astonishing package of economic initiatives that contradicted everything Nixon was supposed to believe but that helped reassert his economic leadership and reclaim the Economic Issue. Connally's package — or parts of it — initially infuriated Meany and precipitated open warfare between organized labor and the administration. But, in 1972, everything, even the economy, worked out for Richard Nixon. That year he made peace with Meany, carried both the labor vote and the white South, and assembled an electoral majority that closely approximated the New Majority of his dreams.

After that everything went wrong. As Watergate was closing in, Nixon had to confront worldwide food shortages, an unprecedented energy crisis, double-digit inflation, and the worst recession of the postwar years. Economic issues, which he always considered regrettable distractions from his main purposes, were back again, this time more dangerous to the health of the nation and to his own prospects than before. Though Nixon cast about for some economic magic to rescue him, as Connally's magic had rescued him in the first term, there was none. Political scandal combined with economic disorder to discredit his leadership, derail his plans for cementing the New Majority, and bring down his presidency in ruins. The economy is seldom the stuff of high political drama, but it assuredly was in the Nixon years.

Attracted by the boldness of Nixon's foreign policy and the debacle of Watergate, historians have largely ignored the role of the economic policy of his administration. My intention is to correct this oversight. Nixon

---

[10] John Ehrlichman, *Witness to Power* (1982), 89.

happened to occupy the presidency at the moment when the postwar boom ground to a permanent halt. He was forced to deal with economic traumas more severe than anything known since the Great Depression. He tried and then discarded all the fashionable economic remedies of his time, unintentionally exposing the poverty of economic theory. He spent countless hours pondering how to prevent the economy from defeating him, how to manipulate foreign trade and monetary issues to woo labor, how to appease the voters with doubtful policies he himself did not believe in, while keeping his conservative base intact. Narrow self-interest usually served as his compass. Once, during the last months of his tenure, he eschewed political advantage for pure principle. The economic policies he pursued had important consequences not only for his own time but for long after. Events of his tenure subsequently inspired the most far-reaching reassessment of economic policy in a generation, preparing the way for Ronald Reagan, a denouement that Nixon had hardly intended. No one, in short, can understand this presidency or attempt its assessment without first reckoning with the economic crises of the period and Nixon's lurching responses. I hope this book provides a crucial piece, too long missing, for solving the puzzle of a pivotal presidency.

# Chapter 1

# Nixon and the Fed

---

## I

When Richard Nixon took the oath of office at the Capitol on January 20, 1969, he placed his hand on the family Bible at Isaiah 2:4: "They shall beat their swords into plowshares and their spears into pruning hooks."[1] The nation was in crisis, Nixon said in his Inaugural Address. "We find ourselves rich in goods, but ragged in spirit . . . We are caught in war, wanting peace. We are torn by division, wanting unity." The answer to these problems could be found in "little things," he said. "To lower our voices would be a little thing."[2] Afterward, at Twelfth Street on the parade route back to the White House, the president's car moved through a hail of sticks, stones, and beer cans, as demonstrators chanted "Ho, Ho, Ho Chi Minh, the NLF is going to win."[3] To quiet the shouting, as Nixon well knew, he would have to end the war in Vietnam.

Ehrlichman's remark that Nixon lived to run for president was a partial truth because it applied to the home front only. On the world scene, Nixon aspired to be a statesman, a bold strategist in the manner of Churchill and de Gaulle, capable of altering history. He believed that the era of the Cold War, dominated by the two superpowers, had given way to a multipolar world in which the relative strength of the United States was declining. To preserve as much of the U.S. position as he could, Nixon hoped to move relations with the Soviets from competition to cooperation by exploiting the Sino-Soviet split. No domestic constituency pressed this policy on Nixon. No one except a few White House confidants knew what he intended to do. Nixon calculated the effects of his every foreign move on domestic politics, of course, and saw peace as a winning issue in the next

---

[1] RN: The Memoirs of Richard Nixon (1978), 366.
[2] Public Papers of the Presidents of the United States: Richard Nixon (hereafter referred to as Pub Paps RN) 1969, 2.
[3] RN: Memoirs, 366.

election. But he shaped his foreign policy not to court the voters; he meant to rally the voters to support his foreign policy. Everything hinged on Vietnam. He could not govern effectively at home unless he ended the war, and he believed that he could not conduct a credible foreign policy unless he ended the war with honor. In 1969, therefore, Vietnam dominated Nixon's presidency.

At the start, Nixon believed that the war would be over within a year. To end it, he would use the carrot and, if necessary, a stick. The carrot would be peace terms so fair that the enemy might actually accept them. If the enemy balked, the stick would be the threat, and perhaps even the reality, of a savage blow to force reconsideration.[4] On May 14, Nixon stated his peace terms: mutual withdrawal of U.S. and North Vietnamese troops from South Vietnam and internationally supervised free elections.[5] Hanoi did not respond. Why should it? On June 8, on the island of Midway where he had gone to confer with President Nguyen Van Thieu of South Vietnam, Nixon unveiled the policy of Vietnamization — the phased withdrawal of U.S. troops and their replacement by South Vietnamese forces.[6] All Hanoi had to do was wait it out.

In Paris on August 4 for a secret meeting with North Vietnamese emissaries, Henry Kissinger, the president's national security adviser, delivered a warning. "I have been asked to tell you in all solemnity, that if by November 1 no major progress has been made toward a solution, we will be compelled — with great reluctance — to take measures of the greatest consequences." The North Vietnamese replied by demanding that the United States withdraw from the South unilaterally and overthrow the Thieu regime.[7] Meanwhile, in Washington, staff work for a savage blow, code-named Duck Hook, was complete. Duck Hook included bombing Hanoi, mining Haiphong harbor, bombing dikes to cause flooding, invading North Vietnam by ground, and possibly undertaking nuclear strikes along the Ho Chi Minh trail, the supply route into South Vietnam.[8]

Duck Hook never happened. By fall, as students returned to the universities and Congressmen to the capital, peace hopes were receding, antiwar sentiment was intensifying, and Johnson's war had become Nixon's war.

---

[4] H. R. Haldeman, *The Ends of Power* (1978), 82–83.

[5] *Pub Paps RN 1969*, 369–375.

[6] Ibid., 443–444.

[7] *RN: Memoirs*, 396.

[8] Seymour M. Hersh, *The Price of Power: Kissinger in the Nixon White House* (1983), 120.

On October 15, 1969, a quarter-million antiwar protesters, joined by un-numbered thousands on campuses and city streets throughout America, demonstrated in Washington for the Vietnam Moratorium. Though the protesters did not know it, their witness forced Nixon to cancel Duck Hook.[9] When he hit back, it was not against North Vietnam but against the antiwar movement. On November 3, 1969, in the most effective tele-vised speech of his presidency, Nixon described his efforts to reach a peace-ful settlement, made the case for peace with honor, and concluded by asking for the support of "the great silent majority of my fellow Ameri-cans."[10] Nixon's appeal rallied the hinterland, notched up his Gallup poll to 68 percent, and won more time for his policy, but he was still bogged down in Vietnam with no apparent way out.[11] At the same time, at home, his hopes were suffering another blow. The economy was turning sour, a development that could do him as much political damage as his failure to break Hanoi.

## II

Reflecting his priorities, Nixon's inaugural address treated the subject of the economy in a single sentence that his own administration would soon expose as inaccurate. "We have learned at last to manage a modern econ-omy to assure its continued growth," he said.[12] There appeared no reason to say any more. Economic issues had played only a small role in the recent campaign. Unemployment was at rock bottom. Inflation still seemed man-ageable, and the economic team he was assembling expected economic growth during the 1970s to be even faster than it had been in the past two decades.

Preoccupied with matters he considered far more important, Nixon barely paid attention to the appointment of the administration's chief economic officials — the secretary of the treasury, the director of the Bureau of the Budget, and the chairman of the Council of Economic Advisers (CEA). Since the days of the Kennedy administration, these three to-gether, formally constituting the Troika, had prepared joint economic fore-

---

[9] *RN: Memoirs*, 402–403. For a quite different account of these events, see Henry Kis-singer, *White House Years* (1979), chap. 8.

[10] *Pub Paps RN 1969*, 909.

[11] *The Gallup Poll, 1935–1971* (1972), 2224.

[12] *Pub Paps RN 1969*, 1.

casts for the president and had served as the principal source of his economic advice. Nixon assumed that he would take care of the areas in which
he was the expert — domestic politics and foreign affairs — and the Troika,
whoever they were, would take care of the economy.

Nixon's only requirement for a treasury secretary was someone who was
not an Eastern banker. Still, it was the chief lobbyist of the ultraestablishment American Bankers Association, Charls Walker, who suggested the
nominee.[13] He was David Kennedy, president of the Continental Illinois
National Bank of Chicago, the eighth largest bank in the United States. At
age 63, the oldest member of Nixon's Cabinet, David Kennedy had served
for a year in the Eisenhower administration as an assistant secretary of the
Treasury and in 1967 had won praise for his work as chairman of the
Commission on Budget Concepts. A moderate Republican with a good
record of civic service in Chicago, Kennedy, white-haired and portly,
seemed safe.[14] But as became all too rapidly apparent, Kennedy was out of
his depth in the Treasury. Even before he was confirmed, he set off a brief
run on the dollar in international currency markets by inexplicably declining to issue the ritual pledge to defend its official price.[15] He then antagonized Congress by his obtuse reluctance to concede that an official who
regulated banks, as he would as treasury secretary, should not own stock,
say, in the Illinois Continental National Bank.[16] Around Washington,
Kennedy quickly acquired a reputation for keeping bankers hours (he left
the office at 5:30 P.M.) and for relying too much on subordinates, especially
Charls Walker, whom he appointed as his undersecretary.[17] More to the
point, the secretary of the treasury was supposed to be the economic strong
man in any administration, a formulator of policy and leading economic
spokesman, but policy was not Kennedy's strong suit, and, as a public
personality, he was nearly invisible. Nixon soon wrote Kennedy off as a
"cipher" and moved him to the top of the list of cabinet offices he plotted
to depose.[18]

For budget director, Nixon chose Robert Mayo, recommended by pow-

[13] RN: Memoirs, 339–340; James Reichley, Conservatives in an Age of Change (1981), 72–
73; Rowland Evans, Jr., and Robert Novak, Nixon in the White House (1971), 25–26.

[14] Wall Street Journal, Dec. 12, 1968, 1.

[15] Ibid., Dec. 18, 1969, 1.

[16] New York Times, Jan. 18, 1969, 1, and 15.

[17] Wall Street Journal, May 27, 1969, 1; New York Times, Sept. 5, 1969, 22.

[18] E-Notes, April 27, 1970.

erful congressional Democrats who remembered Mayo for his nineteen years of capable service in the Treasury.[19] Mayo had left the government in 1960 to become the number-two man under (of all people) David Kennedy at the Illinois Continental National Bank. In 1967, Mayo was also staff director for Kennedy's budget-concepts commission.[20] In Washington, Kennedy and Mayo, whom Herbert Stein described as "mild and retiring characters," were considered a matched pair.[21] "Kennedy is weak and Mayo thinks he's still under him," Nixon complained.[22] Nixon did not like Mayo, who made the mistake of boring him during long sessions on the budget in 1969.[23] Worse, according to John Ehrlichman, Mayo's "mannerisms and odd sense of humor thoroughly alienated Nixon . . . The more Nixon showed signs of annoyance with Mayo's *bonhomie*, the more Mayo compensated by trying to be more humorous and engaging." During the early months of 1970, the president dodged meetings of the Troika for no other reason than to avoid seeing the man.[24] Finally, Mayo demanded an audience with Nixon and got one on March 5, 1970. Mayo used the occasion to complain that Ehrlichman, Nixon's chief domestic adviser, was intruding on his turf and threatened to resign unless his relations with the president improved. "I guess Mayo has got to go," Nixon said after the meeting.[25] Mayo was gone from the Budget Bureau in July 1970, resurfacing shortly as president of the Federal Reserve Bank of Chicago.

For his chairman of the CEA, Nixon took the advice of Arthur Burns, his favorite economist, and appointed Paul McCracken. Nixon had a slight acquaintance with McCracken from the Eisenhower administration, in which McCracken had served for three years as one of the CEA's three members. A onetime Iowa farm boy with a Ph.D. from Harvard, the diminutive McCracken was coordinating Nixon's preinaugural task forces on policy issues when he got his appointment. Nixon accurately described McCracken for the press as a "centrist" and a "pragmatist," who avoided a "doctrinaire" approach to economic issues.[26] Everyone liked McCracken,

[19] Reichley, *Conservatives in an Age of Change*, 73.

[20] *New York Times*, Dec. 12, 1968, 38.

[21] Herbert Stein, "The Organization of Economic Policy-Making" (oral history interview), in Kenneth W. Thompson, ed., *The Nixon Presidency* (1987), 170.

[22] John Ehrlichman, *Witness to Power* (1982), 90.

[23] Reichley, *Conservatives in an Age of Change*, 211–212.

[24] Ehrlichman, *Witness to Power*, 90.

[25] *Haldeman Diaries*, Mar. 5, 1970. Quote in Ehrlichman, *Witness to Power*, 90.

[26] *New York Times*, Dec. 5, 1968, 1, 28.

even Democrats, but McCracken would not satisfy Nixon either. "Paul McCracken is a decent man," Nixon said in a rare compliment, "but he's not strong either."[27] McCracken lacked the gift for crisp and witty memos that Walter Heller had used to amuse and edify President Kennedy, and his eclecticism translated into a lack of steadiness in his policy advice. In meetings McCracken spoke with diffident detachment, his deep voice acting as a soporific. Among those he put to sleep was the president. McCracken would stay through 1971 before returning to his post at the University of Michigan School of Business Administration.

Although Kennedy, Mayo, and McCracken had their problems with the president, they had few problems with each other. Well-acquainted for years, they agreed on most policy issues and enjoyed mutual respect. Ordinarily, the treasury secretary leads the Troika, but because macroeconomics was not Kennedy's long suit, Paul McCracken hosted the group's weekly breakfasts at the Cosmos Club on Massachusetts Avenue.[28] And it was McCracken who was principal architect of Nixon's first economic policy. The consequences of that policy would confirm Nixon's doubts about his economic team and hasten the departure of its members from his government.

## III

Nixon's economic officials approached the problem of economic management conservatively, even humbly. Their conservatism was not the laissez-faire conservatism of Adam Smith, but a conservatism based on appreciation of the complexity of the world and the limits of economic knowledge. As bystanders during the Kennedy and Johnson administrations, they had seen their predecessors brought low by hubris, and they learned lessons then that affected policy when it came their turn to make it.

The Keynesian or so-called new economists in the Democratic administrations of the 1960s had begun with immense confidence in the capacity of their ideas to cure the economy of the business cycle.[29] Locating the source of economic instability in the private sector, the new economists believed that government could fine-tune the economy to keep it running

---

[27] Ehrlichman, *Witness to Power*, 90.

[28] Stein interview, Thompson, ed., *Nixon Presidency*, 170.

[29] The account in these pages of events in the 1960s based on Allen J. Matusow, *The Unraveling of America* (1984), chaps. 2, 6.

smoothly. Their instrument of choice was fiscal policy. When recessions threatened, the government should cut taxes and raise expenditures to increase aggregate demand and maintain employment. When inflation threatened, the government should raise taxes and cut expenditures to reduce aggregate demand, taking pressure off prices. At the urging of new economists, Congress enacted a substantial tax cut in 1964 to put juice into a stagnating economy. When the economy responded with falling unemployment and little inflation, enthusiasts of the new economics hailed the end of the business cycle.

Then everything went wrong. In 1965 President Johnson launched two expensive wars simultaneously, the war on poverty and the ground war in Vietnam. With federal expenditures growing by 60 percent in three years and revenues lagging, the government ran up big deficits; total spending in the economy outpaced production; and inflation began. In 1968 Congress took fiscal aim at excess demand by reducing federal expenditures 6 percent and enacting a temporary one-year tax increase in the form of a 10 percent tax surcharge. (Taxpayers calculated their federal income tax under existing schedules, then added 10 percent.) Keynesian economists feared that Congress was administering an overdose of fiscal restraint, that these measures might cool off the economy so successfully that a recession would result. They were wrong. Despite severe fiscal restraint, the boom got hotter, and inflation accelerated. The tax surcharge had not worked. Arthur Okun, Johnson's last CEA chairman, admitted later, "When we were able to call the policy tune, the economy did not dance to it."[30]

Renegade economists belonging to a school called "monetarism" were hardly surprised. Their chief theoretician was Milton Friedman of the University of Chicago. Friedman argued that the new economists were guilty of false logic in believing that fiscal policy must affect aggregate demand. Take, for example, the 1968 tax increase. The government collected more taxes from taxpayers, reducing the deficit. As a result, the government borrowed less from lenders, freeing funds for expenditure in the private economy. The composition of spending might change, but its total would be altered little. When Friedman correctly predicted the failure of the 1968 tax increase, his stock took off.

Monetarists differed from the new economists most importantly in their view of the business cycle. The private economy was inherently stable, they

---

[30] *Newsweek* (Jan. 24, 1972), 62.

said; governments caused instability. The particular agency of the U.S. government always at fault was the Federal Reserve, keeper of the money supply. When the Fed increased the rate of money growth, output, then prices rose. When the Fed reduced the rate of money growth, output, then inflation slowed down. Forget fiscal policy, monetarists asserted. The Fed's unwitting misuse of monetary policy was the true cause of booms and busts.

In 1968 the economy provided a laboratory to test the rival views of Keynesians and monetarists. Fiscal policy tightened. The Fed eased money. New economists feared a recession. Monetarists predicted an intensifying boom. The accuracy of the monetarist forecast caused a sea change in the intellectual climate. The *New York Times* noted that a few years ago, when the new economists were riding high, the question was, Does money matter? "Today the monetarists have turned the issue almost completely around. The question now being asked is, 'Does spending and tax policy matter at all?'"[31] The policy instrument with potency, it appeared, was money. The way to keep money from destabilizing the economy, Friedman argued, was to deny discretionary authority to the Fed over the money supply and establish a rule that would keep money growing at a steady rate.

Among those falling under the influence of Friedman's ideas in 1969 were the men coming to power in the Nixon administration. A dedicated Republican who advised Nixon during the 1968 campaign, Friedman had close ties to a number of Nixon's advisers and Nixon himself. The president would occasionally phone Friedman to seek his views and invite him to the White House for private consultations. Indeed, Nixon had a monetarist's faith in the potency of money, though he was not entirely sure why, once asking his advisers for help in understanding "the mechanics and logic of monetary policy."[32]

The new administration's general approach to economic policy bore Friedman's stamp. Government was the cause, not the cure, of the business cycle. Government efforts to improve economic performance in the 1960s had failed. Fine-tuning was out; predictable rules to limit fallible policymakers were in. Wage-price guideposts, which the Democrats had used for a while in the sixties to police wage and price decisions, had not worked and would not be revived. Fiscal policy lacked bite and had limited utility. Monetary policy effectively influenced output and prices in the

---

[31] *New York Times*, June 11, 1969, 59.
[32] McCracken for President, Mar. 3, 1970, Memos for President's file, SMOF: McCracken.

short run, and the path of money growth should always be smooth. "We have to avoid the stop-start strategy of seeming to see a recession and stepping on the accelerator—then seeing inflation and stepping on the brakes," Paul McCracken said. "It's like riding in traffic with someone who is learning to drive."[33] Asked to describe his policy views, McCracken replied, "Friedmanesque."[34]

Three days after his inauguration, Nixon met with the Quadriad, which was the Troika plus the chairman of the Federal Reserve System, William McChesney Martin. That meeting set the administration's economic course. The problem, all agreed, was inflation. Excess demand had driven unemployment to an abnormal low of 3.3 percent in January 1969 and raised prices by 4 percent during the previous year. The administration could try to peg unemployment at the current low rate, which would require an accelerating inflation rate, or the administration could try to slow inflation by curbing demand, which would increase unemployment. The Quadriad agreed that the task at hand was "cooling down the overheated economy."[35]

Though the public was not as yet particularly worried about inflation, and Democratic economists took a relaxed view of it, Nixon's advisers were properly worried. Inflation encouraged speculation, discouraged saving and investment, arbitrarily redistributed income, and, if permitted to continue long enough, would undermine social stability. An economic slowdown, the antidote to inflation, would be painful but was nonetheless necessary, the president's advisers agreed. There must be some "malevolent law," said Paul McCracken, "that places Republicans in power when it is hard to be a hero."[36]

McCracken designed the specifics of the administration's anti-inflation policy. Theoretically, he had two choices. He could go "cold turkey,"[37] meaning deflate the boom quickly, suffer a sharp recession, and bring inflation down fast; or he could let the air out of the boom slowly, avoid a

---

[33] Report on Meeting of the Cabinet Committee on Economic Policy, May 16, 1969, Memos for President's file, POF, WHSF.

[34] Herbert Stein, *Presidential Economics* (1988), 140.

[35] McCracken for Stephen Bull, Feb. 6, 1969, President's Meetings—Quadriad Meetings file, SMOF: McCracken.

[36] *New York Times*, Jan. 24, 1969, 17.

[37] The phrase in McCracken's speech before New York Economic Club, Mar. 5, 1969. (Copy furnished me from files of Council of Economic Advisers.)

recession, and keep unemployment within politically tolerable limits. The first was never a real option. The second became the policy which the administration called gradualism.

On February 13, 1969, four days before McCracken was scheduled to unveil gradualism in testimony before Congress, top administration officials discussed it at a meeting of the Cabinet Committee on Economic Policy, chaired by the president. Nixon created this committee in part to appease Commerce Secretary Maurice Stans, his chief fund-raiser, who badly wanted a voice in economic policy but was unwelcome in the Troika. Nixon would endure the meandering monthly discussions of the Cabinet Committee for a year before handing it over to Spiro Agnew and certain death. But while Nixon attended, the Committee served as a forum for the candid expression of views and a place where Nixon could express his concerns about the economy. In one meeting he made clear what he thought economic policy was all about. "You can make every argument in the world economically but you have to consider the political timing," he said. "Whenever political considerations are not present we can afford to look at things purely from an economic standpoint. But that will not be often."[38] Of course, when only economic considerations were present, he was not interested. As McCracken said, "Mr. Nixon may have even had an almost psychological block about economics." He approached the subject "somewhat like a little boy doing required lessons."[39]

Gradualism had political implications that interested Nixon very much. At the meeting of the Cabinet Committee on Economic Policy, the administration's lone skeptic of gradualism was the president himself. As a politician, he knew, even if his economic advisers did not, that the public disliked unemployment more than inflation, and he worried that any policy costing jobs might cost him votes. "When you start talking about inflation in the abstract, it is hard for people to understand," he said. "But when unemployment goes up one half of one percent, that's dynamite." If that were the case, McCracken wondered, how should he handle the topic of unemployment during his forthcoming congressional testimony? "We can hardly say that we can cool down the economy without any adverse effect on unemployment," McCracken observed. Nixon offered McCracken

---

[38] Report of the Cabinet Committee on Economy Policy, Apr. 10, 1969, personal papers of William Safire. Mr. Safire, who kept these minutes, kindly made them available to me.

[39] Quoted in Reichley, *Conservatives in an Age of Change*, 206.

some coaching. "Let's say, 'Our goal is the achievement of more price stability without an increase in unemployment,'" he suggested. "Is that too dishonest? Let's never get into the position where we accept unemployment as a certainty. I don't go along with the idea that sees us as heroes on inflation and villains on unemployment. That will take us to the point where no conservative will ever be elected again. . . The public has had eight years without a recession; and now we have a new Administration, and it has promised better management. We can't allow — Wham! — a recession. We will never get in again."[40] Perhaps if Nixon had had the same confidence in his economic judgment that he had in his judgment on foreign affairs, he would have stopped gradualism on the spot, but at this point he was merely a nervous spectator of the policy that his advisers were advancing in his name.

McCracken explained gradualism before the Joint Economic Committee of Congress on February 17, 1969.[41] To cool the boom, the government would have to reduce aggregate demand, he said. Placing heavy reliance on the Fed's control of money growth, McCracken explained that gradualism would require a policy of moderate monetary restraint through the year. About the effectiveness of fiscal policy McCracken had private doubts, but he was Friedmanesque, not a Friedmanite, which meant that he was not sure. To play it safe, he called for fiscal restraint to accompany tighter money, meaning no budget deficit.

How fast and how much would gradualism bring down inflation? Of the several ways available for measuring price changes, McCracken chose the GNP (gross national product) deflator, which measured prices of all goods produced in the economy, not just consumer goods. McCracken predicted that this inflation rate would fall from 4 percent in 1968 to 3.5 percent in 1969. Internal Troika projections expected a further fall to 3 percent by mid-1970. As for unemployment, McCracken was masterly, even Nixonian, in his evasiveness. "No one can assure that the distortions from 3 years of economic overheating and price inflation can be corrected with no effect on unemployment," McCracken said. The policy of gradualism, he assured an inquiring senator, would not push unemployment "substantially above" the 3 to 4 percent zone of recent years. Troika projections, which

[40] Report of the Cabinet Committee on Economic Policy, Feb. 13, 1969, Safire papers.
[41] McCracken testimony in "The 1969 Economic Report of the President," (1969), Joint Economic Committee, hearings, 284–332.

McCracken did not reveal, estimated unemployment by mid-1970 at 4.4 percent, probably not high enough to cause Nixon political embarrassment in that election year. Democrats as well as Republicans, Arthur Okun as well as Milton Friedman, applauded the policy.[42] "You wait and see," said Charls Walker. "It will work."[43]

## IV

Nixon distrusted his policy of gradualism in part because it assigned to the Federal Reserve and William McChesney Martin the main responsibility for slowing down the economy. A Democrat appointed by Truman in 1951, Martin had played a major role in the nation's economy for almost the whole of Nixon's career. Nixon did not like Martin, whom he considered, in Ehrlichman's phrase, "a stereotypical tennis-playing Eastern Ivy League banker."[44] Mainly Nixon disliked Martin because he blamed him for his defeat in the 1960 election, a defeat whose lingering memory crucially shaped the president's view of political economy.

As the probable candidate of the incumbent party, Vice President Richard Nixon fully expected to benefit from a strong economy in the 1960 election, but in mid-1959, fiscal policy had moved toward restraint, and Martin at the Fed sharply contracted money growth. In March 1960, Arthur Burns, chairman of the CEA during Eisenhower's first term and a life-long student of business cycles, saw signs of trouble. Burns went to Nixon to warn that "we are heading for another economic dip which would hit its low point on October, just before the election." To prevent a recession that could defeat Nixon in November, Burns urged easier money and stepped-up defense spending. Nixon took Burns's recommendations to President Eisenhower, who laid them before an unreceptive cabinet and then buried them. Recalling this episode in his 1962 book *Six Crises*, Nixon wrote, "Unfortunately, Burns turned out to be a good prophet. The bottom of the 1960 dip did come in October and the economy started to move up again in November — after it was too late to affect the election returns. In October, usually a month of rising employment, the jobless rolls increased by 452,000. All the speeches, television broadcasts, and precinct work in

[42] *New York Times*, Feb. 20, 1969, 1; April 26, 1969, 17.
[43] Ibid., Mar. 27, 1969, 20.
[44] Ehrlichman, *Witness to Power*, 247.

the world could not counteract that one hard fact." Nixon reportedly visited Martin after the election and blamed him for the Republican defeat.[45]

Eight years later, as president-elect, Nixon tried to get rid of Martin. At a meeting in New York's Pierre Hotel on December 9, 1968, Nixon told Martin that he intended to appoint none other than Arthur Burns to head the Fed, implying that he would do it as soon as he took office.[46] Martin's term was not scheduled to end until January 31, 1970, and according to Martin's version of the meeting, he declared his intention to complete it. Nixon, for his part, thought Martin agreed to resign in mid-1969 and believed Martin "reneged" when he did not.[47] Whatever was said at the Pierre, Martin would continue to control the levers of monetary policy through 1969, and the fate of gradualism would rest with him. Burns would have to wait.

If not for Nixon's reelection, Burns's career would have been nearing its end. After leaving the Eisenhower administration in 1956, Burns jointly held appointments as a professor at Columbia University and president of the National Bureau of Economic Research, a private research institution. But Burns had developed a taste for public service and the limelight that went with it. With the passing years, he spent ever less time on research and academic business and ever more on blue-ribbon committees and corporate boards. The board of the National Bureau, looking for younger leadership, forced Burns out in 1967. Meanwhile, at Columbia, Burns felt increasingly isolated in a department dominated by model builders and computer pioneers. Burns left Columbia for Stanford University the same year he left the National Bureau, a has-been in his own profession. He was sixty-four years old. But in mid-1969, Burns was back in New York. Nixon was running for president, and Burns was resurrected. Burns was Nixon's

---

[45] Richard Nixon, *Six Crises* (1962), 310; *Annual Report of Council of Economic Advisers 1960*, 44–47; *Annual Report of Council of Economic Advisers 1961*, 28–32 (hereafter cited as *CEA Annual Report*).

[46] Arthur F. Brimmer, "Politics and Monetary Policy: The Federal Reserve and the Nixon White House," (1984), unpublished paper kindly furnished me by the author. Brimmer was a member of the Federal Reserve Board at the time. Brimmer based his account on his conversations with Martin.

[47] For Martin's side, Brimmer, "Politics and Monetary Policy;" for Nixon's expectation that Martin would resign mid-1969, *Haldeman Diaries*, Apr. 23, 1969. Haldeman wrote that Martin "reneged on his agreement to resign in summer to permit Burns to become Fed chairman."

kind of economist, one who understood the political business cycle and wanted to elect Republicans, just as Burns had tried to elect Nixon in 1960. At the Fed, Burns would know what to do. Nixon assigned Burns important tasks in the campaign and in the transition. When Martin refused to resign, Nixon persuaded Burns to join the new administration as counselor to the president with special responsibilities for domestic policy. Mainly, Burns would be on ice until Martin departed.[48]

For Nixon, the wait came to seem overlong. Pedantic and slow-talking, forever filling his pipe, Burns assumed an avuncular manner in dealing with Nixon and wearied him with long lectures. Nixon soon added Burns to the list of people he wished to avoid. Meantime, Burns got tangled in a rivalry with Nixon's house liberal, Daniel Patrick Moynihan, and bungled the assignment of assembling the president's domestic program.[49] Burns did succeed in his primary objective, which was to assure Nixon that when he got to the Fed, he would not be William McChesney Martin. "Eisenhower liked to talk about the independence of the Federal Reserve," Burns said at one meeting of the Cabinet Committee on Economic Policy. "They begin to believe it. Let's not make that mistake and talk about the independence of the Fed again."[50]

In February 1969, a few days after McCracken laid out the essentials of gradualism, Chairman Martin appeared before the Joint Economic Committee to endorse this "very exciting and very constructive effort to disinflate without deflating."[51] Martin had come not merely to pledge fealty to gradualism; he had come to restore the Fed's lost credibility. In 1966 the Fed had undertaken to slow inflation, but when a credit crunch resulted, lost its nerve. In mid-1968, when the Johnson administration feared that too much fiscal restraint would cause a recession, the Fed responded by pouring money into the economy, accelerating the inflation rate. A few weeks before Martin's congressional testimony, Edwin Dale, the economics reporter for the New York Times, stung the Fed with a piece entitled "Laughing at the Fed." Dale wrote, "the easiest laugh around is to ask at a

---

[48] Milton Viorst, "The Burns Kind of Liberal Conservatism," New York Times Magazine, Nov. 9, 1969, 30 ff; Wyatt C. Wells, Economist in an Uncertain World: Arthur F. Burns and the Federal Reserve (1994), chap. 1; Wall Street Journal, May 20, 1969, 1.

[49] See, for example, Haldeman Diaries, Mar. 25, 1969.

[50] Minutes on Meeting of Cabinet Committee on Economic Policy, Feb. 13, 1969, Safire papers.

[51] "The 1969 Economic Report of the President," Joint Economic Committee, 647–708.

party, 'Say, have you heard? The Fed is tightening money.' " The Fed promised terrors, but businessmen kept borrowing, and the money supply kept
expanding, Dale said. "The poor Fed. The butt of jokes. Swarmed by the
Friedman hordes. Uncertain of what it is doing."[52]

Now in the last year of his long tenure, Martin knew that Dale was
right, that the Fed had made mistakes and forfeited respect. He had a final
chance to make amends, and this time he was resolved not to fumble it
away. In Martin's view, the challenge facing the Fed was to break "the
pervasive inflationary psychology" in the corporate community that continued to sustain the boom. To that end he would have to convince the
markets that he meant business, that he would not buckle again. In his
testimony, Martin solemnly promised that the Fed would summon the
"fortitude and patience" to defeat inflation. Whether Martin's effort to
puncture inflationary expectations and Nixon's policy of gradualism were
consistent remained to be seen.

In the boardrooms of the great corporations, they might not have been
laughing at Martin, but they did not believe him. Corporate leaders believed that the government, as it had in the past, would retreat from the
new policy of restraint, rather than risk a recession. If inflation would
indeed continue, the smart move was to borrow as much as possible now
and repay later in cheaper dollars.[53] And that is what businessmen did. In
December 1968, a government survey had revealed that businessmen
planned to increase investment in plant and equipment by a substantial 9
percent during the coming year. In March 1969, despite all that the government had said about cooling down the economy, the survey reported
revised plans to increase investment expenditures by 14 percent.[54] *Business
Week* commented, "Business determination to press on with big spending
plans sets the stage for the great drama of 1969."[55]

In March Martin's fear that he was losing the battle for credibility
intensified. The economy was growing faster than expected, and inflation
was speeding up, not slowing down. The time had come, Martin decided,
for a psychological shock to get the attention of the corporations. Sherman
Maisel, Martin's antagonist on the Federal Reserve Board and a true gradu-

---

[52] *New York Times*, Feb. 3, 1969, 50.
[53] *Newsweek* (Mar. 31, 1969), 63; *Business Week* (Apr. 12, 1969), 23.
[54] *Survey of Current Business* (Dec. 1968), 11; (Mar. 1969), 17; *CEA Annual Report 1969*,
56–57; *Wall Street Journal*, Mar. 14, 1969, 3.
[55] *Business Week* (Mar. 22, 1969), 34.

alist, described Martin's policy as "the idea that what the Fed actually did mattered less than what people thought it was trying to do."[56] On April 3, 1969, the Fed took two highly visible measures to signal resolve. It raised the interest rate it charged on loans to member banks (the discount rate) to the highest level since October 1929, and it raised the percentage of deposits that banks were required to hold as reserves and therefore could not spend or lend.[57]

Martin's action unnerved the president. At a meeting of the Cabinet Committee on Economic Policy on April 10, he asked Herbert Stein of the Council of Economic Advisers what he thought of the decision to raise the discount rate. Stein said that the Fed had made "a psychological gesture" because inflation was stronger than expected. "My feeling," said Stein "is that if they continue with this, it is consistent with our objectives." But Stein's objectives were not Nixon's. "I remember '58," the president said. "We cooled off the economy and cooled off 15 Senators and 60 Congressmen at the same time." Mayo, McCracken, and Charls Walker spoke up for the Fed. Labor Secretary George Shultz, a figure of growing influence, agreed with Nixon. Gradualism meant staying with the same policy, not jacking it around, Shultz said. Burns took the occasion to lay further claim to Martin's job by saying that he hesitated to criticize the Fed, "but there's a hawkish sentiment there. I would have waited until they saw what happened to the [discount] rate before they tightened reserve requirements." Said Nixon, "I want to give a special charge to the Council and to this group — watch this thing."[58]

As the Fed and the corporations continued on their collision course, one tightening credit, the other demanding more of it, possibilities increased for a new credit crunch, a condition in which credit would become so scarce and so expensive that corporate bankruptcies and a financial panic might ensue. As early as January 1969, market interest rates had risen above the legal limit that banks could legally pay on certificates of deposit (CDs) of $100,000 or more. As owners of CDs withdrew them to seek better returns elsewhere, the big New York banks sought replacement funds to meet the voracious credit demands of their corporate customers. The

---

[56] Sherman J. Maisel, *Managing the Dollar* (1973), 242. See Minutes of Federal Open Market Committee (hereafter referred to as FOMC), Apr. 1, 1969, esp. p. 66, for Maisel's views.

[57] *Wall Street Journal*, Apr. 4, 1969, 1, 3; *New York Times*, Apr. 4, 1969, 47, 49.

[58] Report on Meeting of the Cabinet Committee on Economic Policy, Apr. 10, 1969, Safire papers, 47.

banks added to their liquidity by reducing stock purchases, dampening the stock market, and they dumped municipal bonds, damaging the cities.

The main source of replacement funds was Eurodollars, which had rapidly emerged in the late 1960s, accelerating the growing interdependence of world capital markets. Eurodollars were U.S. dollars that flowed into Europe — for example, to pay for U.S. imports — and stayed there as deposits, mainly in the European branches of American banks. By borrowing Eurodollars in 1969, the top dozen New York banks, which supplied the corporations with much of their credit, obtained funds to keep the domestic boom going. The Fed seemed both relieved that Eurodollars were staving off a credit crunch and frustrated that the big banks were using Eurodollars to evade its tight money policy.[59] Eurodollars were one reason for the disheartening news that inflation actually increased from 4 percent in 1968 to an annual rate of 5.2 percent in the second quarter of 1969 (GNP deflator).[60]

While prices and interest rates were going up, stocks and especially bonds were going down, provoking cries of anguish on Wall Street. The Republicans in the big brokerage houses could not believe that an administration they considered their own would cause them such misery. In June, a political operative on the Republican National Committee reported that "Wall Street types" had been "bending my ear unmercifully" with complaints. "The market is down due to loss of confidence in the President," these voices said. "They think he is going too far, too fast in slowing inflation. They feel he is insensitive to Wall Street, its workings, and its influence on the well-being of the country." The president's critics, this report continued, felt that he "has become totally unavailable to the top men on Wall Street including those who supported him politically and financially — often heavily — in the campaign." The president needed to reopen communications with these people, the report concluded.[61] Nixon had already figured that out for himself. Two days before this report was written, he met with the head of the New York Stock Exchange, Bernard "Bunny" Lasker, "to do a little stroking."[62]

---

[59] *Newsweek,* (Apr. 21, 1969), 83–84; *New York Times,* Mar. 12, 1969, 63; *Wall Street Journal,* Mar. 18, 1969, 3; "Euro-Dollars: A Changing Market," *Federal Reserve Bulletin* (Oct. 1969), 765–784.

[60] CEA *Annual Report 1970,* 29.

[61] Dick Garbett to Harry Dent, June 24, 1969, Files: White House Staff Memos, Dent, SMOF: McCracken.

[62] Peter Flannigan for President's file, June 26, 1969, President's Meeting file, POF.

Tensions in the financial markets peaked during the first two weeks in June. As the midmonth deadline for quarterly tax payments approached, corporate demand for credit would intensify, with results many dreaded.[63] Chairman Martin met with big bankers in New York and "really chewed them out" for evading his tight money policy by borrowing Eurodollars.[64] At the same time, Treasury Secretary Kennedy tried to take some of the political heat off tight money by pressuring the banks to keep a lid on the prime rate, the interest rate that banks charge their best corporate customers. On June 8, 1969, the banks responded by announcing an "explosive increase" in the prime to 8.5 percent, the first time in history the rate had jumped a whole point.[65]

On June 11, Burns wrote Nixon, sounding the alarm. "The monetary situation seems to be approaching a critical phase," Burns wrote. "For reasons that you will understand, I do not feel that I should take the initiative in discussing this problem with Bill Martin. I have, however, suggested to both Paul McCracken and Dave Kennedy that they get together with Martin to advise him to keep the discount window open on a uniform basis across the country. I am watching developments in this sensitive area very closely."[66] The subtext, of course, was that once Burns took over the Fed, Nixon's monetary troubles would be over.

The June 16 tax date came and went, and there was no crunch. The main reason was that while the banks had lost $8 billion in CDs during the first six months of the year, they had replaced the loss by borrowing $7.2 billion in Eurodollars. Meanwhile, corporations expanded the loans they made to each other. Total credit available in the United States actually increased during the first half, though not enough to keep up with demand, which is why interest rates rose so high.[67] By June, there were not many Eurodollars left to borrow, and the Fed announced its intention to regulate them in any case.[68] In the second half, demand for loans eased, tensions relaxed, and the financial news retreated to the back pages.

Unlike Martin's critics in the White House, Milton Friedman, staunch defender of gradualism and its chief theoretician, so far approved the Fed's performance. Monetarists paid no heed to interest rates, stock prices, or

---

[63] *Wall Street Journal*, June 9, 1969, 2.

[64] *New York Times*, June 1, 1969, III, 1.

[65] *Wall Street Journal*, June 9, 1969, 3; *New York Times*, June 10, 1964, 1. Quote in *Times*.

[66] Burns for President, June 11, 1969, FI file, WHCF.

[67] CEA *Annual Report 1970*, 34–39.

[68] *New York Times*, June 27, 1969, 1.

financial conditions. They watched only the rate of growth of the money supply. By that standard, the Fed had done well, Friedman said. Money growth had fallen from the inflationary rate of 7.2 percent in 1968 to an annual rate of 4.3 percent during the first half of 1969, the gradualist goal of moderate restraint. After the usual lag of six to nine months, Friedman predicted, the Fed's wise application of gradualism would cool off the boom and slow down prices. In his *Newsweek* column of May 26, 1969, Friedman issued a warning. "It would be a major blunder for the Fed to step still harder on the monetary brakes," he wrote. "This would risk turning orderly restraint into a severe economic contraction."[69]

## V

Nixon always believed that William McChesney Martin would try to ruin him, and in the second half of 1969, he almost did. In June, Martin's mood turned gloomy. In an emotional, extemporaneous speech before an audience of American bankers in Copenhagen, Martin described the U.S. economy as a "house of cards." Lamenting expanded debt and stock speculation, he warned that inflation might require voluntary credit controls, "forced saving," higher taxes, even wage and price controls. If we throw sound policy to the winds, he said, "there is no gadgetry in monetary mechanisms and no device that will save us from our sins." Said Martin, "We're going to have a good deal of pain and suffering before we can solve these things."[70] The point of gradualism, of course, had been to avoid as much pain and suffering as possible, but by then Martin was no longer a gradualist.

"No more economists," Martin liked to say.[71] A banker himself, Martin operated the Fed without a theory and was proud of it. He made policy by keeping in touch with his friends in the financial markets and by intuiting financial conditions. Martin's intuition still told him at midyear that he must break inflationary expectations, whatever the cost. Above all, the Fed must avoid giving any signal that might suggest premature easing and so trigger a new stampede for credit. The false signal that most concerned

---

[69] *Newsweek* (May 26, 1969), 105. For money growth (M1) in 1968, CEA *Annual Report 1970*, 33.

[70] Martin quotes from two separate accounts: *New York Times*, June 21, 1969, 1, 37; *Wall Street Journal*, June 23, 1969, 3.

[71] Quoted in Lawrence Malkin, "A Practical Politician at the Fed," *Fortune* (vol. 83, Apr. 1971), 148 ff.

Martin would be a decline in the federal fund rate, the interest rate that banks charge each other for overnight loans and a rate that the Fed could control precisely. If this rate fell, the markets would conclude that once again the Fed was quitting the fight to avoid the pain. As it happened, demand for credit slackened at midyear, and the federal funds rate sagged. To show resolve, Martin firmed up the federal funds rate, and incidentally all interest rates, in the only way he could. He slashed money growth and grimly kept slashing it through the rest of the year. From 7 percent in the last half of 1968 and 4 percent in the first half of 1969, the annual rate of increase in the money supply, as measured at the time, went nearly to zero. Martin had gone cold turkey.[72]

Since the Fed conducted its operations in secret, outsiders were left to scrutinize monetary clues to decipher its intentions. The first outsider to divine the Fed's shift away from gradualism was Milton Friedman. Things had been going well, Friedman said. Gradualism had, as planned, begun cooling off the economy, just as he said it would. That was why loan demand had turned soft and interest rates, if left to themselves, would be declining. Instead of recognizing success, Martin misinterpreted the downward pressure on interest rates as a failure, as a false signal of premature easing. Consequently, Martin had embarked on the worst possible policy. Writing in *Newsweek* on August 18, 1969, Friedman warned that if the Fed kept aiming at the wrong target and incidentally continued choking off money growth, it would plunge the economy into a recession.[73]

That summer, within the Federal Open Market Committee (FOMC), which steered the Fed's monetary policy, Sherman Maisel of the Federal Reserve Board made Friedman's argument. Though no monetarist, Maisel urged his colleagues to cooperate with the administration on the policy of gradualism. That meant abandoning expectations as the target, letting the federal funds rate decline, and returning to moderate growth in the money supply. Martin was unmoved. According to the minutes of the July meeting,

---

[72] Maisel, *Managing the Dollar*, 243–248. At the time, the estimate of the growth of M1 during the second half was 0.7 percent. One of the problems of trying to manage money was that its measurement was uncertain. Later estimates placed M1 growth at 1.7 percent in the third quarter and 2.1 percent in the fourth (annual rates), still very low rates indeed. Appendix I in Wells, *Economists in an Uncertain World*, conveniently collects revised statistics on M1 growth by quarter for these years. Maisel's account is supported in the Minutes of FOMC during the last half of 1969. I used microfilm copies of FOMC minutes from the National Archives.

[73] *Newsweek* (Aug. 18, 1969), 75.

Martin "did not agree with those, such as Professor Friedman, who argued that it was necessary only for the System to pull the right lever to do an effective job of economic stabilization." In his view, "Inflationary psychology remained the main economic problem." It would be a mistake, he said, "to take any action that might reinforce inflationary expectations just at the time when some weakening in those expectations might be developing." The system had eased too early in 1968 on the basis of mistaken forecasts. He would not ease now on the basis of forecasts that could prove wrong again.[74] In the twilight of his tenure, Martin had become a self-appointed hero in the battle against inflation, a lonely central banker prepared to wring out the economy and purge it of its sins, whatever the cost.

## VI

Among the many officials with their hand in economic policy in 1969, only one emerged with enhanced stature in the eyes of the president. He was George Shultz, a most unlikely Nixonian. Neither an ad man nor a politico, Shultz had a B.A. from Princeton and a Ph.D. from MIT in labor economics. Shultz had served one year on the staff of the Council of Economics when Burns was chairman, and it was Burns who recommended him for the post of secretary of labor in the new administration. Shultz, age 49, was serving as the little-known dean of the business school at the University of Chicago when Nixon nominated him.[75]

In a colorless Cabinet, *Newsweek* remarked, Shultz was the "grayest of the gray."[76] Stiff on a platform, so soft-spoken at meetings that he could hardly be heard, Shultz nonetheless possessed qualities that befit a former captain of Marines, qualities Nixon came to admire: calm under pressure, unswerving loyalty to his chief, willingness to subordinate his ego and personal views to seek consensus. Nixon did not know Shultz when he appointed him, and a labor secretary ordinarily resides in the farthest reaches of the executive branch, but Shultz would become one of Nixon's small inner circle and, in time, the strong man he needed to run economic policy.

Shultz moved up fast because he became Nixon's indispensable ally in the project to build a New Majority. Success in that project hinged on the

---

[74] FOMC Minutes, July 15, 1969, 80–82.

[75] *New York Times*, Dec. 14, 1968, 22; *Wall Street Journal*, June 9, 1969, 1; *Current Biography* (1969), 395–397.

[76] *Newsweek* (Aug. 18, 1969), 19.

courting and winning of George Meany, president of the AFL-CIO. The only member of the new administration who could establish rapport with Meany was Shultz. Despite differences in age, social background, and political affiliation, the ex-plumber and the ex–labor mediator hit it off at once, becoming golfing companions and establishing trusting personal relations. Nixon made Shultz the administration's ambassador to the AFL-CIO, a responsibility that Shultz discharged with such tact and skill that even Nixon admired the performance. It was Shultz who arranged Nixon's briefings for the AFL-CIO Executive Council, his cozy meetings with Meany in the White House, and delicate political matters such as securing labor's support for the Safeguard antiballistic missile.[77] For his part, Shultz completely bought Nixon's line that the white worker was the forgotten American and a choice recruit for the New Majority. When Nixon asked for Shultz's comments on Pete Hamill's article in *New York Magazine* entitled "The Revolt of the White Lower Middle Class," Shultz responded with a major paper. Ethnic white workers "are immigrants, or sons of immigrants, and feel insecure about their own place in the mainstream of American society," Shultz said. "They tend to live in neighborhoods that the blacks are most likely to move into and whose schools black children might attend. They sometimes have jobs that they feel blacks aspire to attain." Shultz proposed an ambitious program to promote interracial communications and to relieve economic pressure on white working-class families.[78]

Nixon admired Shultz, too, because, unlike most of his other department secretaries, Shultz actually got things done. Nixon did not like the Job Corps, so he turned it over to Shultz, who closed inefficient training centers and reorganized the program.[79] Shultz settled politically sensitive labor disputes. He chaired the interagency committee that reviewed the controversial program protecting domestic oil producers from oil imports. He established goals for minority employment in the skilled crafts at federally assisted construction sites, the so-called Philadelphia Plan, which Nixon privately praised as a Machiavellian tactic to pit the NAACP

---

[77] On meetings with Executive Council, Shultz for President, May 2, 1969, and David P. Taylor (Shultz's executive assistant) to John C. Whitaker, Oct. 23, 1969, Records of the Secretary (of Labor), RG 174, N.A.; on meeting of Nixon with Meany, Shultz for President, Mar. 10, 1969, FG 22 file, WHCF; on Safeguard, John C. Whitaker, "Telephone Call, Cabinet," May 5, 1969, FG 22 file, WHCF.

[78] Shultz for President, May 16, 1969, Records of Secretary.

[79] *Newsweek* (Apr. 21, 1969), 34, Kenneth Cole for Shultz, Sept. 15, 1969, FG 22, WHCF.

against the labor unions and split the Democratic coalition.[80] He took on the assignment of refining the administration's welfare reform program, the Family Assistance Plan, at the president's request. "It's still so fuzzy," Nixon said. "Shultz is the one to focus it. He understands it and thinks in precise terms."[81] In May 1969, Nixon asked Shultz to intervene quietly in a socially explosive hospital strike in Charleston, helping to avert violence.[82] That qualified Shultz to chair the Cabinet Committee on School Desegregation in 1970, which worked behind the scenes to facilitate peaceful compliance of Deep South school districts under court order to desegregate.[83] Shultz even put aside his free trade convictions to support import quotas on textiles, which Nixon had pledged to impose for the benefit of South Carolina during the 1968 campaign.[84] Shultz once said, "With the changing political winds, one who sets sail directly toward his goal would never get there. The skill lies in the tacking."[85] Both principled and flexible, Shultz was one of the best appointments Nixon ever made.

Shultz made his bid to move into economic policy on October 7, 1969. By then the economic indicators provided clear evidence that the economy was cooling off. Though capital spending remained strong, consumer spending had weakened. Housing starts, running at the annual rate of 1.7 million in the first quarter of the year, fell to 1.3 million in the last, prompting home builders to descend on Washington for relief.[86] On October 6, the government had announced that the unemployment rate had jumped sharply (if temporarily) from 3.5 percent in August to 4.0 percent in September.[87] Nobody had expected that. The next day Shultz sent Nixon his memo. Nixon had economic advisers, of course, but they were not giving him the kind of advice he wanted or that Shultz thought he ought to have. The secretary of labor had executed an end run around the Troika and the Council of Economic Advisers in a move that would make him a prime-

---

[80] Report of the Secretary of Labor on Accomplishments in 1969, Dec. 19, 1969, Records of the Secretary; on "Machiavellian" Philadelphia Plan, Ehrlichman, *Witness to Power*, 228–229.

[81] H-Notes, July 12, 1969.

[82] Ehrlichman to Bryce Harlow, May 27, 1969; and Harry S. Dent for Shultz, July 14, 1969, Records of the Secretary.

[83] Harry S. Dent, *The Prodigal Returns to Power* (1978), 130–156.

[84] Shultz for President, July 9, 1969, Records of the Secretary.

[85] *Time* (Mar. 25, 1974), 81.

[86] *Wall Street Journal*, Oct. 1, 1969, 10.

[87] *New York Times*, Oct. 7, 1969, 1.

time player in the Nixon White House. Within months Nixon would describe Shultz to Haldeman as the administration's "only really knowledgeable economist."[88]

In his memo Shultz became the first member of the administration to take up Friedman's warning of a recession. "The policy of gradually cooling the economy is beginning to work," Shultz told Nixon, thanks to the policy of moderate restraint in place during the first five months of the year. Beginning in May, "the Fed seems to have abandoned its part of the gradualist policy in favor of one that is sharply more restrictive." The result could be a recession in 1970. "I suggest, therefore, that those in contact with the Fed urge them to return to the gradualist policy immediately."[89]

The similarity of Shultz's views to those of Friedman was not a coincidence. Shultz and Friedman had become friends at the University of Chicago and were so close that when Friedman came to Washington during the Nixon years, he stayed in Shultz's home. Shultz, the disciple, subscribed to both Friedman's free market credo and his theories of the business cycle, but as Friedman himself pointed out, Shultz was no clone. "George is a man of principle," he said, "but he is not an ideolog — like I am."[90]

The Friedmanite message that Shultz delivered on October 7 gave Nixon the excuse he needed to pressure his lieutenants into reassessing economic policy. On a summary of Shultz's views that he forwarded to Arthur Burns, Nixon wrote, "Arthur — I agree. Will it be too late when you take over? Let's hit this with Martin."[91]

A week later, October 15, 1969, Martin was special guest at a meeting of the Cabinet Committee on Economic Policy. Since Nixon himself shrank from face-to-face confrontations, the intrepid Shultz acted as his gladiator. Nixon opened the meeting with a question. "Bill, you going to keep money tight?" Martin replied, "Mr. President, I have been fooled too many times by statistics. We know that the money supply has flattened out. The momentum of inflation was stopped in mid-summer, but the psychology of inflation has accelerated again. When the four percent unemployment figure came out, a lot of people said we would soon be throwing in the towel." He for one would not "relax the pressure prematurely." The risk of "underkill" (inflation) was greater than the threat of "overkill" (recession),

---

[88] *Haldeman Diaries*, Feb. 15, 1970.
[89] Shultz for President, Oct. 7, 1969, President's Handwriting file, POF.
[90] *Business Week* (Mar. 20, 1971), 72.
[91] Ehrlichman for President, Oct. 7, 1969, President's Handwriting file.

Martin said. "I personally discount the threat of recession." Proving how far out of step he was with the president, David Kennedy immediately jumped in to support Martin.

Then, reported the minutes, Shultz began "to needle Martin on his tight money policy." "I think the right policy is moderate restraint, the kind we had in the beginning of the year," Shultz said. "Maybe we should go back to that." When Martin let the remark pass, Shultz persisted. "Maybe we should go back to policies we had earlier — they worked — maybe the new policies are working too well," he said. After the conversation veered in another direction, Shultz waited for an opening and then struck again. "I still think that the Fed's position is too tight," he said. Usually imperturbable, Martin snapped. "There is a disease called Statisticalitis that could wreck us," he said. "This is not a statistical question," referring to the issue of appropriate monetary growth, "it's a judgment question and I have been at this at least as long as you."[92] Two days later, Nixon announced that Burns would replace Martin at the Fed, effective February 1, 1970.[93]

Toward the end of October, Nixon invited Burns, now safely nominated, in for a little chat. "You see to it — no recession," the President said. Martin is "six months too late." Burns replied, "I don't like to be late." Pressing on, Nixon said, Shultz says "turn now." This time Burns did not respond on cue. Sounding rather like William McChesney Martin, Burns said he thought easing now would be bad psychology, that it was time to "show backbone." In that case, said Nixon, the Fed should move in December. Burns countered that interest rates would be down by then, implying that December would not be a good time to ease either. At that moment Nixon may have glimpsed that Burns might not be his pliant tool after all, that the man who as courtier had seconded Nixon's desire to puncture the "myth of the autonomous Fed" might insist no less than Martin on the preservation of the Fed's autonomy.[94] A day later, Burns sent his response to Shultz's memo, which had warned of a recession and urged monetary ease. He had his doubts, Burns said, and so did Paul McCracken.[95]

As the author of gradualism, McCracken might have been expected to lead the charge against Martin's drastic turn toward zero money growth, but Martin had converted McCracken. A month after Shultz warned Nixon of

---

[92] Report on Meeting of the Cabinet Committee on Economic Policy, Oct. 15, 1969, Memo for President's file, POF.
[93] *New York Times*, Oct. 18, 1969, 1.
[94] E-Notes, Oct. 23, 1969.
[95] Burns for Staff Secretary, Oct. 24, 1969, FG 22 file, WHCF.

a recession, McCracken was still backing the Fed — and for Martin's reasons. We are "the legatee of deeply eroded confidence in the future value of money, because this inflation was allowed to run for so long, and skepticism about Washington's will to persevere is pervasive," McCracken wrote Nixon on November 3. "Evidence that the economy is cooling remains only tentative," he said. "Belief that the budget will slip from surplus back to deficit is growing. If on top of that there is premature monetary relaxation, this would congeal fears that Washington has given up, and that we are off to the inflationary races once more." The time to ease was approaching but not yet.[96]

A mere two weeks later, November 15, McCracken wrote Nixon saying that he now saw definite signs of "deceleration" and that we "are in a zone when economic policy ought to be eased." Toward that end, McCracken proposed "quiet talks" with the Fed before the mid-December meeting of the FOMC. By easier money, McCracken meant increasing the rate of money growth from near zero to only 2 to 4 percent. By the standards of monetarism, that was hardly enough. The erstwhile author of gradualism still flew with the hawks.[97]

As December began, Nixon was seized by fear that time was running out, that every day the money supply stayed frozen was a day closer to defeat in the congressional election of 1970. Shultz agreed. "I think it is a matter of great urgency that the Fed get on to a more moderate path now," Shultz wrote on December 1. "Continuation of the Fed's present policy will lead only to continuation of the bankrupt policy of extremes — and they will be extremes that will hurt us all."[98] On December 11, five days before the next scheduled meeting of the FOMC, Nixon authorized McCracken to begin "quiet talks" with the Fed.[99] Nixon himself called a Quadriad meeting for the fifteenth, presumably to apply some last-minute pressure on William McChesney Martin.[100] To no avail. Martin would not yield, at least not now. Maybe in January, the last month of his tenure.

---

[96] McCracken for President, Nov. 3, 1969, Draft Memo for President's file, SMOF: Mc-Cracken.

[97] Ibid., Nov. 15, 1969, BE 5 file, WHCF.

[98] Shultz to Kenneth Cole, Dec. 1, 1969, (CF) FI file, WHSF.

[99] Cole to McCracken, Dec. 11, 1969, FI file, WHSF.

[100] McCracken for President, Dec. 12, 1969, FG 131, WHCF. This memo offers Nixon suggestions for discussions at the Quadriad. In addition to the budget, McCracken wrote, "The posture of monetary policy should also be discussed in the light of the budget and economic picture."

In the days that followed, Nixon vented his anxieties in the privacy of the Oval Office. He phoned Friedman, who told him that Martin was "a fine guy but usually wrong."[101] He met with McCracken, who now took the view that six more weeks of tight money would cause a recession next fall.[102] We "*can't* have a recession," Nixon told Haldeman and Ehrlichman. Burns "*must* loosen."[103] The "need for a Republican Congress," he said, must be "superior" to the goal of fighting inflation.[104] Absent from Nixon's remarks was evidence of that fortitude and patience that Martin had pledged in February and that the corporations believed would vanish at the first sign of hard times.

Later in December 1969, speaking of the Council of Economic Advisers, Nixon told an aide, "They don't have any influence."[105] No wonder. At the beginning of the year, McCracken had sold gradualism with an optimistic forecast on output and prices. After slowing down in the first half, output would pick up during the second half, McCracken had said. Instead, fourth-quarter output actually declined by 1.4 percent (annual rate), and the recession that McCracken said would not happen, began. As for inflation — the target of gradualism — its rate did not fall, as McCracken had predicted. It picked up speed — the GNP deflator increasing from 4 percent in 1968 to 4.5 percent in 1969. The Consumer Price Index (CPI) told an even more depressing story, with prices rising from 4.7 to 6.1 percent.[106] Nixon was not really surprised. Instinct honed by a lifetime in politics had defended him against the optimism of his advisers. He had mistrusted their policies all along, expected recession, and anticipated betrayal by the Fed. In his darkest ruminations, not even Nixon had imagined a scenario that would produce by year's end both recession and inflation, two conditions once considered mutually exclusive but now conjoined to embarrass his economists and threaten his party with defeat in the coming election.

---

[101] E-Notes, Dec. 19, 1969.
[102] Ibid., Dec. 20, 1969.
[103] Ibid., Dec. 19, 1969.
[104] Ibid., Dec. 20, 1969.
[105] Ibid., Dec. 19, 1969.
[106] *Annual Report of CEA*, 229.

# Chapter 2

# The Fiscal Ironies of 1969

---

## I

Though the Nixon team took office with firm views on monetary policy, fiscal policy was another matter. Keynesians in the Kennedy and Johnson administration had believed that tax and spending decisions, embodied in the federal budget, could stabilize the economy. When higher taxes and less spending failed to curb inflation in 1968, old faiths suddenly came into question, and eclectic economists, including those coming to power with Nixon, were left wondering what to do. Ready or not, the new administration had to have a fiscal policy. The team faced two questions. Should it enlist the budget in the fight against inflation? That was the economic question. And for what purposes should the revenues be spent, once collected? That was the political question. Throughout 1969, even as it became entangled with the mysteries of monetary policy, the Nixon administration confronted budget issues no less vexing. This time, however, it was Congress, not the Fed, that caused all the trouble.

Liberals, mainly Democrats, had clear positions on fiscal issues. Despite past failures, they retained a dogged faith in the capacity of fiscal policy to stabilize the economy. But liberals cared more about the purposes of spending than its effects on aggregate demand. These were the years of ghetto riots, of angry protests by the militant poor, of bitter criticism against the military-industrial complex. The overriding fiscal purpose of the liberals was to fund bold new programs that would help the disadvantaged and save the cities. To pay the bill, they would shift budgetary priorities away from foreign wars back to the home front. Given their revulsion against Vietnam and the pressing nature of ghetto problems, liberals advanced their fiscal views with no small degree of urgency.

Conservatives, mainly Republicans, disputed liberal fiscal policy root and branch. Said Milton Friedman, "we simply do not know enough to be able to use deliberate changes in taxation or expenditures as a sensitive stabilizing mechanism."[1] But the main problem of the budget, said conservatives, was the threat posed by its growth to the liberties of the people and the efficiency of the market. In 1964, as a candidate for president, Barry Goldwater had campaigned on an idea of Friedman's that became part of the conservative credo. Goldwater recommended a 5 percent across-the-board cut in income taxes each year for five years to slow the growth of government and strengthen private initiative.[2] Federal programs to remedy social problems were a waste of money anyway, conservatives said, because so few of them actually worked. Thus, liberals would spend growing revenues to remedy social ills, and conservatives would return these revenues to the people in the form of lower taxes.

Nixon was neither a liberal nor the conservative of popular belief. He was a politician bent on preempting the center of American politics to build a New Majority. In addition to social conservatism, waving the flag, and playing the race card, Nixon sought center ground by judicious expansion of the welfare state. It was no part of Nixon's initial purpose to cut taxes or slash expenditures, as conservatives were urging. He knew that spending money was more popular than pinching pennies, and he favored balancing the budget only so long as it did not cost him votes. If the administration's anti-inflation policies were not working, Nixon said in 1969, "let's build some dams."[3] As a man of the center — a conservative man with liberal views — Nixon intended to address the nation's domestic ills with programs of his own, programs with a Republican cast to be sure, but programs that would cost money nonetheless.

Though Nixon would resist liberal efforts to cut deeply into defense spending, fiscal trends for which he was not responsible did in fact shift priorities away from war during the nearly six years he was in office. Mainly because Vietnam wound down and uncontrollable expenditures under existing domestic programs rapidly increased, defense spending would decline from 46 percent of the federal budget to 30 percent, whereas spending on human resources would rise from 33 to 50 percent.[4] But Nixon was not content merely to sit passively while domestic spending automatically es-

---

[1] Milton Friedman, *Capitalism and Freedom* (1962), 78.

[2] Milton Friedman, "The Goldwater View of Economics," *New York Times Magazine*, Oct. 11, 1964, 35 ff.

[3] Report on Meeting of the Cabinet Committee on Economic Policy, Nov. 13, 1969, Safire papers.

[4] *Budget of the United States, Historical Tables: Fiscal Year 1997*, 45, 46.

calated. He wanted to find money to do something new, something distinctively his own. To that end, during his first year, he emerged as the defender of the revenues and even came close to asking Congress for a tax increase.

At the outset, Nixon's theoretician of the budget was Herbert Stein, who had good credentials for the job. Stein had never held an academic post, but for two decades had been the fiscal specialist for the Committee for Economic Development, a private organization funded by progressive businessmen and located in Washington. During these years, Stein learned the ways of politics, developed a reputation as a good economist, and authored a well-regarded book in 1964 called *The Fiscal Revolution in America*. Stein was serving as a fellow at the Brookings Institution when, on the advice of Milton Friedman, Nixon drafted Stein to prepare budget studies, first for the campaign, then for the preinaugural transition.[5] In 1969, Stein, a registered Democrat, joined the Council of Economic Advisers.

Like CEA chairman Paul McCracken, Stein approached economic policy in a moderate and eclectic manner. Unlike McCracken, Stein liked politics, took pleasure in making speeches, and enjoyed the thrust and parry of partisan debate. Often described as owlish in appearance, Stein was a master of a deadpan humor that assured him distinction in a notably humorless administration. Though Nixon never included Stein in his inner circle, he liked him. When McCracken resigned in 1971, Nixon would appoint Stein as the chairman of the CEA, a post he would hold until the end.

Stein's task, as he saw it at the outset, was "to rehabilitate fiscal policy and bring it back from the nihilistic state into which it had fallen at the end of 1968."[6] In his preinaugural reports, Stein acknowledged that the past few years had "greatly weakened confidence" in compensatory fiscal policy. As a result, "we are left without any standard and generally accepted guide to fiscal policy." Stein agreed with Nixon's other advisers that monetary policy was the tool of choice, but he was not prepared to write off fiscal policy altogether. "It is still not safe to assume that major changes in the relation between taxes and expenditures have no effect on economic activity, employment, and prices," Stein said.[7] In fact, Stein believed that wide swings

---

[5] *New York Times*, Feb. 18, 1969, 20; *Current Biography* (1973), 389–392.

[6] Herbert Stein, "The Rehabilitation of Fiscal Policy," speech before the National Association of Savings Banks, May 26, 1969, provided me from files of CEA.

[7] "Fiscal Policy for the New Administration," Dec. 2, 1969, Task Force on Budget Policy file, Transitional Task Force Reports, NPMP.

in the budget had been the major reason for the Fed's unfortunate habit of speeding up and slowing down money growth. "If we want monetary policy to behave in a reasonably stabilizing way we should not ask it to contend with highly unpredictable and variable fiscal policy," Stein said. Accordingly, to keep fiscal policy from destabilizing the economy, Stein proposed a rule. In normal times, he said, fiscal policy should aim "to achieve a moderate, predictable and stable budget surplus."[8] A budget surplus would augment the nation's savings, providing funds for investment, especially investment in housing, which was then in short supply.

How should the administration spend the new revenues that an expanding economy would yield? Here Stein believed that the administration would need explicit priorities to help clarify choices. Stein's own priorities were hardly Republican but quite Nixonian. Ranking them only behind national security, Stein listed expenditures that would contribute "significantly to meeting the new aspirations of the disadvantaged without disappointing the expectations of the rest of society," a statement neatly balanced in the political center and expressive of Nixon's actual intentions.[9]

Wanting to be an activist president, Nixon needed to know how much revenue he had to spend. Optimism on the point ran high at first, mainly because of the so-called peace dividend. In January 1969, the outgoing Johnson administration released a study concluding that if the war in Vietnam ended immediately, defense spending would decline by $19 billion in two and a half years — enough to fund Nixon's initiatives and provide a budget surplus besides.[10]

A few weeks after Inauguration Day, Nixon appointed Stein to chair the Interagency Study Group on Post-Vietnam Planning to examine, among other things, the peace dividend. Stein presented the preliminary findings of the Study Group on May 18, 1969, at a meeting of the Cabinet Committee on Economic Policy. His was a depressing story. Assume a truce in June 1969. Because of scheduled military pay raises and commitments already made to build new weapons systems, net defense spending would decline only $5 billion by fiscal 1973. That sum would in turn be swallowed up by uncontrollable increases in existing domestic programs — mainly en-

---

[8] Stein, "Rehabilitation of Fiscal Policy."

[9] "Budget Policy for Early 1969," Nov. 5, 1969, Task Force on Budget Policy file.

[10] *New York Times*, Jan. 17, 1969, 16.

titlement programs such as social security, public assistance, Medicare, and Medicaid. The only dividend that Nixon could count on was a growth dividend — that is, increases in revenues resulting from increases in GNP. Assuming no new federal programs and a robust economy, the growth dividend would produce a surplus of $23 billion to spend in fiscal year 1973 (FY 73), but visible claims on the budget so far exceeded that amount that the administration could face an estimated deficit that year of $14 to $19 billion.[11]

"What happened to the peace dividend?" Nixon asked Stein after his presentation to the Cabinet Committee. "The peace dividend will be there," Stein replied, "but we have already committed it." Commerce Secretary Maurice Stans thought the administration had better begin dispelling the public's illusion "that there are billions available ahead," but Nixon rejected passive acceptance of Stein's conclusions. "We can't resign ourselves to what we are doing and the way we are doing it, including the tax system," he said. Picking up the hint, McCracken said, "To get room, we have to raise taxes" — a proposal anathema to any true conservative. "I am not sure you may not have to have it," Nixon said. "The only way to get an increase in revenue" was to find some new form of taxation, "and don't let that out of this room." The more Nixon warmed to the subject, the less he was ready to acquiesce in fiscal inertia. "We must not become captives of the forces we inherited," Nixon went on. "If we just 'manage it better,' we will have failed. . . As an administration, we'll either ride only with the same programs, managing it five percent better but down that same road that leads to the precipice, or we can seize the moment and control the destiny of the country." Nixon closed the meeting saying, "We have to be bold." By boldness, he meant shaking up the bureaucracy, encouraging new ideas, and, of course, finding the revenue to realize them.[12]

Stein's Post-Vietnam Study Group had discovered a truth that would cast a shadow over budget making for the indefinite future. Before the mid-1960s, thanks to economic growth, government revenues tended to outpace expenditures in normal times, providing funds for new programs.

---

[11] Memo from Stein to Cabinet Committee on Economic Policy, May 13, 1969, (CF) FG 238, WHSF. This includes Stein's summary of FY 73. Other reports, not entirely consistent, are dated May 5, 1969 (Safire papers), and May 28, 1969, Cabinet Committee on Economic Policy file, SMOF: Stein.

[12] Report of the Meeting of the Cabinet Committee on Economic Policy, May 28, 1969, Safire papers.

After that, entitlements whose claims on revenues were open-ended tended to drive expenditures faster than revenues, producing chronic deficits and limiting new initiatives. The final report of the Post-Vietnam Study Group, presented at a meeting of administration officials at the Western White House in August 1969, underscored the point. By 1974–1975, the report said, projected federal revenues would grow sufficiently to cover the cost of existing programs and a few of Nixon's, but only $13 billion more would remain to satisfy claims of $100 billion for new spending plus a surplus for housing.[13] Breaking the bad news to the press after the meeting, Presidential Counselor Daniel Patrick Moynihan said, "I'm afraid the peace dividend tends to become evanescent like the morning clouds around San Clemente."[14]

## II

Even as they peered into the bleak fiscal future, Nixon and his advisers faced the problem of a role for fiscal policy now. What, if anything, should the budget contribute to the policy of gradualism? More specifically, what should the administration do with the 10 percent tax surcharge — due to expire on June 30, 1969 — that Lyndon Johnson had sponsored in 1968 to cool off the economy? The surcharge had helped shift the budget from a $25 billion deficit in FY 68 to an estimated $3 billion surplus in FY 69, but it had also failed to slow the boom or curb inflation. Furthermore, Nixon had campaigned against the surtax during the recent election, saying, "I will allow the 10 percent surcharge to expire as scheduled on June 30 or will reduce it significantly."[15] Once elected, Nixon was not sure. Stein took the position that extending the surcharge was consistent with the administration's gradualist objectives.[16] Other advisers urged him to get rid of a tax that practically everyone loathed, in particular the voters who had to pay it.

One of the peculiarities of the American government was that Nixon did not prepare the budget for next fiscal year — FY 70, beginning July 1, 1969. Lyndon Johnson did. In his last weeks in office, Johnson leaned

---

[13] Herbert Stein, Maurice Mann, and Murray Weidenbaum to Cabinet Committee on Economic Policy, Aug. 11, 1969, Cabinet Committee on Economic Policy file.

[14] *New York Times*, Aug. 26, 1969, 1, 28.

[15] Ibid., Oct. 27, 1968, III, 14.

[16] "Fiscal Policy for the New Administration," Dec. 3, 1968.

toward recommending extension of the surcharge for another year but hesitated to endorse so unpopular a measure in his farewell budget if Nixon really intended to scrap it. The president-elect preferred to duck the whole issue. Intermediaries trying to resolve these differences had no easy time of it. "I don't know of any two men who hated the surtax more than the two Presidents," one reported. Finally Johnson and Nixon got on the phone and settled the matter themselves.[17] Johnson asked Congress to extend the 10 percent tax surcharge for one more year, and Nixon, hedging, issued a statement saying that pending a review by his administration, "I will support the president's suggestion that the surcharge be extended."[18] Nixon's options remained open.

Once in office, Nixon's advisers launched the policy of gradualism, including for safety's sake, a bow to fiscal restraint, which meant either keeping the surcharge or slashing expenditures. In one of his first acts, Nixon ordered the departments to review their budgets with an eye to cutting them. The departments sent back requests for more money. In despair, Budget Director Robert Mayo, a true believer in fiscal frugality, met with Nixon on March 7, 1969, to seek his backing for "drastic cuts." Nixon took the occasion to let Mayo know he was not really interested. According to the notes of the meeting, "the President cautioned against the practice of reducing expenditures so much that the national economy suffers." Small cuts, yes, Nixon implied, but nothing so drastic that it caused a recession or antagonized the voters. Mayo dutifully agreed, "and as the President began looking over the papers on his desk — and packing his briefcase for the Florida trip — the meeting came to a close."[19]

On March 26, 1969, Nixon did what his economic advisers now told him he must do. He sent Congress a request to extend for one more year the unloved 10 percent tax surcharge, an action that *Newsweek* described as "surely the least popular of his young administration."[20] Nixon followed up on April 12 by proposing to cut the budget that Johnson had submitted for next year from $197 billion to $193 billion. The surcharge plus the budget cut would yield an estimated budget surplus in FY 70 of nearly $6 billion,

[17] *Newsweek* (Jan. 27, 1969), 78.

[18] *New York Times*, Jan. 15, 1969, 21.

[19] Alexander Butterfield for President's file, Mar. 7, 1969, Memos for the President's File, POF.

[20] *Pub Paps RN 1969*, 253–255; *Newsweek* (Apr. 7, 1969), 60.

"the fourth largest in our history," the president boasted.[21] Privately, Nixon admitted to Republican congressional leaders that the budget cuts were disappointing and that some of them "aren't going to stand up."[22]

Only weeks after sending Congress his request for the surcharge extension, Nixon amended it. The surcharge, it turned out, was no sure thing. Since Democrats outnumbered Republicans in the House by 243 to 192, the administration would have to fish for support among the opposition. Meeting with administration officials in mid-April, Wilbur Mills, the powerful Democrat who chaired the House Ways and Means Committee, suggested the bait. Couple repeal of the investment tax credit with the surcharge, Mills said, and you pick up a hundred Democrats.[23]

Sponsored by President Kennedy in 1962, the investment tax credit permitted businessmen to deduct 7 percent of the cost of new plant and equipment from their federal taxes. In essence, the credit was a tax cut for business. Though the corporations originally had preferred other forms of tax relief, they soon learned to love this one. By the late 1960s, liberal Democrats, in an anticorporate mood, had turned against the investment tax credit as an unjustified giveaway and aimed to repeal it.

Mills's suggestion that the administration sponsor repeal of the credit for the sake of the surcharge touched off a heated debate in the administration, which was not resolved until Nixon himself heard the arguments at a fifty-five-minute meeting in the White House on April 21, 1969. Charls Walker, the Treasury strong man, made the case for repeal, that is, for raising taxes on the president's business constituents. "Social priorities today call not for strong stimulus to equipment spending," Walker said, "today's needs are for help to the cities, to the disadvantaged, and to those in poverty." Repeal of the investment tax credit would yield $3 billion for these purposes, as well as dampen the investment boom currently fueling inflation. Not least, Walker said, repeal could "be the clincher in achieving passage" of the surcharge.[24] Arthur Burns argued the negative. Though he

---

[21] *Pub Paps RN 1969*, 278–280.

[22] Patrick Buchanan for President, Apr. 15, 1969, Memo for President's File, POF.

[23] Draft Memo from Charls Walker to President, Apr. 16, 1969, Agency File: Treasury Dept. 1969–1970, SMOF: Stein. Walker mentioned here the meeting with Mills and Mills's prediction of 100 Democrats' votes.

[24] These quotes taken from Walker's Draft Memo; for participants in the meeting, President's Daily Calendar, Apr. 21, 1969.

was willing to consider suspension of the tax credit, he opposed repeal with some passion. Burns made the traditional Republican argument that higher taxes on business would hinder investment and cramp long-term economic growth.[25]

But this was not a traditional Republican administration. Later that day Nixon surprised official Washington by resubmitting the tax surcharge in a package with repeal of the investment credit. In FY 70, revenues gained from repeal would make possible reduction of the tax surcharge from 10 percent during the first half of the year to 5 percent the second. After that, Nixon said, he intended to use the $3 billion in revenue from repeal of the tax credit for his program of revenue-sharing with state and local governments and for tax credits to encourage private investment in poverty areas.[26] Herbert Stein explained the president's decision a few days later. "It seemed at least to some of us who were involved in the discussions that there were more important things at this juncture in history to do with the Federal budget, with the national output, than to make even more rapid a rate of growth that is already very rapid or making larger a gross national product in 1975 or 1980, which already in any case is going to be a staggering size."[27]

Nixon hoped that his support for repeal of the investment tax credit would rally liberal Democrats to the tax surcharge. But the hundred Democratic votes Mills predicted proved a mirage. The liberals, it turned out, wanted much more than repeal of the credit and intended to hold the surcharge hostage until they got it. Senator Edward Kennedy set the ransom price in a speech before the Detroit Economic Club in April. The surcharge, said the senator, must be linked to "at least a first step toward basic tax reform," that is, the achievement of greater equity in the tax code by closing loopholes.[28]

A single remark had triggered the tax reform furor of 1969. In January, outgoing Secretary of the Treasury Joseph Barr told Congress that 155 taxpayers with incomes over $200,000, including twenty-one millionaires, had paid no income taxes in 1967. Said Barr, "We face now the possibility of a taxpayer revolt if we do not soon make major reforms in our income

---

[25] For an account of the meeting, Rowland Evans, Jr., and Robert D. Novak, *Nixon in the White House* (1971), 194–195.

[26] *Pub Paps RN 1969*, 310–313.

[27] *New York Times*, Apr. 25, 1969, 65.

[28] *New York Times*, Apr. 9, 1969, 28.

taxes."[29] As angry letters flooded Washington, liberal Democrats rushed to lead a tax reform crusade that soon enlisted nearly everybody. Yielding to the pressure, Nixon informed Wilbur Mills in February 1969 that he would submit one package of tax reforms at the end of the current House session and another in 1970.[30] Nixon himself had little interest in tax reform, and not because he liked loopholes. "Once in 1969," Stein recalled, "during a discussion of ways to close tax loopholes he said that whatever we did would not matter because sophisticated lawyers would find a way to beat the system. He attributed this wisdom to his recent experience practicing law in New York."[31]

Once liberals demanded tax reform as the price of the surcharge, the Treasury moved up Nixon's timetable and began working round the clock on an "interim" tax reform package for quick submission to Congress. On April 21, in the same message that sweetened the surcharge with repeal of the investment tax credit, Nixon submitted an interim tax reform package in a separate bill. Joining the movement to curb the tax-dodging rich, Nixon proposed tightening up on charitable deductions, tinkering with a few lesser inequities of the tax code, and limiting the amount of income that wealthy taxpayers could shield from taxation. For good measure, he included a recommendation (the low-income allowance) that would eliminate 5 million low-income families and individuals from the tax rolls.[32] Nixon was becoming the Republican Robin Hood.

Liberals were not satisfied by mere interim tax reform. If they gave him the surcharge now, could they trust Nixon to submit a full menu of reforms later? On May 14, 1969, fifty-four liberal Democratic House members petitioned Ways and Means, where tax legislation originates, to hold up the surcharge until tax reform was safe.[33] Because tax reform legislation would take months to pass and because the surcharge was scheduled to expire on June 30, the most the liberals would consider was extension of the surcharge for a month at a time until they got the reforms they wanted.

---

[29] Ibid., Jan. 18, 1969, 15.

[30] Memo from Bryce Harlow to Staff Sec., Feb. 23, 1969, President's Meeting File, POF.

[31] Herbert Stein, *Presidential Economics*, 2d rev. ed. (1988), 137.

[32] Nixon proposed "setting a 50% limitation on the use of the principal tax preferences which are subject to change by law." He called this "in effect a 'minimum income tax.'" *Pub Paps RN 1969*, 310–313.

[33] *New York Times*, May 15, 1961, 1.

Over the Memorial Day weekend, passage of the surcharge in any form became doubtful when congressmen visiting their home districts encountered stiff tax resistance — a mood confirmed a few weeks later in a Gallup poll showing 38 percent in favor of the surcharge, 51 percent against.[34] Though Wilbur Mills had declared for the surcharge, he did not like to lose and now was inclined to lock up the surcharge in his committee.[35] For Nixon, the stakes had become more than just the surcharge. This was his first test in Congress, and he would have to win it or lose all hope of leading the divided government.

An administration that in January had considered abandoning the surcharge defended it in June as if Western civilization hung in the balance. On June 10, top Nixon officials held a joint press conference to make the case for the temporary tax increase. The newspapers gave the story little play.[36] On June 11, Treasury Secretary David Kennedy appeared before the liberal Democratic Study Group to implore its members to support the surtax now and trust the president to do the right thing on tax reform later. "We think you're conning us," Congressman John Brademus replied.[37] On June 12, a bipartisan group of House leaders went to the White House to hear McCracken, Kennedy, and William McChesney Martin predict doom unless Congress passed the surcharge. Without more revenue to prevent a budget deficit, these worthies warned, prices would keep climbing, inflationary psychology would be rekindled, and America's global position would deteriorate.

At this meeting, not unmoved, the Democratic House Whip Hale Boggs offered a deal. At the moment, the surcharge bill was packaged only with the investment tax credit. If Nixon added one other feature, Boggs said, the Democratic leadership would back the surcharge without waiting for tax reforms. All Nixon had to do was shift the low-income allowance for the poor from the tax reform bill to the surcharge bill. Majority Leader Carl Albert predicted a hundred Democratic votes for the surcharge with this change. Nixon sealed the bargain on the spot.[38] The administration, it

---

[34] *Congressional Quarterly Weekly Reports* (June 20, 1969), 1076; for Gallup poll, *New York Times,* July 3, 1969, 14.

[35] *New York Times,* June 8, 1969, 1.

[36] Ibid., June 11, 1969, 1.

[37] Ibid., June 12, 1969, 1.

[38] Buchanan for President, June 12, 1969, Memos for the President's file, POF. This is a report of the leader's meeting.

appeared, had finally severed the link between the surcharge and reform. But the AFL-CIO pressured liberal Democrats to stand firm for tax reform, and Southern Democrats continued to oppose the surcharge no matter how it was sweetened. In the end, Mills released the amended bill from his committee, but Boggs and Albert could deliver only a ragtag group of Democratic regulars to support it.[39]

On June 30, facing defeat of the surcharge later that day on the House floor, Nixon invited to breakfast the one group of congressmen who might yet rescue the tax bill. His twenty-three guests were all conservative Republican congressmen who opposed higher taxes on principle and had either decided to vote against the surcharge or were leaning that way. Declaring that his leadership was at stake, the president pleaded for support on grounds of party loyalty.[40]

That afternoon, at the conclusion of five hours of tense debate, the surcharge failed in the first vote by 201 to 194. Behind the House rail, a group of Republican conservatives drew straws to see who would switch votes and save the president.[41] On the second vote, the surcharge squeezed through 210 to 205. Only fifty-three Democrats voted for the bill. Only nine of Nixon's twenty-three breakfast guests voted against him.[42] "We didn't twist any arms but we did beat a few heads," Nixon quipped.[43]

Because the surcharge bill still had to pass the Senate and because existing authority for the surtax would expire the next day, Congress rushed through emergency legislation to extend the surcharge for one month, giving the Senate time to deliberate on the full one-year extension. On July 31, the Senate gave Nixon only part of what he wanted by passing a bill with a single provision — extension of the 10 percent tax surcharge through December 1969. If Nixon wanted his 5 percent surcharge for the second half of the fiscal year (January–June 1970), he would have to keep his promise on tax reform. The House accepted the Senate bill in early August, leaving Nixon no choice except to sign. The budget surplus that Nixon had predicted in April for the next fiscal year still remained in doubt.

---

[39] *Newsweek* (July 7, 1969), 69.

[40] Bryce Harlow to Staff Secretary, Aug. 11, 1969, President's Meeting file, POF. This is a report on June 30 meeting.

[41] *Newsweek* (July 14, 1969), 22.

[42] *Cong Rec* (1969), 17874–17875.

[43] Memo from Jim Keough, July 10, 1969, Memos for President's File, POF.

## III

On August 3, 1969, three days after congressional passage of the six-month surcharge extension, Ways and Means reported a 368-page tax reform bill that narrowed a lot of loopholes but made the tax code even more tangled than before. Among other things, the bill increased taxes on capital gains, imposed federal taxation on interest from state and municipal bonds (later dropped), limited the amount of income that the wealthy could shield from taxation, and tightened tax preferences benefiting the oil industry. At the last minute, Ways and Means also added to its tax reform legislation odds and ends originally in the House surcharge bill but cut out of the six-month extension: repeal of the investment tax credit; removal of low-income taxpayers from the tax rolls; and, most important to the administration, extension of the tax surcharge at a 5 percent rate for the last six months of the fiscal year. The surcharge and tax reform were now in the same bill.[44]

But a funny thing happened to the bill on the way to the House floor. Both Wilbur Mills and the administration had intended the tax reform provisions to be revenue-neutral. On the one hand, Congress would raise new revenue by closing loopholes; on the other, it would provide tax relief for selected taxpayers in equal amount. Ways and Means originally reduced taxes only in the form of the low-income allowance for the poor and a generous increase of the standard deduction, which would benefit taxpayers in the five lowest brackets. Discipline in the committee began to crack when repeal of the investment tax credit was suddenly added to the bill. Nixon had intended to use revenues gained from repeal to do good works. But the Ways and Means Committee, playing to the public's hatred of taxes, promptly sacrificed revenue from repealing the tax credit by cutting income tax rates on all but the bottom five brackets, already beneficiaries of the increased standard deduction.[45] With a stroke of the pen, the committee had wiped out $3 billion in revenue that Nixon had been counting on and given tax breaks to practically everybody in the country.

As Mills discovered when he took his bill to the House Rules Committee, not quite everybody. Liberal Democrats on the Rules Committee pointed out that Ways and Means had overlooked homeowners with in-

---

[44] "Tax Reform Act of 1969," Aug. 3, 1969, House Report 91–413.
[45] "Tax Reform Act of 1969," 211–212.

comes from $8,000 to $12,000. Mainly in the bottom five brackets, these taxpayers would obtain no relief from the more generous standard deduction because they itemized to deduct mortgage interest. Mills had neglected precisely the voters for whose political allegiance Nixon and the Democrats were then in combat. Mills blamed the oversight on a staff misunderstanding. "That was a very remarkable misunderstanding," Congressman Richard Bolling said. "I'd say so myself," Mills replied. Hastily reassembling during the lunch break, Ways and Means made amends by cutting the tax rates in the bottom five brackets by 1 percent each. In twenty minutes, Nixon had lost another $2.4 billion.[46]

The administration watched distraught as Congress transformed tax reform into tax relief. The 5 percent surcharge for the last half of FY 70 was safe, but at what cost? In FY 72, the committee would give away an estimated $3.2 billion from repeal of the investment tax credit and $3.7 billion in net additional tax relief. At a time when his advisers were telling Nixon that the peace dividend had evaporated, Congress was threatening to reduce revenue by nearly $7 billion below Nixon's April expectation. As Stein explained, that was "about one-third of the increased revenue that would otherwise have been available after meeting the built-in cost increases of existing non-defense programs."[47] Unfortunately, Stein said, getting Ways and Means to give up tax relief would be about as easy as taking "a beefsteak back from a Great Dane."[48]

On August 7, 1969, the House passed the tax bill and sent it on to the Senate. The bill would shore up revenues in the short run with the 5 percent tax surcharge but would squander them in the long run with tax cuts. Four days later, Nixon submitted to Congress two expensive new programs — revenue sharing and a guaranteed income for low-income families — which, if enacted, would ultimately add $9 billion to the federal budget at current levels of income.[49] A president presumed to be conservative wanted to save the revenues to pay for deeds such as these, but the Democrats in Congress were bent on frittering away the revenues.

---

[46] *Washington Post*, Aug. 6, 1969; 1; *Wall Street Journal*, Aug. 6, 3; *New York Times*, Aug. 3, 1; Aug. 6, 1; *Congressional Quarterly Almanac* (1969), 610. Quotes in CQ.

[47] Stein, "Economic Implications of the House of Representatives Tax Bill," Aug. 23, 1969, FG 3-3, Bureau of Budget, NA.

[48] Stein for President, Aug. 1, 1969, Memos for President's file, Aug. 1, 1969, SMOF: Houthakker.

[49] *Pub Paps RN 1969*, 647–654, 665–668.

IV

On September 4, 1969, Treasury Secretary David Kennedy appeared before the Senate Finance Committee to present at last the administration's full menu of tax reforms and to critique the House tax bill under consideration, a bill recognized by everyone as the most important of the congressional session. Kennedy attacked the House bill on two grounds. It cut revenues when the country had pressing domestic needs, and it suffered from an imbalance between tax reductions for individuals and tax increases on business, tilting the bill too far toward consumption and away from investment. Kennedy proposed to remedy these flaws by a less generous increase in the standard deduction and a cut of two percentage points in the corporate income tax. Congress ignored both recommendations. Kennedy also tried to chip away at tax reform, for example, by weakening the provision in the bill to raise taxes on capital gains.[50] Commented the *New York Times*, the Nixon administration did "after all consist of people who think like Republicans."[51]

On one important tax reform issue Secretary Kennedy misread Nixon's intentions. In the 1968 campaign, Nixon had pledged in Texas to protect the most notorious loophole in all the tax code — the 27.5 percent depletion allowance for the oil industry. The House committee had reduced the allowance to 20 percent, and though Nixon privately was prepared to accept this reduction, he wanted the treasury "to go easy" on other oil tax preferences. As Nixon told one Treasury aide, he wished to help a Houston congressman named George Bush run for the Senate next year.[52]

In his Senate testimony Secretary Kennedy accepted too readily the cut in the depletion allowance and favored other provisions tightening tax treatment of oil income. Furious, the chairman of the Republican party's Finance Committee in the Southwest, William Leidtke of Pennzoil, wrote

---

[50] "Tax Reform Act of 1969," Committee on Finance, Senate hearings (1969), 510 ff.

[51] *New York Times*, Sept. 7, 1969, IV 3.

[52] Memo from Edwin Cohen to the Secretary, Sept. 16, 1969, FI 11, WHCF. Cohen, the Treasury's tax expert, summarized his part in oil tax-reform events in this memo, including his conversation with Nixon, who said to "go easy" on oil and that "he wanted to help George Bush run for the Senate." Nixon also told Cohen to accept the reduction in the oil depletion allowance to 20 percent, but clearly expected Cohen to back off on another loophole for "intangible drilling expenses." Kennedy failed to make a pro forma gesture on the depletion allowance and presented a watered-down reform on expensing intangibles that angered the industry. The final bill cut the depletion allowance from 27.5 percent to 22 percent.

Bush to say that Kennedy's testimony would cost Nixon both campaign contributions and votes in Texas and hurt Bush's chances for a Senate seat. Bush promptly forwarded the letter to the White House.[53] In the end, the Senate Finance Committee took a lot of the bite out of the bill's oil provisions, and the unfortunate Kennedy had to eat crow at a meeting with big independent oil operators in Bush's home.[54]

"The heat is off tax reform," one congressman noted, but the fever to please the voters by cutting taxes had not abated. Discipline held in the Finance Committee, but Chairman Russell Long foresaw a breakdown on the Senate floor. "After all," Long said, "we're entitled to have some fun too."[55] Indeed, the Senate would treat the tax bill in the fashion of a legislature in a banana republic. Senator Albert Gore, an anticorporate liberal from Tennessee facing an uphill battle for reelection in 1970, believed that the bill did not "give tax relief to the guy who needs it most — the man living in the suburbs in his little house with a big mortgage and filled with children."[56] In a move that transformed the debate and ultimately the bill, Gore proposed in committee to eliminate across-the-board rate reduction from the House bill and concentrate relief on taxpayers of modest means by increasing the individual exemption. Since 1948, each taxpayer had been permitted to exempt $600 from taxation for himself and for each dependent. Gore proposed increasing the exemption to $1,250. There was only one problem, said the Treasury's tax expert, Edwin Cohen. Gore's proposal would cost the Treasury $20 billion — or one-quarter of current revenues from the income tax. A scaled-down version of the Gore proposal barely missed committee approval.[57]

Senators began having fun on the floor in early December when Gore successfully moved to strike across-the-board tax reductions and replace them with an increase in the personal exemption from $600 to $800. At a stroke, the Senate transformed a bill that provided tax relief for all classes to one that provided relief only for those at or near the bottom of the

---

[53] Memo from Bush to Harlow, Sept. 15, 1969, with attachment, Liedtke to Bush, Sept. 5, 1969, FI 11 file, WHCF. Bush wrote on Liedtke letter, "This is a *good* letter on my favorite subject. Whoops, another mortar attack coming in — back under the desk! Hastily, George."

[54] Bush to Kennedy, Nov. 12, 1969, BE 4/Oil, WHCF.

[55] *New York Times*, Oct. 10, 1969, 1, 33.

[56] Ibid., Dec. 14, 1969, IV, 1.

[57] For Cohen's testimony, "Tax Reform Act," Senate hearings, 509–510. *Congressional Quarterly Weekly Report* (Nov. 7, 1969), 2189. The committee voted 8–8 to reject an increase to $850 by 1972.

50  NIXON'S ECONOMY

income scale.[58] Once the Gore amendment passed, a reporter noted, "an 'anything goes' attitude swept the Senate like a grass fire."[59] Senators began approving new tax breaks as well as other doubtful amendments, including a huge 15 percent increase in social security benefits without a corresponding increase in social security taxes.[60]

The bill, which the Senate approved on December 11, 1969, was a fiscal calamity. It cut revenues by $3 billion more than the House bill had done, meaning that by FY 72 Nixon would have $10 billion less in revenue than he had expected in April.[61] At his press conference on December 8, a reporter asked, "Sir, if the final version of the tax reform bill now pending in Congress includes the Senate-adopted $800 exemption provision and the 15 percent social security increase, can you sign it?" Not noted for terseness, Nixon replied simply, "No."[62] The next day the president told aides to leave the bill "screwed up" so he could veto it.[63]

The House-Senate conference committee that met to resolve differences over the bill restored a measure of sanity. The committee knocked out giveaways voted in the Senate and reworked the Gore amendment by cutting the increase in the personal exemption from $800 to $750 and phasing it in over three years. This change plus the temporary 5 percent surcharge meant that the bill would add $3.7 billion to the revenues during the current fiscal year (FY 70), but by FY 72 would cost Nixon $7 billion.[64] As for tax reform, the scholar Joseph Pechman pronounced the bill's provisions "a weak brew compared to what most people would identify as a prescription for tax reform."[65] On December 20, Congress ended its yearlong struggle over taxes by passing the bill and sending it to the president, whose intentions were not at all certain, even to him.

To sign or not to sign. That question occupied much of Christmas week, 1969. Nixon had his own reason for disliking the tax bill. After Gore got rid of rate reduction, the main relief provisions were removal of the poor from the income tax and the increased personal exemption. The bill helped a lot

[58] Cong Rec (1969), 36671–36676.
[59] New York Times, Dec. 7, 1969, IV, 1.
[60] Congressional Quarterly Weekly Report (Dec. 12, 1969), 2526–2531.
[61] Cong Rec (1969), 40703.
[62] Pub Paps RN 1969, 1005.
[63] E-Notes, Dec. 9, 1969.
[64] "Tax Reform Act of 1969," House Report No. 91-782.
[65] Washington Post, Dec. 16, 1969, A14.

of poor people, but it did not help the people he hoped to recruit to the New Majority, the people "in the middle," Nixon told the Troika. "They pay income taxes. They are hardest hit living in the cities . . . We have to do something for *them*. I'm for helping the poor but we must be political — must speak to our constituency. The tax bill doesn't help."[66] Ultimately his decision on signing hinged on how he weighed the short-term revenue gain against the long-term loss.

It was a close call, but he decided to go with the short-term gain. Without the $3.7 billion in net additional revenue this current fiscal year, all hope was lost for the fading budget surplus. Corporations would see a deficit as a sign of weakening will in the anti-inflation fight. Arthur Burns, not yet installed at the Fed, was threatening to keep money tight if fiscal policy went soft. Social security recipients would be angry at the loss of increased benefits provided in the bill, and Congress would have wasted a whole year on tax legislation if Nixon vetoed. "Sign the tax bill," Mc-Cracken advised on December 26. "Clear the air. Build the case for easier money."[67] In a statement on December 30, 1969, Nixon said he was signing despite the bill's harmful long-term effect on the budget and inflation because "it is a necessary beginning in the process of making our tax system fair to the taxpayer."[68] Privately, he denounced the Tax Reform Act of 1969 as "an attorney's paradise."[69]

V

As the battle over taxes was reaching its climax in Congress, Nixon's advisers were deep in preparation for the budget he would submit in January 1970 for the fiscal year beginning next July (FY 71). The more they looked at the numbers, the more they saw red ink, not only in the next fiscal year but for the current one. Back in April 1969, Nixon had predicted a surplus in FY 70 of nearly $6 billion. To help achieve it, he had cut $4 billion from Johnson's budget. In July, only a few weeks into FY 70, uncontrollables were rising so much faster than expected that Nixon had to cut out another $3.5 billion, mainly from defense.[70] Congress kept appropriat-

---

[66] E-Notes, Dec. 26, 1969.
[67] Ibid., Dec. 26, 1967.
[68] *Pub Paps RN 1969*, 1044–1046.
[69] E-Notes, Dec. 26, 1969.
[70] *Pub Paps RN 1969*, 536–538.

ing more than he requested, and revenue estimates for the year were falling. Even with passage of the 5 percent surcharge, the surplus would turn into a $2.8 billion deficit by the end of the fiscal year.

Looking ahead to FY 71, the picture was gloomier still. With expenditures estimated at $207 billion and revenues at $200 billion, Nixon faced the prospect of submitting a budget with a deficit amid the struggle against inflation and the effort to establish fiscal credibility with the skittish business community. Supported by fellow Troika members David Kennedy and Robert Mayo, in late November Paul McCracken sent Nixon memos on the budget so starkly outlining the alternatives that they got Nixon's full attention. Given the looming deficit, McCracken offered the president three options. He could fiddle with the numbers to present a budget for FY 71 with an illusory balance. He could cut spending to create a real balance, a task that "seems, and possibly is, impossible." Or he could raise taxes, which was the option favored by the Troika. McCracken urged "laying it on the line," explaining the fiscal realities to the American people, and proposing a new tax, perhaps a Value-Added Tax, or VAT, similar to a tax now widely used in Europe. He knew this was "strong medicine," McCracken said, but he believed that the country would "respond affirmatively."[71]

Nixon circulated McCracken's views for comment. George Shultz[72] and Arthur Burns[73] wrote back to challenge McCracken's position. Taking the classic conservative position, both opposed new taxes because they opposed big government, urging reduced spending instead. For FY 71, Burns wanted to force expenditures below $200 billion, a target he said, "of great psychological importance." If he did not get a tight budget, the Fed chairman-designate implied, Nixon would not get easy money. Shultz and Burns also took the opportunity to oppose the budget rule that had been the administration's informal guide since the Council of Economic Advisers had proposed it early in the year. "The policy of a modest surplus as

---

[71] McCracken for President, Nov. 17, 1969 and Nov. 26, 1969, (CF) BE 5 file, WHSF. Quote on impossibility of cutting, Nov. 17; on laying it on the line, Nov. 26.

[72] Memo from Shultz to Cole, Nov. 25, 1969, (CF) BE 5 file, WHSF; memo from Shultz to Cole, Dec. 6, 1969, Records of Secretary, DOL.

[73] Memo from Burns to Staff Secretary, Nov. 25, 1969, (CF) BE 5 file; memo from Burns to Staff Secretary, Nov. 30, 1969, same file. For Burns's hint at connection between tight budget and easier money, "Nomination of Arthur F. Burns," Committee on Banking and Currency, Senate hearings (1969), 14–16.

standard practice seems to me unworkable and represents an unrealistic expectation," Shultz said. If the budget ran a surplus, Congress would never consider it an addition to saving but would either spend it or give it away in tax reduction. Burns, too, dismissed the idea of a regular budget surplus, calling it "a little romantic." Thus, at the end of 1969, the administration was still searching for fiscal first principles, a quest that would persist through the Nixon years and never come to closure.

Though Nixon's advisers were divided on the issue, the Treasury and the Troika worked through December on a possible tax increase that would free the president from his fiscal dilemma. The chief candidate was Mc-Cracken's favorite, the Value-Added Tax. To calculate this tax, each business firm would subtract from sales revenues the cost of purchases from other firms and pay a tax on the remainder.[74] A VAT of 1 percent would yield $5 billion in revenue. As late as December 30, when it summed up the arguments for signing the Tax Reform Act, the Troika still hoped that Nixon would ask for new taxes in the next budget to make up the lost revenue.[75]

But Nixon was not ready. Key advisers opposed any tax increase, Congress was inhospitable, and 1970 was an election year. In a long meeting on December 26, Paul Volcker of the Treasury stated that there was "no political support for the Value-Added Tax." McCracken added, "or any tax." Then, said Nixon, let's wait until next year. In any case, asking for a tax increase before a congressional election would be politically "incredible," he said.[76] Nixon was not burying the idea, merely postponing an alternative to the vanished peace dividend and the revenue squandered by the profligate Congress. Though the VAT would resurface for serious White House consideration in future years, the time never seemed right to propose it.

Fiscal ironies abounded in 1969. Richard Nixon, arch Republican, wanted to extend Lyndon Johnson's tax surcharge, spend money for good works, repeal the pro-business investment tax credit, defend the revenues, and maybe even raise taxes. His main antagonists were liberal Democrats, whose fiscal performance in 1969 had been less than responsible. The most

---

[74] McCracken for President, Dec. 24, 1969, Memos for President's file, SMOF: Houthakker.

[75] Kennedy, Mayo, McCracken for President, Dec. 30, 1967, Memos for President's file, SMOF: Houthakker.

[76] E-Notes, Dec. 26, 1969.

scathing critique of that performance was delivered by one of their own, Charles Schultze, a director of the Budget Bureau under Lyndon Johnson. Writing in the *Washington Post* on December 19, Schultze said it made sense for conservatives, who opposed government, to cut taxes. "Yet why are the liberals not only following this strategy but leading the parade? . . . There is much brave talk of 'new priorities.' But with large tax cuts enacted, there will simply not be the revenues available to pay for these new priorities. When the chips were down on tax cuts, those who *talked* about priorities for pollution control and education and an end to hunger *voted* for a different set of priorities — for beer and cosmetics and whitewall tires."[77] Schultze neglected to note that practically the only other people in Washington who were making this point worked in the Nixon White House.

---

[77] *Washington Post*, Dec. 19, 1969, A22.

# Chapter 3

# Election Year 1970

---

I

Richard Nixon had participated in political campaigns every two years since 1946. It was what he lived to do. In 1970, he would be campaigning to elect Republicans to Congress, especially to the Senate, where for the first time in years his party had a chance to take control. At stake in the upper chamber were thirty-five seats, twenty-five held by Democrats, many of them vulnerable. If the Republicans could achieve a net gain of seven, the Senate would belong to them. Republicans had some cause for optimism. Nixon had rallied the Silent Majority and undercut the antiwar opposition by his program of phased withdrawals of U.S. troops from Vietnam. In addition, the mood of the country was becoming increasingly conservative on issues of race and culture — the Social Issue — on which Republicans would base their campaign. But Nixon himself was not optimistic. Signs of recession were multiplying; and a recession, he knew, would kill his party's chances in the fall.

In January 1970, as his advisers were preparing the economic game plan for the year ahead, Nixon brooded in the White House over the inadequacies of gradualism. Meeting with McCracken while Haldeman took notes, he sought reassurance. "The P kept asking Paul to explain why we hadn't solved the inflation problem, and asking if he still felt we were doing the right thing. Paul hesitated before saying yes, thus shaking the P's confidence a little. P made point that he never heard of losing an election because of inflation, but lots were lost because of unemployment or recession. Point is, he's determined not to let the war on inflation get carried to the point that it will lose us House or Senate seats in November." A few weeks later, Nixon issued instructions to Haldeman and Ehrlichman. "Made point to E very strongly," Haldeman noted, "that our concern must not be inflation but recession. Pay lip service to inflation fight but don't let it run danger of a recession." The administration had to turn the economy around now, "while not appearing to do so . . . Wants E to ride it continuously, and really crack the whip." These were empty orders. None of the president's advisers shared Nixon's doubts about gradualism, and Nixon lacked sufficient confidence in his own economic judgment to force a change by himself. "Feels 1970 will be the worst year," Haldeman recorded. "Will have inflation/recession."[1]

The Council of Economic Advisers did not agree. In February 1970, Paul McCracken was back with another cheery forecast. In his view, declining output in the last quarter of 1969 did not signal a recession. Thanks to the Fed's policy of zero money growth during the last half of 1969, the movement of output would be "essentially lateral" during the first half of 1970, but it probably would not fall. During the second half, McCracken said, output would resume expanding but at a pace slow enough to accommodate a reduction in the inflation rate. The CEA's forecasting model punched out the numbers. Real GNP would grow approximately 2 percent for the year, unemployment would rise no higher than 4.6 percent, and the inflation rate as measured by the GNP deflator would decelerate from nearly 5 percent at the end of 1969 to 3 to 3.5 percent in 1970. All this assumed, of course, that Arthur Burns and the Fed would supply enough money to avoid a recession.[2]

When McCracken presented his forecast to the Joint Economic Committee of Congress in February 1970, Wisconsin Democrat William Proxmire mocked it. Gradualism was doing to Nixon what Vietnam had done to Johnson, Proxmire said. In 1965, the Johnson administration "gave us body counts in Vietnam, you are giving us kind of economic body counts on the drop in production . . . the drop in new orders . . . the drop in corporate profits, and now, of course, a rise last week in unemployment." Proxmire did not trust McCracken's forecast in 1970 any more than he had trusted his forecasts in 1969.[3] As it turned out, Proxmire — and Nixon — were right. The economy would fall into recession in 1970, with unemployment rates

---

[1] *The Haldeman Diaries*, Jan. 9, Feb. 6, and Jan. 8, 1973.
[2] *CEA Annual Report 1970*, 57–60; McCracken testimony in "The 1970 Economic Report of the President," Joint Economic Committee, hearings (1970), 2–6; for unemployment estimate, McCracken remark at Cabinet Meeting, Jim Keough for President's file, Feb. 18, 1970, Memos for President's File, POF.
[3] "The 1970 Economic Report of the President," Joint Economic Committee, 14.

far in excess of McCracken's prediction and an inflation rate that stubbornly refused to fall.

McCracken's forecasts would damage the CEA's reputation, not least with the president, and would help to discredit gradualism. In fact, there was nothing wrong with gradualism except the forecasts. When compared to the cycle of booms and busts that followed, gradualism would later seem the height of wisdom. The CEA's mistake at the time was to miscalculate how long it would take gradualism to produce results and how high the costs would have to go. These errors were understandable. The CEA expected the rate of inflation to decelerate quickly once output slackened because that was how inflations had behaved in the recent past. But the current inflation had persisted longer than previous episodes, its momentum was greater, and the inflationary expectations it generated were more deeply baked into the public's psychology. Moreover, even as gradualism cooled demand, long-accumulated costs continued to percolate through the system. As McCracken himself explained, "prices and costs may increase 'today' because other prices and costs increased 'yesterday.'" A demand-pull inflation had become a cost-push inflation, and it would take a lot longer to unwind than Nixon's economists imagined.[4]

The CEA had reasons, too, for underestimating the costs of gradualism in unemployment. By fiat, the Kennedy and Johnson administrations had declared the rate of unemployment consistent with stable prices (the so-called natural rate) to be 4 percent. When Nixon took office, unemployment stood at 3.3 percent. The Council reasoned that if demand slackened enough to raise unemployment just a little above 4 percent, the economy would quickly disinflate and then move back toward equilibrium. In fact, analysis would soon demonstrate that the rate of unemployment consistent with stable prices was not 4 percent but 5 percent. To slow inflation, therefore, unemployment would have to rise above 5 percent and in fact would get all the way to 6 percent by the end of 1970 — a politically damaging rate made all the more so because the administration said it would not happen. If the Fed's tight money policy during the last half of 1969 had not precipitated a recession, the process of disinflating might have proceeded

---

[4] The process described in Phillip Cagan, *Persistent Inflation: Historical and Policy Essays* (1979), 150–152. See also CEA *Annual Report 1971*, 60–61. McCracken quote, "The 1970 Economic Report of the President," Joint hearings, 4.

more gently, and unemployment might not have gone so high. Even so, gradualism would still have exacted pain in excess of the administration's assurances.[5] Economically, gradualism made sense, but because its costs turned out to be more than the public was willing to pay, gradualism threatened Nixon with defeat in the coming congressional election.

## II

Nixon's fading hopes for rescue from a recession resided in Arthur Burns, who was preparing in January 1970 to take over the chairmanship of the Fed from William McChesney Martin. Nixon appointed Burns precisely to assure the Fed's cooperation with his purposes, but Nixon already had cause to doubt Burn's gratitude and his willingness to play the role of loyal lieutenant. The immediate source of tension was the budget for FY 71, which Nixon would send to Congress in February 1970. Through much of 1969, Burns had been the White House hawk on expenditures, fighting and losing battles against new programs that threatened to unbalance the budget. In the weeks before he moved to the Fed, Burns pointed the gun of the money supply at Nixon to get his way at last on expenditures. Unless Nixon held spending under $200 billion in the coming budget, Burns said, he would have to defend credibility in the anti-inflation fight by keeping money tight.[6] Because Nixon desperately wanted easy money and wanted it quick, he had no choice except to cooperate in the purposes of Arthur Burns.

By early January, to appease Burns, Budget Director Robert Mayo succeeded in squeezing estimated projected expenditures in FY 71 from $212 billion to $203.7 billion, a figure Mayo regarded as rock-bottom. Burns

---

[5] On the natural rate, Herbert Stein, *Presidential Economics*, 2d rev. ed. (1988), 140–142; George L. Perry, "Changing Labor Markets and Inflation," *Brookings Papers on Economic Activity* (No. 3, 1970), 411–439. The natural rate rose because of a recent influx into the labor market of women and teenagers, groups with higher rates of unemployment than adult males. Stein explained the CEA view of the relation between inflation and unemployment under gradualism: "the faster the inflation rate diminished, the more the unemployment rate would exceed the natural rate but the shorter would be the period of excess unemployment." Herbert Stein, "Achieving Credibility," William Fellner, ed., *Contemporary Economic Problems 1980* (1980), 39–75.

[6] "Nomination of Arthur F. Burns," Committee on Banking and Currency, Senate hearings (1969), 14–16.

demanded a further cut of $4 billion. When Mayo countered instead with a series of relatively painless tax increases to balance the budget, Burns rejected them too. No expenditures cut, no money.[7] Finally, at a long meeting with Nixon and his advisers on January 13, 1970, Burns got his pound of flesh — or most of it. Nixon cut the budget to $200.3 billion, mainly by postponing for six months a scheduled pay raise for federal employees.[8] One result was that in February 1970 Nixon was able to submit a budget with a paper-thin surplus of $1.3 billion. Another was that in March underpaid postal workers in New York City went on strike for higher pay, forcing Nixon first to call in the U.S. Army and then to agree to a budget-busting wage settlement. Nixon would say with some accuracy and no little bitterness that Burns "had brought on the strike."[9]

On January 31, 1970, Burns was finally sworn in as the chairman of the Fed at a ceremony in the White House. Nixon took the occasion to remind Burns why he had appointed him in the first place. Noting the applause in the room for Burns, Nixon called it "a standing vote of appreciation in advance for low interest rates and more money." Nixon allowed that he had "strong views" on the economy and "would convey them privately and strongly to Dr. Burns . . . I respect his independence," Nixon said with a forced jocularity that no one misunderstood. "However, I hope that independently he will consider that my views are the ones that should be followed."[10] Puffing on his pipe amid the nervous laughter, Burns remarked laconically, "What we need now is just one bit of luck."[11]

After the ceremony, Nixon repaired to his office with aides to discuss the economy. "This is Arthur Burns's time," Nixon reflected. "The Fed has the fate of the economy in its hands." No one could know for sure how long it would take easier money to revive output, but if Burns "leaned in thirty to sixty days" toward ease, there might yet be "no recession."[12] At the January meeting of the Federal Open Market Committee (FOMC), Martin

---

[7] This account of the budget battle drawn from *Newsweek* (Jan. 19. 1970), 70; (Jan. 26, 1970), 64; *National Journal* (Feb. 17, 1970), 270–271; *Wall Street Journal*, Jan. 6, 1970, 3; Rowland Evans, Jr., and Robert D. Novak, *Nixon in the White House: The Frustration of Power* (1971), 202–203; James Reichley, *Conservatives in an Age of Change* (1981), 212.

[8] E-notes, Jan. 13, 1970.

[9] Ibid., Mar. 31, 1970.

[10] *Pub Paps RN 1970*, 44–46.

[11] Burns quoted in *Newsweek* (Feb. 9, 1970), 67.

[12] E-Notes, Jan. 13, 1970.

himself had made a gesture toward relaxing the money supply, but it had been slight and contradictory.[13] If the Fed were to turn, Burns would have to turn it.

On February 10, 1970, Burns presided over his first meeting of the FOMC, which set the System's monetary policy. He wasted no time in demonstrating how different he would be from William McChesney Martin. Martin had disdained economists and forecasts; made policy on the basis of his feel for the money markets; rejected the monetarist target of the money supply; and sought to tame the current inflation by breaking inflationary expectations, no matter the cost. Burns was an economist who had made his reputation in forecasting. Though not a rigid monetarist, he had been influenced by his former student and Vermont neighbor, Milton Friedman. It was time, Burns believed, to give the money supply its due. At the February meeting of the FOMC, Burns forecast a possible recession and made the case for ease in terms of increasing the growth rate of money. If the committee "failed to agree on a gentle, gradual move toward less firm conditions," he warned, it might be forced to a policy of drastic ease in only a few months.[14]

A majority of the members disagreed. Inflation, not recession, remained their concern, and they opposed any policy that might revive inflationary expectations. A determined chairman could usually find the votes he needed to prevail, and Burns was determined. After a debate, which Sherman Maisel described as "the most bitter I experienced in my entire service on the FOMC,"[15] a divided committee voted to set a moderate target for money growth of 4 percent, up from current estimates of near zero in the past six months. This was exactly the target favored by the CEA. Burns would attempt to rescue Nixon after all.

At first, that was not obvious to the White House. For some weeks gyrations in the money supply obscured the Fed's real intentions. "Monetary policy continues to portray an uncertain course," McCracken told Nixon on March 9, 1970. "If our basic game plan goes awry, there is high probability that the problem will have its roots here."[16] In the middle of the month Nixon assured nervous Republican congressional leaders that he

---

[13] FOMC minutes, Jan. 15, 1970, 101. The Committee's directive specified for the first time the money supply as a target.

[14] FOMC minutes, Feb. 10, 1970, 84–86, 92–93.

[15] Sherman Maisel, *Managing the Dollar* (1973), 248–250.

[16] McCracken for President, Mar. 9, 1970, (CF) BE file, WHSF.

intended to avoid a recession at all costs but left no doubt where the blame would be if he failed. "The President said that he felt our fate was right with the Federal Reserve."[17] Early in April the monetary clouds finally lifted. McCracken reported, "it is now clear that some easing is underway. If continued at the initial rate, the easing could be substantial."[18] By then Nixon knew that the turn at the Fed had come too late to help him in November. Contrary to the CEA's optimism in February, output had declined in the winter for the second straight quarter. By journalistic rule of thumb, declines in two consecutive quarters constituted a recession.

Nixon found consolation in a letter he received from Milton Friedman on April 3. Praising the Fed's new course, Friedman wrote to shore up Nixon's always shaky commitment to gradualism. It was too late now to prevent a recession, which "will clearly affect adversely our political fortunes in the Fall's election," Friedman said. Nevertheless, the administration must resist the "catastrophic" temptation to run up budget deficits and pump up the money supply beyond Burns's sensible target. The consequences of "drastic easing" would be open inflation of 5 to 10 percent, a sharp contraction to combat it, or the "imposition of price and wage controls in the vain hope that they would work" — options, Friedman emphasized, that would hurt in the presidential election year of 1972. ("Correct," Nixon wrote in the margin.) If the administration stayed on the path of moderate money growth, Friedman said, the economy in 1972 "would be expanding rapidly in real terms, with prices nearly stable." Friedman concluded, "Success is in sight, but it will require continued determination and political courage to reap the reward of the policies followed so far."[19]

Nixon found Friedman's views highly encouraging, and for the moment he accepted the role of steady and brave economic statesman in which Friedman had cast him. In commenting on Friedman's letter to a member of the White House staff, Nixon amended Friedman's advice in one regard. If he told Burns merely to be moderate, Burns would tend to be too cautious. "Therefore, we should urge him to do more, and he will end up doing a moderate amount."[20]

---

[17] Buchanan for President, Mar. 17, 1970, Memos for President's file, POF (notes of meeting).

[18] McCracken for President, Apr. 7, 1970, (CF) BE 5 file, WHSF.

[19] Friedman for President, Mar. 13, 1970, attached to a summary, Ehrlichman for President, April 3, 1970, BE 5 file, WHCF.

[20] Ken Cole to Flanigan, Apr. 9, 1970, Flanigan 1970 file, SMOF: McCracken.

Buoyed by Friedman, Nixon was in surprisingly good spirits at his cabinet meeting on April 13. He regretted, he said, that the economic downturn would hurt the chances this year of good friends like George Bush, running for the Senate in Texas. If there was anything he could do to improve the economy by November, he would do it. The Fed, as usual, had kept money too tight too long, and there was no quick way to undo the damage. "Now that Arthur Burns is over there, maybe that kind of thing will be remedied," he said. Of course, echoing Friedman, "if the Board loosens up too much, the result might be an overheated economy and the same old problem in 1971." When Nixon again expressed high hopes for Burns, George Shultz interrupted and broke the mood. "Well," said Shultz, "Arthur has a way of holding the money supply as a hostage — saying that 'if you don't behave, I'll tighten up on money,' and in fact in that way he's trying to run the whole executive branch with the Federal Reserve." Nixon slapped the table. "When we get through," he said, "this Fed won't be independent if its the only thing I do in this office."[21]

## III

By the spring of 1970, as the parties were gearing up for the fall campaign, euphoric Democrats sensed that they had the winning issue. "For Democratic politicians, happiness is higher unemployment, shrinking overtime pay, rising prices, lofty interest rates, and tight money," observed the *Wall Street Journal*. Explained an adviser to Democratic congressmen, "The guy who is worried about crime and about the blacks moving into his neighborhood might . . . be tempted to vote Republican, but his paramount interest is his pay check. When he loses overtime pay, his standard of living is hurt, and he's going to blame the Administration for it. We'll see to that."[22] Presidential hopeful Edmund Muskie declared, "in the 1920s it took Republicans eight years to go from prosperity to unemployment and now they've learned to do it in one year." Joseph Califano, counsel of the Democratic party, called Nixon a "Herbert Hoover in TV makeup."[23]

Nixon had not only caused the recession, the Democrats claimed, but

---

[21] Jim Keough for President's File, Apr. 13, 1970, Memos for President's File, POF.

[22] *Wall Street Journal*, Apr. 3, 1970, 1, 31.

[23] Califano quote, *Business Week* (May 2, 1970), 15; Muskie quote, *Wall Street Journal*, Apr. 3, 1970, 31.

he was so paralyzed by his conservative ideology that he refused to take the one step that could stop inflation painlessly. Instead of waiting for fiscal and monetary policies to do their slow work, the administration should intervene directly in markets to prevent unjustified increases in prices and wages. In the language of economists, the Democrats wanted Nixon to fight inflation with incomes policy. Incomes policy emcompassed a wide variety of options: "jawboning," meaning efforts to talk down individual wage and price decisions; wage-price guideposts, which established economy-wide standards for socially responsible decisions by unions and corporations; and even mandatory wage and price controls. As early as February 1970, Henry Ruess, a leading Democratic spokesman in Congress on economic issues, said, "Many of us, on the Democratic side, feel that policies of fiscal-monetary austerity by themselves are not enough to do the job, and that what the President should do immediately is to impose an across-the-board freeze for at least 6 months, so that sound fiscal, monetary, incomes, and supply policies could take hold."[24] Of course, the president had no legal authority to freeze prices and wages. Before the year was over, the Democrats would fix that.

Nixon had stated his view of incomes policy at his first press conference in January 1969. "I do not go along with the suggestion that inflation can be effectively controlled by exhorting labor and management and industry to follow certain guidelines," the president said. Corporate and labor leaders "have to be guided by the interests of the organizations that they represent."[25] Nixon knew that the Kennedy administration had established wage-price guideposts in 1962 but that the rising tide of inflation had swept them away in 1966. He also knew that recent experiments with incomes policy in European countries had all failed. Nonetheless, the Democrats pressed the issue with increasing insistence through the 1970 election year.

The politics of incomes policy was complex. Democrats demanded it, though the chief target of incomes policy would be the labor unions, and Republicans resisted it, though the chief proponents of incomes policy were some of the nation's leading businessmen. The main reason why prices kept rising through 1970, despite gradualism, was the big wage increases that workers were demanding and getting. The workers had a good

---

[24] "The 1970 Economic Report of the President," Joint Economic Committee hearings, 26.

[25] *Pub Paps RN 1969*, 22.

case. During the early stages of the Vietnam inflation, unions had signed long-term contracts locking workers into wages that failed to keep pace with prices. Indeed, from 1965 to 1969, the real wage of the average factory worker actually fell by eighty-two cents a week.[26] When the old contracts expired, unions demanded catch-up wage increases. Non-union workers needed to catch up too. And catch up the workers did. In 1969 the average nonfarm worker in the private economy received a huge 7.2 percent increase in compensation, nearly double the increase of four years before. Because productivity per worker did not rise in 1969, the entire increase in compensation added to average unit costs.[27] Businesses either had to absorb added costs at the expense of profits, which had been declining, or they had to raise prices, which in the main they chose to do, even though demand for goods was slackening.

In mid-1969 Peter Flanigan, the White House liaison with the business community, reported to Nixon that "many of our faint-hearted supporters in the business area feel that 'something has to be done' . . . Because this feeling has become so widespread among businessmen and others, I believe that some harmful political fallout can occur by not publicly urging unions and industry to moderate wage and price demands."[28] Flanigan was the first of Nixon's advisers to buckle under the pressure to do something about wages.

The Council of Economic Advisers adamantly opposed incomes policy. To the extent it made a difference, the CEA argued, government meddling in the price system would distort the allocation of resources, encourage overexpansive fiscal and monetary policies, and in the end fail to achieve its purpose. But the CEA knew it was in a race. If gradualism did not soon produce results, Nixon would eventually yield to the pressure and become entangled in a mistaken effort to police the price system. The CEA's strategy was to play for time by making small concessions. Herbert Stein recalled, "The administration was like a Russian family fleeing over the snow in a horse-drawn troika pursued by wolves. Every once in a while they throw a baby out to slow down the wolves, hoping thereby to gain enough time for most of the family to reach safety. Every once in a while the administration would make another step in the direction of incomes pol-

---

[26] *New York Times*, Jan. 11, 1970, XII, 12.
[27] CEA *Annual Report 1970*, 53; CEA *Annual Report 1972*, 231.
[28] Flanigan for President, July 25, 1969, FG 238 file, WHCF.

icies, hoping to appease the critics while the demand-management policy would work."[29]

Nixon began feeding the wolves in September 1969, when he created the feeble Construction Industry Collective Bargaining Conversion in a vain effort to promote reasonable wage settlements in construction.[30] In October 1969, disturbed that business and labor were "going merrily on their way pushing up prices and wages,"[31] Nixon wrote 2,200 business and labor leaders to argue that restraint was in the best interests of each.[32] Early in 1970, he appointed a subcabinet committee to investigate a series of spectacular copper price increases.[33] In the spring the administration quietly threatened to abandon quotas on imported steel unless domestic steel companies stopped raising prices.[34] The price that engaged the personal attention of the president himself was the price of meat.

During the winter of 1970, meat prices were the single most important cause of the surging Consumer Price Index and the source of considerable anger among housewives. Nixon wanted to force down meat prices by relaxing quotas on imported meat.[35] But powerful Republican senators from the Midwest, acting for the cattle lobby, blocked him. ("They all wear silver buckles and bring me lamb," Nixon said of the cattlemen. "I don't like lamb.") Agriculture Secretary Charles Hardin suggested a more politically convenient culprit. The retail food industry, Hardin claimed, had refused to pass declining cattle prices on to consumers in the form of lower beef prices. Then, said Nixon, on February 2, 1970, "Kick the chain stores."[36]

Learning two weeks later that meat prices had not budged, Nixon became so agitated that he ordered Hardin to lower meat prices before Monday or he would issue a public statement "blasting" the chains. Dismayed, Peter Flanigan confided to McCracken, "There is nothing that

---

[29] Stein, *Presidential Economics*, 157.

[30] *Pub Paps RN 1969*, 735–736.

[31] Report on Meeting of the Cabinet Committee on Economic Policy, Sept. 19, 1969, Safire papers.

[32] *Pub Paps RN 1969*, 812–814.

[33] *Wall Street Journal*, Jan. 12, 1970, 2.

[34] Colson for Flanigan, Mar. 18, 1970, White House Staff files, SMOF: McCracken; Flanigan for President, Apr. 30, 1970, FE 4/Steel file, WHCF.

[35] Timmons for Colson, Mar. 10, 1970, (CF) BE 5-2 file, WHSF; John Whitaker to Staff Sec., Mar. 7, 1970, same file; Harlow for President, Mar. 19, 1970, same file; Palmsby for Colson, Mar. 10, 1970, same file.

[36] E-Notes, Feb. 2, 1970.

Hardin can do in a free society to bring down prices by Monday."[37] Meat prices did not come down, and there was no blasting. McCracken, for his part, irritated the president by submitting a report that puzzled over the widening spread between farm and retail meat prices but found no evidence of "profiteering or collusion by retailers."[38] As a young man working in father's independent grocery, Nixon had acquired strong opinions of his own concerning the food industry. The day after hearing from McCracken, Nixon wrote an aide, "I have still not had a report that I consider to be adequate on meat prices. I think you will find that chain stores who generally control these prices nation-wide are primarily dominated by Jewish interests. These boys, of course, have every right to make all the money they want, but they have a notorious reputation in the trade for conspiracy."[39] Nixon ordered the unfortunate McCracken to call in chain-store executives and demand an explanation of the spread between cattle and beef prices.[40] He was in the process of maneuvering the Justice Department into an investigation preliminary to an antitrust suit when meat prices fell of their own accord.[41] The episode mainly served to underscore the wisdom of keeping politics out of the price system.

Throwing morsels to the wolves failed to satisfy even a renegade faction within Nixon's own cabinet. Winston Blount of the Post Office, John Volpe of the Transportation Department, George Romney of Housing and Urban Development, and Maurice Stans of Commerce joined forces early in 1970 to pressure Nixon into some form of incomes policy. Each of them occupied a post on the far ramparts of the administration, each resented his exclusion from Nixon's inner counsels, and each was positioned to see the current cost-push inflation as an intolerable problem. Blount and Volpe had made their fortunes in the construction industry, where wage settlements currently bordered on the outrageous. Inflation was killing home building, which Romney's department was charged to foster. And Stans, Nixon's fund-raiser and a former investment banker, reflected the views of

---

[37] Flanigan for McCracken, Feb. 19, 1970, FG 63 file, WHCF.

[38] McCracken et al. for President, Mar. 14, 1970, (CF) BE 5-2 file, WHSF.

[39] President for Flanigan, Mar. 16, 1970, (CF) BE 5-2 file, WHSF.

[40] Henrik Houthakker to Egil Krough, Apr. 30, 1970, White House Staff Memos: Zeigler-Garment, SMOF: Stein; Houthakker for Flanigan, Mar. 20, 1970, CEA Staff Memos file, SMOF: McCracken.

[41] E-Notes, Mar. 16, 1970; Bud Krogh to Houthakker, Apr. 20, 1970, White House Memos, Zeigler-Garment file; John Brown for Ehrlichman, Apr. 3, 1970, (CF) BE 5-2 file, WHSF; Flanigan for Staff Secretary, Mar. 18, 1970, (CF) BE 5-2 file, WHSF.

corporate leaders bent on restraining wages by any means possible. Writing Nixon in early February 1970, Blount, Volpe, Romney, and Stans proposed that the president issue wage-price guideposts and appoint a commission to investigate violators.[42]

Nixon was tempted. The dissidents "are worth talking to" he told Haldeman. He did not "necessarily buy Shultz and McCracken," who were opposing incomes policy on free market grounds.[43] After McCracken weighed in with written counterarguments,[44] Nixon decided, "McCracken is right." Romney, never one of Nixon's favorites anyway, was making "a grandstand play."[45] At a cabinet meeting on February 18, Romney shattered the usual false harmony by challenging the "lack of policy in the wage-price field" at a time when "some very inflationary wage settlements" were looming. McCracken responded with the argument most likely to impress the president. "If we set guidelines, they will be broken and then the question will be asked: Mr. President, what are you going to do about that? And in that way, we will have forced the President into a corner." When Romney pressed his point, Nixon shot back, "What wage-price policy ever worked?" "The British Plan," Romney replied. "Oh, no. Now, George," said Nixon, who in this case was better informed, "don't tell me about British wage-price policy. I know about that. It didn't work."[46]

Nixon had quelled the dissidents but only for the moment. Meanwhile, the Democrats kept up the drumbeat for incomes policy. With Gallup showing more people favoring controls than opposing them, the Democrats attempted to embarrass the president in August 1970 by adding to a routine bill an amendment granting him discretionary authority for six months to impose mandatory controls on wages and prices. Democrats said that now "the president will have all the necessary weapons needed to control inflation."[47] Republicans denounced the measure as demagoguery. It occurred to neither that Nixon might actually use the authority so cynically bestowed upon him.

---

[42] McCracken for President, Feb. 16, 1970, Memos for the President's file, SMOF: McCracken; H-Notes, Feb. 18, 1970.

[43] H-Notes, Feb. 15, 1970.

[44] McCracken for President, Feb. 16, 1970.

[45] H-Notes, Feb. 18, 1970.

[46] Keough for President's file, Feb. 18, 1970, Memos for President file, POF (notes of Cabinet Meeting).

[47] *Congressional Quarterly Almanac 1970*, 430–435.

## IV

During the winter of 1970 the public feared merely a recession. By spring the financial community feared a panic that could trigger the next Great Depression. The crisis that gripped the economy began with a crisis in Indochina. Nixon had apparently neutralized the war issue by gradually winding down U.S. military operations. But on April 22, 1970, buried in his announcement of plans to bring home another 150,000 troops within a year, Nixon issued a warning. "If I conclude that increased enemy action jeopardizes our remaining forces in Vietnam," Nixon said, "I shall not hesitate to take strong and effective measures to deal with that situation."[48] As he spoke, Communist troops in Cambodia were threatening to overrun a right-wing military regime that one month before had ousted the neutralist government of Prince Norodom Sihanouk. Fearing that a Communist Cambodia would become a vast staging ground for North Vietnamese attacks on South Vietnam, prolonging the war, Nixon secretly decided on April 26 on U.S. intervention to prevent the collapse of the Cambodian government.[49] Nixon realized that escalating the war might recharge the peace movement. What he did not foresee was the devastating consequence of escalation on American financial markets.

Stocks had been slumping for more than a year. The Dow-Jones industrial average, which at the crest of the bull market in December 1968 had stood at 985, had fallen to 800 in December 1969, hurt by tight money and flattening output.[50] The market rallied in March 1970 but fell back in mid-April on disappointing reports of corporate earnings. When the Dow fell twenty-seven points during the two days of April 27 and 28 to close to 724, tension gripped Wall Street. Because brokerage houses carried much of their capital in stocks, the decline in the market threatened to bring down enough of them to initiate a chain reaction, culminating in a general financial panic.[51] Nixon blamed unsteadiness in the markets on lack of confidence. "The financial houses must be reassured," he said.[52] On April 28 the president made some news by telling a visitor, "Frankly, if I had

---

[48] *Pub Paps RN 1970*, 373–377.

[49] *RN: Memoirs of Richard Nixon* (1978), 446–450; Henry Kissinger, *White House Years* (1979), 483–505.

[50] Dow-Jones industrial averages for every day included at end of annual volumes of *Wall Street Journal Index*.

[51] *Wall Street Journal*, Apr. 28, 1970, 1.

[52] E-Notes, Apr. 27, 1970.

any money, I'd be buying stocks right now." The next day the market rose thirteen points.[53]

Nixon killed his own rally on April 30, 1970, with the stunning announcement that he had ordered U.S. troops into Cambodia to wipe out border sanctuaries, used by the North, he said, for attacks on South Vietnam and on the Cambodian government.[54] Nixon acted without the support of his secretaries of state and defense, without consulting Congress, and without fully grasping the outrage he would provoke. The result was the greatest crisis of Nixon's first term. Student protesters paralyzed great universities. The Vietnam Moratorium Committee, which two weeks before had announced that it was closing down, orchestrated a week of demonstrations in the capital. Congressmen from both parties submitted resolutions to get U.S. troops out of Cambodia, and on May 4, at Kent State University in Ohio, National Guardsmen brought the war home by killing four unarmed students on their own campus. Student strikes immediately erupted in colleges and universities across America. "The country is virtually on the edge of a spiritual — and perhaps even a physical breakdown," said New York Mayor John Lindsay. Not even Nixon's promise on May 8, 1970, to terminate the Cambodian operation by June 30 quelled the furor.[55]

As the political crisis deepened, so not coincidentally did the crisis of stocks and bonds. The day of Kent State the Dow fell seventeen points, the largest single one-day decline since Kennedy's assassination. Nervous markets edged toward disorder. John Kenneth Galbraith, liberal Democrat and author of a famous book on the Great Depression, feared that the "insanity" of 1929 might be reoccurring.[56] David Rockefeller of the Chase-Manhattan Bank and a pillar of the Republican establishment, warned that "a lot of people" were talking about a possible collapse.[57] In the Bankers Club on Wall Street, luncheon patrons cursed "the damn Nixon bear market," while pollster Louis Harris found that 78 percent of corporate executives blamed Nixon's policies for the continuing stock market decline.[58]

Democrats exploited the turmoil by redoubling their attacks on Nixon's

---

[53] *New York Times*, Apr. 29, 1970, 1, 65.
[54] *Pub Paps RN 1970*, 405–410.
[55] *Newsweek* (May 11, 1970), 24 ff; (May 18, 1970), 26–30.
[56] *New York Times*, May 3, 1970, III, 1.
[57] *Wall Street Journal*, May 11, 1970, 3.
[58] *Newsweek* (May 4, 1970), 73; *New York Times*, May 11, 1970, 22.

economic policies, particularly his refusal to adopt incomes policy. No less a figure than Senate Majority Leader Mike Mansfield came out for wage and price controls. The Democratic National Chairman, Larry O'Brien, blaming hard times on "Nixonomics," told an audience of Democrats, "There is one way out of this economic bog. The president can still enlist the responsible majority of business and labor leaders in the effort to bring the wage-price spiral under control."[59] Not all those favoring incomes policy, of course, were Democrats. David Rockefeller joined the chorus in May.[60] And so did Arthur Burns, whose apostasy at the moment of his greatest peril the president considered the unkindest cut of all.

As a private economist in the 1960s, Burns had been the most effective critic of the Kennedy-Johnson incomes policy, arguing in traditional Republican fashion the folly of tampering with free markets.[61] Once Burns knew that he would be taking over the Fed, his views changed. Because easier money would be his first objective, Burns developed an interest, while still on Nixon's staff, in collateral policies that might help restrain the possible inflationary consequences. Closeted with Nixon in the Oval Office in September 1969, Burns confided his fear that next year we "could have both unemployment and inflation." "God, I know," said Nixon. It's "heresy," Burns confessed, "but I'm even thinking of wage and price controls."[62]

Still, it came as a shock when, on May 18, 1970, in the midst of Cambodia and the commotion on Wall Street, Burns told an audience of bankers in Hot Springs, Virginia, that while incomes policy had achieved little in other countries, it should remain a policy option here. "We should not close our minds to the possibility that an incomes policy, provided it stopped well short of direct price and wage controls and was used merely as a supplement to overall fiscal and monetary measures, might speed us through this transitional period of cost-push inflation," Burns said.[63] Nixon, furious, ordered Ehrlichman to "freeze" Burns out for a while "unless he serves our purpose."[64] Burns, contrite, sent word claiming that the

---

[59] *New York Times*, May 22, 1970, 51.

[60] *Business Week* (May 30, 1970), 108.

[61] Burns's 1964 paper on the subject published in Arthur F. Burns, *Business Cycle in a Changing World* (1969), chap. 9.

[62] E-Notes, Sept. 11, 1969.

[63] Burns's speech reprinted in Arthur F. Burns, *Reflections of an Economic Policy Maker* (1978), 91–102.

[64] E-Notes, May 19, 1970.

press had misconstrued his remarks.[65] Delighted, the Democrats welcomed Burns to the rank of Nixon critics. Indeed, some in the White House believed that Burns had spoken as he did to curry favor among his new-found friends in the Democratic congressional leadership.[66]

Remarkably, Nixon emerged from the Cambodian episode not all that scathed. Youth might vilify him, but the spectacle of privileged students in sometimes violent opposition to their own government helped rally the "constituency of the uneducated" to the president's side. AFL-CIO president George Meany backed Nixon on Cambodia, as did most of the union officials in his federation. Construction workers were especially emphatic in their patriotism. On May 8, a few hundred flag-waving hard hats descended on New York's financial district to beat up dozens of student demonstrations at a noontime rally and then stormed city hall to raise the flag, which had been flying at half-mast for the four dead at Kent State.[67] When the construction unions followed by calling a pro-war parade on May 20, more than 150,000 turned out to march down Broadway for flag and country.[68] A grateful Nixon invited the leaders of the Building and Construction Trades Council of Greater New York to the White House, where he briefed them on Cambodia, and they presented him with a hard hat.[69] The Social Issue still had some kick after all.

As for the stock market, the feared earthquake never came. Nixon, for one, did his part. On May 27, 1970, following a two-day tumble of stock prices that carried the Dow-Jones average all the way down to 621, the president hosted a White House dinner for forty-five of the nation's top business and financial leaders. After the beef Wellington and the Château Lafite-Rothschild '62, Nixon expounded on his Cambodian policy for nearly an hour. More important, Arthur Burns spoke for three minutes to say that the Fed was "going to continue to work against inflation, but we do have flexibility, and we are prepared to use it if necessary."[70] That same day, in what *Business Week* called a "fantastic rebound," the market shot up thirty-two points.[71] By the end of the month, the Dow had climbed back to

---

[65] Flanigan for President, May 20, 1970, BE 5-3 file, WHCF.

[66] Roger A. Freeman for McCracken, May 21, 1970, White House Staff Memos, Flanigan file, SMOF: McCracken.

[67] *New York Times*, May 9, 1970, 1.

[68] Ibid., May 21, 1970, 1.

[69] Colson for President's file, May 26, 1970, Memos for President's file, POF.

[70] *New York Times*, May 28, 1970, 1; *Newsweek* (June 8, 1970), 71 ff.

[71] *Business Week* (June 6, 1970), 19.

700, students were going home for the summer, and the troops were beginning to pull out of Cambodia. Preliminary data for the spring quarter would shortly reveal that real output had actually expanded, if only by less than half of 1 percent.[72] The recession might already be over. Nixon had apparently ridden out the storm.

V

But not quite. On May 3, four days after Nixon launched the Cambodian incursion, the *New York Times* reported that as bad as the bear market was, "the Street is full of talk that other, far more serious problems, are lurking just beneath the surface . . . Put bluntly, responsible analysts are beginning to ask whether there is a danger of a 'liquidity crisis' — perhaps even approaching the magnitude of those that periodically sent business through the wringer in the latter part of the 19th century."[73] Liquidity referred to the ability to raise cash to pay debts as they fell due. After a year of tight money, heavy corporate borrowing, and falling profits, the business system was low on cash and fearful that there might not be enough in a pinch. With bank credit scarce thanks to the Fed, corporations were borrowing huge sums from each other in the form of commercial paper, that is, unsecured promissory notes redeemable in 270 days or less. From April 1968 to April 1970, the value of commercial paper rose from $17.5 billion to $38 billion, even as the cash needed to redeem the paper was drying up. Here was yet another scenario for a depression.[74] If a substantial number of corporations that had issued commercial paper got nervous, declined to roll it over, and demanded redemption in cash, a chain reaction of bankruptcies could follow, carrying down the whole economy. Said Telford Gaines, a former senior staff economist of the Fed and vice president of Manufacturers Hanover, "if it is not a 'crisis,' it is as close to one as any of us except our elderly colleagues are able to remember from personal experience."[75]

The Council of Economic Advisors took these fears seriously. In mid-May, Paul McCracken informed the cabinet that the Fed's prolonged policy of tight money may have produced "too high a degree of 'liquidity dehydration.'" By midyear, "the ratio of money supply to gross national product

---

[72] *Survey of Current Business* (July 1970), 1.
[73] *New York Times*, May 3, 1970, III, 1.
[74] *Wall Street Journal*, June 23, 1970, 2; June 12, 1970, 1.
[75] *New York Times*, May 3, 1970, III, 1.

could be very thin." "Are you saying that the growth of money supply might not be enough?" Nixon asked. "Yes," McCracken replied. "You have a lot of company on that," Nixon said.[76] A month later McCracken was sufficiently alarmed to propose "a one-shot substantial expansion of the money supply" to restore liquidity. Shultz, loyal Friedmanite that he was, opposed that proposal as a violation of the monetarist principle of steady money growth. "I lean more to McCracken," Nixon informed Flanigan.[77] But only Burns could settle the matter, and he agreed with Shultz.

If the economy really was tottering, the Penn Central Company just might bring it down. In February 1969, the mighty Pennsylvania Railroad had merged with the reluctant New York Central to form the seventh largest corporation in America. It was a bad marriage from the start. By the end of 1969, in a soft economy, the company's railroad operations were losing money, while its real estate subsidiary could not generate nearly enough cash to cover the losses.[78] In 1970, to service its exploding debt, the company intended to roll over $200 million in commercial paper and float a $100 million bond issue. After the company reported big first-quarter losses, the bond issue was doomed. By mid-May, creditors had called in $50 million of the company's commercial paper, with $75 million due on June 30. Because the company did not have the cash, bankruptcy loomed, and the feared chain reaction in the commercial paper market might finally commence.[79]

On May 19, 1970, David Bevin, chief financial officer of the Penn Central, met in Washington with Treasury Secretary David Kennedy. Bevin's mission was to persuade the Nixon administration to bail out his railroad. Bevin made the case not on behalf of the Penn Central but on behalf of an endangered America. If the Penn Central defaulted, Bevin said, the ripple effect could devastate the country's financial structure. Kennedy "paled perceptibly," Bevin recalled, and enlisted on the spot.[80] On May 26, 1970, the day the Dow hit bottom, high administration offi-

[76] Keough for President's File, May 19, 1970, Memo for President's files, POF.

[77] McCracken for President, June 13, 1970, President's Handwriting file, POF; Flanigan for President, June 22, 1970, same file.

[78] Stephen Salsbury, *No Way to Run a Railroad* (1982), esp. chaps. 9 and 10; Rush Loving, Jr., "The Penn Central Bankruptcy Express," *Fortune* (vol. 82, Aug. 1970), 105 ff; *Business Week* (June 27, 1970), 96–100.

[79] *Wall Street Journal*, May 27, 1970, 17.

[80] Salsbury, *No Way to Run a Railroad*, chap. 12.

cials agreed to a bailout of the Penn Central. Flanigan reported the reasons to the president. "Given the 'delicate health' of the economy at this time, the large amount of commercial paper which the Penn Central has out-standing, and the fact that the Penn Central is the country's largest rail-road, all agree that there is very real risk to the economy of the Penn Central being allowed to go into reorganization." The proposed instrument of rescue was the Defense Production Act of 1950, which authorized the Defense Department to guarantee bank loans to defense industries.[81] If the Defense Department would declare the Penn Central a defense industry and guarantee its loans, the road would be saved.

On June 19, 1970, bank officials ready to furnish federally guaranteed loans to the Penn Central sat in the company's Philadelphia offices await-ing word from Wshington to proceed. They were still waiting when Under-secretary of Defense David Packard strode into the White House and firmly declined to underwrite any loans for the company. The Penn Central, after all, was neither a good credit risk nor even a defense industry, and the department's friends in Congress had turned against the bailout. Denied backing from the administration, the Penn Central now had no option except to declare bankruptcy, which it did on Sunday, June 21, 1970.[82] Said the prominent economic writer Eliot Janeway, "This will prick the balloon."[83]

With Penn Central creditors holding commercial paper that they could not redeem and the economy facing a cash shortage, panicky corporations might all begin dumping their paper at once. "As working capital disap-peared and customers were lost," Sherman Maisel of the Federal Reserve Board said in describing the worst-case scenario, "corporations unable to borrow would shut down. Massive unemployment could ensue."[84] Every-

---

[81] Flanigan for President, June 4, 1970, Memos for President file, Alpha Subject files, Haldeman: SMOF. The plan called for DOD to guarantee loans only temporarily. The administration would submit legislation to Congress that would authorize the Transportation Dept. to guarantee up to $750 million in loans, taking over the guarantees of DOD. See also Melvin Laird for Flanigan, June 3, 1970, White House Staff Memos, Flanigan file, SMOF: McCracken; *Congressional Quarterly Weekly Report* (June 26, 1970), 1633; *Wall Street Journal* (June 11, 1970), 3; Joseph R. Daughen and Peter Binzen, *The Wreck of the Penn Central* (1971); "Department of Defense Appropriations for 1971," Committee on Appropriations, House Hearings (1970), 1011–1040.

[82] *Business Week* (June 27, 1970), 100; Daughen and Binzen, *Wreck of the Penn Central*, (1971), 297–298.

[83] *Newsweek* (June 29, 1970), 62.

[84] Maisel, *Managing the Dollar*, 8.

thing depended on the banks. Corporations with lines of credit to the banks would seek to draw on them to pay off their paper. But would the banks have the money?

One day after the Penn Central failed, Arthur Burns called an emergency meeting of the Federal Reserve Board. Burns regarded "a gradual erosion of confidence" as the most likely consequence of the Penn Central failure. But he did not rule out the possibility of "a collapse in markets that could come quickly."[85]

The board took two emergency steps. It sent word to its member banks that the discount window was wide open, meaning that the Fed would make loans to the banks to ease the liquidity shortage, and it raised the legal limit on interest rates that the banks could pay to attract large certificates of deposit. Though nervous corporations dumped $6 billion in commercial paper during the next three months, the banks had the cash to fund their redemption. Banks got the cash by borrowing $1 billion from the Fed and by selling $11 billion in new CDs.[86] After it was over, there was some doubt that cash had been all that scarce and considerable suspicion that the economy had experienced merely a "pseudo-crisis."[87] Because no crisis had occurred, Burns took credit for the happy ending.[88]

The episode had consequences for the Fed's management of the money supply. For one thing, it tempered Burns's enthusiasm for monetarism. If Burns had followed pure monetarist doctrine, he would have ignored the commotion in financial markets and stuck to steady money growth. Instead, faced with an apparent emergency, he pumped money into the markets at a generous rate. As a result, the money supply during 1970 grew not by 4 percent, the February target, but by 5.5 percent, a high rate by histor-

---

[85] "Excerpts from the Minutes of the Meeting of the Board of Governors of the Federal Reserve System on June 22, 1970," Box B 89, Penn Central file, Burns Papers, Ford Library.

[86] Maisel, *Managing the Dollar*, 9.

[87] The CEA surveyed 535 corporations during 1969 and 1970 and found that few of them were actually starved for cash. *CEA Annual Report 1971*, 169–178. Anna J. Schwartz, *Money in Historical Perspective* (1987), 283–284. Schwartz calls the episode a "pseudo-crisis." For views at the time on whether there was a real crisis, *Wall Street Journal*, June 12, 1970, 1; June 16, 1970, 18. In August 1970, economists of the Federal Reserve Bank of New York said that concerns over liquidity were exaggerated. *Wall Street Journal*, Aug. 6, 1970, 2.

[88] Burns's testimony in "The 1970 Midyear Review of the State of the Economy," Joint Economic Committee, hearings (1970), esp. 581–583; also Leonard Malkin, "The Practical Politician at the Fed," *Fortune* (vol. 83, April 1971), 148 ff; Maisel, *Managing the Dollar* (1973), 9–10.

ical standards. Whether it would be high enough to satisfy Nixon remained to be seen.

## VI

The spring crisis had a profound effect on the White House. No longer content to be a mere spectator of a policy that was losing him votes, Nixon was ready to make changes, beginning with his advisers. Budget Director Robert Mayo and Treasury Secretary David Kennedy "must go," Nixon decided.[89] Though Kennedy would survive through the year, Mayo went in June 1970 as part of major executive reorganization, which folded the Budget Bureau into a new superagency called the Office of Management and Budget (OMB). Intended to strengthen the president's management of the bureaucracy, OMB would never fulfill the hope of its architects.[90] But Nixon wished to launch OMB properly with a first-class director. He considered John Connally, ex-governor of Texas; Kenneth Rush, once his law professor at Duke; and even Lee Iacocca, president of Ford Motor Company. On June 10, one day after Mayo learned he would not get the job, Nixon announced that OMB's first director would be George Shultz, the secretary of labor who had become one of Nixon's most trusted advisers. "As a known quantity," Haldeman noted, "he's the safest, and we know P can work with him."[91]

When Shultz took over OMB on July 2, he did not move into the Old Executive Office Building with his new agency but into an office in the White House near the president. Along with Haldeman, Ehrlichman, and Kissinger, George Shultz would become one of the handful of officials through whom Nixon ran his government. Above all, Nixon hoped Shultz would take over economic policy. It was Shultz, not McCracken, who would call meetings of the Troika and act as first among equals in that body, and Shultz on whom Nixon expected to lean for economic advice.

Stein and McCracken had known Shultz for years. Shultz had even written the introduction to Stein's first book. Nonetheless, though its members admired Shultz for his ability as a manager, there was no joy at the CEA on his ascendance. Untrained in macroeconomics, Shultz had done

---

[89] E-Notes, April 28, 1970.

[90] Larry Berman, *The Office of Management and Budget and the Presidency, 1921–1979* (1979), chap. 5.

[91] *Haldeman Diaries*, Jan. 10, 1970; Apr. 21, 1970.

his professional work on labor.[92] In the CEA's view, Shultz lacked the professional qualifications for the role of Nixon's chief economic adviser. Divisions quickly emerged among these old friends, not so much about power and turf but about policy.

There was, for example, the question of a fiscal rule. In 1969, while still in the Labor Department, Shultz had challenged the CEA's rule of a stable, predictable, and moderate budget surplus in normal times. Congress would squander any surplus, Shultz believed, probably by spending it to swell a government already too big. The fate of the CEA's rule was sealed in May 1970, when the Troika tried to rescue a surplus by proposing either a tax increase or an expenditure cut. Nixon refused to adopt either course. Congress would not increase taxes during an election year, he said, and a deficit might help counter the recession.[93] The surplus rule was dead.

No sooner did Shultz take over OMB than he convinced Nixon to adopt the fiscal rule he favored. Nixon announced the new rule in a statement on the budget, July 18, 1970. "Except in emergency conditions," the president said, "expenditures must never be allowed to outrun the revenues that the tax system would produce at reasonably full employment."[94] In other words, it did not matter if the budget was actually balanced, only that it would be in balance if the economy were operating at full employment. Milton Friedman had proposed a variant of the rule long ago and still believed in it. Herbert Stein had also proposed the rule long ago but had come to consider it flawed.[95] Though Stein was supposed to be the administration's fiscal expert, Nixon, following Shultz, adopted the full employment budget.

Nixon would remain faithful to the full-employment balance rule only for little more than a year. For the present it served a number of his purposes. The rule limited expenditures to revenues that would be collected at full employment, assuring some fiscal discipline. It provided a justification for the current deficit ($23 billion in FY 71), which resulted from a revenue

---

[92] Stein interview with the author, Aug. 3, 1993.

[93] Flanigan for President, May 5, 1970, (no file info.). E-Notes, May 5, 1970.

[94] *Pub Paps RN 1970*, 600–602.

[95] Stein pointed out that the rule was inadequate "in a world of inflation because a budget that was balanced at high employment with a serious inflation going on, and balanced by the effect of the inflation itself, was not a satisfactory condition to aim at." *Presidential Economics*, 140. For other critiques of full-employment budget, Arthur Okun and Nancy Teeters, "The Full Employment Surplus Revisited," *Brookings Papers on Economic Activity* (No. 1, 1970), 77–110; Alan J. Blinder and Stephen M. Goldfield, "New Measures of Fiscal and Monetary Policy, 1958–1973," *American Economic Review* (vol. 62, Dec. 1976), 781–796.

shortfall in a recession-plagued economy, and the rule permitted Nixon to claim that he was balancing at least some budget. Fiscal conservatives, who still believed that the actual budget was the one to balance, were not impressed. At a cabinet meeting in August 1970 Postmaster General Winston Blount, a fiscal conservative, listened to Shultz explain the new fiscal rule and then remarked, "A lot of this is economic bullshit."[96]

The main difference betwen Shultz and the CEA concerned the status of gradualism. Though the CEA had authored gradualism in 1969, it was Shultz who proved the more loyal proponent. Following Friedman, Shultz believed that the administration should stick unwaveringly to the full-employment balance rule and that the Fed should stick unwaveringly to money growth at a 5 percent annual rate. The private economy would do the rest. If the Fed strayed from its present steady course and began pumping up money to speed the decline of unemployment, Friedman warned in July, "another inflationary binge" would likely result.[97]

Shaken by the spring crisis and by an unemployment rate that had risen above 5 percent, the CEA had had its fill of gradualism. Seizing on a fluke decline in the inflation rate at midyear, the council decided that prices were no longer the country's number-one economic problem. Unemployment was. The council believed that the president himself had signaled the new target of policy. In an offhand remark at his press conferences of July 20, 1970, Nixon said that full employment was "a goal we think we can achieve during fiscal 1972," in other words, on the eve of the presidential election.[98]

In the CEA's view, the goal of full employment by mid-1972 would not be feasible if the economy just "rocks along."[99] To get back down to 4 percent unemployment in two years would require precisely the pump priming that Friedman and Shultz were warning against. Pushing expansion as hard as they had recently pushed gradualism, the Council urged money growth at the sky-high annual rate of 7 to 8 percent.[100] Stein wrote Shultz, "We are willing to take the risk that pumping the economy up to full employment, over the course of two years, will cause inflation to accel-

---

[96] E-Notes, Aug. 5, 1970.
[97] *Newsweek* (July 7, 1970), 663–665.
[98] *Pub Paps RN 1970*, 603.
[99] McCracken for President, Aug. 23, 1970, McCracken Meetings Files, Presidential Meetings–Quadriad file, SMOF: McCracken.
[100] McCracken for President, July 11, 1970, President's Handwriting file, POF.

erate again. We believe that this risk is not great, but it is not zero."[101] Stein had two reasons for believing that the risks of inflation would not be great. First, during the early stages of recovery, productivity would rise, cutting labor costs and easing price pressures. Second, though output would be increasing, it would remain below potential long enough for inflation to subside. But Stein knew it was a gamble. Gambling when the stakes were boom and bust, however, was not something Shultz was prepared to do. "We worked so hard to get here," he said, "let's not blow it."[102]

Nixon, therefore, was still without a solution to his economic problem. The man he trusted was Shultz, but Shultz was counseling patience, though Nixon, who kept time by the political clock, believed that time was running out. The CEA, whose members he did not much respect, were now the ones telling him what he wanted hear. When McCracken wrote Nixon in July recommending a sizable increase in money growth, Nixon scribbled a note to Peter Flanigan, "Pete, I agree with Paul. Let's keep the heat on."[103]

Then, in August 1970, a spate of favorable statistics temporarily relieved the tension. Meeting in San Clemente that month with the cabinet, the president boasted that his administration "may be the first modern administration not to act hit or miss;" consequently, we "may have price stability and full employment — if the Fed doesn't act like a bunch of fools. Big if."[104] Nixon meant, of course, that all might yet be well by the 1972 election. For the election closer at hand, the economy would be the obstacle he must overcome.

# VI

On his San Clemente vacation in August, Nixon read a book called *The Real Majority*, whose authors were Richard M. Scammon and Ben J. Wattenberg, two self-styled independent Democrats. The book was a manual on how to win elections in the decade of the seventies. Winning elections meant capturing the center, and the center was up for grabs. The voter in the center, said Scammon and Wattenberg, was a mythical "forty-seven-year-old housewife from the outskirts of Dayton, Ohio, whose husband is a

---

[101] Stein for Shultz, June 29, 1970, Office of Director files, OMB, NA.
[102] *New York Times*, July 19, 1970, 56.
[103] McCracken for President, July 11, 1970.
[104] E-Notes, Aug. 5, 1970.

machinist."[105] Since the New Deal, the Democrats had had her vote on the Economic Issue, but the disturbances of the 1960s had created a new issue, the Social Issue, which presented the Republican party with a historic opportunity. If the Republicans successfully combined conservatism on the Social Issue with liberalism on the Economic Issue, they would win the housewife from Dayton and become the new majority party.

Nixon could, of course, have written the book himself. *The Real Majority* was less a manual of instruction than a description of the politics that he was already practicing. But the book excited him nonetheless. "P talked about Real Majority and need to get that thinking over to all our people," Haldeman recorded in his diary entry for August 28. "Wants to really ram this home and make all decisions based on it . . . Wants to hit pornography, dope, bad kids."[106]

In the election at hand, the best Nixon could do with the Economic Issue was to try to neutralize it. Peter Flanigan, he said, should "run a daily program — bang, bang, bang," to pin inflation on the Democrats and accuse them of "running down America" with scare talk of a recession. Flanigan responded by organizing a nine-man team of economic officials for forays into major cities to dine with the "shakers and doers" and explain Nixon's economic policies.[107] As for the Social Issue, Nixon planned a bare-knuckles campaign. He told Haldeman to tie the Democrats to peace protesters. "Get a goon squad to start roughing up demonstrators," he said. Use the VFW or hard hats to do the job. "No insults to the president . . . Get some stuff out that commies are doing demonstrations. Encourage police to arrest demonstrators."[108]

Nixon agreed with Scammon and Wattenberg that the key to building a Real Majority — or the New Majority — was the blue-collar worker. Accordingly, Nixon kicked off his campaign by hosting an extravagant Labor Day dinner at the White House for seventy-five labor leaders and their wives. The guest of honor was the irascible autocrat of the AFL-CIO, George Meany. Nixon toasted Meany on this occasion as "a pillar in the storm — strong, full of character, devoted to his church, devoted to his

---

[105] Richard M. Scammon and Ben J. Wattenberg, *The Real Majority* (1970), 70.

[106] *Haldeman Diaries*, Aug. 28, 1970.

[107] H-Notes, July 23, 1970; Flanigan for Kennedy, Stans, John Mitchell, McCracken, Charls Walker, Maurice Mann, Stein, Weinberger, and Paul Volcker, Aug. 5, 1970, BE 5 File, WHCF.

[108] H-Notes, July 24, 1970.

family, . . . standing with the President and his country when he felt that served the interest of freedom." Meany replied by saying that no matter how political they were, every president he had known wanted to be the best president he could be, "and let me tell you, Franklin Roosevelt, he was just as tricky a politician as anyone who bore the name of Tricky Dick."[109] Nixon was no doubt relieved after that to repair to the South Lawn where he joined 6,000 union functionaries and their families for a performance of Tchaikovsky's 1812 Overture, complete with live cannon.[110]

In quest of a Republican Senate, Nixon sent Vice President Spiro Agnew on the road in September to establish this campaign theme. "We believe in representing the poor too, and we do," Agnew said, opening his campaign in Springfield, Illinois. "But the time has come for someone also to represent workingmen of this country, the forgotten men of American politics, white collar and blue collar."[111] "Written off by the old elite," Agnew went on, "the workingman has become the cornerstone of the New Majority."[112] In San Diego, Agnew asked whether America would be led by a president elected by the majority, or would "we be intimidated and black-mailed into following the path dictated by a disruptive radical and militant minority — the pampered prodigies of the radical liberals in the United States Senate?"[113] Though GOP hopes for capturing the Senate soon dissipated, the Social Issue seemed to be taking hold, and polls showed the Republicans making significant gains.[114]

In the end, the Economic Issue bit more deeply. On September 15, 1970, unluckily for Nixon, 344,000 members of the United Auto Workers began a six-week strike of General Motors (GM), costing workers $12 million a day in wages, GM suppliers $200 million a week in sales, governments $100 million in revenues,[115] and the GNP $12 billion in lost auto production and distribution.[116] Week by week through the fall, augmented by the strike, unemployment crept upward until it reached 6 percent in December. Among blue-collar workers, the prize quarry of the campaign,

---

[109] White House Press Release, Sept. 7, 1970, no file info, SMOF: Colson.

[110] *New York Times*, Sept. 8, 1970, 1, 20; *Time* (Sept. 14, 1970), 16.

[111] *Wall Street Journal*, Sept. 11, 1970, 1.

[112] *Washington Post*, Sept. 11, 1970, A 10.

[113] Ibid., Sept. 12, 1970, A 2.

[114] *Time* (Sept. 21, 1970), 15.

[115] *New York Times*, Sept. 20, 1970, III, 1.

[116] CEA Annual Report 1971, 35.

unemployment rose to 7.5 percent in the fourth quarter, up from 3.9 percent in 1969.[117] As measured by the GNP deflator, inflation also behaved
badly. Prices, which had slowed at midyear, spurted temporarily at an annual rate of 6.3 percent during the fall quarter of 1970 — compared to
McCracken's forecast of 3 to 3.5 percent.[118]

Through most of 1970, analysts had debated whether the economy was
really in recession. After declining in the fall of 1969 and in the winter of
1970, output increased slightly during the spring and summer quarters. The
GM strike resolved all uncertainties. Mainly because of the strike, real
output fell in the fall quarter at an annual rate of 4.1 percent.[119] The
National Bureau of Economic Research, official arbiter of these matters,
would declare the downturn of 1970 to be a true recession, the fifth, though
also the mildest, of the postwar period.

The GM strike and the grim economic news doomed Nixon's hopes for
major inroads among middle-income blue-collar workers. A Harris poll
reported that only 35 percent of the public gave Nixon high marks for
handling the economy. Labor leaders whom Nixon had courted in September fled back to the Democrats in hard times, and the Social Issue faded.[120]
Covering the Midwest, a political reporter located the typical American
voter, who was not a housewife in Dayton, but Mike Mango, a real teamster
from Akron. Mr. Mango despised antiwar demonstrators and thought National Guardsmen had been "100 percent right" to fire on students at Kent
State. But the economic downturn had cut into his overtime pay, forcing
his wife back to work for the first time in twenty-two years to keep their
three children in Catholic school. Mike Mango was voting for Howard
Metzenbaum, Democratic nominee for the U.S. Senate from Ohio.[121]

Nixon knew in October that the Economic Issue was killing him.
"Every statistic this month is bad," he told Ehrlichman. He wanted action
but felt himself "drifting" toward the riverbank.[122] Nonetheless, hoping at
least for a net gain of four seats in the Senate, the president commenced a
three-week campaign trip on October 17 that covered 17,000 miles in

---

[117] *Monthly Labor Review* (July 1971), 97, Table 5.

[118] For the year the GNP deflator (as revised) rose 5.5 percent in 1970 compared to 4.7
percent in 1969. The Consumer Price Index gave a more favorable result, with prices rising
by 5.5 percent in 1970 compared to 6.1 percent in 1969 (Dec.–Dec.).

[119] For GNP deflator, *Survey of Current Business* (June 1972), 15, Table 19. For the year,
output fell 0.6 percent.

[120] *New York Times*, Oct. 18, 1970, IV, 8; *Wall Street Journal*, Oct. 21, 1970, 1.

[121] *New York Times*, Oct. 29, 1970, 48.

[122] E-Notes, Oct. 23, 1970.

twenty-two states and astonished reporters by its reckless expenditure of the president's energies.[123] Advance men made sure small groups of demonstrators were admitted to distant corners of Nixon's halls, where their muffled chants provided him his foil.[124] "And, my friends, I say that the answer to those that engage in disruption, to those that shout their filthy slogans, to those that try to shout down speakers," he said, "is not to answer in kind, but go to the polls on election day and in the quiet of that ballot box stand up and be counted, the great silent majority of America."[125] On October 29, in a carefully staged encounter, Nixon left the municipal auditorium in San Jose, California, where demonstrators under television lights had been permitted to stand behind barricades near his car. Climbing atop it, Nixon glowered at his youthful adversaries, flashed his "V" salute, and said to no one in particular, "That's what they hate to see." As he sped away, demonstrators pelted his car with eggs and rocks,[126] providing him with dramatic material for a nationwide televised appeal on election eve for the votes of middle America.[127]

The tactic failed. When the votes were counted, the Republicans gained only two seats in the Senate and lost nine in the House, where the average Democratic margin of victory increased by an impressive 3 percent over 1968.[128] Though Nixon put the best possible spin on the results, he knew he had been defeated, and he knew why. "A Republican administration with any kind of economic slowdown is a disaster," he told Haldeman two days after the election. "Without economic drag, [we] would have carried both House and Senate."[129] Unless he neutralized the Economic Issue before 1972, his reelection, not to speak of the New Majority, stood imperiled. Somehow he had to stop the drift. Haldeman reported in his diary on November 18 that the president was "seriously considering complete change in advisors, since they failed in the one prime objective he set, to keep unemployment under 5 percent in October. Doesn't want to take any chance on screwing up 1972."[130]

---

[123] *New York Times*, Oct. 25, 1970, IV, 1.
[124] *Time* (Nov. 2, 1970), 6–7; *New York Times*, Oct. 30, 1970, 1.
[125] Quote in *Pub Paps RN 1970*, 898; *Time* (Nov. 9, 1970), 14–15.
[126] *New York Times*, Oct. 30, 1970, 1; Oct. 31, 1970, 12.
[127] *Pub Paps RN 1970*, 1033–1039.
[128] *New York Times*, Dec. 9, 1970, 1.
[129] H-Notes, Nov. 5, 1970.
[130] *Haldeman Diaries*, Nov. 18, 1970.

## Chapter 4
# The Decline and Fall of Gradualism

---

### I

A week after the 1970 Congressional election, on the plane to Paris for de Gaulle's funeral, Nixon considered the stakes in the 1972 campaign. The Democratic aspirants to replace him would be utterly "irresponsible domestically" and "extremely dangerous internationally," he said. "They would have to learn what I knew when I came in" — namely, that "America has only two more years as the number one power" and that we either "make the best deals we can between now and 1975 *or* increase our conventional strength. No Democrat can sell this to the country. Therefore, the economy must *boom* beginning July 1972."[1]

Trusting the boom entirely to his current economic team was a risk Nixon was not prepared to take. "Problem is not just advice, it's that they don't get in and fight," he told Haldeman.[2] Nixon had already purged Robert Mayo from the Budget Bureau. Now he would have to replace David Kennedy, his nearly invisible secretary of the treasury. On November 19, 1970, Nixon met Kennedy to coax his resignation, but encountering resistance, shrank from a confrontation and botched the job.[3]

Nixon was still pondering the Treasury problem later in the day when he met with the President's Advisory Council on Executive Reorganization to receive its final report. The subject of reorganizing the government bored him, and the garbled presentation of the council's chairman, Roy Ash, did not help matters. Then John Connally, the handsome and forceful ex-governor of Texas, took over. A conservative Democrat appointed to the Advisory Council at Nixon's instigation, Connally snapped the meeting to attention with a persuasive brief on the political merits of consolidating the executive departments. After past sessions of the council, Nixon

---

[1] E-Notes, Nov. 11, 1970.
[2] *Haldeman Diaries*, Nov. 18, 1970.
[3] Ibid., Nov. 19, 1970.

had taken Connally aside for political conversation. On this occasion Connally's bravura performance inspired Nixon to consider an intriguing possibility.[4]

At Nixon's suggestion Connally stayed over till the next morning for a chat. There were only two jobs in the administration worth taking, Connally told Nixon — secretary of state or secretary of the treasury.[5] That very day Nixon confided to Haldeman that "somehow" he had to find a way to get Connally for the Treasury.[6] Nixon was still playing with the idea on November 30, 1970, when the White House announced Connally's appointment to the Foreign Intelligence Advisory Board. Leaders of the Texas Republican party, including Senator John Tower and George Bush, were furious that Nixon should confer such distinction on their worst enemy. Only weeks before, Connally protégé Lloyd Bentsen had defeated Bush for a U.S. Senate seat.[7] Undeterred, Nixon offered Connally the Treasury on December 4. Only Haldeman knew. Connally said he would think it over.[8]

That night, flying to Washington after a speech in New York, Nixon closeted himself with Haldeman to avoid the cabinet officers on board. Connally was the topic on his mind. Haldeman should call Connally, Nixon instructed, to tell him he "is desperately needed" in the Treasury now "and for another more important position in the future . . . he wants you here as counselor, advisor and friend. He wanted me to say that I hope and pray you won't turn him down. He's fought a long, lonely fight, has no one in the Cabinet to talk to . . . he wants you because he thinks you're the best man in the country that he could have as his advisor in national and international affairs. He feels you're the only man in the Democratic Party that could be President . . . In some way, the P has a simpatico feeling for you. Please don't turn him down on this . . . The P doesn't have a man in the whole shop that he respects in this way . . . He's not interested in the idea of political purposes either in Texas or to get a Democrat in the Cabinet . . . He wants you because of what you are."[9] Haldeman made these

---

[4] Andrew Rouse for the President's File, Nov. 19, 1970, Memos for President's file, POF; James Reston, Jr., *The Lone Star: The Life of John Connally* (1989), 376–377, 379.

[5] Reston, *Lone Star*, 379–380.

[6] H-Notes, Nov. 20, 1970.

[7] *Haldeman Diaries*, Dec. 1, 1970; Reston, *Lone Star*, 380.

[8] Ibid., Dec. 4, 1970; H-Notes, Dec. 4, 1970.

[9] Ibid., Dec. 4, 1970.

points in a phone call to Connally at eleven o'clock the next night, and "interestingly enough," Haldeman notes, "he seems to be favorably inclined towards taking the job." On December 7, 1970, Connally took it.[10] "I've never seen P so pleased—from a personal standpoint," Haldeman wrote. "Think this can make the difference."[11]

Though Connally could not be sworn in for two more months, Nixon could hardly wait to spring his surprise. Much spade work had to be done first. On Wednesday, December 9, Nixon offered Bush the post of United Nations ambassador, which, as Haldeman observed, "will help when the Connally blow strikes."[12] On Friday, December 11, screwing up his courage, Nixon told David Kennedy he was out on February 1. Later in the day, the president apprised Shultz of the impending change, which implicitly threatened Shultz's position as the president's economic point man. "George reacted with total impassivity, and betrayed no emotion," Haldeman wrote in his diary. "The P and I both concluded that he was not particularly pleased by the Connally plan."[13] The big day was December 14, Monday. Nixon personally broke the news of the appointment to John Tower, informed an astonished group of cabinet officers and congressional leaders, and relished the surprise of White House reporters when he paraded Connally into the press room and introduced him as his new secretary of the treasury.[14]

Nixon had good reason for his awe of John Connally. Son of a sharecropper, Connally had been president of the student body at the University of Texas, sometime lieutenant of Lyndon Johnson, servant of the Texas oligarchy, briefly secretary of the navy under Kennedy, and the dominant politician in Texas during his three terms as governor from 1963 to 1969. One of the bullets that Lee Harvey Oswald fired at a moving car in Dallas on November 22, 1963, passed through Connally's back, nearly killing him, even as it made Connally a national figure. Increasingly alienated by the leftward drift of the Democrats through the sixties, Connally had given such tepid support to the national ticket in 1968 that his ultimate political loyalties had come into question. That was why Nixon, who did not know Connally, had tapped him for the Ash Council.[15] Once the two men got

---

[10] Ibid., Dec. 5, 1970; Dec. 7, 1970.
[11] H-Notes, Dec. 7, 1970.
[12] *Haldeman Diaries*, Dec. 9, 1970.
[13] Ibid., Dec. 9, 1970; Dec. 11, 1970.
[14] Ibid., Dec. 14, 1970.
[15] Reston, *Lone Star*, 375–376.

acquainted, Nixon felt Connally's star power. Henry Kissinger wrote later, "Connally's swaggering self-assurance was Nixon's Walter Mitty image of himself. He was one person whom Nixon never denigrated behind his back."[16]

Nixon had reasons other than personal admiration to appoint Connally. He yearned to recruit conservative southern Democrats to the New Majority, and Connally was a leading southern Democrat. He hoped to recover Texas from the Democrats in 1972 and believed Connally could help him do it. He scorned his small-minded Vice President Spiro Agnew and plotted to place Connally on the 1972 ticket in his stead. He thought Connally would add glamour to a drab cabinet, help him with congressional Democrats, engineer a public relations campaign to improve the president's image, and provide sage political advice. Most of all, Nixon appointed Connally to relieve his deep concern about the economy. True, Connally was not a banker or a financier, and he knew little of economics, but he would understand the crucial point — which was, as Nixon once said, "we are in a continuous campaign."[17] Here at last was the man to smite the critics, tame Arthur Burns, and nourish the boom Nixon needed for reelection. The policies of Nixon's current advisers might yet work, of course. He would wait and see. If not, if the gradualist game plan that he called the "Ohio State strategy of three yards and a cloud of dust" faltered, Nixon finally had a player who could throw the long bomb.[18]

## II

In the weeks after the 1970 congressional election, the United States stood at something of an economic crossroads. In 1969 Nixon had mounted the policy of gradualism to combat the Vietnam inflation and restore stability. The result had been a recession he had not wanted, but a recession that nonetheless had been the mildest of the postwar era. At relatively little cost, the administration had reduced excess demand and now stood on the brink of a noninflationary recovery. But the achievement would take time. Shallow recessions are followed by slow recoveries, and the lingering effects of cost-push inflation would keep the inflation rate uncomfortably high well into 1971. Impatient critics would demand pump priming to bring

---

[16] Henry Kissinger, *White House Years* (1979), 951.

[17] *Haldeman Diaries*, Mar. 25, 1971.

[18] Herbert Stein interview in Erwin C. Hargrove and Samuel A. Morley, *The President and the Council of Economic Advisers* (1984), 367.

down unemployment and controls to bring down inflation. If Nixon had the courage to resist, he could halt the cycle of stop and go and initiate an era of economic stability. If he flinched, if the political calendar forced him to reinflate, the economy could slip dangerously and rapidly out of control. Decisions that the president would make in the coming months would determine the fate of the American economy for years.

Nixon himself set the standard of recovery from the recession. The president's advisers had been assuming since July 1970 that his goal was 4 percent unemployment by mid-1972. Nixon offered clarification at an October meeting of the Troika. "The important thing in his view," summarized the note-taker, "was that unemployment be coming down and the mood of the country be buoyant." The team took that to mean a 4.5 percent unemployment rate midway through the presidential election year.[19] The question was this: To get there, should policy stay the present course or pump up demand?

On November 19, 1970, Milton Friedman visited the White House once again to offer reassurance and firm up the president's commitment to gradualism. At the time, output was declining, unemployment and inflation were rising, and Nixon was still reeling from his recent election setback. In stunning contradiction to everything else the president was hearing, Friedman said, "Things are going quite well." The recession was draining away inflation, while the Fed's 5 percent money growth assured a healthy expansion of output. If Nixon would ignore the mood swings of Wall Street and the short-sighted criticism of the commentators, if he continued to resist excessive fiscal-monetary stimulus and stuck with gradualism, he could steer the economy to a soft landing.[20] After Friedman left, Nixon remarked to Haldeman, "It was nice to have someone say we're doing things right." But he himself clearly had doubts. "P still concerned about '72. Can't afford to risk a downtrend, no matter how much inflation."[21]

Nixon nonetheless stayed with gradualism in the months after the congressional election because George Shultz, a Friedman disciple, was still

[19] On significance of Nixon's July 20 news conference remark, McCracken for President, Aug. 23, 1970, Memos for President's file, SMOF: McCracken; Flanigan to Files, Oct. 13, 1970, Memos for President's file, POF.

[20] Shultz for President's file, Nov. 19, 1970, Memos for President's file, POF; Friedman elaborated these views in letter from Friedman to David Kennedy, Dec. 12, 1970, Friedman (4) file, Box K12, Burns Papers, Ford Library.

[21] Haldeman Diaries, Nov. 19, 1970.

his man on the economy. Shultz had been the first to warn Nixon of the coming recession in 1969 and had proved his ability in many assignments since. Insecure in his own judgment on economic matters, Nixon had moved Shultz from the Labor Department to the Office of Management and Budget in July 1970, made him unofficial head of the Troika, and expected to rely on him for economic advice. Late in 1970, Shultz offered his prescription for the year ahead. It was the prescription of a gradualist. Shultz proposed a tight budget with a $5 billion full-employment surplus and a money growth of 6 percent—enough, Shultz said, "to make the economy really move."[22]

Within the administration, Shultz's chief opponent was the Council of Economic Advisers. The original architects of gradualism, McCracken and Stein had emerged from the traumas of the Cambodian spring deeply shaken and ready to cut loose from their own policy. Gradualism had produced more unemployment than they were prepared to tolerate and might, if continued, cost their chief his reelection. McCracken and Stein understood that pumping up demand might reignite inflation but, given the stakes, considered the risk small and in any case worth taking. Thus, while Shultz favored a surplus in the full-employment budget, the CEA wanted to spend every last dollar permissible under the full-employment balance rule. Instead of 6 percent money growth, the CEA urged at least 8 percent, which had been the rate in 1968 when prices spun out of control. Nixon's intuitions coincided with the CEA's advice, but it was Shultz whose judgment he trusted and Shultz who mainly prevailed.

Nearly as concerned to reelect the president as the president himself, Herbert Stein kept trying. Late in December 1970, the administration was deep in discussion on how to get to 4.5 percent by mid-1972. Everyone agreed that on the path to this goal dollar GNP would have to grow by 9 percent to $1,065 billion in 1971.[23] The issue was how to get to $1,065 billion. Stein renewed his pleas to the Troika for more stimulus, repudiating without embarrassment positions he had only recently held. "I think the situation is serious and getting more serious every day," Stein wrote. "And despite what seems to be adequate agreement on the need for more expan-

---

[22] Ed Harper for President's file, Dec. 12, 1970, Memos for President's file, POF; Flanigan for President's file, Nov. 19, 1971, Memos for President's file, POF.

[23] Memo from Troika Staff to Troika, Dec. 4, 1970, McCracken-President Meetings–Quadriad file, SMOF: McCracken; McCracken for Ehrlichman, Dec. 11, 1970, FG 131, WHCF.

sive policy, we are not getting more expansive policy and don't seem about to get it." Present policies, he said, were likely to yield unemployment above rather than below 5.5 percent by mid-72. The way out was easier money, which Stein would now go to any lengths to obtain.

Money should grow at a rate of 8 percent in the coming year, Stein said, and the Fed should be so informed. If the price of the Fed for faster money growth was an incomes policy, "I think we should pay the price." If the Fed "cannot be persuaded or bribed," the administration had two alternatives: It could try to pump up demand on the fiscal side, which Stein doubted would work unless the Fed cooperated, or the administration could force its will on the Fed "by an open attack."[24] Stein won a small victory in the following days when the president opted to seek a balanced full-employment budget for the next fiscal year rather than the small surplus that Shultz preferred.[25] But Nixon declared no wars on the Fed and acquiesced to the gradualist money target of 6 percent, which Shultz told Nixon was enough to produce the target GNP of $1,065 billion.

In truth, virtually no one outside the Office of Management and Budget, including Milton Friedman, believed that a balanced full-employment budget and 6 percent money growth would generate a $1,065 billion GNP in 1971. Shultz believed it because he had found an economist who assured him 6 percent would do the job. He was Arthur Laffer, age 30, a former Shultz protégé at the University of Chicago, now on academic leave to fill the new post of OMB economist. Later famous as author of the Laffer Curve, which helped persuade Ronald Reagan to cut taxes in the mistaken belief he could also increase revenue,[26] Laffer was completing work on an econometric model in December 1970, whose astonishing policy implications Shultz brought directly to Nixon.[27] Laffer's single four-equation model, a radical variant of monetarism, indicated that a 1 percent increase in money growth would produce an instantaneous 1 percent growth in real GNP. Applied to 1971, Laffer's model meant that to achieve the administration's goal of 6 percent real growth in 1971, the money supply had only to grow by the gradualist target of 6 percent. Add 3 percent inflation resulting from the lagged effect of past inflations, and you get a rise in

[24] Stein for Kennedy, McCracken, Shultz, Dec. 21, 1970, CEA Staff Memos, Stein, SMOF: McCracken.

[25] Flanigan for President's File, Dec. 24, 1970, Memos for President's file, POF.

[26] Current Biography (1972), 212–215.

[27] E-Notes, Dec. 15, 1970.

money GNP of 9 percent — or $1,065 billion.[28] Wits had a merry time with OMB's model, one of them describing it in the *New York Times* as "Laffer's new magic money machine."[29] It was a phrase that would haunt the model for the fifteen minutes of its fame.

Though economists inside and out of the administration scoffed at the model, nothing, not even the authority of Friedman himself, could dissuade Shultz from placing a reckless wager that Laffer was right and everybody else was wrong. How did Laffer's model become Shultz's folly? Laffer thought he knew. "Thousands of people work days and nights to get those other models out," Laffer said. "He can't understand them, but he can understand this easily."[30] No doubt there was another reason. Laffer appeared to lend the support of science for the gradualist target of 6 percent money growth that Shultz already favored, furnishing him the wrong reason for the right policy. Of course, if GNP fell off Laffer's predicted path, the enemies of gradualism would have an even stronger case than before for priming the pump.

Early in 1971 Nixon unveiled for the coming year an economic program that was appropriately gradualist but whose true character he tried to conceal behind a facade of buoyant rhetoric. In his State of the Union Message, the president promised "a new prosperity: more jobs, more income, more profits, without inflation and without war." Claiming "expansionary policies" to accomplish this goal, the president cited the commitment of the Federal Reserve to supply enough money and his own full-employment budget, "a budget designed to be in balance if the economy were operating at its peak potential," he explained. The arresting feature of the full-employment budget was the license it gave even a Republican president to run an actual deficit in slack times. Because times would still be slack in 1971, Nixon submitted a budget for FY 72 with an estimated actual deficit of $11.6 billion. He even boasted of it. Said Nixon, "By spending as if we were *at* full employment, we will help *bring about* full employment," a line that made his economists cringe.[31] Nixon casually informed one interviewer, "I am now a Keynesian in economics."[32] In fact, Herbert Stein had

---

[28] Arthur Laffer to Director (Shultz), Dec. 11, 1970, with paper describing his model attached; Arthur B. Laffer and R. David Ransom, "A Formal Model of the Economy," Feb. 26, 1971.

[29] *New York Times*, May 16, 1971, III, 16; *Washington Post*, Feb. 14, 1971, M 1.

[30] Lawrence Malkin, "Practical Politician at the Fed," *Fortune* (May 1971), 148 ff.

[31] *Pub Paps RN, 1971* 52; for budget number, *Pub Paps RN 1971*, 82.

[32] *New York Times*, Jan. 7, 1971, 19; *Business Week*, (Jan. 16, 1971), 22.

pioneered the full-employment budget in 1947, and Keynes's leading critic, Milton Friedman, had long supported a similar fiscal rule.[33]

No one was fooled by Nixon's assurances of expansiveness. Burns had promised Nixon only 6 percent money growth, which his own CEA considered inadequate, and his budget had a lot less kick than Nixon claimed. The stimulus of the budget depended on the magnitude of its shift toward ease from one year to the next. As a study of the Brookings Institution noted, the full-employment budget would swing from a surplus of $1.4 billion this year to a surplus of $0.1 billion in the next — "not enough by itself to provide a significant stimulus to the economy."[34] Nixon's Keynesian critics argued that a vigorous recovery from the 1970 recession required not the balanced full-employment budget that Nixon had submitted but a substantial full-employment deficit.[35]

Under duress from the White House, the CEA reluctantly published the administration's precise forecast for 1971 in its February annual report, a forecast the CEA did not believe attainable under gradualism. The report acknowledged that mainstream forecasters were predicting a GNP of only $1,045–$1,050 billion during the current calendar year. "This is a possible outcome," said the CEA, with studied ambiguity. "However, it seems more likely that with present policies the outcome would be higher than that and could be as high as $1,065 billion."[36]

Noting the scorn that greeted the forecast, which only Shultz and Laffer believed, Stein called it "an instant sensation . . . the best known GNP number in history."[37] Business Week said that the administration had gone out on a "very exposed limb." House Democratic leader Hale Boggs was reminded of Alice in Wonderland.[38] Paul Samuelson wondered why the forecast had not inspired "a rash of quiet or indignant resignations from scholars of impeccable probity," referring of course to McCracken and Stein.[39] Stein managed to recover some honor for the CEA in a speech in

---

[33] Herbert Stein, Fiscal Revolution (1969), 220–232; Milton Friedman, "A Monetary and Fiscal Framework for Economic Stability," American Economic Review (1948), 245–264.

[34] Charles L. Schultze et al., Setting National Priorities: The 1972 Budget (1971), 8.

[35] "The 1971 Economic Report of the President," Joint Economic Committee, hearings (1971), testimony of Arthur Okun, 452; Robert Eisner, 500–502; George Perry, 537.

[36] CEA Annual Report 1971, 84.

[37] Stein speech before National Agricultural Outlook Conference, Feb. 23, 1971. Copy provided by CEA.

[38] Business Week (Feb. 6, 1971), 16.

[39] Newsweek (Mar. 8, 1971), 81.

February that began loyally by defending the $1,065 billion forecast and then veered off to attack the Laffer model, unnamed of course, that had ground out the number. Said Stein,"We do not believe . . . a one percent increase in money yields a one percent increase in GNP . . . we do not believe that the effect of money on the GNP is instantaneous."[40] Whether gradualism according to Laffer could move the economy along Nixon's required path remained to be seen. In case it did not, on February 11, 1971, John Connally was sworn in as secretary of the treasury.

## III

"The first months of 1971 were the lowest point of my first term as President," Nixon wrote in his memoirs. "The problems we confronted were so overwhelming and so apparently impervious to anything we could do to change them that it seemed possible that I might not even be nominated for reelection in 1972."[41] His approval rating had fallen to a new low of 52 percent in December; and Senator Edmund Muskie, the Democratic front-runner for 1972, had pulled even with him in the Gallup poll. Nixon cited the economy as a prominent reason for his difficulties.[42] Contemporary accounts agreed, *Newsweek* warning in January 1971, "If there is not sustained pick-up in the months ahead, the economy could turn out to be Richard Nixon's 'Vietnam.' "[43]

Nixon himself diagnosed the economic malady as a "psychological recession," which was why he emphasized confidence.[44] Confidence must radiate outward from the White House through the entire administration and into the country beyond. It had to begin with the president, who could initiate its revival by projecting an image of strong leadership, countering the sense of economic drift. In the context of early 1971, strong economic leadership could mean only one thing—taking decisive action to slow inflation, which had risen at a 5.5 percent rate (CPI) in 1970. So far, Nixon, acting in accord with the precepts of gradualism, had made only modest gestures toward an incomes policy. As 1971 began, the wolves were closing in fast, and the time had clearly come to throw them real meat.

---

[40] Stein Speech, Feb. 23, 1971.
[41] *RN: Memoirs* (1978), 497.
[42] *New York Times*, Dec. 17, 1970, 37; George H. Gallup, *Gallup Poll* (vol. 3, 1978), 2284.
[43] *Newsweek* (Jan. 25, 1971), 27.
[44] E-Notes, Dec. 15, 1970.

One day in January 1971, Nixon mused, "People want controls (of the other fellow). What do we do about it?" Shultz replied, "Find things to do that show we care." Nixon had a better idea. "We have to kick someone," he said.[45] That month Bethlehem Steel raised structural steel prices by 12 percent, and the other steel companies were poised to follow suit.[46] Nixon kicked the industry by canceling negotiations in Frankfurt to extend an agreement limiting steel imports into the United States. Bethlehem quickly backed down by halving its price increase, and Nixon looked like a leader.[47]

No one doubted that the crucial test of Nixon's leadership on the inflation front was the construction industry, the nation's largest, where first-year negotiated wage and benefit settlements were averaging 18 percent — more than double average settlements in manufacturing. Ten thousand craft locals with more than 3 million members in the highly fragmented construction industry were engaged in a game of leapfrog to determine which of them could score the biggest contracts, even though unemployment in the industry was rising.[48] White House discussion had gone round the problem for months, without resolution. For one thing, Nixon was grateful to the hard hats for their support of his Cambodian invasion and harbored hopes of recruiting them into the New Majority. For another, the sheer multiplicity of powerful union locals might frustrate efforts at federal control. In January 1971, Nixon invited building contractors and union leaders to the White House to plead for a voluntary solution.[49] When that failed, he decided that in the interest of confidence he would have to quell his aversion to incomes policy and take decisive action.

Nixon had two choices. He could freeze construction prices and wages under authority granted him by Congress in August 1970. That would appear strong but might prove impossible to enforce. Or he could suspend the Davis-Bacon Act. Passed in 1931, Davis-Bacon effectively required contractors to pay union scale on federal and federally assisted construction projects — 30 percent of all construction in the country. Insulated by Davis-

[45] Ibid., Jan. 15, 1971.

[46] New York Times, Jan. 12, 1971, 1; Wall Street Journal, Jan. 13, 1971, 3; Business Week (Jan. 16, 1971), 22.

[47] New York Times, Jan. 13, 1971; Jan. 19, 1971, 1; Jan. 20, 1971, 43; Newsweek (Jan. 25, 1971), 64.

[48] Time (Feb. 15, 1971), 72.

[49] Secretary of Labor for the President, Jan. 15, 1971, Pres. Meetings–McCracken, SMOF: McCracken.

Bacon from nonunion competition, unionized federal contractors had no incentive to resist wage demands that they could easily pass on to the government in higher construction costs.[50] Suspending Davis-Bacon would address the problem of escalating wages only indirectly, but by threatening protected markets it might prompt the unions to cut a wage deal. Though many of his advisers preferred to freeze construction wages, on February 23, 1971, Nixon suspended Davis-Bacon.[51] A few days later in Des Moines, a group of hard hats joined in unlikely alliance with student demonstrators to pelt the president's limousine with snowballs.[52]

No less unhappy was the gang of four in Nixon's cabinet, which had conspired a year before to pressure him into an incomes policy and gone down again fighting for a freeze on construction wages. Romney, Volpe, Stans, and Blount reunited on March 5, 1971, at a secret meeting in Romney's office to conspire for a wage freeze in construction. They decided to meet again and this time to invite the nation's most famous advocate of incomes policy, Arthur Burns.[53] At that point, Romney decided he had better tell presidential counselor John Ehrlichman what was afoot.[54] "It's an end run of the system," Nixon stormed when he learned the news. "Burns can't be in on it. He *can't* be." Nixon ordered Ehrlichman to crash the group's next meeting and tell the conspirators "that they are nothing but a damn secret splinter group."[55] "Talk about a skunk at a garden party," recalled Ehrlichman of his uninvited visit; "I was it."[56] Meanwhile, Nixon had decided to undercut "the cabal" by hastily calling a cabinet meeting to clear the air and reestablish his authority.[57]

On March 26, 1971, sullen barons of the realm gathered to confront the sovereign who despised them. The meeting featured a report by Labor Secretary James Hodgson, who outlined an impending agreement with the unions that vindicated Nixon's approach. Suspending Davis-Bacon, said Hodgson, got the attention of the unions "the way a two-by-four gets the

---

[50] McCracken for President, Nov. 25, 1971, President's Handwriting file, POF.
[51] *Pub Paps RN 1971*, 199–200.
[52] *Newsweek* (Mar. 15, 1971), 25.
[53] Stein to Blount et al., Mar. 11, 1971, attached to Ehrlichman for McCracken, Mar. 24, 1971, FG 6-3, WHCF.
[54] Ehrlichman for President, Mar. 18, 1971, attached to Ehrlichman for the President, Mar. 25, 1971, Ehrlichman Chron file, WHSF.
[55] John Ehrlichman, *Witness to Power* (1982), 107–108.
[56] Ehrlichman interview in Kenneth W. Thompson, ed., *The Nixon Presidency* (1987), 131.
[57] E-Notes, Mar. 25, 1971.

attention of a mule." In return for reinstatement of Davis-Bacon, the national union chiefs had agreed to cooperate with a Construction Industry Stabilization Committee, to be created by executive order and empowered to enforce wage guideposts at federal and federally assisted construction projects. Commerce Secretary Maurice Stans asked whether creation of this committee precluded a wage-price panel for the whole economy. "Nothing in it precludes anything," Hodgson replied. Nixon interrupted. "There is," he said. "I won't go for it. That precludes that."[58]

After Nixon created the Construction Industry Stabilization Committee, a measure of order returned to construction. Average first-year negotiated wage and benefits settlements came down from 19 percent to 11 percent.[59] Some argued that if a wage-price board could help construction, then a general wage-price board, relying on voluntary compliance, might work economywide. Nixon had explained to the cabinet why this would not likely be so. The difference between construction and other industries, he said, is that in construction, "you can stick Davis-Bacon to them." People are good, Nixon added, "not because of love but because of fear."[60] Though Nixon's intervention in construction had achieved a modest success, pressure for a more thoroughgoing incomes policy kept building, and confidence in the president's economic leadership remained low.

Concern with confidence explained Nixon's obsession with Harold Goldstein, the economist in the Bureau of Labor Statistics, whose job it was to brief the press on the government's monthly consumer price and unemployment statistics. Nixon was highly sensitive to coverage of these numbers and believed that the bureaucracy should massage them to suit his political purposes. Goldstein had seen presidents come and go for twenty-four years and intended to explain the statistics as he always had, without varnish.

Month by month, Nixon's anger at Goldstein grew. In July 1970, when the Consumer Price Index rose only slightly, the press headlined not the size but the fact of another increase. "P has always been convinced we are

[58] R. K. Price, Notes for President's file, Mar. 26, 1971, Memos for President's file, POF.

[59] *CEA Annual Report 1972*, 74–75; Albert Rees, "The Construction Industry Stabilization Committee: Implications for Phase II," *Brookings Papers on Economic Activity* (no. 3, 1971), 760–765; also D. Q. Mills, "Explaining Pay Increases in Construction, 1953–1972," *Industrial Relations* (vol. 13, May 1974), 196–201.

[60] Price, Notes, Mar. 26, 1971.

jobbed by the Bureau of Labor Statistics [BLS]," Haldeman wrote in his diary.[61] In November 1970, when the BLS published a statistic before the White House could devise a public-relations plan, Haldeman wrote, "He's convinced they sabotage us."[62] On February 5, 1971, at the same time Secretary Hodgson was proclaiming a small drop in unemployment as "of great significance," Goldstein was telling reporters that the drop was only "marginally significant."[63] The next day, according to Haldeman, Nixon wanted "some action taken immediately to get rid of Goldstein, who he feels is the same guy who screwed us back in the later years of the Eisenhower Administration."[64] In March 1971, when Goldstein gave the latest unemployment statistic a different spin from Hodgson, Goldstein told a reporter, "It is not my job to support the Secretary's statement or not. My job is to help you understand the figures."[65] Two weeks later, Hodgson announced cancellation of regular BLS briefings "to avoid the awkwardness of subjecting the professional staff to questions with policy implications." Goldstein denied he felt awkward.[66]

There was a postscript. In July 1971, at a time when Nixon desperately needed some good economic news, the BLS announced the biggest one-month drop in unemployment in nine years — "obviously a big story for us," Haldeman wrote. "Unfortunately, as usual, the Bureau of Labor Statistics screwed it up and said that it wasn't really important because it was due to a statistical quirk. This drove the P right up the wall tonight, and he started hounding [White House aide Charles] Colson on the phone every couple of minutes demanding that we get Goldstein fired."[67] By then Goldstein had come to embody three of Nixon's most despised enemies — Democrats, bureaucrats, and Jews. Four times that month Nixon asked Haldeman for the number of Jews in the BLS. To smoke out "Jewish cabals," Haldeman

---

[61] *Haldeman Diaries*, July 21, 1970.

[62] Ibid., Nov. 24, 1970.

[63] *Washington Post*, Mar. 20, 1971, reprinted in "Discontinuance of Monthly Press Briefings by Bureau of Labor Statistics on the Consumer Price Index and Employment Figures," Government Operations Committee, House hearings (1971), 82–83. The article quotes remarks of Feb. 5.

[64] *Haldeman Diaries*, Feb. 6, 1971.

[65] *Newsweek* (Mar. 15, 1971), 77.

[66] Hodgson's statement reprinted in "Discontinuance of Monthly Press Briefings," House hearings, 81.

[67] *Haldeman Diaries*, July 2, 1971.

ordered Frederic Malek of the White House staff to conduct an "ethnic" survey of the BLS.[68] The efficient Malek reported back on July 27, 1971, that of the top thirty-five people in BLS, twenty-five were Democrats. "In addition," Malek said, "13 of the 35 fit the demographic criterion which was discussed."[69] In October Goldstein was reassigned to another bureau, where, presumably, he could no longer undermine Nixon's campaign to restore confidence.[70]

# IV

Nixon was under no illusion that confidence alone could solve his problems. In the end the actual performance of the economy would determine his political fate. Fiscal policy would have some effect on that performance, but as 1971 began, everybody in the White House continued to believe that the money supply was the main event. Though Shultz and the CEA might disagree on how much money the Fed should print, both were still essentially Friedmanesque in their views. Indeed, the months after the 1970 election were the high tide of monetarism in the Nixon administration.

Tides recede and so did this one. In the laboratory of the economy, monetarist ideas would be put to the test and by mid-1971 apparently found wanting. Critics had long held that Friedman, the high priest of monetarism, underestimated the problem of measuring money, overestimated the power of the Fed to control the money supply, and was dead wrong in believing that the Fed by itself could raise or lower output in the short run by raising or lowering the quantity of money. The events of 1970 and 1971 did not conclusively prove the case against monetarism, but they did undermine the credibility of monetarist theory, even in the White House.

With money the issue, the spotlight shone again on Arthur Burns. Burns would not rank among the Fed's abler chairmen. Abrasive and autocratic, he was insensitive to the collegiality so prized by the institution he led. Political to the core, he was too ready to sacrifice clarity for surface harmony in the policy directives of the Federal Open Market Committee,

---

[68] H-Notes, July 5, 24, 25, 30, 1971.

[69] Malek to Haldeman, July 27, 1971, Alpha Name file, Malek, SMOF: Haldeman.

[70] Reprinted from *Congressional Record* in "Discontinuance of Press Briefings," House hearings, 89–91; *New York Times*, Oct. 9, 1971, 1.

too concerned with reconciling conflicting external pressures.[71] Critical of monetarist doctrines, he had no fixed monetary principle of his own, except a determined eclecticism that translated into unsteadiness of purpose. No man in public life spoke more eloquently or urgently against inflation than he. Yet during the eight years of his leadership, the Fed would become the very engine of inflation he had determined it must not be. Nearly a year after he appointed Burns to the Fed, Nixon offered his assessment. "Pessimistic" and "volatile," Burns panicked easily and felt pressure from the Fed staff and the business community, Nixon said. "Has vanity. Wants to help us. A bad mix."[72]

In the weeks after the 1970 election, relations between Burns and Nixon, tense for months, got worse. It infuriated Nixon that, while his advisers were debating 6 percent or 8 percent, the money supply had apparently not grown at all since August. Burns disclaimed responsibility, arguing that the Fed was generously providing the banking system with reserves, but people were not borrowing. It was not the Fed's fault, therefore, that the money supply stayed stuck.[73] Nixon's advisers, for their part, suspected Burns of intentionally cutting money growth to raise interest rates in the interest of strengthening the balance of payments, about which Nixon cared nothing. There was something to this.[74] At the November 17, 1970, meeting of the top-secret FOMC, Burns resisted too steep a decline of interest rates in part to keep dollars from flowing abroad.[75] "He'll get it right in the chops," Nixon fumed. Had the time come "to take the Fed on?" he wondered. Should he "give the Fed a good kick now?"[76] Despite this bravado and two days of preparation,[77] when Nixon met Burns by the fire in the Oval Office on November 20, 1970, it was Burns who did most of the talking.[78]

---

[71] William Greider, *Secrets of the Temple: How the Federal Reserve Runs the Country* (1987), 340–341.

[72] E-Notes, Dec. 23, 1970.

[73] Burns's views discussed in his absence at White House meeting, E-Notes, Nov. 11, 1970.

[74] The White House theorized that Alfred Hayes and the New York Fed, which carried out the system's open market operations, intentionally sabotaged the FOMC's directions to pursue its own international objectives. The White House further theorized that Burns was Hayes's accomplice. E-Notes, Nov. 11, 17, 19, 1970; Shultz for the President, Nov. 18, 1970, FG 131, WHCF.

[75] FOMC Minutes, Nov. 17, 1970, 44–45, 65, 103–104.

[76] Nixon's threat, E-Notes, Nov. 16, 1970.

[77] E-Notes, Nov. 17, 19, 1970.

[78] Ibid., Nov. 20, 1971.

Within days, Nixon learned that the Fed had not been following a "zero growth policy" after all. Revising its money supply series, the Fed now reported that money had actually grown at the ample rate of 5.6 percent (annual rate) during the first three quarters of 1970. During the last quarter, it would grow not by zero but by 3.5 percent.[79] Money had not increased as fast as the administration wanted, but it had increased faster than the old statistical series had indicated. Nixon was perplexed. The revisions raised questions about how much was really known about the facts, he said to McCracken. "We seemed, in short, to be having difficulty not only figuring out where we might go but where we have been."[80]

Nixon and Burns met again on December 15, 1970. Only days before, the two men had publicly taken differing positions on the appropriateness of incomes policy. If Burns brought up the balance of payments problem, Nixon blustered prior to the meeting, "I'll unload on him like he's never had."[81] But this time Burns brought good news. That morning the Fed had voted to target money growth at 6 percent, which happened also to be the target of George Shultz and Arthur Laffer.[82] The White House and the Fed, it appeared, were at last on the same monetary page.

Through February 1971 Nixon looked for the money Burns had promised in December but could not find it, at least not money as the White House measured money.[83] M1 (checking accounts plus currency in circulation) was growing not at 6 percent but only at the annual rate of 3.5 percent. With recovery foremost on his mind and more money essential for its achievement, Nixon decided in early March to turn up the heat on the Fed. One morning Burns received a visit from White House aide Peter Flanigan, who annoyed him by persistently arguing for more money. Then in the afternoon Burns had lunch with George Shultz, who asked him pointedly why the money supply was misbehaving. Years later Burns recalled the episode. "I said, 'This is the second time today that I've heard from the White House. Once is too many, and twice is completely unacceptable. I'm going to tell the President that if he ever again sends one of his assistants to talk to me on this question, I'll throw him out bodily.' And

[79] McCracken for President, Nov. 27, 1970, Memos for President's file, SMOF: McCracken.

[80] McCracken for President's File, Nov. 27, 1970, President's Meeting file, POF.

[81] E-Notes, Dec. 15, 1970.

[82] Ehrlichman for President's File, Dec. 17, 1970, BE 5, WHCF; FOMC minutes, Dec. 15, 1970; E-Notes, Dec. 15, 1970.

[83] Laffer and Stein, Feb. 19, 1971, CEA-Troika Memos, Troika 1971 file, SMOF: Stein.

I told Nixon that."[84] In retaliation Nixon considered unleashing John Connally on the chairman of the Federal Reserve.[85]

There was more than one way to measure money, as Milton Friedman reminded both Shultz and Stein in February 1971. The White House was fixated on M1, but there was M2, which included not only checking accounts but savings deposits. That season it made all the difference which definition of money one chose. M1 had been growing slowly, as the White House said, but M2 had been growing since the summer of 1970 at the astonishing annual rate of 10 percent. Friedman explained the divergence. Though market interest rates had been coming down, banks and savings institutions had kept up their rates to win back savers. The result was a massive shift out of other financial assets, including checking accounts, into savings deposits. Thus, M1 was down, M2 was up. The White House believed the economy was starving for money, at least starving for M1. Friedman believed the economy was awash in money, or at least in M2. Friedman attributed the explosion in M2 ultimately to the easy money policy of the Fed and warned the White House that, if the Fed kept it up, "inflation is bound to be reignited."[86] Thus, Nixon's Friedmanesque advisers found themselves at odds with Friedman, and Nixon was left to wonder whether money was too tight or too easy, whether the Fed was strangling recovery or overheating the economy, whether he should measure money as his advisers measured it or as Friedman did. In fact, the White House brushed off Friedman's views and continued to press the Fed for faster M1 growth.

Though Burns defended the Fed's policy in public, by early 1971 he had in fact become an internal critic of its performance. By now past his anxiety over the balance of payments, Burns no less than Nixon wanted faster domestic recovery.[87] Like Nixon, he had come to believe that M1 growth was too slow. Burns's conversion to an expansionist policy had two sources. The Fed staff was predicting a recovery so anemic that unemployment

---

[84] For this episode and the quote, John T. Woolley, *Monetary Politics: The Federal Reserve and the Politics of Monetary Policy* (1984), 157–158.

[85] E-Notes, Mar. 8, 1971.

[86] Friedman to Shultz, Feb. 9, 1971, attached to Stein to Shultz, Feb. 16, 1971, Correspondence Files, Economists, Friedman, SMOF: Stein; Friedman to Stein, Feb. 22, 1971, same file; Friedman to Shultz, Feb. 22, 1971, Friedman (4) file, Box K12, Burns papers, Ford Library.

[87] FOMC minutes, Feb. 9, 1971, Apr. 6, 1971, 54–56.

would increase from its current 6 percent level to 6.7 percent by the end of the year.[88] And Burns did, after all, feel the heat from Richard Nixon. He said as much at the meeting of the FOMC in January 1971. The public's confidence in the Federal Reserve remained strong, Burns said, but as a result of recent feeble performance of M1, "the Administration's confidence in the system was weakening." Moreover, he himself was "greatly disturbed by the shortfalls of the money aggregates from the Committee's targets at a time when economic conditions were deteriorating." To strengthen "credibility," Burns urged the FOMC "to make up the recent shortfall." Following Burns's lead, the FOMC raised the target from 6 percent to 7.5 percent money growth for the first quarter of 1971 to get back on path.[89] Burns was not the only member of the Fed feeling White House pressure. Sherman Maisel, a member of the Federal Reserve Board in this period, wrote subsequently, "With less emphasis on money in the Administration, I believe the swing votes in the center would probably have opted for tighter money."[90] By the time Nixon sent Flanigan and Shultz to badger Burns for more money in March, Burns and his colleague had already embarked on a course of monetary appeasement.

It was one thing to set a monetary target, another to meet it. Through the first two quarters of 1971, the Fed would miss badly, failing once more to master the powerful tool it wielded. During the winter quarter, the FOMC aimed for M1 growth of 7.5 percent (annual rate) but got a dangerously inflationary 8.9 percent.[91] During the spring quarter, the Fed lowered the target to 6 percent but got 11 percent, mainly because Burns had become more concerned by interest rates than the money supply. When market interest rates began climbing in March, Burns spied a threat to the infant recovery. Leaning against the rise by accelerating money growth, the Fed inadvertently pumped up M1 far beyond the target. Over both quarters, M1 grew at an annual rate of 10 percent, the fastest six-month growth since World War II. M2 more than kept pace at 15 percent.[92] Burns had fallen

[88] Ibid., Jan. 12, 1971, 30.

[89] Ibid., 37, 64–65.

[90] Sherman S. Maisel, *Managing the Dollar* (1973), 278–279.

[91] *Federal Reserve Bulletin* (May 1971), 368.

[92] FOMC minutes, Apr. 6, 1971, 80–82; May 11, 1971, 51, 73–74; June 8, 1971, 22–27; *Federal Reserve Bulletin* (Aug. 1971), 641–643; Phillip Cagan, *Persistent Inflation: Historical and Policy Essays* (1979), 123–124; for postwar record growth, letter of economist Allan Meltzer, *New York Times*, Aug. 10, 1971, 30.

into the trap that Friedman had warned against. He had forgotten the money supply and focused on the interest rate.

In the White House, the Council of Economic Advisers welcomed the accidental money spurt as evidence of great wisdom and suggested that the president write Burns a letter of appreciation.[93] Friedman did write Burns, not in appreciation, but to say he was "apalled" at the Fed's reckless performance. By committing the classic blunder of trying to slow interest rates, Friedman warned, the Fed was feeding steam into the boiler so fast it risked an inflationary explosion by the end of the year.[94]

The puzzle was that, despite M1 growth in excess of 5 percent during 1970 and 10 percent during the first half of 1971, the engine still continued to sputter. At the June 1971 meeting of the FOMC, the Fed's chief economist admitted bafflement. "Why is it that the very high recent growth rates of money . . . fail to produce a satisfactory real performance?" asked Charles Partee. "Why does the real economy not show vigorous growth that generally has characterized postwar recoveries?"[95] By every tenet of monetarism, high rates of money growth in 1970 and 1971 should by now have produced a vigorous expansion. In February Friedman believed that money growth much lower than the actual growth would cut unemployment.[96] In fact, unemployment with high money growth would still be stuck on 6 percent at the end of the year, and real GNP would grow by only 2.7 percent. What had happened? Why had monetarist predictions strayed so far off the mark?

The crucial premise of monetarism was, in Friedman's words, that "people seem to be extraordinarily stubborn about the real amount of money they want to hold."[97] When the Fed increased the money supply, it followed that people would eventually hold more money than they wanted. To reduce money balances to their desired level, they would increase spending, stimulating the economy. But through the first half of 1971, people did not spend the money the Fed was printing up so copiously. Fearful of hard times that year, the public achieved the highest savings rate

---

[93] McCracken for President, May 18, 1971, Memos for President file, SMOF: McCracken. Draft letter to Burns attached.

[94] Friedman to Burns, Apr. 12, 1971, Friedman (4) file, Box K12, Burns papers; also Friedman to Burns, Apr. 26, 1971, Friedman (3) file; Friedman column, *Newsweek* (May 3, 1971), 81.

[95] FOMC minutes, June 29, 1971, 24.

[96] Friedman to Shultz, Feb. 9, 1971.

[97] Milton Friedman, *Dollars and Deficits* (1968), 108.

of the postwar era.[98] Saloman Brothers estimated in March that individuals had saved a massive $35 to $40 billion in the preceding six months, compared to $3.2 billion during the corresponding period a year before.[99] In the jargon of economics, Friedman expected the demand for money to be stable, but in 1971 the public's demand for money had increased. With less spending than the monetarists expected, recovery sputtered.

Of course, the increased money balances people were holding might be spent later, meaning that Friedman might be wrong in the short run but right on the ultimate consequence of easy money. Leonard Silk, economic correspondent of the *New York Times*, succinctly described the problem that this uncertainty posed for policy. "Are we in fact sitting on a liquidity time bomb that will again produce an explosive effect on inflation?" Silk wondered. "Or are we caught in a liquidity trap from which, not more money, but only a change in fiscal policy—more government spending or lower taxes—can rescue us?"[100] Given the recent difficulty of measuring money, controlling the supply of money, and predicting the effects of money on the economy, even some of the president's Friedmanesque advisors were ready to entertain the fiscal alternative. On departing the government at the end of the year, Paul McCracken was asked by an interviewer if he were as Friedmanesque as when he started. "I would say less," McCracken replied. He found the case "a little less clear that if you simply have the monetary expansion, you produce the expansion" of the economy.[101]

## V

But George Shultz never wavered in the faith. By spring it was clear that Laffer's equations had gone wrong, that the economy had already fallen off the path of a $1,065 billion GNP in 1971, and that inflation was still too high. Amid a growing clamor for bigger budget deficits and price-wage controls, Shultz delivered a notable defense of gradualism on April 22 in a speech before the Economic Club of Chicago. "With each passing day the pressures mount to alter course," Shultz said. Though there were problems,

[98] *CEA Annual Report 1972,* 212.
[99] *New York Times,* Mar. 30, 1971, 47.
[100] Ibid.
[101] *Wall Street Journal,* Dec. 31, 1971, 2.

output the first quarter had advanced, and inflationary pressures were abating. Shultz opposed an incomes policy, warned against the inflationary consequence of full-employment deficits, and pleaded for "time and the guts to take the time" to permit the administration's policies to work. Summing up his credo in a vivid nautical metaphor, Shultz said, "Those of you familiar with sailing know what a telltale is — a strip of cloth tied to a mast to show which way the wind is blowing. A captain has the choice of steering his ship by the telltale, following the prevailing winds, or to steer by the compass. In a democracy, you must keep your eye on the telltale, but you must steer by the compass. That is exactly what the President of the United States is doing. The voice from the bridge says, 'Steady as you go.'"[102]

But the Council of Economic Advisers thought that it made no sense to follow a steady course if it would not take you where you wanted to go.[103] In June 1971, the CEA renewed its challenge to gradualism. That month the economy was moving at a crawl, employment hit 6.2 percent, business was scaling back plans for new investment, and clear evidence of a declining inflation rate had yet to emerge. Only a housing boom fueled by low interest rates was keeping the recovery alive. "We have now reached a critical juncture in economic policy," McCracken wrote Nixon, tacking with the prevailing winds. Once opposed to fine-tuning on grounds that it destabilized the economy, the CEA now pressed for 7.5 percent money growth over the next year. Once doubtful of the efficiency of fiscal policy, the CEA proposed to stimulate the economy by a $8 billion tax cut, though the full employment budget had already shifted into deficit. And in a shocking repudiation of the CEA's free market principles, McCracken informed the president, "With no joy, I have concluded that we must even be prepared at a suitable time to invoke wage and price controls."[104]

But the CEA had jumped the gun. Nixon was not ready, and neither was John Connally, especially given the source of the advice. Connally was furious at McCracken for proposing early in June to move international

---

[102] "Address of George Shultz before Economic Club of Chicago," Apr. 22, 1971, OMB — Records of Director (69:1), 47.

[103] Stein to Shultz, Apr. 21, 1971, Policy and Programs file, SMOF; Stein.

[104] For McCracken quotes, McCracken for the President, June 14, 1971, President's Handwriting file, POF; for recommendations on money and budget, Stein for the President, June 25, 1971, plus attachment, Stein for McCracken and Shultz, June 24, 1971, CEA Staff Memos, Stein, SMOF: McCracken.

monetary issues out of the Treasury,[105] and he so disdained the CEA that McCracken suspected Connally of planting stories of a Treasury plot to abolish it.[106] The CEA compounded its problems in mid-June by failing to meet Nixon's exacting public-relations standard. When someone in the CEA neglected to praise a favorable statistic in a press interview, Colson wrote McCracken a nasty little note asking for the name of the perpetrator.[107] Then, on June 17, McCracken gave an interview of his own to the *New York Times*, hinting at uncertainty. "We have to recognize that the expansion is not yet moving fast enough to eat into the unemployment picture," McCracken said. "And I think it is important for us to achieve the degree of economic expansion which will do it." Sometime in July or August, McCracken continued, the president would decide whether to propose some new stimulus like a tax cut. The *Times* remarked that McCracken "had supplied the first official word that the Administration was dissatisfied with the economic pace."[108] The financial press blamed the ensuing thirty-five point drop in the Dow on the mild "trauma" of the McCracken interview, which had suggested drift and division.[109]

McCracken's interview provoked a fierce reaction in the White House. To repair the damage to confidence and assert leadership, Nixon decided to quash his unfortunate CEA chairman. Since the sooner this was done the better, he moved the midyear review of the economy and budget from July to June. The review began Wednesday evening, June 23, 1971, with a cruise aboard the presidential yacht *Sequoia*. Shultz, Connally, Ehrlichman, and Flanigan were invited. McCracken was not.[110] The meeting moved for the weekend to Camp David, Nixon's retreat in the nearby Catoctin Mountains of Maryland. On Saturday, McCracken came to make the case for tax cuts; Shultz opposed them, and Connally was uncommitted.[111] McCracken went home, and the rest stayed through Sunday. At the meeting's conclusion, Nixon said his "guess as of now" was that, barring a

---

[105] McCracken for President, June 2, 1971, President's Handwriting file, POF; Connally for President, June 8, 1971, declassified by Treasury.

[106] McCracken interview in Hargrove and Morley, *The President and the Council of Economic Advisers*, 336.

[107] Colson to McCracken, June 16, 1971, White House Staff files, Colson, SMOF: McCracken.

[108] *New York Times*, June 18, 1971, 17.

[109] *Business Week* (June 26, 1971), 21.

[110] *Haldeman Diaries*, June 23, 1971.

[111] *Business Week* (July 3, 1971), 14–15.

steel strike, "we will have a very buoyant fall, not in July and August, but . . . starting in September."[112] The president decided that policy was already expansive enough, that public musings by members of the administration on future moves had created economic uncertainty, and that from now on only one man should be the administration's economic spokesman — John Connally.[113] Ehrlichman recalled, "I was sent to tell George Shultz that in meetings with outsiders he was henceforth to defer to Connally. George didn't much like that."[114]

On Monday morning, down from the mountain, Nixon assembled senior members of the White House staff in the Cabinet Room to continue the humiliation of Paul McCracken. Nixon sat alone on one side of the long table. Loud claps of thunder sounded overhead. Two weeks before, the *New York Times* had published the first installment of the top-secret *Pentagon Papers*, inspiring the president's extraordinary effort to plug leaks. The dark soliloquy Nixon delivered on the meaning of loyalty and discipline was meant primarily for McCracken but not only for McCracken. There would be no wage-price board and no change in tax policy at this time, and there would be no discussion of a possible change later, Nixon said. Debating issues in the press eliminated options, blunted the impact of decisions, and undermined confidence. "To have confidence, there must be certainty," Nixon went on. "To have certainty, there must be one voice, one man, the Secretary of the Treasury, as the economic spokesman. He doesn't leak in advance, doesn't whine around." When he had been vice president, Nixon recalled, if he disagreed, "by God I always told the President, never the press." There will be "no more of this crap." There will be a "united front from everyone in the Administration." There will be no more guidance for the press. "If you can't follow this, get out. None of you is responsible, I am."[115] It was a performance that even John Connally might admire, which was probably its point.

That afternoon Connally made his debut as the administration's economic spokesman at a press conference called to announce the decisions of the weekend. The president had come to the conclusion, Connally said,

[112] *Haldeman Diaries*, June 27, 1971.

[113] Shultz for President's file, June 26, 1971, Memos for President's file, POF. Shultz misdated the meeting by a day.

[114] Ehrlichman, *Witness to Power*, 260.

[115] There were three similar accounts of these remarks. I drew on all three. *Haldeman Diaries*, June 28, 1971; E-Notes, June 28, 1971; H-Notes, June 28, 1971.

"that No. 1, he is not going to initiate a wage-price board; No. 2, he is not going to impose mandatory price and wage controls; No. 3, he is not going to ask Congress for any tax relief; and No. 4, he is not going to increase federal spending." Radiating confidence, Connally declared that the economy was receiving "enormous" fiscal and monetary stimulus and that only time was needed to turn the economy around. "It is not like a yo-yo," he said.[116] With the declaration of the so-called four noes, Connally gave gradualism Richard Nixon's categorical endorsement, good, as it turned out, only for six more weeks.

Connally's "virtuoso sales performance"[117] could not disguise the fact that the administration had chosen to do nothing except stick with the policy of gradualism, by then rapidly losing public favor. Arthur Okun, one of Lyndon Johnson's CEA chairmen, remarked, "As an American I am disappointed. As a professional economist I am very disappointed. But as a Democrat I have to be delighted."[118] No one, of course, was more disappointed than Paul McCracken, who tried to resign a few weeks later but at Nixon's request agreed to stay on to the end of the year.[119]

## VI

Gradualism was the policy only as long as Connally said it was. Since taking over the Treasury in February 1971, Connally had met Nixon's every expectation. An exciting political personality who entranced official Washington, he had a quick, retentive mind and a superb public presence. They loved him in the Treasury, where he put in eighteen-hour days learning the job, encouraged open and intense debate, and moved the agency to the center of the action. And they loved him in Congress for his bonhomie, his mastery of arcane subjects, his committee appearances without the usual phalanx of aides to coach him. "When you got used to the Texas accent, it became apparent that here was a very sharp mind," said Murray Weidenbaum, an assistant Treasury secretary. "You'd give him two fat brief-

---

[116] Connally's press conference covered in several sources, with excerpts. For four noes and "enormous" stimulus, *Newsweek* (July 12, 1971), 67; and *Business Week* (July 3, 1971), 15. For yo-yo quote, *New York Times*, June 30, 1971, 18.

[117] *Business Week* (July 3, 1971), 15.

[118] *Time* (July 12, 1971), 55.

[119] McCracken for President, Aug. 4, 1971, Memos for President's file, SMOF; McCracken. This memo reports conversation held July 22.

ing books the night before he was to testify before a committee, and when you talked to him the next morming, you knew he'd read them."[120]

Accomplished as a public performer, Connally proved no less adept as an inside operator. He would brook no intermediary between him and the president, not even the mighty Haldeman, whom he regularly bypassed to get to Nixon and whom he once kept waiting half an hour for an appointment at the Treasury.[121] He won respect by taking on the really hard problems, like the bailout of the failing Lockheed Corporation. He asserted control over economic policy by the simple gesture of moving meetings of the Troika from the Cosmos Club to the Treasury's dining room, and he solidified his hold on the president by combining shameless flattery with Nixon's public-relations obsession. Connally spent endless hours with Nixon plotting a campaign to market the president's image by telling the true but unknown story of Nixon the man — a man of guts, compassion, intelligence, spartan in his habits, a keen judge of people, warm, yet ruthless when he had to be. It was a story apparently unknown even to Nixon's closest associates. Within a month of joining the administration, at Nixon's instigation, Connally spoke at a secret dinner for the senior White House staff on the subject of Richard Nixon, "the most misunderstood man in public life."[122] Shortly afterward Connally edified the cabinet with a similar testimonial. To those who wanted to know about him, Nixon would say, "Talk to Connally. He understands me."[123]

Connally came to Washington with no fixed convictions about economic policy. In fact, he openly boasted that he had no fixed convictions about anything. "I can play it round or I can play it flat, just tell me how to play it," Connally liked to say.[124] He began by listening, learning, keeping open all options. When aides assumed in February 1971 that Connally would oppose legislation extending the president's power to impose price and wage controls, Connally set them straight. "If the legislature wants to give you a new power — you take it," he said. "Put it in the corner like an old shotgun. You never know when you might need it. Besides, we might want to use this."[125] By the time Congress extended the president's author-

[120] *Time* (Oct. 18, 1971), 18.

[121] Reston, *Lone Star*, 395.

[122] Ibid., 389–394. Reston's account confirmed in H-Notes for this period.

[123] Ibid., 394.

[124] Quoted in Stein, *Presidential Economics*, 162.

[125] Reston, *Lone Star*, 396–397.

ity to impose controls in May 1971, with Connally's support, it remained an open question whether Connally would use the power or not.[126] At Camp Daivd late in June, he was still not sure, though he and Nixon had begun seriously to consider the possibility. The economic picture was too murky, the politics uncertain. He would wait a little longer for the dust to settle.

By July 1971, labor strife threatened Nixon's hopes of cooling inflation. Major strikes broke out in copper, communications, the railroads, and the West Coast docks, with a potentially crippling steel strike looming at the end of the month.[127] In the White House, the president's advisers divided over taking on labor. No friend of unions in Texas, Connally favored resisting their demands.[128] Charles Colson, Nixon's henchman in building the New Majority, counseled peace for the sake of the labor vote. Nixon agreed with Colson, though claiming a more high-minded purpose. It was a matter of the workers's superior patriotism, he said. Working people, "who offer their backs and their brawn," had stood up for their country in time of crisis — men of character and strength, like George Meany, teamster president Frank Fitzsimmons, and Peter Brennan of the building trades — "all Irish Catholics, probably hard-boiled Democrats." We must not attack the unions, Nixon concluded, "regardless of politics."[129]

With the administration on the sideline, one by one the strikes of July ended in victories for the workers.[130] In steel, management might have taken a strike, but in the last hours of negotiation, Labor Secretary Hodgson appealed for peace at any price. The price turned out to be a contract featuring a 15 percent first-year wage increase.[131] Nixon could hardly complain when a day later U.S. Steel announced price increases of 8 percent.[132] Militant labor was still driving cost-push inflation, and Nixon still had no program to stop it. Public confidence in the game plan reached a new low.

The man most disturbed by these wage developments was Arthur Burns. Though the Fed had recently been more than accommodating on

---

[126] "To Extend Standby Powers of the President to Stabilize Wages and Prices," House hearings, Committee on Banking and Currency (1971), esp. p. 5.

[127] *Business Week* (July 10, 1971), 18; (July 17, 1971), 33–34; *Newsweek* (July 26, 1971), 55.

[128] Connally argued for a tough stand in Quadriad in May. See Stein for President, May 21, 1971, Memos for President's file, POF.

[129] Colson for the President, July 21, 1971, President's Meeting file, POF.

[130] *Business Week* (July 24, 1971), 13–15.

[131] *Business Week* (Aug. 7, 1971), 17–19; *Wall Street Journal*, Aug. 2, 1971, 3.

[132] *Wall Street Journal*, Aug. 3, 1971, 1.

money, relations between Burns and Nixon were never worse than in July 1971. Burns publicly attacked the Camp David decision not to employ incomes policy.[133] The Fed cast a pall over recovery by raising the discount rate on July 15, citing as one reason "concern over the continuation of substantial cost-push inflation."[134] And Burns irritated the president with some gloomy congressional testimony on prices.[135] "Try to get Arthur to make just one speech saying what is good with the economy," Nixon said.[136]

Nixon had been threatening a showdown with the Fed almost from the day he took office. Now furious at Burns, Nixon decided at last to play hardball. On July 20, he told aides he would neither see Burns, approve his request for a raise, nor consult him concerning a vacancy on the Federal Reserve Board. Connally would try to fill the vacancy with "the easiest money man he can find." "If you know a crazy," Nixon said to Shultz, "let John Connally know."[137] In late July, on Nixon's instructions, Colson planted stories, easily traceable to the White House, that Nixon was planning to attack the Fed's independence and had turned down Burns's request for a $20,000 raise because it was inconsistent with Burns's repeated pleas for wage-price restraint.[138] Stung by the charge of greed, Burns protested to sympathetic White House aides that he had not requested a raise for himself, only for his successors. "I hope Colson can sleep nights," he said.[139]

The attack on Burns backfired. The spectacle of the president and the chairman of the Federal Reserve in a gutter brawl so disturbed Wall Street that the Dow-Jones plunged twenty-seven points in three days.[140] Peter Flanigan reported to Nixon that even his strong supporters in the financial community felt "that with confidence precarious in both the dollar and business expansion, a battle between the White House and the Fed under-

---

[133] *Newsweek* (July 12, 1971), 67.

[134] *New York Times*, July 16, 1971, 1.

[135] "The 1971 Midyear Review of the Economy," Joint Economic Committee, hearings (1971), 252–254.

[136] H-Notes, July 25, 1971.

[137] E-Notes, July 20, 1971.

[138] William Safire, *Before the Fall: An Inside View of the Pre-Watergate White House* (1975), 491–496, in the chapter, "Hardball." See also Charles Colson, *Born Again* (1977), 62–63. For instruction to Colson, HRH (Haldeman), Talking Paper, Charles Colson, July 26, 1971, Chron file, SMOF: Haldeman. *New York Times*, July 29, 1971, 45; July 30, 1971, 43.

[139] Safire to Haldeman, Aug. 3, 1971, Safire file, Alpha Name file, SMOF: Haldeman.

[140] *New York Times*, July 30, 1971, 43.

mines essential stability."[141] As a result, in his press conference of August 4, Nixon was forced to exonerate Burns on the issue of his salary increase and to praise him as "the most responsible and statesmanlike of any Chairman of the Federal Reserve in my memory."[142] A grateful Burns called the White House to say, "This just proves what a decent and warm man the President is."[143] It is hard to know which of the two men was more insincere.

The quarrel between Nixon and Burns was essentially a quarrel over policy. Burns believed that the Fed had done as much as it could through easy money to promote recovery and that a more expansive fiscal policy was now in order. Moreover, he no longer favored merely a voluntary wage-price board but, in private at least, a full-scale, mandatory wage-price freeze. Ironically, even as Nixon launched open hostilities against Burns in July, he was preparing to adopt Burns's policy prescriptions.

Nixon abandoned gradualism in the wake of his dramatic announcement, from a television studio in Burbank, California, on July 15, 1971, that he would visit the People's Republic of China next February.[144] Anticipating domestic political benefits, he told Kissinger on the plane back to Washington that "we were in a deteriorating position, and we really needed something to change this situation, because we were bleeding to death slowly."[145] But Nixon learned that he was still bleeding when Republican leaders at a White House briefing on July 20 spent more time complaining about the economy than they did extolling his China policy.[146] "After this meeting," Nixon recalled, "Connally and I concluded that the time had come to act."[147] Nixon told Connally to think in terms of a wage-price freeze.[148]

Since March, with Connally's encouragement, a small group of Treasury officials, headed by Paul Volcker, had been working on contingency plans for this moment.[149] On July 27, a week after deciding to shift course,

[141] Flanigan for the President, Aug. 3, 1971, (CF) FG 131, WHSF.
[142] *Pub Paps RN 1971*, 855.
[143] Safire to Haldeman, Aug. 5, 1971, Safire file, Alpha Name file, SMOF: Haldeman.
[144] *Pub Paps RN 1971*, 819–820.
[145] *Haldeman Diaries*, July 18, 1971.
[146] Ibid., July 20, 1971.
[147] *RN: Memoirs*, 518.
[148] H-Notes, July 23, 1971.
[149] Thomas Auston Forbord, "The Abandonment of Bretton Woods: The Political Economy of U.S. International Monetary Policy," Ph.D. diss., Harvard University (1980), 164–167.

Connally put the pieces of the plan together for Nixon.[150] "By nature, he always favored the 'big play,'" Nixon wrote of Connally in his memoirs, "so I had expected that he would recommend something bold. But even I was not prepared for the actions he proposed."[151] The next day, John Petty of the Treasury recalled, "Connally came into a meeting between Volcker and me saying, 'Go ahead with the plans. I got Nixon's agreement on the wage/price freeze, the budget cuts, and the gold window last night. Shultz doesn't know yet.'"[152] The gold-window decision meant that the United States would terminate its commitment to exchange gold for dollars on demand by foreign central banks, thereby foreclosing a possible run on the nation's gold hoard.

Connally's package intended nothing less than to address the full range of the country's economic problems, domestic and foreign, by a policy reversal so dramatic that it would confound the administration's enemies and amaze its friends. On August 2, 1971, Connally presented Nixon the completed plan at a long meeting, and then the two informed Shultz,[153] a practical man above all and a good soldier, who did not resign his post upon the repudiation of his gradualist policies but stayed on to help execute the new ones. Connally, the man without whom Nixon could not have made the big play, was now in command.

Connally's political timing was impeccable. On August 1, 1971, the *New York Times* observed, "It may well be, as President Nixon's top aides have been suggesting, that with more patience and persistence, everything will work out fine. But the ranks of the doubters seem to be growing steadily and substantially."[154] The Harris poll gave Nixon a 73 percent negative rating on his economic performance that month,[155] and Gallup reported that 50 percent favored a wage-price freeze. Even Republican stalwarts were jumping ship.[156] Republican Senators Hugh Scott and John Tower,

---

[150] On July 27, 1971, Connally met with Nixon for fifty-five minutes. Given other evidence in Forbord, it was at this meeting that Connally must have unveiled the preliminary plan, but no independent confirmation exists. See President's Daily Calendar.

[151] *RN: Memoirs*, 518. Nixon makes this statement in regard to a report he says Connally made to him unveiling the full package on Aug. 6. Nixon got his dates confused. We know from Haldeman's diary that Nixon got Connally's full report on Aug. 2 and from Forbord that he got a preliminary look a few days before.

[152] Forbord, "Abandonment of Bretton Woods," 261.

[153] *Haldeman Diaries*, Aug. 2, 1971, Aug. 3, 1971.

[154] *New York Times*, Aug. 1, 1971, III, 1.

[155] Ibid., Aug. 10, 1971, 21.

[156] *Gallup Poll* (vol. 3), 2315.

one a liberal, the other a conservative, had joined to sponsor legislation cutting taxes.[157] On August 3, a day after the steel settlement, twelve Republican senators announced that they would introduce a bill to create a wage-price review board.[158] At his news conference on August 4, Nixon said he would keep an open mind on the review board but was "unalterably opposed" to "permanent wage and price controls."[159] Nobody asked what he thought of a temporary wage and price freeze.

Despite the mounting pressure to do something, once Nixon and Connally secretly decided to abandon "steady as you go," they were in no particular hurry. Not only did Connally's package need more staff work, but the president felt he should wait to close the gold window until Congress returned from its summer recess on September 8, and he thought next January might be a good time to impose the wage-price freeze.[160] On August 6, when Nixon showed signs of impatience, Connally advised that "it's better to just let things sit and simmer for the time being, and actually let them get worse . . . because if they are worse, then the move will look all that much better when it's made."[161] Connally was due to leave for an extended Texas vacation that day but sensed uneasy vibrations in world money markets and delayed. He finally left on August 10.

Connally was back on Thursday, August 12. Paul Volcker, fearing deterioration of the dollar's position in foreign money markets, decided the United States could wait no longer to close the gold window. Connally "says there's no panic," Haldeman recorded in his diary, "but it's getting worse and worse, and we're losing the initiative."[162] Meeting at 5:30 that afternoon, Nixon and Connally decided to move on the whole package and to move now. Wrote Haldeman, "We were going to pack up the key people — including Arthur Burns and the key Treasury and economic group — go to Camp David tomorrow afternoon, spend the weekend there, and get it worked out, and make the announcement on Monday. We'll cover the whole thing when we do it, apparently, so its going to be quite an earthshaking operation."[163] This time, when Nixon came down from the

---

[157] *Business Week* (July 10, 1971), 29.
[158] *New York Times*, Aug. 4, 1971, 16.
[159] *Pub Paps RN 1971*, 856.
[160] On January freeze, *Haldeman Diaries*, July 23, 1971.
[161] Ibid., Aug. 6, 1971.
[162] Ibid., Aug. 12, 1971.
[163] Ibid., Aug. 12, 1971.

mountain, he would shake the domestic economy, challenge the existing international economic order, and vastly enhance his chances for reelection. The burden of gradualism would be lifted from him at last.

## VII

In July 1971, as Nixon was preparing to give up on gradualism, Friedman wrote a column in *Newsweek* praising him as a leader of "vision and courage" for resisting the pressure and staying the course. Nixon's reward, said Friedman, was an economy that was now performing well. "Inflation has slowed, although less than all desired and many expected." The recovery had been appropriately moderate, which meant that prices could cool down as unemployment fell. "What we need now to complete the treatment," said Friedman quoting his friend George Shultz, " 'is the time and the guts to take the time, not additional medicine.' "[164]

Friedman overstated the accomplishments of gradualism to date, but he was most likely right about the direction of things. As he told Nixon in June during the last visit he would ever pay him in the White House, "there's lots of steam in the boiler."[165] From the hindsight of a decade, the distinguished economist Robert J. Gordon would write, "it is hard to avoid the conclusion that the boom of 1972–73 was primarily due to the influence of the acceleration of monetary growth in 1971."[166] If Nixon had really had the "courage and vision" to wait, the public would have finally begun to spend its swollen money balances, in all likelihood providing Nixon with the expansion he wanted, when he wanted it.

Inflation too would have cooled. Through mid-1971, the price signals were mixed. The Wholesale Price Index accelerated. The Consumer Price Index slowed erratically. The GNP deflator revealed a declining inflation rate. The Personal Consumption Deflator hardly budged. Taken together, the data meant that the inflation rate had at least stopped rising and probably had begun to subside.[167] There was a logic at work that would have unwound inflation in the months ahead even without controls.

---

[164] *Newsweek* (July 26, 1971), 62.

[165] Shultz, Meeting with Friedman, June 8, 1971, Memos for President's file, POF.

[166] Robert J. Gordon, "Postwar Macroeconomics: The Evolution of Events and Ideas," in Martin Feldstein, ed., *The American Economy in Transition* (1980), 101–162.

[167] Cagan, *Persistent Inflation*, 148–149; Gordon, "Postwar Macroeconomics," 140–142; CEA *Annual Report* 1972, 40–44.

Though compensation per worker rose nearly as fast in 1971 as in 1970, output per worker rose significantly. Consequently, labor cost per unit, which had risen by 7 percent in 1970 rose by only 3.5 percent in 1971. With the push of labor costs on prices weakening, price increases would have slowed on their own.[168]

The public refused to judge the policy a success, not only because evidence to substantiate the claim was still lacking, but because the public had an unrealistic standard of economic performance. Through most of the rest of the 1970s the 6 percent unemployment rate and 5 percent inflation of 1971 would seem less the evidence of a failed policy than an outcome devoutly to be wished. But in 1971 the standard was the mid-1960s, when the Kennedy tax cut, easy money, and low inflationary expectations had produced the happy but fleeting result of 4 percent unemployment and 3 percent inflation. That moment attained the status of a norm, and Nixon was politically stuck with it. In truth, he was producing a success that looked like a failure. Through 1971 no man in the White House had attacked the policy of gradualism more aggressively than Herbert Stein. Later he would admit, "In fact, the country was not suffering any severe injury from the process of gradualism."[169]

For losing heart prematurely, Nixon deserved little blame. Not an economist but a politician, he simply refused to bet his reelection on good times that seemed a dimming prospect. Moreover, he abandoned gradualism only after practically every prominent Democrat, most professional economists, a growing number of Republicans, much of the corporate community, his own CEA, Arthur Burns, and the public demanded that he do so. For the next cycle of stop-and-go, which his new policies would help initiate, there was blame enough for nearly everyone.

---

[168] CEA Annual Report 1973, 231; Phillip Cagan, "Controls and Monetary Policy," in Cagan et al., A New Look at Inflation (1973), 1–34, esp. pp. 10–12; Marvin Kosters, Controls and Inflation (1975), 9–10; Cagan, Persistent Inflation, 21.

[169] Herbert Stein, "Price-Fixing as Seen by a Price-Fixer, Part II," in American Enterprise Institute, Contemporary Economic Problems (1978), 121.

# Chapter 5
# Trade, Politics, and the New Mercantilism

---

Two different crises converged at Camp David in August 1971. One was the collapse of domestic support for the policy of gradualism. The other was the collapse of foreign confidence in the dollar, along with the first U.S. trade deficit since 1893. Though they had different histories, both crises offered Nixon an opportunity to retrieve the Economic Issue from the Democrats before election '72. At home, he would pump up the economy and clamp on controls. Abroad, he would launch an export crusade to create jobs for Americans — at the expense, to be sure, of America's allies. Influenced by John Connally, the president would embrace a mercantilist paradigm that subordinated international money and trade issues to his domestic political purposes, not the least of which was creation of a New Majority. With customary candor, Connally summed up the nationalist mood that would grip the administration in the year of Camp David. "My basic approach is that the foreigners are out to screw us," Connally told a group of Treasury consultants. "Our job is to screw them first."[1]

## I

Nixon took power at the end of the era of U.S. domination of the world economy. For a quarter century, Americans had used this domination for the political purpose of building the Western alliance and containing the Soviet Union. The United States had financed European reconstruction after the war and had aggressively promoted reduction of trade barriers to achieve allied interdependence.[2] So dominant was the American economy through the 1950s that the United States tolerated discrimination by client

---

[1] Connally quoted in John S. Odell, *U.S. International Monetary Policy* (1982), 263.
[2] Robert O. Keohane and Joseph S. Nye, Jr., *Power and Interdependence: World Politics in Transition* (1977); Robert Gilpin, *The Political Economy of International Relations* (1987). For critical treatment of the United States as hegemon, David Calleo, *The Imperious Economy* (1982).

states against its exports and even encouraged creation in 1958 of a customs union with protectionist potential called the European Economic Community (EEC). But economic liberalism was the dominant trend, with tariff barriers falling drastically and trade within the alliance expanding rapidly.[3] Under U.S. leadership, Western Europe recovered its elan, achieved security, and experienced two decades of unprecedented economic growth.

During the 1960s, European dependence on the United States diminished.[4] Europe's fear of a Soviet invasion faded. Soviet achievement of nuclear parity sapped the credibility of the U.S. nuclear deterrent, and Europe, along with Japan, developed industries capable of challenging the United States in the markets of the world. Europeans inevitably began chafing under continuing American hegemony. In 1966 President Charles de Gaulle of France asserted the sovereignty of France against the United States by blocking the integration of NATO military forces.[5] Beginning in 1969, West Germany launched its policy of *Ostpolitik,* an independent approach to both East Germany and the Soviet Union for improved relations. Great Britain moved away from its special relationship with the United States and toward the continent by applying for membership in the EEC, which it got in 1971. The EEC itself defied U.S. hopes by adopting a highly protectionist policy against U.S. agricultural exports and by negotiating preferential trade arrangements with former European colonies in Africa and with nations bordering on the Mediterranean Sea. As Nixon took office, economic tensions were seriously eroding the integrity of the Atlantic alliance.[6]

Nixon was initially less disturbed by these tensions than any of his postwar predecessors would have been. As a statesman, he conceived his purpose not to resist the emergence of a multipolar world but to manage its consequences. To that end, he focused most of his attention on the triangular relationship of the United States, the USSR, and the People's Republic of China. Insofar as he considered Western Euope, Nixon was prepared to

---

[3] For a good survey of these developments, W. M. Scammell, *The International Economy Since 1945,* 2d ed. (1983), chaps. 1–5.

[4] Benjamin J. Cohen, "The Revolution in Atlantic Economic Relations: A Bargain Comes Unstuck," in Wolfram F. Hanrieder, ed., *The United States and Western Europe* (1974), 56–173.

[5] Edward A. Kolodziej, *French International Policy under De Gaulle and Pompidou* (1974).

[6] Richard N. Cooper, "Trade Policy is Foreign Policy," *Foreign Policy* (Winter 1972–1973), 18–36; David Calleo and Benjamin M. Rowland, *America and the World Political Economy: Atlantic Dream and National Realities* (1973), 126–168.

accept a diminished role for the United States and to relegate to bureaucrats the resolution of economic disputes, which he initially dismissed as issues of low diplomacy.

So far as free trade was concerned, Nixon paid it ritual lip service. At a press conference soon after taking office, he said, "I believe that the interest of the United States and the interest of the whole world will best be served by moving toward freer trade rather than toward protectionism."[7] But Nixon had no intentions of acting on this platitude, in part because the politics of free trade was changing. Organized labor, whose support he intended to court, had backed free trade as long as U.S. industries dominated world markets. By the late 1960s the U.S. trade surplus was vanishing, and imports were threatening such oldline American industries as steel, autos, electrical appliances, and sectors of the textile industry. Accordingly, the AFL-CIO defected to the cause of protectionism. In 1968, with labor's support, one-third of the U.S. Senate cosponsored legislation to impose mandatory quotas on steel imports, forcing President Johnson to negotiate voluntary restraints with foreign steel makers.[8] (Legislated quotas were in violation of international trade rules; voluntary quotas were not.) Meanwhile, domestic pressure for import quotas to protect other industries was rapidly building.

In February 1969, Nixon, in office only a month, toured Western Europe to meet heads of state and discuss issues of mutual concern, including trade. "I pointed out the great pressures we are under here for quotas on imports," Nixon reported to his advisers on his return, "and I told them this is not the time for new breakthroughs in trade procedures. There will not be a new Kennedy Round — that's not in the cards — it's time to digest what we already have on the plate."[9]

Nixon was not only unwilling to champion lower trade barriers; he was quite prepared to sacrifice liberal trade principles whenever it suited his domestic political purposes. This first became clear in the notorious case of textiles, where his implacable determination to impose import quotas nearly wrecked the world trade system. The object of Nixon's textile policy was to secure the political support of the senior senator from South Car-

---

[7] *Pub Paps RN 1969*, 74.

[8] William Scheuerman, *The Steel Crisis: The Economics and Politics of a Declining Industry* (1986), 57–61.

[9] Report on Meeting of Cabinet Committee on Economic Policy, Mar. 7, 1969, Safire papers.

olina, Strom Thurmond. Hero to much of the white South, Thurmond had bolted the Democratic party over civil rights in 1948 to run as the Dixiecrat candidate for president and then bolted the party for good in 1964 to join the Republicans. In 1968, Nixon secured Thurmond's support for the Republican nomination by promising an administration that would give Thurmond a sympathetic hearing on civil rights and protection for the textile industry, which accounted for 40 percent of South Carolina's manufacturing jobs. It was a bargain that yielded Nixon handsome returns. Thurmond used his immense prestige to contain a boom for Ronald Reagan among southern delegates at the Republican convention, and in the fall he campaigned effectively to contain the Wallace challenge to Nixon in the Deep South.[10] Once in office, Nixon saw Thurmond as a key ally for gathering disaffected white southerners into his New Majority. To enlist Thurmond in the cause, Nixon would first have to deliver on textiles.

Nixon quickly discovered that the leading textile exporting nation — Japan — was little disposed to assist him. Virtually a client of the United States during the first two postwar decades, Japan, like Western Europe, had depended on the United States for military protection and economic nurture and, even more than Europe, had yielded to its benefactor on matters of mutual concern. In the late 1960s, by now an emerging economic colossus, Japan had grown resentful of its status as America's junior partner. Revived Japanese nationalism, craving respect and equality, demanded defense of the nation's textile industry against Nixon's desire to constrict it, even though textiles had ceased to be on the cutting edge of Japan's economic development and in a few short years would no longer rank as an important Japanese export.[11]

It did not help Nixon that his case for protection lacked merit. Because import quotas on cotton textiles were already in place, at issue were manmade fibers — notably polyesters, acrylics, and nylons — which had brought prosperity to the U.S. textile industry in the 1960s. Foreign man-mades accounted for a mere 4.2 percent of U.S. consumption in 1969, refuting industry claims of ruin by import.[12] Only particular segments of the indus-

---

[10] Harry S. Dent, *The Prodigal South Returns to Power* (1978), chap. 5, 198–207; for Nixon's public pledge on textiles, see Text of a Telegram from Richard M. Nixon, Aug. 21, 1968, Textile file, Houthakker Subject files, SMOF: Houthakker.

[11] The textile account in this chapter relies on I. M. Destler, Haruhiro Fukui, and Hideo Sato, *The Textile Wrangle: Conflict in Japanese-American Relations, 1969–1971* (1979).

[12] "Tariff and Trade Proposals," Committee on Ways and Means, House hearings (1970), 1326–27, 1487.

try could claim injury, in particular, small labor-intensive firms specializing in inexpensive sweaters, shirts, and children's wear.[13] Though the Japanese were willing to negotiate voluntary quotas on specific product categories, U.S. industry leaders demanded a comprehensive agreement, imposing specific limitations on every category of Japanese man-made textiles, even those where no import competition existed. Nixon felt politically obliged to obtain a comprehensive agreement. The Japanese government felt politically obliged to resist.

Though negotiations stalled through most of 1969, the basis for a settlement eventually emerged. Japan's prime minister, Eisaku Sato, cared less about textiles than he did about the end of the U.S. occupation of Okinawa and its return, nuclear-free, to Japan. Nixon cared less about Okinawa than he did about a textile agreement that would satisfy Strom Thurmond. In November 1969, at a summit meeting in Washington, Nixon and Sato conducted a secret Okinawa-for-textiles deal. The communiqué concluding these talks pledged the United States to enter negotiations for the return of Okinawa but, at Sato's insistence, said nothing about textiles, in deference to the approach of Japanese elections in December. No sooner did Sato return to Japan, however, than rumors spread that he had sold out Japanese textiles. Lacking authority to seal the deal himself and the courage even to admit he made it, Sato reneged. Nixon never forgot and one day would exact his revenge.[14]

Disappointed with Nixon, the U.S. textile industry next turned for help to Congress, where the key legislator was Wilbur Mills, the Democratic chairman of the House Ways and Means Committee, then at the height of his power. Though a free trader on principle, Mills improbably aspired to be the South's candidate for president at the 1972 Democratic convention, a goal he might advance by becoming a hero of the textile wars. In April 1970, Mills proposed legislation that would unilaterally impose U.S. quotas on imported textiles in violation of international trade rules. To broaden support of this measure, Ways and Means also added to the bill import quotas to protect the shoe industry. Mills was playing a complex and dangerous game. Personally opposed to legislated quotas, he sponsored them now only to pressure the Japanese into negotiating a voluntary quota agree-

---

[13] Rush Loving, Jr., "What the Textile Industry Really Needs," *Fortune* (vol. 84, Oct. 1970), 84 ff.

[14] Destler et al., *Textile Wrangle*, chaps. 5, 6; Henry Kissinger, *The White House Years* (1979), 325–340.

ment. But Mills was too clever. The Japanese remained unmoved, and in June 1970 the frustrated Nixon administration surprised Mills by endorsing his bill, or more precisely, its textile provision. Mills now found himself reluctant sponsor of quota legislation that might actually pass.[15]

Free traders in the government feared that the Mills bill might prove the opening shot in a worldwide trade war. Paul McCracken warned Nixon that Japan might retaliate against legislated quotas by restricting U.S. wheat imports, and the EEC might seize on the precedent of unilateral quotas to discriminate against U.S. soybeans. "As we have already threatened retaliation against their automobile industry in the event they take steps against our soybean market," McCracken said, "the seeds of a chain reaction are present."[16] Expressing a widespread fear, the Fed's chief international economist wrote Arthur Burns, saying that passage of legislated quotas "would be the most important backward step in post–World War II international policy."[17]

The quota issue soon began spinning out of control. Seizing on the Mills bill, protectionists in Congress used it to mount a frontal attack on the entire postwar trade regime. In July 1970, Ways and Means added an extraordinary provision to the trade bill triggering mandatory quotas on every imported good whose share of the U.S. market exceeded 15 percent.[18] This was too much for Nixon, who publicly threatened to veto any bill that went beyond textiles "because that would set off a trade war."[19] In November 1970, the House nonetheless passed the Mills bill, imposing mandatory quotas on textiles and shoes and including a modified trigger provision. Many House Democrats voted for the bill, hoping to force Nixon into a veto that would jeopardize his courtship of the South. Congress mercifully adjourned in December before the Senate could act, rescuing Nixon from a protectionist challenge that his own textile policy had made possible.[20]

Nixon's determination to pay off Strom Thurmond remained undiminished. Indeed, the nationalism of his textile policy had come to reflect his

---

[15] Destler et al., *Textile Wrangle*, 180–207.
[16] McCracken for the President, July 2, 1970, TA 4 file, WHCF.
[17] Robert Solomon to Burns, June 16, 1970, no file information, Burns papers.
[18] *Congressional Quarterly Weekly Report* (Aug. 28, 1970), 2135–2137.
[19] *Pub Paps RN 1970*, 606.
[20] *Congressional Quarterly Weekly Report* (Nov. 20, 1970), 2811–2812, (Dec. 18, 1970), 3003–3006; (Dec. 25, 1970), 3047.

general views on trade, increasingly similar to those of the average congressman. In August 1970, Nixon told a group of advisers that the United States had lost competitive advantage except in agriculture and advanced technologies. If U.S. productivity did not increase, there would be a new round of tariffs, he said. The United States needed a study that would answer these questions: "What is the U.S. competitive position? What should our own policy be regarding quotas? . . . What are the facts?"[21] The nominal leader of the liberal regime was ready to reexamine first principles.

## II

Money no less than trade had become a source of acrimony within the Atlantic alliance during the 1960s.[22] Monetary issues were economic, of course, but they were also political, increasingly so, because many Europeans came to view the international monetary system as yet another instrument of an obsolete American hegemony. That system derived loosely from an agreement negotiated in 1944 by forty-three nations at a resort hotel in Bretton Woods, New Hampshire. The founding fathers intended to design a monetary regime that would be proof against the competitive currency manipulations and exchange controls that had hampered world trade and retarded recovery during the Great Depression. At Bretton Woods, participating nations pledged to convert the currencies of other nations into their own at fixed rates of exchange. Fixed exchange rates and free convertibility, they believed, would facilitate the flow of goods and private capital across national boundaries in an open-trade world, promoting prosperity for all.

Bretton Woods never intended any one currency to have more privileges and responsibilities than any other, but almost immediately the dollar assumed the key role in the new system. This was the accidental consequence of a shortage of monetary reserves in Europe following World War II. Reserves were a necessary precondition of foreign trade. If a nation spent more abroad than it received, it had to cover the deficit by drawing

---

[21] E-Notes, Aug. 7, 1970.

[22] On the international monetary system, Robert Solomon, *The International Monetary System, 1945–1981* (1982); Benjamin J. Cohen, *Organizing the World's Money* (1977); Leland B. Yeager, *International Monetary Relations*, 2d ed. (1976); Judy Shelton, *Money Meltdown: Restoring Order to the Global Currency System* (1994); CEA Annual Report, 1973, chap. 2.

down its reserves, gold being the traditionally acceptable means of payment. European nations had exhausted most of their gold during the war. Only the United States, which possessed 60 percent of the world's official gold in 1945, was prepared on the demand of foreign central bankers to exchange gold for dollars — at a rate of $35 per ounce. Here was the solution to the reserve shortage: Because the dollar was as good as gold, the dollar would become the world's main source of monetary reserves.

As the one currency as good as gold, the dollar became not only the reserve currency but the lynch pin of the fixed-exchange-rate regime. The value of the dollar was determined by its fixed gold price. Other nations established the value of their currencies in fixed relation to the dollar. To maintain the par value of, say, the yen at 360 to the dollar, the central bank of Japan was obliged under the rules of the system to intervene in the free currency market, buying or selling dollars for yen to keep the yen from falling or rising. At the center of the system, the dollar, like the sun, stood still.

Through the 1950s, the United States obligingly met Europe's need for monetary reserves by running deficits in its balance of international payments. In other words, the United States spent more dollars for imported goods, foreign investments, foreign military and economic aid, and foreign travel than it received, mainly from exports of goods and from earnings on its foreign investments. From 1950 through 1958, the U.S. payment deficit averaged $1.2 billion annually, providing reserves that lubricated world trade and facilitated European growth. In 1958, finally holding adequate dollar reserves, nations in the system abandoned exchange controls and embarked on the Bretton Woods regime of fixed exchange rates and free convertibility. Almost immediately the economist Robert Triffin located a potentially fatal dilemma. If dollars kept accumulating abroad, foreign central banks would soon own more dollars than the United States could redeem in gold, threatening the regime with collapse. If the United States reduced its payments deficit, world reserves would cease to grow fast enough to sustain expanding trade and investment.[23]

From 1958 through 1960, the U.S. payment deficit increased to an annual average of $3.6 billion, turning the dollar shortage into a dollar glut. European central banks responded by exchanging unwanted dollars for U.S. gold, reducing U.S. gold reserves from $22 billion to $17 billion in three years.[24] Despite determined efforts by Presidents Kennedy and

---

[23] Robert Triffin, *Gold and the Dollar Crisis: The Future of Convertibility* (1960).
[24] Yeager, *International Monetary Relations*, 570–571.

Johnson to contain the dollar outflow, principally by placing restraints on U.S. foreign investment, the deficits persisted and so did the threat to America's gold supply. Indeed, by 1964, dollar holdings of foreign central banks exceeded the value of all the gold in Fort Knox.[25]

In the mid-1960s, European critics, led by de Gaulle, objected not only to the economic but to the political consequences of dollar domination. The dollar, they charged, enjoyed "exorbitant privileges." When any other nation except the United States ran a payments deficit, it had to deflate its economy or in other ways reduce imports in order to conserve reserves. Because the dollar was the reserve currency, the United States could escape the discipline the system imposed on others. The United States could print up as many dollars as it wished and use them to sop up imports, buy up European industries, and pay for misguided military adventures like Vietnam. Of course, foreign central banks, which absorbed excess dollars that their citizens did not want, had the formal right to exchange them for U.S. gold, but if foreign central bankers actually did so, the United States would close the gold window, and the system would collapse. Because Bretton Woods, for all its faults, received much of the credit for postwar prosperity, sober central bankers shuddered at the prospect of life without it. Except for the French, who did not have many dollars to convert, central bankers hesitated to ask for gold and instead lent their dollars back to the United States by purchasing Treasury bills and other short-term credit instruments, which at least earned them interest. In the words of Jacques Rueff, de Gaulle's economic adviser, the American payments deficit was a forced loan from American's allies — "a deficit without tears."[26] At a press conference on February 4, 1965, de Gaulle proposed to escape the domination of the dollar by returning to gold, "whose nature does not alter, which may be formed equally well into ingots, bars or coins, which has no nationality and which has, eternally and immutably, been regarded as the unalterable currency *par excellence*."[27]

Despite de Gaulle's early complaints, Bretton Woods became Europe's nightmare only during the Vietnam boom of the late 1960s in America. The boom sucked imports into the United States, and it inflated U.S. prices, hurting exports. As a result, the U.S. trade surplus shrank, and the

---

[25] Paul Volcker and Toyoo Gyohten, *Changing Fortunes: The World's Money and the Threat to American Leadership* (1992), 32.

[26] Jacques Rueff, *The Monetary Sin of the West* (1972), 23. Rueff provides outline of European critique in parts 1 and 2.

[27] De Gaulle's press conference reprinted in Rueff, *Monetary Sin*, 70–74.

U.S. payments deficit ballooned. As the volume of unwanted dollars flowing into Europe grew, the value of the dollar in the currency markets sagged. In accord with its obligations under Bretton Woods, the German Bundesbank, for example, had to intervene in the currency markets to support the fixed rate of exchange between the mark and the dollar. The Bundesbank supported the dollar by printing up marks to buy dollars. Printing up ever more marks for this purpose meant German inflation.[28] The founders of Bretton Woods envisioned a system that would promote harmonious economic relations among nations. As the system forced them to import U.S. inflation, many Europeans came to regard America as a monetary predator.

## III

By the time Nixon took office, the Bretton Woods system was under considerable stress. Though he had only a tenuous grasp of the issues, the president did have ideas. He considered the payments deficit of marginal importance, regarded gold as a monetary anachronism, periodically expressed a desire for an entirely new system that would avoid annoying crises, and insisted that international economic issues remain subordinate to his domestic economic objectives. Most of all, Nixon did not wish to waste his time on a topic that seemed to him inconsequential and boring. After a year in office he wrote his aides, "What really matters in campaigns, wars, or in government is to concentrate on the big battles and win them." Concerning economic matters, he would take personal responsibility for decisions bearing on inflation and recession. But, he continued, "I do not want to be bothered with international monetary matters . . . and I will not need to see the reports on international money matters in the future." Turn the issue over to Arthur Burns, he suggested, but not to the treasury department. "I feel that we need a new international monetary system and I have so instructed in several meetings. Very little progress has been made in that direction because of the opposition of the Treasury."[29]

By tradition the dominant agency in the government on world financial matters, the Treasury kept control despite Nixon wishes. Inside the

---

[28] Harold van B. Cleveland and W. H. Bruce Brittain, *The Great Inflation: A Monetarist View* (1976).

[29] President for Haldeman, Ehrlichman, and Kissinger, Mar. 2, 1970, Memos from the President file, Apha Subject file, SMOF: Haldeman.

Treasury, the key man was Paul Volcker, undersecretary for monetary affairs. Tall at six feet seven inches, given to rumpled suits and cheap cigars, Volcker did not look much like the pillar of the East Coast banking establishment that he was. Educated at Princeton and Harvard, Volcker had moved easily during a brilliant career among the New York Federal Reserve, the U.S. Treasury, and the Chase-Manhattan Bank. Charls Walker of the ultraestablishment American Bankers Association and soon to be Volcker's colleague in the Treasury recommended him for the post of undersecretary, and despite Nixon's aversion to nominal Democrats and associates of David Rockefeller, Chase's chairman, Volcker got the job.[30] Nixon never liked Volcker, whom he regarded, not unfairly, as the main obstacle to his desire for monetary change. But Treasury Secretary David Kennedy delegated to Volcker, the expert, all matters at the Treasury regarding international money. One of Volcker's first tasks was to head an interagency task force to canvass monetary options for the president.

On June 23, 1969, the so-called Volcker Group presented its report to the president.[31] The report acknowledged that the dollar's status as the reserve currency did indeed confer on the United States the special privileges that de Gaulle said it did. To pursue its foreign objectives, the report pointed out, all the United States had to do was to print dollars, which foreigners had to accept in payment whether they wanted dollars or not. Unfortunately, the volume of unwanted dollars in foreign hands was now placing the system under insupportable strain, the report said. The dollar was de facto inconvertible into gold, and Europeans regarded the U.S. payments deficit as "a transmission belt for passing our inflation" onto the rest of the world. Conceding that change in the system was now unavoidable, the Volcker report considered the possible options, with an eye to preserving the current privileges of the dollar as long as possible. The options were to devalue the dollar, break the link between gold and the dollar, or adopt incremental reform.

Technically, devaluation meant raising the dollar price of gold. Practically, devaluation meant that the value of the dollar would decline relative to other currencies. The dollar would buy less abroad than it did

---

[30] *Current Biography* (1973), 425–428; Volcker and Gyohten, *Changing Fortunes*, 63–64.

[31] Basic Options on International Economic Monetary Affairs, June 23, 1969, Treasury Dept., provided me by the Treasury. For an excellent explication, Joanne S. Gowa, *Closing the Gold Window* (1983).

before, and the mark and the yen, for example, could buy more in the United States. Fewer imports and more exports would reduce the U.S. payments deficit and restore equilibrium. Devaluation was indeed a way out of the present problem but not one that the Volcker Group wanted to take. For one thing, changing the price of gold would require the consent of the Democratic Congress, risking a politically damaging debate — the crucial point so far as Nixon was concerned. For another, other nations were unlikely to stand still and permit the United States to expand its exports at their expense by devaluing the dollar. Hendrik Houthakker of the Council of Economic Advisers asked a responsible official of the European Economic Community in April 1969 what Europe would do if the United States devalued. "He stated flatly that all European currencies would be devalued by the same percentage in the same day," Houthakker recalled.[32] There were other reasons not to devalue, which the report did not mention. While it was true that devaluation of the dollar would increase exports and thus create jobs, devaluation would also mean that more exports would be required to obtain the same volume of imports, reducing the American standard of living. Devaluation would, moreover, have inflationary effects, because the price of imports would rise, along with the price of domestic goods that competed with imports. Finally, devaluation would be an admission of economic mismanagement and damage the prestige of the United States.

Closing the gold window was Volcker's second option. Currently, foreign holdings of dollars dwarfed the U.S. gold hoard, and the dollar was de facto inconvertible into gold. What if the United States abandoned the fiction of convertibility altogether? What if it simply closed the gold window, refusing to exchange gold for dollars? The dollar would remain the world's reserve currency, with all the privileges that entailed, and the last infringement on America's monetary freedom would be gone. Though tempting, this option had its problems too. If the United States unilaterally ended the gold convertibility of the dollar, other nations would consider it a hostile act — unless, of course, some kind of crisis developed, giving the United States no choice. Keep the gold window open for now, the report advised, but be prepared to close it if necessary.

The Volcker Group's preferred option was "evolutionary reform,"

---

[32] Hendrik S. Houthakker, "The Breakdown of Bretton Woods," in Werner Sichel, ed., *Economic Advice and Executive Policy* (1978), 45–64.

whose advocates wished to retain the essentials of the current system but add a saving flexibility. The Bretton Woods agreement had theoretically provided for flexibility by providing that any nation in fundamental monetary disequilibrium could adjust the value of its currency — devaluing in case of a chronic payments deficit, revaluing upward in case of a chronic payments surplus. In practice, no one wanted to adjust, and from 1961 until 1967, when the British devalued the pound, no one did. Countries running chronic payments deficits resisted devaluing because, though devaluation would help exports, it would worsen the terms of trade and injure prestige. Countries running a chronic surplus resisted upward revaluation because, while revaluation would make imports cheaper and improve the terms of trade, it would raise export prices, damaging powerful domestic industries that sold abroad. The point of evolutionary reform was to overcome the system's resistance to adjustment by encouraging frequent but small changes in the value of currencies, removing the trauma. From the point of view of the United States, said the report, the advantage of evolutionary reform was to retain "for an indefinite period a major role for the dollar and monetary leadership of the United States."

Nixon went into his meeting with the Volcker Group without either reading its report or receiving a briefing on its contents. Except to wave off a dissenting plea by Arthur Burns for devaluing the dollar, he decided nothing and gave no direction. By default, then, Nixon returned the international monetary issue to the despised Paul Volcker.[33]

Given the contents of the Volcker report, Volcker might have been expected to pursue the option of evolutionary reform. In fact, the report reflected the consensus of the group, not Volcker's personal views. Speaking later of the reform option, Volcker said, "We never expected very much from that effort but did it to keep people quiet. It was an exercise we had to go through."[34] Discussion of reform proceeded within the government and in various forums abroad, but because the Treasury dragged its feet, got nowhere. The problem with the reform option, Volcker believed, was that frequent changes in exchange rates would only encourage speculators betting on adjustments to attack weak currencies, further destabilizing the system. Europe's central bankers agreed. Shaking a finger in Volcker's face,

---

[33] Thomas A. Forbord, "The Abandonment of Bretton Woods: The Political Economy of U.S. International Monetary Policy," Ph.D. diss., Harvard University (1980), 74.

[34] Ibid., 142.

one of them said, "If all this talk about flexible exchange rates brings down the system, the blood will be on your American head."[35]

Though Volcker was notorious in the government for playing "his cards very close to his vest," his views were clear enough.[36] He had grown up with Bretton Woods, believed in fixed exchange rates, and had seen crises in the system come and go. If the United States tamed inflation, he believed, the system might yet right itself. He did not want to close the gold window, reform the system, or devalue the dollar. He also opposed removing the restrictions on U.S. foreign investment that the Johnson administration had imposed and that Nixon had pledged during the 1968 campaign to rescind. Volcker's policy, then, was muddling through.[37] Of course, from the perspective of European critics, muddling through meant retaining the "exorbitant privileges of the dollar" for as long as possible, which was, in fact, one of Volcker's purposes.

Muddling through worked well enough in 1969 because interest rates in the United States were high as a result of the Fed's tight money policy that year. Economists had believed that the value of currencies would be established by such fundamentals as the balance of trade and long-term foreign investment, but the advancing integration of world capital markets and the growth of large pools of short-term capital added tremendous volatility to currency values and vastly complicated the efforts of central bankers to manage the system. In 1969 billions of so-called Eurodollars, dollars on deposit mainly in the branches of U.S. banks in London, sloshed across the Atlantic to New York, where short-term interest rates were higher. A dollar shortage, of all things, developed in Europe, prompting European central bankers to feed dollars from their reserves into the market to relieve the demand. That year official dollar holdings of foreign central banks declined by $2.7 billion, and gold flowed *into* the United States.[38]

The year 1970 should also have been a good one for the dollar. As a result of the U.S. recession, Americans spent less for imports, and the U.S. trade balance improved, but by midyear U.S. short-term interest rates fell below European rates, and most of the dollars lent in 1969 to the United

---

[35] Volcker and Gyohten, *Changing Fortunes*, 68.

[36] Forbord, "Abandonment of Bretton Woods," 110.

[37] For a public statement of Volcker's views, see his testimony in "The Balance of Payments Mess," Joint Economic Committee, hearings (1971), 82–104.

[38] International Monetary Fund, *Balance of Payments Yearbook: 1969–73* (vol. 26), Table 1; CEA Annual Report 1970, 126–130.

States made the return trip to London. In 1970 enough of these returned dollars found their way into foreign central banks to swell foreign dollar reserves by $9.8 billion, an increase three times as large as had occurred in the worst previous year.[39] Expanded holdings of U.S. dollars meant more European inflation. Now even Volcker began to harbor private doubts about the viability of Bretton Woods.[40]

## IV

In 1971, the climactic year of his economic management, Nixon abandoned the postwar liberal ideal of a harmonious trade world in favor of a nationalist conception of U.S. interests. Western Europe and Japan were now considered not so much trading partners but rivals to be subdued. The *Wall Street Journal* reported at midyear, "The United States government is getting ready for a new cold war against the rest of the free world . . . Spurring Washington to act is a vision that Europeans deride as 'the American nightmare': a dark picture of a world in which other nations combine the newest technology with lower wages to rout U.S. goods from both home and foreign markets."[41] This nationalist turn owed something to Nixon's own inclinations and a great deal to two advisers who joined his administration in February 1971, John Connally and Peter G. Peterson.

Late in 1970, Nixon was looking for someone to appoint as a White House assistant for foreign economics and as the first executive director of the Council for International Economic Policy (CIEP), a new agency proposed by the Ash Council on executive reorganization to coordinate and focus the various federal agencies operating in this area. After the distinguished Chicago economist George Stigler declined the post, George Shultz suggested Peterson.[42] Son of a Greek immigrant, Peter Peterson graduated from Northwestern in 1947 and twelve years later was executive vice president of the Chicago-based firm, Bell and Howell, then primarily a manufacturer of camera equipment. As president of the company beginning in 1961, Peterson diversified and expanded its operations, doing well enough to be called "the most brilliant" businessman of his generation.

---

[39] CEA *Annual Report 1971*, 139–142; *New York Times*, Oct. 6, 1970, 69; IMF, *Balance of Payment Yearbook*, Table 1.
[40] Volcker and Gyohten, *Changing Fortunes*, 72–73.
[41] *Wall Street Journal*, June 18, 1971, 1.
[42] E-Notes, Dec. 28, 1970.

Shultz and Peterson had become acquainted at the University of Chicago in the 1960s, where one had been dean of the business school and the other a university trustee.[43] "Trade is a two-way street," Nixon told Shultz. If Peterson was "a total free trader," he "can't have the job." In fact, Peterson did not yet have any deep views on the international economy, and Nixon did not really expect much of him. "He'd be all right," Nixon said; "he wouldn't bother me."[44] On January 19, 1971, one day before the *New York Times* published a front-page story on the drift and failings of his foreign economic policy,[45] Nixon announced Peterson's appointment.[46]

The Nixon White House never felt entirely comfortable with Pete Peterson. He had been the protégé of Senator Charles Percy, the liberal Republican and past president of Bell and Howell, who had first spotted Peterson and brought him into the company. Nixon despised Charles Percy. Once in Washington, Peterson mingled easily at Georgetown parties with liberals, Democrats, and columnists. Nixon loathed Georgetown, into which no true Nixonian would ever voluntarily tread. In time, Nixon came to doubt Peterson's loyalty and suspect him of the deadly sin of leaking. Within a year, he would bounce Peterson out of the White House and into the Commerce Department, but before his exile, Peterson would enjoy a brief moment of influence and help Nixon crystallize his nationalist intuitions into a coherent set of economic ideas. The Council on International Economic Policy, incidentally, proved just one more failed attempt to impose order on the fragmented bureaucracy.[47]

As his first assignment Nixon asked Peterson to conduct a study of the changing world economy. Plunging into terra incognita, Peterson emerged in April 1971 with a confidential report, which, one reporter wrote, "bowled over" the president.[48] Indeed, Nixon was so intrigued that for a brief time that spring he elevated Peterson to the status, in William Safire's

---

[43] *Current Biography* (1972), 349–351; *New York Times*, Jan. 26, 1971, 16; *Wall Street Journal*, July 6, 1971, 1.

[44] E-Notes, Dec. 28, 1970; Jan. 11, 1971.

[45] *New York Times*, Jan. 20, 1971, 1.

[46] *Pub Paps RN 1971*, 42–43.

[47] I. M. Destler, *Making Foreign Economic Policy* (1980), 213–214; Dominic Del Guidice, "Creation and Evolution of the Council on International Economic Policy," in Commission on the Organization of the Government for the Conduct of Foreign Policy, Appendices, (vol. 6, June 1975), 110–123.

[48] *Wall Street Journal*, June 18, 1971, 1.

phrase, "of number one intellectual concubine,"[49] spending time with his new assistant to ponder how to keep the United States number one. Nixon even set up meetings in the White House for Peterson to display his array of colored charts on the world economy for members of the president's staff, congressmen, labor leaders, and others. These charts argued an early version of a thesis that would soon become an article of popular belief, the thesis of America's competitive decline. "I think of what happened to Greece and Rome," the president told a group of media executives in Kansas City that year, "and, as you see, what is left — only the pillars."[50]

Peterson's charts showed America's diminishing share of world output, her slower rate of economic growth compared to all other developed nations except Britain, her dead-last ranking in gross investment, and her shrinking proportion of the world's export trade. Although U.S. exports had increased 110 percent since 1964, Germany's had gone up 200 percent, and Japan's 400 percent. In 1970 Americans bought 49 percent of their sewing machines from abroad, 52 percent of their black and white televisions, 70 percent of their radios, and 100 percent of their 35-mm cameras. Once America's superiority had seemed unassailable. Now it appeared that Japan would surpass the United States in per capita income by the year 2000. It would take more than devaluation of the dollar to restore the competitiveness of U.S. exports, Peterson said. The problems were more fundamental than that. America would have to challenge the unfair conduct of its competitors and restore the dynamism of American enterprise by adopting what would later be called industrial policy.[51]

It did not hurt Peterson with the president that Connally entirely agreed with his thesis. "JC buys Peterson's ideas," Nixon said in May.[52] These ideas helped Connally define his purpose as the nation's finance minister and lent point to his tenure. Together, Connally and Peterson set out to warn the nation of its imperiled position and fashion appropriate policies of rescue. To be sure, the alliance was merely one of ideas. When

---

[49] Safire, *Before the Fall* (1975), 498.

[50] *Pub Paps RN 1971*, 812.

[51] Peterson's April 1971 memo to Nixon remains classified. A published version appeared in December 1971, Peter G. Peterson, *The United States in the Changing World Economy* (vol. 1) and *Background Material* (vol. 2). Parts of this paragraph drawn from charts in volume 2.

[52] E-Notes, May 21, 1971.

Peterson threatened to encroach on the Treasury's monopoly of international monetary issues, Connally cut his legs off.

Peterson and Connally believed that America's former clients, once recipients of so much American benevolence, were now following pernicious policies to fleece Uncle Sugar. Said Peterson, "our partners no longer need special crutches. In fact, as is sometimes the case, patients may be inclined to throw them at the doctor."[53] Thus, the nations of Western Europe were restricting U.S. agricultural exports. They had entered bilateral agreements with Mediterranean and African countries harmful to U.S. trade interests. They had devised discriminatory arrangements insulating them from all but 7 percent of Japanese exports, whereas the United States had to absorb 30 percent. And they paid only $800 million of the $1.7 billion annual cost of stationing U.S. troops on their soil for their own protection.[54] Peterson conceded that the United States actually enjoyed a surplus in its trade with Western Europe, but he warned against the protectionist drift of the European Economic Community and urged measures to halt it.

The stunning emergence of Japan as a trade power did most to shatter American complacency and fuel a sense of grievance. The United States had paid little attention to Japanese trade until 1965, when Japan's exports to the world surged to $7 billion, and the U.S. trade balance with Japan slipped into deficit for the first time. In 1971 the value of Japan's exports to all nations exceeded $23 billion, and the U.S. trade deficit with Japan reached $3 billion, approximately equal to the U.S. deficit with the world.[55] By then Japan, Inc. had emerged as the latest version of the Yellow Peril. Following a policy of mercantilism, Japan's business-government alliance had mounted a drive to develop and promote exports, while keeping out the goods of others. Peterson's favorite example of Japanese unfairness was autos. Though Japanese auto exports had captured 20 percent of the Los Angeles market in 1970, General Motors, the largest U.S. exporter of cars, had only 0.1 percent of the entire Japanese market.[56] *Time* quoted an

---

[53] Don Bonafede, "White House Report," *National Journal* (vol. 3, Nov. 13, 1971), 2238–2248. Bonafede quoted from the confidential Peterson memo.

[54] "Foreign Trade," Committee on Finance, Senate hearings (1971), 19.

[55] Gary R. Saxonhouse, "A Review of Recent U.S.–Japan Economic Relations," *Asian Survey* (vol. 12, Sept. 1972), 739; U.S. Department of Commerce, *Business Statistics, 1973*, 110, 115.

[56] Peterson, *United States in the Changing World Economy*, vol. 2, 21.

unnamed cabinet officer, who sounded suspiciously like John Connally, as saying, "The Japanese are still fighting the war, only now instead of a shooting war, it is an economic war. Their immediate intention is to try to dominate the Pacific and then perhaps the world."[57]

Connally and Peterson in effect announced that the days of U.S. benevolence were over. Said Connally, other nations "have grown accustomed to our being relaxed, fairly generous, always forgiving, always easy in our dealings with them. Consequently, they have built up tariff arrangements, they have built up trade restrictions against U.S. goods . . . And they expect us to like it."[58] The appropriate U.S. response was not to erect trade barriers of its own (except in retaliation) or to offer reciprocal concessions. The appropriate response was to bludgeon other nations into playing by fair rules. During the first half of 1971, the United States pressed Germany to pay more for U.S. troops stationed in its territory. Connally mused aloud that perhaps the United States should pull the Sixth Fleet out of the Mediterranean to protest Europe's preferential trade relations with countries in that region.[59] When Japan only partially met U.S. demands to relax import restrictions, the administration broke off negotiations in July, threatening retaliatory measures that could initiate a trade war.[60]

Connally and Peterson did not blame America's decline solely on unfair foreigners. Americans, it appeared, were going soft. "The simple fact is that in many areas other nations are out-producing us, out-thinking us, and out-trading us," Connally told Congress.[61] America would have to increase investment, raise productivity, and get "off its back and on its feet and back to work."[62] For the Japanese, especially, Connally felt both resentment and grudging admiration. Said Connally, "the people themselves, very frankly, are more industrious than we are, and they work harder than we do, they save more than we do."[63] One way to beat Japan was to copy her, or at least to copy the Japanese model of government guidance to achieve export supremacy. In violation of the free-market credo of the Republican party,

---

[57] *Time* (May 10, 1971), 85.
[58] *U.S. News and World Report* (Apr. 12, 1971), 55.
[59] *Washington Post*, Apr. 26, 1971, A4.
[60] *Business Week* (July 3, 1971), 64–70; *Wall Street Journal* (Aug. 13, 1971), 5.
[61] "Foreign Trade," Senate hearings, 19.
[62] Connally speech at meeting of International Bankers Association, Dec. 2, 1970, copy in White House Staff files, Connally file, SMOF: McCracken.
[63] "Foreign Trade," Senate hearings, 75.

Connally and Peterson considered subsidies for research and development that would enhance U.S. competitiveness. They favored special tax policies to encourage exports, and they proposed suspending the antitrust laws to permit firms in the same industry to cooperate, in the fashion of Japanese cartels, for the conquest of foreign markets.[64] "I'm not for a Japanese transplant," Peterson said. "But in a high technology world that is changing fast, we ought to ask, 'What kind of planning for the future is appropriate, given the kind of economic system we have?' "[65] According to the *Wall Street Journal*, Peterson had lately been punctuating his conversation with an occasional "ah so."[66]

One reason Connally and Peterson got Nixon's attention was that they helped him make the connection between commercial policy and American power, between issues he had once considered low diplomacy and the U.S. role in world affairs. In extemporaneous remarks to the Productivity Commission in June 1971, Nixon showed himself an apt pupil. "It's terribly important that we be #1 economically because otherwise we can't be #1 diplomatically or militarily . . . As distinguished from other great powers throughout civilization, we did not ask for our position of power, nor did we even have a policy for acquiring the power. It fell into our lap. For the next quarter century let us see to it that we do play this role . . . I have been more melodramatic than I meant to be, but if the moment comes when we are not competitive, our standard of living will go down, inflation will go up, and something will go out of the American spirit . . . The future of the economy is in our hands — and also the future of peace."[67]

It was the implications of the Peterson-Connally analysis for domestic politics that most intrigued Nixon. During the spring and summer of 1971, when Nixon was acutely worried about unemployment, Peterson told him that every extra billion in U.S. exports created 60,000 to 80,000 new jobs. In the public version of his report, published in December, Peterson wrote, "If our exports were now in adequate surplus (i.e. our trade balance had shifted from deficit to the size of surplus needed to bring an overall payments balance into equilibrium), the direct and indirect job effects of that surplus would have added between 500,000 and 750,000 men and women

---

[64] *Business Week* (May 22, 1971), 19–20, (July 3, 1971), 67; *Wall Street Journal*, July 6, 1971, 1.

[65] *Business Week* (July 3, 1971), 70.

[66] *Wall Street Journal*, July 6, 1971, 12.

[67] Productivity Meeting, June 29, 1971, Memos for President's file, POF (Safire's notes).

to the employed labor force."[68] Nixon found this estimate so interesting that according to one account, he "underlined it and for weeks showed it to all visitors."[69] Speaking to Peterson in July, Nixon said that in the past the United States had used trade for foreign policy; now we "must use it as instrument of our domestic policy, *e.g.* jobs."[70] Once he grasped the implications of economic nationalism for his domestic purposes, Nixon committed wholeheartedly to the Peterson-Connally thesis.

Of course, an export crusade would not create more jobs overnight or maybe even in time for the next election. The mere prospect of such a crusade would help the administration politically, especially with the labor unions, many of which also equated exports with jobs and favored nationalist policies to expand foreign markets. In other words, a trade offensive could help Nixon recruit workers to the New Majority. This was a point Connally hit hard. At the Camp David economic meeting late in June 1971, Nixon sent Haldeman to Connally's cabin to sound him out on the kind of leader Nixon should be. Haldeman summarized the conversation in his diary. Connally "feels strongly we shouldn't overlook international trade as a domestic issue . . . He feels that we have to have some restrictions on imports, and this would be popular domestically." The president "can win labor by showing an interest in protecting their jobs. We don't have to solve the problem, just work towards it, showing visible understanding and articulation. For example . . . taking them Peterson's charts and showing what we're trying to do, being on the side of the angels even if we don't win."[71] A few weeks later, at a meeting to discuss the administration's labor policy, Connally said the president could "get to the labor rank and file, especially on the issue of jobs, and particularly, on the American position in the world economy, i.e., our trade relations. On that issue, labor will be our strongest ally."[72]

Academic economists around the president scorned the Peterson report as the work of misguided amateurs, the latest version of the mercantilist fallacy. Circa 1630, the writer Thomas Mun summed up the essence of mercantilism: "The ordinary means therefore to increase our wealth and treasure is by foreign trade, wherein we must ever observe this rule: to sell

---

[68] Peterson, *United States in Changing World Economy*, 41.
[69] Martin Mayer, *The Fate of the Dollar* (1980), 183.
[70] E-Notes, July 27, 1971.
[71] *Haldeman Diaries*, June 27, 1971.
[72] Ibid., July 21, 1971; Colson for President, July 21, 1971, President's Meeting file, POF.

more to strangers yearly than we consume of theirs in value."[73] It followed that governments should intervene in the market to promote and defend exports.

Classical economists had thoroughly discredited the logic of this view except with governments and the public. In competitive markets, industries rise and fall all the time. Whenever imports serve the American consumer better than domestically produced goods, U.S. capital and labor should shift to more efficient uses. By specializing in what they can most efficiently produce, trading nations maximize prosperity for all. Nations export not to create jobs; they export to satisfy wants with as little effort as possible. That view of foreign trade went virtually unchallenged among mainstream economists, regardless of their differences on other issues. "As you know I find many of the propositions in your essay unconvincing," Herbert Stein wrote Peterson. Urging him to seek "more concentrated input from economists," Stein reminded Peterson that international economics had been intensively studied for 200 years and that most economists agreed on the subject. "It would be a shame not to know what the discipline has to say," Stein scolded.[74]

Providing Peterson with an elementary economics lesson, the CEA's Hendrik Houthakker wrote of his report, "One would get the impression from this presentation that the main purpose of our foreign trade is exports, which of course is putting things on their head. We need imports because they enable us to get things cheaper than their cost of production here . . . If you are going to show this briefing material to Congress it is very important that it is not biased in a mercantilist direction. The notion that we need foreign trade only because we have to be nice to foreigners is a pernicious one that has done a great deal of harm, quite apart from being absurd from a logical view."[75] The way to fix the problem of declining competitiveness was not by trade wars or industrial policy, the economists said, but by correcting the overvalued dollar.

Critics of the Connally-Peterson thesis challenged in particular the contention that foreigners had stacked the deck against an innocent America. In May 1971, Houthakker told Congress that the United States was

---

[73] Quoted in Paul R. Krugman and Maurice Obstfeld, *International Economics: Theory and Practice* (1988), 508; see Hans O. Schmitt, "Mercantilism: A Modern Argument," *The Manchester School* (vol. 47, June 1979), 93–111.

[74] Stein for Peterson, July 16, 1971, Agency Files: CIEP, SMOF: Stein.

[75] Houthakker for Peterson, April 22, 1971, CIEP Subject File, SMOF: Houthakker.

just as guilty as foreign governments of restricting imports. "The severity of these restrictions is hard to measure, but in the aggregate they come close to canceling each other out," he said. Houthakker cited a State Department study showing that the United States employed sixty-seven quantitative restrictions on trade and covered a larger percentage of industrial imports with quotas than any other nation. The United States also had a larger number of high tariffs than its major trading partners as well as a somewhat larger number of low tariffs.[76] In the liberal view, if the United States retaliated against the trade restrictions of others by imposing still more restrictions of its own, it would right no wrongs, penalize American consumers, and hasten the development of trade blocs inimical to U.S. interests.

"Liberal trade policy is a triumph of pure reason over common sense," the economist Richard N. Cooper once wrote. "Everyone who is not an economist thinks he knows imports reduce profits and jobs."[77] Taking the side of common sense, Peterson, Connally, and Nixon decided to force open foreign markets for American exports. Their efforts partook of economic illiteracy. Speaking once of a crucial concept in international economics, Connally said, "Senator, that's the theory of comparative advantage. In the first place, the reason I do not understand it is that I am not an economist. But if I were an economist, I would not want to understand it because I do not believe it is going to work."[78] Neither did Nixon. Against the advice of his own economists, the president moved toward that showdown with the rest of the trading world that his mercantilist advisers, Peterson and Connally, were now urging on him.


# V

The xenophobia descending on the White House was not unconnected to Nixon's continuing quest for textile quotas. At no time during this dispute did the administration acknowledge any contradiction between its protests against the protectionism of others and its own effort to protect the American textile industry. Rather, it all seemed part of a single effort to bend

---

[76] "Foreign Trade," Senate hearings, 254–255.
[77] Richard N. Cooper, "Comment," in Robert E. Baldwin and Anne O. Krueger, *The Structure and Evolution of Recent Trade Policy* (1984), 27.
[78] "Foreign Trade," Senate Committee, 58.

the trading world to America's will. It mattered not the diplomatic cost. Nixon would get his way.

It vastly complicated Nixon's problem that in the winter of 1971 Wilbur Mills again took over the textile issue. Though he reintroduced his bill mandating textile quotas, Mills hoped to keep it off the House floor, where protectionists might capture it, as they had in 1970. To this end, Mills approached leaders of the Japanese textile industry through an intermediary to warn against legislated quotas and to urge Japan to impose voluntary quotas on itself. Mills believed he had Nixon's support for the initiative but neglected to keep the administration informed as he proceeded. On March 8, 1971, in an apparent triumph for Mills, the Japanese Textile Federation announced a voluntary three-year program that would limit the growth of Japan's textile imports to the United States by 5 percent the first year and 6 percent in each of the next two. Sato's government immediately endorsed this solution and so did Mills.[79] Because the agreement lacked ceilings on specific product categories, the American Textile Institute claimed that Japan remained free "to wreck entire segments of the domestic industry" and bitterly opposed it.[80]

Shultz, Peterson, Kissinger, and McCracken nevertheless urged Nixon to accept the Mills agreement.[81] If he did, the president could bury an issue that threatened costly damage to the world trade system and avoid antagonizing Mills, whose cooperation Nixon needed on pending legislative issues. But the opinion that counted was Strom Thurmond's. On March 9, 1971, Thurmond wrote Nixon saying, "There is no question that the Japanese proposal is totally inadequate if the American textile industry and its hundreds of thousands of employees are to be protected from the increasing unfair competition of Asian imports."[82] Two days later, at a meeting of his advisers, Nixon angrily denounced Mills for interfering in U.S. foreign policy and selling out "too cheap." Sato "shook hands on a deal" in 1969, and he, Nixon, would not "let Mills undercut it."[83] That afternoon the White House issued a statement rejecting the Mills agreement.[84]

---

[79] Destler et al., *Textile Wrangle*, 251–266; *Wall Street Journal*, Feb. 26, 1971, 14.

[80] *Newsweek* (Mar. 22, 1971), 79.

[81] Destler et al., *Textile Wrangle*, 269; McCracken for President, Mar. 10, 1971, Textiles file, SMOF: Flanigan.

[82] Thurmond for President, Mar. 9, 1971, Textiles file, SMOF: Flanigan.

[83] E-Notes, Mar. 11, 1971.

[84] *Pub Paps RN 1971*, 423–424.

Having obtained what he considered a good deal for the textile indus-try, Mills no longer felt obligated to support his quota bill. As Mills told Peterson, "Those greedy bastards . . . will not get *any* quota legislation passed until a voluntary approach is given a fair chance."[85] Blocked by Japan from obtaining a satisfactory voluntary agreement and prevented by Mills from obtaining legislated quotas, the administration turned next to a law already on the books, authorizing the president to impose quotas on any nation holding out against a multilateral pact to limit textile imports. Nixon sent emissaries to Korea, Taiwan, and Hong Kong to line them up for an agreement that would be prelude to imposing unilateral quotas on Japan. These nations too declined to help Nixon pay off a campaign debt.[86] Meanwhile, on July 15, 1971, Nixon devastated Sato and undercut the basis of postwar Japanese foreign policy by announcing his forthcoming visit to China, without even the courtesy of prior notice. This became known in Japan as the first Nixon Shock. During the second week in August 1971, Nixon's advisers were deep in debate on his remaining op-tions to impose unilateral quotas on textiles, all of doubtful legality.[87] They were close to a decision on August 13 when Nixon decided to pack up his advisers and go to Camp David. There the textile issue would become enveloped in a far larger showdown, not only with Japan but with the rest of America's trading partners.

## VI

Through the first half of 1971, trade problems but not money ranked high on Connally's agenda. By contrast, the Council of Economic Advisers believed that the main problem of trade *was* money. Because fixed ex-change rates kept the dollar above its real market value, U.S. exports were too expensive and imports too cheap. If currency values were realigned and the dollar devalued, America's trade position would materially improve, the economists said. Connally dismissed currency realignment as so much "monetary magic" and opposed devaluation. Money itself, he said, "cannot produce, increase efficiency, or open markets abroad."[88] With Connally

---

[85] Peterson for President, Mar. 11, 1971, Notes on Meetings with President, SMOF: Ehrlichman.

[86] Destler et al., *Textile Wrangle*, 283–285.

[87] H-Notes, Aug. 1, 12, 1971.

[88] "Foreign Trade," Finance Committee, Senate hearings (1971), 21.

indifferent, the administration confronted the advancing decay of Bretton Woods without clear direction, and even responsible officials differed not only on what policy should be but what it actually was.

Some commentators described U.S. policy as "benign neglect," a phrase used by Daniel Patrick Moynihan to describe Nixon's policies on race but in this case meaning, "The dollar is our currency but your problem."[89] The chief theoretician of benign neglect was the Harvard economist Gottfried Haberler, who had chaired Nixon's preinaugural task force on the balance of payments.[90] Advocates of benign neglect held that the United States should ignore the payments deficit. Let America pursue its national objectives as it wished, and let other nations manage the monetary consequences as best they could. Nations running a payments surplus with the United States faced three choices: They could absorb excess dollars, inflating their currencies. They could revalue their currencies upward, pricing exports higher and imports from America lower. Finally, they could impose controls to restrict the inflow of American capital. If countries with payments surpluses attempted to escape these costly alternatives by demanding gold for dollars, the United States would close the gold window, placing the world on a pure dollar standard. In other words, there was really nothing the United States should do about the dollar glut except enjoy it. The policy of benign neglect received widespread support among U.S. academic economists, whose monetary patriotism was one of the era's more remarkable features. Inside the government, the CEA not only advocated benign neglect but assumed that it was administration policy. Europeans detested the very phrase.

Paul Volcker denied that benign neglect was or should be the policy.[91] Dedicated to Bretton Woods, he hoped to ride out the storm until the system recovered equilibrium. There was no crisis, Volcker said, only a temporary emergency created by short-term capital movements. In contrast to advocates of benign neglect, Volcker opposed the revaluation of surplus currencies, principally the mark and the yen, which would only

---

[89] Charles A. Coombs, *The Arena of International Finance* (1976), 219.

[90] Gottfried Haberler and Thomas Willett, *A Strategy for the U.S. Balance of Payments Policy* (1972); Haberler, *U.S. Balance Payments and the International Monetary System* (AEI Reprint No. 9, Jan. 1973); *Washington Post*, May 23, 1971, G1. Another influential case for benign neglect was Lawrence B. Krause, "A Passive Balance of Payments Strategy for the U.S.," *Brookings Papers on Economic Activity* (1970), 339–368.

[91] "Balance of Payments Mess," Finance Committee, Senate hearings, 82–104.

encourage further speculation. He regarded the closing of the gold window as an apocalyptic plunge into the unknown, to be avoided if at all possible. In addition, he was willing to make small gestures to show that the United States cared, provided such gestures did not hinder the domestic economy. Thus, in 1971, the U.S. government issued $3 billion in special bonds to sop up some of Europe's unwanted dollars, in effect trying to empty the ocean with a thimble. Embattled Europeans saw little difference between benign neglect and the Volcker policy of muddling through. In either case, the U.S. posture was passivity in the face of the havoc that its own monetary laxity had created.

If any man was responsbile for the unraveling of Bretton Woods in 1971, it was, ironically, Arthur Burns, passsionate advocate of fixed exchange rates and gold. It was Burns's easy money policy at the Fed during the first half of the year that caused a steep decline in U.S. interest rates, prompting a massive outflow of short-term capital from the United States in search of higher returns elsewhere. In 1970 foreign central banks had reluctantly absorbed $10 billion in support of the sagging dollar. In 1971 they absorbed $30 billion, one cause for accelerating foreign inflation rates.[92]

Burns was afflicted by pangs of conscience at the meeting of the Federal Open Market Committee on April 6, 1971. Wishing to avoid the appearance of benign neglect, he proposed raising the federal funds rate from 4 percent to 4.25 percent to slow the dollar outflow so destabilizing to foreign economies. The rate increase that Burns favored was less than the one favored by Arthur Hayes of the New York Fed, who would have risked a slowdown of the domestic economy for the dollar's sake. Burns made clear that he wanted to raise rates only temporarily and reminded his colleagues of the Fed's great mistake in 1931 when it aborted recovery at home to save the dollar abroad.[93] Burns, then, would do little more than Volcker to save the system they both loved. Most economists would agree that Burns was right to give priority to the domestic economy, given the relatively small size of the economy's foreign sector. But in 1971, a slowdown in money growth would have served both Bretton Woods and the domestic economy equally well.

---

[92] Yeager, *International Monetary Relations*, 516–517. This figure owed something to the "Eurodollar Carousel," by which central banks lent dollars and then unwittingly repurchased them, an error corrected in May 1971. See Yeager, 435.

[93] FOMC minutes, Apr. 6, 1971, 56.

In the spring of 1971, the death watch for Bretton Woods began. On May 3, after months of massive dollar inflows occasioned by low U.S. interest rates, German Finance Minister Karl Shiller set off a speculative frenzy by hinting at revaluation of the mark. The Bundesbank bought $1.2 billion on May 4, as speculators unloaded dollars to buy marks that might soon appreciate. The bank took in another billion during the first forty minutes of trading the next day and then closed German currency markets. On May 7 and 8, Western Europe's finance ministers met to seek a common escape from dollar domination but could unite only in their common hostility to benign neglect. Electing to cut loose from the dollar, the Germans stopped buying them and freed the mark to find its market value.[94] That is, they floated the mark. At a Quadriad meeting in the White House on May 12, 1971, McCracken welcomed the German float, Volcker regretted it, and Nixon warned against tightening monetary policy for external reasons, with effects "adverse to our domestic economic interests."[95] After the value of the floating mark appreciated by 4 percent against the dollar, a measure of calm returned to the markets.[96]

Amid diplomatic discord and economic uncertainty, the American Bankers Association hosted an international banking conference in Munich in late May 1971. Visiting Americans were embarrassed by the refusal of restaurants to accept their travelers checks and by talk in the corridors of the coming dollar devaluation.[97] The last speaker on the conference program was John Connally, making his European debut. Despite a touch of the flu, Connally delivered his blunt remarks with such force that he created a lasting image of himself, in his own words, as "the bully boy on the manicured playing fields of international finance."[98] Declaring that monetary disturbances were merely symptomatic of deeper problems, he blamed the U.S. payments deficit on the unfair behavior of the allies and recited a by-now familiar litany of American complaints: EEC discrimination against U.S. farm products, Japanese protectionism, European discrimination against Japanese exports, Canadian tariffs on American cars, the re-

---

[94] Solomon, *The International Monetary System,* 178–179; *Wall Street Journal,* May 5, 1971, 2; Susan Strange, "The Dollar Crises of 1971," *International Affairs* (vol. 48, Apr. 1972), 191–215, esp. pp. 200–202.

[95] McCracken for President's file, June 8, 1971, Quadriad file, SMOF: Houthakker.

[96] Coomb, *Arena,* 213; *Newsweek* (May 24, 1971), 71–72.

[97] *Business Week* (May 29, 1971), 17–18.

[98] Harry Brandon, *The Retreat of American Power* (1973), 228.

fusal of U.S. partners to pay their fair share of the common defense. Calling on the other nations to right these wrongs, Connally stated that the United States could no longer afford benevolence and must now look to its own interests. Concerning dollar devaluation, which many in Europe favored as a solution to the dollar crisis, Connally said that in any negotiation "there are necessarily some unalterable positions of any participant. Believing this, I want without arrogance or defiance to make it abundantly clear. We are not going to devalue. We are not going to change the price of gold."[99] Connally himself had added this defiant pledge to the draft of the speech that Volcker had written for him. Volcker, who knew that devaluation was a real possibility, asked Connally if he really wanted to take such a stand. "That's my unalterable position today," Connally replied. "I don't know what it will be this summer."[100]

In June 1971, the signs briefly turned favorable for the dollar — converging interest rates in the United States and Europe, higher inflation abroad than in the United States, the apparent success of the German float. But on July 10, 1971, Volcker received advance notice of some bad news. The U.S. trade balance, which had produced a $2.7 billion surplus in 1970, had become a $597 million deficit in June, with the looming prospect of the first year-long trade deficit since 1893. It was a Saturday morning, and Volcker's Treasury colleague William Dale was at home when Volcker called him back to the office. "When I got there," Dale recalled, "Volcker asked me what size deficit for June would set exchange markets rocking. I told him the size I thought would do this . . . He said, 'You got it.' He then directed me to do a plan for closing the gold window and said, 'This time it's for real.' "[101]

Volcker intended to close the gold window before the United States was forced to do it, then undertake a diplomatic offensive to realign currencies and correct the overvalued dollar. But Connally had other ideas. He, too, was ready for decisive action but not for the "monetary magic" of dollar devaluation. To solve the trade problem, Connally preferred instead to force the others into opening their markets to more American goods. This feat he would accomplish by employing a blunt weapon in the form of a temporary 10 percent border tax on imports, in effect doubling the average

---

[99] John Connally, "Mutual Responsibility for Maintaining a Stable Monetary System," May 28, 1971, reprinted in *U.S. Department Bulletin* (vol. 65, July 12, 1971), 42–46.

[100] Volcker and Gyohten, *Changing Fortunes*, 75.

[101] Forbord, "Abandonment of Bretton Woods," 243–244.

effective tariff on dutiable goods. To get rid of the border tax, foreigners would have to make the concessions on trade that Connally was demanding. Devaluing the dollar, Connally believed, might damage U.S. prestige and hurt the president politically. The border tax would appeal to nationalist sentiment and boost Nixon's popularity. When Connally asked Volcker to begin work on the border tax option, Volcker balked. Not only would the border tax be protectionist, but, by reducing imports, the tax would strengthen the dollar at the very time the United States should be seeking its devaluation. "I hoped I had been convincing and that Connally's request would go away," Volcker recalled. But Connally insisted, and Volcker got to work on the border tax.[102]

Sometime in July 1971, Connally changed his mind about the gold window, deciding both to close it *and* to impose the 10 percent border tax. Connally never explained the reason, but that month he did read a report by Treasury consultant Edward Bernstein, arguing that a dollar depreciation of 12 to 15 percent could stimulate domestic recovery by adding 500,000 jobs, reducing the unemployment rate by 0.5 percent. C. Fred Bergsten, who had handled international monetary matters on Kissinger's National Security Council staff until he resigned in May 1971, said later, "Connally decided devaluation was the thing to do after he read Eddy Bernstein's analysis in mid-July . . . This analysis convinced Connally that the devaluation was good politically. Connally always looked at the politics of the economics."[103] At a time when 5 million Americans were unemployed and the economic issue was killing Nixon, Bernstein's report appar-

---

[102] Ibid., 245–247; Volcker quote, Volcker and Gyohten, *Changing Fortunes*, 76.

[103] Forbord, "Abandonment of Bretton Woods," 249. See Bergsten's interpretation in "The New Economics and U.S. Foreign Policy," *Foreign Affairs* (vol. 50, Jan. 1972), 199–222; see also Bergsten, *Dilemmas of the Dollar* (1975), 92. For an elaboration of Bergsten's views, see Haberler, *U.S. Balance of Payments*, 184. Students of this subject disagree sharply on whether Connally did or did not have domestic political motives. Linda S. Graebner, "The New Economic Policy, 1971," in Commission on the Organization of the Government for Control of Foreign Policy, Appendices (vol. 3, June 1975), 160–184, cites an interview with Bergsten to argue that Connally's motives were domestic. Odell, *U.S. International Monetary Policy*, 233–239, 263–267, discounts domestic factors, citing lack of interest group pressures. Odell cites an interview with Herbert Stein that rejects the domestic politics thesis. Odell also notes that the domestic implications of Nixon's international measures were not mentioned at Camp David. Susan Strange, "The Dollar Crisis, 1971," *International Affairs* (vol. 48, April 1972), 191–211, emphasizes Nixon's desire to "reinforce public belief in his own leadership" and discounts purely economic considerations (p. 204). These authors did not have access to the *Haldeman Diaries* or Ehrlichman's notes, which support the primacy of domestic political motives.

ently persuaded Connally that the job benefits of dollar depreciation exceeded the costs to U.S. prestige.

On August 2, 1971, Connally presented to Nixon his complete package for a dramatic new direction in the administration's foreign and domestic economic policies. Nixon signed off immediately on wage-price controls, tax cuts, and closing the gold window, but not the border tax, which he approved later.[104] Connally's measures would not only silence the critics on the inflation-unemployment front, but the foreign components of the plan would appeal to the president's blue-collar constituency. Connally, said Volcker, "sold it as a package that would help the domestic economy and place Nixon in a strong political position."[105]

Nixon and Connally intended to close the gold window on September 8, 1971, the day Congress returned from summer recess, but developments in the money markets altered this timetable. On July 28, the government published the bad news of the June trade deficit, and speculators began dumping dollars.[106] On August 5, the *Wall Street Journal* reported that the White House and the Treasury "responded with 'sullen no comments' to the current currency turmoil rather than with the ringing reassurances of past years that the dollar has a uniquely 'immutable' value."[107] On August 6, the Joint Economic Committee of Congress issued a report endorsing devaluation, further increasing a speculative fever that forced foreign central banks during the next week to absorb $3.7 billion.[108] "We were on the brink of a market panic that willy-nilly would force us off gold," Volcker recalled. "If we were going to take the initiative suspending the convertibility of dollars for gold and present it as the first step of a considered and constructive reform package, the decision could not wait until September. I called Connally and told him so."[109] Connally received Volcker's call on August 12 as he began his Texas vacation. Returning immediately, Connally was back in the White House for the afternoon meeting that persuaded Nixon to "pack up the key people" and take them secretly to Camp David.[110]

---

[104] Forbord, "Abandonment of Bretton Woods," 260.

[105] Ibid., 255.

[106] *Wall Street Journal*, July 29, 1971, 1.

[107] Ibid., Aug. 5, 1971, 1.

[108] Ibid., Aug. 9, 1971, 3; Coombs, *Arena of International Finance*, 215; "Action Now to Strengthen the Dollar," Joint Economic Committee, Report (Aug. 1971).

[109] Volcker and Gyohten, *Changing Fortunes*, 76.

[110] *Haldeman Diaries*, Aug. 12, 1971.

The next morning, only hours before the helicopters took off for the mountains, Charles Coombs of the New York Federal Reserve was in Volcker's office, making a last plea to keep open the gold window and save Bretton Woods. Interrupting the meeting to take a call, Coombs returned, despondent. The British had just asked to exchange $3 billion of their reserves for U.S. gold, Coombs reported. In fact, the British had not asked for gold but for a routine guarantee of the dollars they were holding against loss in case the United States devalued. The United States offered to cover $750 million instead of the $3 billion requested, and the British accepted. "The message to Coombs had apparently gotten a bit garbled," Volcker wrote later.[111] Connally left for Camp David, therefore, fortified with misinformation to confirm his belief that foreigners were out to screw us unless we screwed them first.

Coombs, who had charge of international monetary transactions for the Federal Reserve System, later denied the existence of any crisis that August. No central bank was asking for appreciable quantities of U.S. gold, and none was likely to make the request that would topple the system. Said Coombs, "despite monetary hysteria in the markets, the foreign central banks displayed a remarkable degree of coolness and forbearance."[112] Though Combs might have been right, his implicit conclusion that Bretton Woods could have survived for a prolonged period was not. Volatile short-term capital movements had made fixed exchange rates increasingly difficult to defend and would have broken the system sooner or later. Nixon closed the gold window when he did not only because he thought he had to but because he wanted to. It was his opening move in a historic offensive to correct the overvalued dollar and reorder the trading world to serve his political purposes. Breaking with the liberal premises of postwar U.S. foreign economic policy, he had adopted the mercantilist paradigm, which he hoped would keep the United States number one and help rally a New Majority in '72.

---

[111] Coombs, *Arena of International Finance*, 218; Forbord, "Abandonment of Bretton Woods," 228–229; Volcker and Gyohten, *Changing Fortunes*, 77; Brandon, *Retreat of American Power*, 224–226. Quote, Volcker and Gyohten.

[112] Coombs, *Arena of International Finance*, 215.

## Chapter 6

# Camp David

---

### I

On Friday, August 13, 1971, William Safire, one of Nixon's speech writers, found himself spirited off by helicopter to the president's retreat at Camp David for purposes unknown. Safire asked his seatmate on the trip, Herbert Stein, what was up. "This could be the most important weekend in the history of economics since March 4, 1933," Stein replied. "We're closing the banks?" Safire joked. "Hardly," Stein said. "But I would not be surprised if the President were to close the gold window." Safire, who did not know what the gold window was, asked Stein how to explain it to a layman. "I wouldn't try," Stein shouted over the whirr of the blades. "That's why you're along."[1]

At 3:15 P.M., when Nixon called for order in the living room of his Camp David cabin, eleven men took their seats. Connally, Shultz, Mc-Cracken, Peterson, Stein, and Volcker were there, as well as Haldeman, Ehrlichman, and Safire of the White House staff, and Arthur Burns, only weeks before victim of a White House smear. Though important foreign policy issues would be considered that weekend, neither Secretary of State William Rogers nor National Security Adviser Henry Kissinger attended: Rogers, because Nixon usually excluded State from crucial decisions; Kissinger, because he had little interest in international economics and was leaving the next day for secret negotiations in Paris with the North Vietnamese. Sitting at Nixon's right, Connally was clearly the man in charge. Connally was the quarterback of the team, Nixon would say later. "I was more like the coach."[2] Nixon opened by enjoining strictest secrecy and briefly surveying the issues.[3] Connally, taking over, then led a discussion of nearly four hours, which everyone in the room believed would make his-

---

[1] William Safire, *Before the Fall* (1975), 510.

[2] *Time* (Aug. 30, 1971), 6.

[3] The sources for this meeting are Safire's notes, extensively excerpted in *Before the Fall*, 511–518; Haldeman's long diary entry for August 13; and Haldeman's handwritten notes.

tory. The responsibility was "sobering," Safire remembered. "It was also more fun than any of the men there had ever had in their lifetimes."[4]

Camp David was an unusual way to conduct the government's business. The agenda had emerged mainly from the private conversations of Nixon and Connally. The regular departments were excluded; the usual staff work had not been completed; and everything had to be decided in two days, leaving scant time for analysis. Despite the gravity of the issues, Nixon cared less for the particulars of the decisions he would make than for the image of action they would project, action that he would dramatize at the climax of the weekend in a televised speech to restore his leadership and dispel the gloom enveloping his administration. The group at Camp David "acquired the attitude of scriptwriters preparing a TV special to be broadcast on Sunday evening," Stein recalled. "The announcement — the performance — was everything. It had to be as dramatic and smooth as possible, with no loose ends trailing. But it was not regarded as a step in the continuing process of government. After the special, regular programming would be resumed."[5]

Connally began by ticking off in summary fashion the elements of the new program, each of which he had publicly said the president would not do. To cool inflation, a freeze on prices and wages. To stimulate the economy and reduce unemployment, a series of tax cuts for business and individuals. To "attack the root cause of the dollar problem," close the gold window and impose a 10 percent border tax on imports.[6] As others would note, the elements of the package cohered. Tax cuts would stimulate demand, and the international measures would raise prices — together justifying a price-wage freeze of three-month duration to counter these new inflationary pressures.

The freeze was the least debated feature of the program, though no administration had ever before imposed price and wage controls in peacetime, and many in the room regarded the freeze with repugnance. "What worries me," Nixon said, "is putting the economy in a strait jacket under the control of a bunch of damn bureaucrats for any length of time."[7] The purpose of the freeze was to puncture the inflationary expectations sus-

---

[4] Safire, *Before the Fall*, 522.

[5] Herbert Stein, *Presidential Economics*, 2d rev. ed. (1988), 176–177.

[6] *Haldeman Diaries*, Aug. 13, 1971.

[7] Safire, *Before the Fall*, 516. On staff work for the freeze in the days before August 15, Robert H. Peritt, Jr. and Robert C. Dresser, "Policy Planning," in Office of Economic Stabilization, *Historical Working Papers on the Economic Stabilization Program* (1974), 17–18.

taining cost-push inflation. The problem of the freeze, as Shultz said, was "how do you stop it when you start?"[8] That crucial question got short shrift. The president's men decided that there would be time enough during the ninety-day freeze to design the next phase of controls, probably a voluntary wage-price review board. Recalled Stein, "The imposition of the freeze was a jump off the diving board without any clear idea of what lay below."[9]

The improvisational style of Camp David was evident in the package of fiscal measures adopted there. To stimulate the economy, Connally proposed a series of tax cuts that included reinstating the investment tax credit for business, canceled at Nixon's request in 1969; advancing by a year tax reductions already scheduled for individuals in 1973; and repealing the 7 percent excise tax on the sale of new cars. "For every 100,000 cars we don't sell," Connally said, getting carried away, "we lose 20,000 jobs."[10] In 1969 Nixon had fought to rescue the revenues from a tax-cutting Congress so he could do good works. Now, to advance his reelection, he would give away the revenues himself.

But there was a problem. Connally's tax cuts would simulate the economy, but they would also bust Nixon's full-employment budget. Under the administration's self-imposed fiscal rule, expenditures must not exceed revenues that would be collected at full employment. To honor this rule, the conferees at Camp David decided to match tax cuts with expenditure reduction. This mix made some sense politically because it saved a balanced budget, but it made no sense economically because cuts in expenditures would cancel the stimulus of tax cuts. The fiscal package, however, was not what it appeared. Nixon expected, indeed hoped, that Congress would enact larger tax cuts than he would request, and he knew that most of the proposed spending reductions were either illusory or unlikely to win Congressional approval. If it treated his proposals as anticipated, Congress would choose deficit spending over his balanced fiscal package, which is what Nixon really wanted. How much stimulus did the economy need? How big should the deficit be? These matters went undiscussed at Camp David because no one there had done the necessary homework.[11] As for the balanced full-employment rule, it had lasted barely a year.

---

[8] Safire, *Before the Fall*, 516.
[9] Stein, *Presidential Economics*, 178.
[10] Safire, *Before the Fall*, 511.
[11] Ibid., 515; *Haldeman Diaries*, Aug. 15, 1971, For quote, Stein, *Presidential Economics*, 178.

Connally's international proposals provoked the only real debate at the Camp David meeting. McCracken noted a contradiction. On the one hand, the point of closing the gold window was to depreciate the dollar; on the other, the 10 percent import surcharge — or border tax — would reduce demand for imports, strengthening the dollar. "I know it's inconsistent; you are right," Connally acknowledged. "But the tax may make a change in the exchange rate possible," meaning that he would use the border tax as a weapon to force other countries into accepting the currency realignment he wanted.[12] Paul Volcker, who recoiled from the naked nationalism of the border tax, argued for holding it in reserve as a threat rather than deploying it at the onset. Nixon settled that argument himself. "The border tax is not too damned aggressive, just aggressive enough," he said.[13]

But the main event at Camp David featured Burns versus Connally on the subject of gold. In most respects, Camp David was Burn's vindication. Inside the White House in 1969, Burns had unsuccessfully fought Nixon's decision to repeal the pro-business investment tax credit. Now Nixon would seek to reinstate it. More recently Burns had urged both price controls and tax cuts, and Camp David was nothing if not Nixon's admission that Burns was right on both counts. But Burns fought a losing battle to keep open the gold window. Burns had the typical central banker's faith in the importance of gold as a bulwark against inflation, and he believed that the ruthlessness of closing the gold window without first warning the Allies would damage multilateral cooperation and perhaps inspire a protectionist backlash against the United States. McCracken once said of Burns that if he "wants to give a performance worthy of Sophocles, he can do it."[14] At Camp David, on behalf of gold, he did.[15] Burns's main point was that the president's other measures would probably render closing the gold window unnecessary. "You will be doing something dramatic," said Burns, addressing Nixon, "wage and price policy, a border tax. You will order a cutback in government spending. These major actions will electrify the world. The gold outflow will cease. If I'm wrong, you can close the gold window later." Safire's notes recorded the ensuing discussion.[16]

---

[12] Safire, *Before the Fall*, 513.

[13] Ibid., 515.

[14] McCracken interview in Erwin C. Hargrove and Samuel A. Morley, eds., *The President and the Council of Economic Advisers* (1984), 352.

[15] For Burns quotes in this paragraph and the following long exchange, Safire, *Before the Fall*, 513–515.

[16] *Haldeman Diaries*, Aug. 13, 1971.

THE PRESIDENT: If we do all these things, speculators may say, "Next, they'll close the gold window," and there would be a run.

BURNS: Then you would close the gold window. What's to lose by waiting?

CONNALLY: What's our immediate problem? We are meeting here because we are in trouble overseas. The British came in today to ask us to cover $3 billion, all their dollar reserves. Anybody can topple us — anytime they want — we have left ourselves completely exposed.

BURNS: But all the other countries know we have never acted against them. The good will . . .

CONNALLY: We'll go broke getting their good will.

VOLCKER: I hate to do this, to close the window. All my life I have defended exchange rates, but I think it is needed.

CONNALLY: So the other countries don't like it, so what?

BURNS: They can retaliate.

CONNALLY: Let 'em. What can they do?

BURNS: They're powerful. They're proud, just as we are . . .

CONNALLY: We don't have a chance unless we do it. Our assets are going out by the bushel basket. You're in the hands of the money changers. You can see the result of this action will put us in a more competitive position.

BURNS: May I speak up for the "money changers"? The central bankers are important to you. They would be pleased at this action, short of closing the window.

In the course of the debate, Burns shrewdly played on Nixon's fears of political injury if he quit the gold standard. The public would condemn him for abandoning gold and for devaluing the dollar, Burns said. *Pravda* would hail these developments as a sign of disintegrating capitalism. The stock market might crash. "It will be exploited by the politicians, hated by business and financial people," he said. Nixon, who had gone to Camp David prepared to close the gold window, was shaken. "The media will be vicious," he said. "I can see it now: 'He's devalued the dollar.'" Volcker had a thought. "There's a certain public sentiment about a cross of gold," he said. The president grimaced. "Bryan ran four times and lost," he said.[17]

When the meeting broke up at 7:00 P.M. for dinner, Burns stayed be-

---

[17] Safire, *Before the Fall*, 514–515.

hind to make a last plea for gold and also to tell the president he would back him whatever he decided.[18] With that pledge, Burns gave Nixon what he wanted from Camp David above all. Burns was back on the team. As Nixon told some of his advisers that weekend, Burns was getting so much from the program "he can't run to the Hill and piss on it."[19] That night, alone in his cabin while the others dined together, Nixon called Safire on the phone. "You know," said the president, "Arthur is a fine man. Really, a fine man. Tell him I said that." As for gold, Nixon now leaned toward Burns.[20]

Nixon was the principal writer for his most important speeches. Few would be more important than the speech he would give at the conclusion of this weekend. He began composing at 3:00 A.M. on Saturday, awakened Haldeman by phone at 4:30 to read him choice passages, and called again at 8:40 with the instruction that Safire should preserve his "gutsy rhetoric" and to report that he was now leaning again to Connally's view of gold — "take the risk and take the heat." He was clearly pleased with his night's work. "This'll put the Democrats in a hell of a spot, this whole speech," he said.[21] That afternoon he decided finally to close the gold window. Nobody asked what kind of monetary system he envisioned to replace the one now being interred, and nobody knew. As Safire said, "we were winging it."[22]

Saturday afternoon Nixon met with the subcommittees assigned to wrap up the details. By dinner it was all finished. At 9:00 P.M. Haldeman, Ehrlichman, and OMB's Caspar Weinberger went to Nixon's cabin to talk politics. The night was hot, but they found the president by the fire in an otherwise darkened room "in one of his sort of mystic moods," Haldeman noted. The president said that, as the second Roosevelt had done, they had to raise the spirit of the country. Change the spirit, he said, "and then the economy could take off like hell." "Let America never accept being second best," he said. "We must try to be what it is in our power to be."[23]

At 9:00 P.M. Sunday, August 15, 1971, back at the White House, Nixon

---

[18] Ibid., 515.

[19] E-Notes, Aug. 14, 1971.

[20] Safire, *Before the Fall*, 519. On Nixon leaning to Burns, *Haldeman Diaries*, Aug. 13, 1971.

[21] *Haldeman Diaries*, Aug. 14, 1971.

[22] Safire, *Before the Fall*, 522.

[23] *Haldeman Diaries*, Aug. 14, 1971.

went on television to deliver a historic speech. Though hesitant to preempt the popular Western *Bonanza,* he felt he had to make his announcement before the markets opened on Monday morning.[24] Masterful as an exercise in rhetoric, the speech accomplished Nixon's purpose of seizing the offensive and appearing in command. To achieve prosperity without war, he said, the "time has come for a new economic policy for the United States." Outlining his fiscal measures, the president proposed cutting taxes to create jobs and cutting expenditures to restrain inflation. Calling inflation "one of the cruelest legacies of the false prosperity" created by the Vietnam war, he announced a ninety-day freeze of prices and wages and asked corporations to freeze dividends. The real genius of the speech was to turn the closing of the gold window from defeat into victory. Nixon accomplished this by blaming the plight of the dollar not on U.S. monetary and fiscal policies but on an alleged all-out war against the dollar by unnamed "international money speculators." To defend the dollar against these enemies, Nixon announced that he was suspending "temporarily the convertibility of the dollar into gold or other reserve assets." In an attempt at demystification, he said, "Let me lay to rest the bugaboo of what is called devaluation." Foreign cars and trips abroad would cost more. "But if you are among the overwhelming majority of Americans who buy American-made products in America, your dollar will be worth just as much tomorrow as it is today." Unfortunately, this was not true.

In discussing the 10 percent import tax, Nixon shifted the target from money speculators to friendly nations, whose "unfair exchange rates" he called a major reason for America's eroding trade balance. "When the unfair treatment is ended" he said, "the import tax will end as well." As a result of America's help, the industrial nations of Europe and Asia had regained vitality and become "our strong competitors." It was now time for them to assume their fair share of the burdens of the common defense, establish fair exchange rates, and play by equitable trading rules. "There is no longer any need for the United States to compete with one hand tied behind her back," he said. He intended his new economic program "to help us snap out of the self-doubt, the self-disparagement that saps our energy and erodes our confidence" and accept the challenge to stay "number one in the world's economy."[25]

---

[24] Stein, *Presidential Economics,* 177.
[25] *Pub Paps RN 1971,* 886–890.

## II

How would the headlines read? Nixon wondered. "Would it be 'Nixon Acts Boldly'? Or would it be, 'Nixon Changes Mind'?"[26] After all, only months before John Connally had solemnly proclaimed that the administration would not impose wage-price controls, cut taxes, or devalue the dollar. Now Nixon was proposing to do them all. As it turned out, doing things he said he would never do proved wildly popular. On August 16, staging a Nixon Rally, the stock market jumped thirty-two points, the largest one-day gain in history to date.[27] "Prez Changes Economic Game Plan," Variety headlined. "New Score Is Dow 32, Nixon 72."[28] In another of his dazzling performances, John Connally briefed the press that afternoon on the New Economic Policy — or simply the NEP — a label that the administration learned to its embarrassment Lenin had used first. "There's nothing, as the wise saying goes, there's nothing constant except change," Connally said. "The American people would think they have a dope for a President if they had one that they thought would take a position and never change it."[29]

At a cabinet meeting that same day, Nixon recounted the drama of the weekend, and Burns delivered a little speech saying that Nixon had "electrified the nation" and "given a tremendous lift of confidence to business and financial leaders."[30] White House aides, calling influentials around the country, did indeed encounter enthusiasm bordering on euphoria. Alfred Sindlinger, Nixon's favorite pollster, conducted a telephone survey and reported that 75 percent backed the president's program. "In all the years I've been doing this business — more than 15 — I've never seen anything this unanimous," Sidlinger said, "unless maybe it was Pearl Harbor."[31] Nixon, said the banker Gabriel Hauge, had "lanced the boil of pessimism."[32]

Support was not quite unanimous. Liberal Democrats and conservative Republicans both expressed degrees of opposition, though for different reasons. Stunned by Nixon's appropriation of their best issue, Democrats sought to recover by attacking the NEP on grounds of equity. Freezing

---

[26] RN: Memoirs (1978), 520.
[27] New York Times, Aug. 17, 1971, 47.
[28] Quoted in New York Times, Aug. 22, 1971, IV, 1.
[29] New York Times, Aug. 17, 1971, 1.
[30] H-Notes, Aug. 16, 1971.
[31] Wall Street Journal, Aug. 17, 1971, 3.
[32] Hauge quoted in "The New Economic Policy," Fortune (Vol. 84, Sept. 1971), 65.

prices and wages was fine, but what about interest, dividends, and profits? Creating jobs was worthy, but why then, in the name of economy, did the president promise to cut employment in the federal government?"[33] Cutting taxes to stimulate the economy was needed, but Nixon's cuts offered "raw meat for business," while "the consumer gets little more than a soup bone."[34]

More disappointed in the NEP than any Democrat was Milton Friedman, who had only recently praised the president for his steadfast adherence to gradualism. Amid his crowded calendar on August 16, Nixon asked Shultz to call Friedman "and try to soothe him a bit by pointing out the realities of our declaring a wage-price freeze," and to tell him that because the Democrats were going to impose permanent wage-price controls, it "was imperative that the President beat them to the punch with a temporary move."[35] Unpersuaded by this doubtful defense, Friedman savaged the wage-price freeze in his *Newsweek* column of August 30. "Sooner or later, and the sooner the better," he said, "it will end as all previous attempts to freeze prices and wages have ended, from the time of the Roman Emperor Diocletian to the present, in utter failure and the emergence into the open of the suppressed inflation."[36]

But it was precisely the freeze that was the main reason for the NEP's initial popularity. In fact, only one interest group in America opposed the freeze — union labor. Everybody knew the real purpose of the freeze. It was to halt the excessive wage settlements driving up cost-push inflation. That was why corporations cheered the freeze and why the unions might well kill it. At Camp David, Shultz expected the worst. "A freeze will stop when labor blows it up with a strike," he said. "Don't worry about getting rid of it — labor will do that for you."[37] Whether the unions killed it or not, the freeze placed Nixon at odds with labor, derailing his cherished plans to build a New Majority. Forced to choose between his short-term goal of surviving in 1972 and his long-term goal of party realignment, Nixon could only choose survival.

---

[33] *New York Times*, Aug. 22, 1971, 1.

[34] "The President's New Economic Program," Joint Economic Committee, hearings (1971), 5.

[35] H-Notes, Aug. 16, 1971; Haldeman to Shultz, Aug. 16, 1971, Chron file, SMOF: Haldeman.

[36] *Newsweek* (Aug. 30, 1971), 22.

[37] Safire, *Before the Fall*, 516.

Assuming that Nixon would never impose price-wage controls, George Meany, the seventy-seven-year-old president of the AFL-CIO, had recently endorsed a freeze on condition "that the sacrifice was equal to everybody concerned."[38] Once Nixon did the unthinkable, Meany condemned the freeze on grounds of equity. Freezing wages but not dividends, interest, or profits, Meany said, was "Robin Hood in reverse, robbing the poor to pay the rich."[39] (In fact the administration had statutory authority only to control prices, wages, salaries, and rents.) A few days into the freeze, the administration deepened its rift with labor by ruling that 1.3 million workers scheduled to receive previously negotiated wage increases during the freeze could not receive them. If the administration "wants war, it can have war," United Auto Workers President Leonard Woodcock warned.[40]

Meeting with Connally and Charles Colson on August 17, Nixon decided to fight back. They would attack Meany on the grounds that he "was the one who asked for wage and price control to begin with, that it was dishonest and hypocritical for him now to attack us on it."[41] Later that day Connally charged that Meany was "out of step" with labor's rank and file, and Labor Secretary James Hodgson weighed in with a similar blast.[42] Open war, it appeared, had broken out. When Shultz and Hodgson went to AFL-CIO headquarters to explain the president's program, one official told Shultz, "When you take your ass out of here, get measured for a pair of tin pants because you are going to need them."[43] Despite all the angry talk, the unions bowed to the popularity of the freeze, deciding to save their big guns for the inevitable battle over Phase II of the controls program. Once the unions acquiesced in the freeze, the only question became whether it would work.

A wage-price freeze was a blunt instrument capable of much damage. A freeze would lock in some prices and wages that needed to be raised, abrogate contracts, and prevent the price system from allocating resources efficiently. Nonetheless, this freeze succeeded. For one thing, it was simple.

---

[38] New York Times, July 12, 1971, 1.

[39] Newsweek (Sept. 6, 1971), 46.

[40] New York Times, Aug. 19, 1971, 1; Arnold Weber and Daniel J. B. Mitchell, The Pay Board's Progress: Wage Controls in Phase II (1978), 5. Congress subsequently authorized payment retroactively of most wage increases lost as a result of the freeze.

[41] Haldeman Diaries, Aug. 17, 1971.

[42] New York Times, Aug. 18, 1971, 1.

[43] Quoted Joseph C. Gouldner, Meany (1972), 428.

The Cost of Living Council (COLC), which Nixon appointed from among administration officials to oversee the program, froze everything except raw foods and imported goods and then ignored the numberless appeals for relief. Employing minimal enforcement machinery, the administration relied mainly on voluntary compliance, which it got. During the three months of the freeze, the Consumer Price Index rose at an annual rate of 1.6 percent, compared to 4.0 percent in the six preceding months. Average hourly compensation for labor rose by 0.6 percent, annual rate, against 6.2 percent.[44] It helped that pressure on prices was diminishing anyway and that the freeze ended in the nick of time. As Arnold Weber, who served as executive director of the COLC, reported, "the difficulty of sustaining uniform general policies increased geometrically as the freeze progressed. By the end of the 90 days, the COLC was running out of thumbs to plug the dike."[45] Though Nixon reaped the political benefits of the freeze, he himself stayed aloof from the whole business, except to ask on one occasion whether it was necessary to freeze the salaries of pro football players. Assured that it was, he said, "I guess you're right. But whatever you decide to do, leave me out of it."[46]

What would the administration do for an encore? This had been one of the great unanswered questions of Camp David, though the general assumption had been that some kind of voluntary wage-price review board might succeed the freeze. By the time Herbert Stein assumed leadership of a task force to plan Phase II of controls in September 1971, a quick return to the market was no longer politically feasible. "The freeze had instantly become the most popular economic action of government that anyone could remember," Stein recalled. "There was widespread public rejoicing that at last the government was protecting the people."[47] The administration concluded that it had no choice except to devise a comprehensive, mandatory controls system, complete with complex rules and bureaucrats to administer them. Stein, the public official, now found himself drafting a controls program that Stein, the economist, utterly detested.

Once again the overriding question was the attitude of organized labor.

---

[44] Arnold Weber, *In Pursuit of Price Stability: The Wage-Price Freeze of 1971* (1973), 34.

[45] Weber, *In Pursuit of Price Stability*, 83.

[46] Ibid., 21–22 (footnote).

[47] Herbert Stein, "Price-Fixing as Seen by a Price-Fixer: Part II, " in William Fellner, ed., *Contemporary Economic Problems* (1978), 113–135. On planning Phase II, Peritt and Dresser, "Policy Planning," 22–24.

"No program works without labor cooperation," Nixon said.[48] On September 10, Nixon, Stein, and other administration officials met with a delegation of labor leaders to negotiate the next phase of controls. By Meany's account, the president began with "soothing words about wanting to tell labor his long-standing plans." Meany raised his hand to interrupt. "If you are going down the route of government control, we'll fight you," he said. Meany stated his nonnegotiable demand. "We told them we would suggest the establishment of an independent voluntary agency free from government control, of a tripartite nature, similar to the Wage Labor Board of World War II." Anything else would be "the first step toward fascism."[49] Meany's terms shaped the proposal for Phase II, which Stein presented to Nixon on October 5, 1971.[50] Nixon remarked to Stein on receiving it, "It's a good thing it is we who are doing this because if this baby seems to be getting too strong we can strangle it in the cradle." Observed Stein, "But of course we couldn't."[51]

In a televised speech on October 7, Nixon unveiled a Phase II crafted to Meany's specification. Meany cared nothing about how prices were controlled, everything about wage controls. Therefore, Nixon created two separate entities: the Price Commission to control prices, and the Pay Board to control wages. All seven members of the Price Commission would represent the public interest, but the fifteen members of the Pay Board would consist of five each from labor, business, and the public. In this way labor would have a hand in its own regulation. Nixon threw Meany additional concessions in the form of a Government Committee on Interest and Dividends to monitor these areas and promised that the Price Commission would roll back the prices of firms earning "excess profits." As soon as the country no longer needed controls, Nixon said, he would get rid of them.[52]

Meany was not satisfied. In a press briefing after the president's speech, Stein said that the COLC, created to oversee the program, would retain residual authority over the Price Commission and Pay Board. Meany, who wanted total autonomy for the Pay Board, charged a double-cross and

---

[48] H-Notes, Oct. 12, 1971.
[49] Quoted in Gouldner, *Meany*, 432.
[50] Stein for Staff Sec., Oct. 14, 1971, White House Staff Memos: Huntsman, SMOF: McCracken (Summary of Oct. 5 meeting).
[51] Stein interview in Kenneth Thompson, ed., *The Nixon Presidency* (1987), 181–182.
[52] *Pub Paps RN 1971*, 1022–1026.

threatened to walk.[53] Preferring appeasement to war, Nixon initialed a memo on October 11, which Shultz and Hodgson personally delivered to Meany, effectively granting both the Pay Board and Price Commission full independence to make decisions on individual prices and wages.[54]

With the ninety-day freeze set to expire on November 13, 1971, there remained little more than a month to appoint members of the Pay Board and Price Commission, recruit staff, and formulate rules for Phase II. On Shultz's recommendation, Nixon appointed C. Jackson Grayson, dean of Southern Methodist University's business school and an accountant, as chair of the Price Commission. Grayson later confessed, "my knowledge of economics and past price controls programs was abysmal."[55] No plausible candidate wanted the job of heading the Pay Board, which contained built-in labor opposition, including Meany himself. Desperate, the administration gave the job to a sixty-seven-year old federal judge named George H. Boldt, an amiable man with no qualifications except his friendship with John Ehrlichman's family in Seattle. Asked why he was appointed, Boldt replied, "I haven't the foggiest."[56] Under tremendous time pressure, the Price Commission and Pay Board worked in a fever to frame their separate regulations for achieving Nixon's announced goal of an inflation rate of 2 or 3 percent by the end of 1972.

Things went badly for Judge Boldt and the Pay Board from the start. Convinced that Nixon had stacked the deck against labor with his appointments of the Board's public members, Meany barely spoke to them.[57] On November 8, 1971, when the Board met to conclude its rancorous discussion of Phase II wage regulations, Meany sat sullenly in an overcoat until placated by a warmer room. That meeting produced a compromise guideline calling for annual increases in labor compensation of 5.5 percent—2.5 percent for anticipated inflation, plus 3 percent for an anticipated increase in productivity. (The guideline was later increased to 6.2 percent.) On one point the Board sharply divided. With the five labor members opposed, the Pay Board majority voted to deny workers retroactive payment of wage increases that had been scheduled to take place during the freeze but had been cancelled by the freeze. Less than $1 billion

[53] *New York Times*, Oct. 8, 1971, 1.
[54] Weber and Mitchell, *Pay Board's Progress*, 20–21.
[55] C. Jackson Grayson, Jr., *Confessions of a Price Controller* (1974), 9.
[56] *Time* (Nov. 1, 1971), 30.
[57] Quoted in Gouldner, *Meany*, 438.

was at stake, but labor considered retroactive payment a matter of principle.[58] "They have abrogated our contracts," Meany said before departing by train for Bal Harbor, Florida, and the opening of the AFL-CIO annual convention on November 18, 1971.[59]

Though Nixon had been invited to address this convention, he felt that he would be casting "pearls before swine" and did not want to go. But Shultz, Ehrlichman, and Charles Colson thought that if he faced down his labor antagonists like "Daniel into the Lion's Den," he would score a major public-relations coup.[60] So at the last minute, Nixon agreed to speak. Relegating Nixon to a spot on the program's second day, Meany himself opened the convention before a thousand cheering delegates with a long harangue, presenting a distorted history of the Pay Board and charging the administration with a "crackdown of labor." Labor's position on the Pay Board, he said, would be one of noncooperation until the sanctity of contracts was upheld. "If the president doesn't like the terms we lay down here, let him kick us off."[61]

By now convinced that his two-year courtship of Meany was hopeless, Nixon decided to cast the sometime plumber from the Bronx, with his beefy jowls, big black cigar, and cranky demeanor, as the foil in his battle for the NEP. Meany played his assigned role with relish. For Nixon's appearance at the Americana Hotel, Meany banned TV cameras, canceled "Hail to the Chief," and provided the president with a one-sentence introduction.[62] His voice shaky,[63] Nixon said he would discard his prepared text and speak "straight from the shoulder."[64] The delegates laughed when he called the freeze "a remarkable success," and they groaned when he suggested they ask their wives if they doubted him.[65] Defiantly Nixon told them that he had an obligation to make the stabilization program work "and to the extent that my power allows it, I shall do exactly that." His speech concluded, Nixon began shaking hands with the delegates — until

---

[58] Weber and Mitchell, *Pay Board's Progress*, chap. 2.
[59] *New York Times*, Nov. 9, 1971, 1.
[60] *Haldeman Diaries*, Nov. 17, 1971.
[61] Meany's speech quoted extensively in Gouldner, *Meany*, 439, 445. For "kick labor off" quote, *New York Times*, Nov. 19, 1971, 1; A. H. Raskin, "George Meany's Way Isn't the President's," *New York Times Magazine*, Jan. 23, 1972, 10 ff.
[62] *Haldeman Diaries*, Nov. 19, 1971; Gouldner, *Meany*, 446.
[63] *Time* (Nov. 29, 1971), 29.
[64] *Pub Paps RN 1971*, 1118–1125.
[65] *New York Times*, Nov. 20, 1971, 1.

Meany gaveled for order and hustled him out of the room. "We will now proceed with Act II," Meany said.[66] If Nixon had been play-acting, so had Meany, who had no intention of boycotting the Pay Board, at least not yet.

Amid these theatrics, Phase II, which commenced on November 14, 1971, faced its first test. The Pay Board had established a guideline of 5.5 percent for annual compensation negotiated in new labor contracts, but hundreds of thousands of workers were scheduled to receive more generous raises under contracts already negotiated. The Pay Board decided to challenge only those increases that failed the test of reason. In its first case the Pay Board undermined all credibility by voting 10 to 5 to approve a grossly unreasonable 17.5 percent increase in hourly compensation for bituminous coal miners in West Virginia, negotiated by the union and the coal companies literally on the eve of Phase II.[67] The coal companies immediately turned to the Price Commission for permission to raise coal prices and recover the costs. Under its regulations, which related price increases to cost increases, the Price Commission could have granted the full request, which is what the White House wanted it to do.[68] But the Price Commission declared its independence from the Pay Board and indeed from the rest of the administration by cutting the companies' price request nearly in half, forcing them to eat a chunk of the wage settlement.[69] "We have to stop somewhere," said Price Commission chair Jack Grayson.[70] The public, which opposed higher coal prices, indeed opposed higher prices for anything, applauded Grayson for saving Phase II at birth.

As a matter of policy, Phase II was not really worth saving. Observed the Yale economist James Tobin, "The administration has undertaken an adventure in a controlled economy that is designed to diminish the rate of inflation from 4% plus to 3% minus per year. What are the great benefits of so modest a difference in the speed of inflation?"[71] Inflation was unwinding anyway. Controls could suppress the price level only temporarily. The program was so bafflingly complex that in the first two weeks, the Price Com-

---

[66] For Meany quote, *Time* (Nov. 29, 1971), 29; *New York Times*, Nov. 20, 1971, 1.

[67] Weber and Mitchell, *Pay Board's Progress*, 139–152.

[68] Grayson, *Confessions*, 12–14. For a discussion of Phase II regulations, Robert F. Lanzillotte, Mary T. Hamilton, and R. Blaine Roberts, *Phase II: The Price Commission* (1975), chap. 3.

[69] Price Commission News Release, Dec. 1, 1971, Wage-Price Freeze file, SMOF: Solomon; Grayson, *Confessions*, 97–100.

[70] *New York Times*, Dec. 5, 1971, IV, 2.

[71] *Business Week* (Nov. 13, 1971), 110.

mission received 400,000 requests for clarification.[72] And, as in all controls episodes, distortions and inefficiencies would hinder the business system, though clever lawyers would ingeniously twist the regulations to say pretty much what clients wanted. Such logic as there was in Phase II derived entirely from the political calculations of Richard Nixon.

## III

Politics was also the principal inspiration of the NEP's fiscal package. The Democrats had demanded an activist fiscal policy, so Nixon gave them one. The package was not what they had in mind, the Democrats countered, because it provided no net stimulus for the lagging economy. "I hope the President is kidding when he suggests that the tax cuts must be matched fully by Federal expenditure cuts and elimination of one in twenty of Federal workers," wrote Paul Samuelson.[73] "Such a recipe, taken literally would not add a single job." But Nixon was only kidding, as became clear when his proposed expenditure cuts evaporated without a trace. He called on Congress to save money by postponing enactment of revenue sharing and welfare reform, which would not pass that year anyway. He ordered a 5 percent reduction in federal employees by June 1972, which never happened. He proposed delaying a wage increase for federal employees, which Congress declined to do.[74] Soon all that was left of the fiscal package was the tax cuts, meaning that the economy would get that dose of deficit spending demanded by most Democrats and privately desired by the president.

While favoring tax reduction, liberal Democrats took issue with the particular cuts Nixon proposed. Nixon's cuts favored business. Democrats favored helping the nation's working people. For once disdaining subterfuge, the administration admitted that its tax proposals were indeed probusiness. Connally noted that profits had fallen by 10 percent during the last four years and now stood lower as a percentage of GNP than any time

---

[72] Grayson, *Confessions*, 89.

[73] *New York Times*, Aug. 22, 1971, III, 4.

[74] For a description of the administration's expenditure cuts, "Tax Proposals Contained in the President's New Economic Policy," Committee on Ways and Means, hearings (1971), 304. The administration's goal was to reduce federal employment this fiscal year by 66,000 jobs, as Shultz explained in "Tax Proposals." The actual reduction was 8,000, as revealed in U.S. Dept. of Labor, *Employment and Earnings* (July 1972), 50.

since 1938. In 1969 Nixon had sponsored a major tax bill that provided tax relief for individuals, while actually raising business taxes. The time had come to redress the balance, Connally said. Cutting taxes on business would increase profits, which in turn would increase investment and employment.[75] Despite liberal complaints, Congress passed Nixon's tax cuts substantially as he proposed them and even added a provision that legislated faster tax write-offs by business for losses from depreciation, something Nixon had tried to do more generously on his own earlier in the year, only to have his authority challenged in court. The combined effect of liberalized depreciation and a 7 percent investment tax credit produced a $5.4 billion tax cut for business during calendar 1972 — a reduction of approximately 12 percent. By contrast, individuals received a cut of only $3.2 billion. Add in $2.6 billion for repeal of the auto exise tax, and the total cut exceeded $11 billion.[76]

Nixon hoped that Congress would assist his reelection by cutting taxes even more than he requested and was disappointed in October 1971 when the House did not. No less disappointed, Paul McCracken complained to the president that Congress would probably not provide "the amount of fiscal stimulation for the economy we had counted on." Perhaps, McCracken speculated, the Democrats "may be coming to the view that action to pump up the economy helps the Administration more than it helps them." With recovery still sluggish, "if Congress moves to increase the size of the tax reduction package, we should not resist," McCracken said. "I agree," Nixon replied.[77] But the final tax bill that Congress passed in December provided slightly fewer cuts than Nixon had requested in August.

As it turned out, that was too much. Even as the government was preparing a remedy for a sluggish economy, the long-awaited boom, as yet undetected, had already begun. Real GNP was growing at a 6.6 percent annual rate during the last quarter of 1971, nearly double the previous quarter, and would keep gaining steam. Meanwhile, the full-employment

---

[75] "The President's New Economic Program," Joint Economic Committee, 7–16.

[76] Nixon had proposed an investment tax credit of 10 percent the first year and 5 percent thereafter. Congress enacted a straight 7 percent credit. Concerning liberalized depreciation, Congress legislated approximately half the amount Nixon had tried to provide on his own authority early in 1971. Wilbur Mills explained the final bill in *Cong Rec* (Dec. 9, 1971), 45852–45855. See *Congressional Quarterly Almanac 1971*, 440–456. Mills's estimates of tax cuts differs from CQ because CQ includes liberalized depreciation. Nixon's proposals would have cut business taxes by 20 percent, including his depreciation effort.

[77] McCracken for President, Oct. 19, 1971, President's Handwriting file, POF.

budget swung from virtual balance in calendar 1971 to a $8.4 billion deficit in 1972.[78] The timing was all wrong. Tax cuts and deficit spending were the last thing the economy needed now, but the deficit and the boom that it fed would help reelect Nixon, and that after all was the point.

## IV

The international component of the NEP was not only an incident of Nixon's reelection campaign but an attempt to force a fundamental shift in world power relations. Politically and economically America's postwar dominance was waning. Germany and Japan had emerged to challenge the United States in the world market, the nation's trade surplus had disappeared, and its balance of payments deficit had swollen to gargantuan proportions. Under stress from these developments, the Bretton Woods international monetary regime had become dysfunctional. According to the rules of that system, other nations were expected to maintain the value of their currencies in fixed relation to the dollar. The dollar had ceasd to be worth as much as fixed exchange rates said it was, obligating the Germans and the Japanese, especially, to undertake expensive — and inflationary — currency transactions in defense of existing parities. Everyone regretted the resulting disequilibrium in the world trade and payments system, but no one could summon the will to correct it.

The problem was that the overvalued dollar conferred costs and benefits in approximately equal measure on surplus and deficit countries alike. For the United States, the overvalued dollar hurt exports by pricing them high, which was bad, but it lowered the price of imports, foreign investments, and foreign wars, which was good. For surplus countries, principally Germany and Japan, the overvalued dollar meant low prices for exports to America, providing a competitive advantage to powerful export industries. That was good. But the resulting inflow of dollars with no place to go had the effect of inflating local currencies. That was bad. Every country resented the costs of disequilibrium, but none wished to give up its benefits. The man who broke the impasse was John Connally.

Taking a fresh look at monetary and trade arrangements, Connally had come to the conclusion that the costs of the current system to the United

---

[78] For the CEA's preliminary estimate of calendar 1972 full-employment deficit and a discussion of the effects of overwithholding that year, CEA *Annual Report 1973*, 41. I use revised estimate of full-employment deficit in CEA *Annual Report 1976*, 55.

States had long since exceeded the benefits. Like the president, Connally's chief concern was domestic unemployment, a concern intensified during 1971 by the lingering effects of the recent recession and the approach of an election year. The point of trade and monetary arrangements, Connally believed, must be to expand U.S. exports, hence creating new jobs for Americans. To achieve his mercantilist ends, he would seek to change the rules of the game and break down barriers to U.S. goods in foreign markets. The allies, he knew, would resist him, and conventional diplomatic negotiations would fail to bring them around. Therefore, to get his way he would have to create a crisis. On August 15, 1971, Nixon effectively declared economic warfare against his astonished allies by closing the gold window unilaterally and imposing a 10 percent border tax on imports, throwing world money markets into turmoil and threatening allied prosperity. Connally never doubted that his offensive would succeed, provided the country gave him time. Because of the size and relative self-sufficiency of its economy, the United States would feel the effects of the crisis much less than the others and only had to wait until they were forced to sue for peace on his terms.

Connally could embark on his remarkable offensive because he had the confidence of Richard Nixon. But there were limits on how far the president would permit Connally to go, as he implied in a conversation with Henry Kissinger and Peter Peterson on August 27, 1971. His first priority was the domestic economy, Nixon said, and the second was "international affairs . . . Then and only then do we worry about the international monetary situation."[79] In other words, if Connally's efforts should conflict with his other objectives, the president would not hesitate to rein in his favorite minister.

On the day that Nixon announced the NEP, stock markets throughout Europe crashed, and currency markets closed. Meeting in Brussels on August 18, the economic ministers of the European Economic Community struggled to find common ground for defense against America's nationalist assault. That assault included not only closing the gold window and imposing the border tax, but a 10 percent cut in foreign aid, a new tax dodge for U.S. corporations to subsidize exports, and an investment tax credit that applied only to machinery made in America. Internally divided on countermeasures, the ministers departed Brussels without agreement, leaving

---

[79] *Haldeman Diaries*, Aug. 27, 1971.

each nation to grope through the debris of Bretton Woods as best it could. When currency markets reopened after a week, central bankers abandoned their obligation under Bretton Woods to defend fixed exchange rates and instead let their currencies float, within limits, against the dollar in the private currency markets.[80] Connally's moves had forced an unwilling and unprepared Europe into uncharted waters.

Connally's chief target was Japan, the nation running the largest trade surplus with the United States. On July 15, Nixon had undercut the basis of Japan's foreign policy with the surprise announcement of his forthcoming visit to the People's Republic of China. On August 15, ten minutes before Nixon knocked the props from under the Japanese economy, Secretary of State William Rogers phoned Premier Sato to suggest he listen to another speech by the president. "Not again," said Sato, shaking his head.[81] Japanese stocks tumbled on news of the gold window, and Japanese pride was wounded when U.S. emissaries, sent abroad to explain the NEP, conspicuously omitted Tokyo from their itinerary. Japan knew what the Americans wanted anyway. They wanted revaluation of the yen, which would raise the price of Japanese goods in the U.S. market, help U.S. industries compete, and save blue-collar jobs in America.[82] Thus began the second Nixon Shock.

Japan was determined to resist. Only recently recovered from the devastating effects of World War II, the Japanese regarded their current prosperity as tenuous at best and their current trade surplus as merely temporary — a cushion against the next cycle of hard times. More dependent on the U.S. market than any European country, Japan clung to the fixed parity of 360 yen to the dollar for the advantage it provided to exports and as guarantor of stable trade relations in an otherwise turbulent commercial world. Japan's initial response to the American measures was to keep currency markets open and aggressively purchase dollars with yen to defend 360 to 1. In two weeks the Bank of Japan bought a staggering $3.4 billion, increasing its foreign reserves by 42 percent and inflating the money supply. On August 27, Japan abandoned the absurdly expensive effort to peg the yen and shifted to a managed float, which permitted the yen to drift up but

---

[80] *New York Times,* Aug. 17, 1971, 1; Aug. 20, 40; Aug. 21, 1; *Newsweek* (Aug. 30, 1971), 16–18.

[81] *Time* (Aug. 30, 1971), 17.

[82] *Manchester Guardian,* Aug. 18, 1971, 1.

under limits imposed by the Japanese government — a "dirty float" in the American vernacular. After three weeks of floating, the yen appreciated 6 percent against the dollar, far from the American goal of 25 percent.[83]

Connally first confronted his adversaries in mid-September at the regular meeting of the Group of Ten in Lancaster House, a nineteenth-century mansion near Buckingham Palace in London. The Group included the finance ministers and central bankers of the leading industrial nations — the United States, Germany, Japan, Britain, Canada, France, Italy, Belgium, Sweden, and the Netherlands. Many of the worldly politicians and bankers in this club, wrote the British journalist Henry Brandon, considered Connally "a figure out of an Edna Ferber novel, a character whose rascality they both admired and loathed."[84] Connally's performance in London did nothing to repair his image. "We were generous in our years of prosperity, and now we expect to be generous in sharing our problems," Connally said. "That's what friendships are for."[85] If the others wanted the United States to lift the 10 percent border tax, they would have to realign their currencies to effect dollar depreciation, remove obstacles to U.S. exports, and assume more of the financial burden for maintaining the common defense. The end result of these concessions, Connally said, must be a shift in the U.S. payments deficit from a deficit of $9 billion to a surplus of $4 billion — a huge $13 billion swing — to be accomplished almost entirely by an increase in U.S. merchandise exports, which is to say, by increasing U.S. employment at the expense of allied jobs. The number $13 billion, Connally warned, "isn't being produced as a negotiating figure, it states our position accurately."[86] "Intransigence," snapped Finance Minister Giscard d' Estaing of France as he stalked from one meeting.[87] "A severe setback," said the *Manchester Guardian* of the London meeting.[88]

By then everyone understood that some currency realignment would be the outcome of the current crises. There were two ways to accomplish this realignment. The United States could devalue the dollar by raising its gold price in official transactions from $35 an ounce to, say, $38 an ounce, or the

[83] Robert C. Angel, *Explaining Economic Policy Failure: Japan in the 1969–1971 International Monetary Crisis* (1991), preface, chap. 5.

[84] Henry Brandon, *The Retreat of American Power* (1973), 228.

[85] *Newsweek* (Sept. 27, 1971), 82.

[86] *Wall Street Journal*, Sept. 16, 1971, 2.

[87] *Newsweek*, (Sept. 27, 1971), 83.

[88] *Manchester Guardian*, Sept. 17, 1971, 10.

others could revalue their currencies upward while the dollar stood still. European leaders insisted that the United States devalue by raising the dollar price of gold. That way in the next election they could lay the blame for declining exports and employment in their home markets on the United States. The United States insisted that the gold price of the dollar remain unchanged and that the others revalue upward. In this way the United States would safeguard its prestige, reduce the monetary role of gold, and most important to Nixon, keep the issue out of the Democratic Congress, which would have to legislate any change in the gold price and which might use gold to hurt him. The debate between the United States and the allies over gold was not economic but political. Concerning the economic aspect of the argument, Milton Friedman wrote, "What conceivable difference can it make to the United States, or to other countries, if we don't sell gold to foreign governments at $35 an ounce or if we don't sell gold to them at $38 an ounce?"[89] It mattered not how the dollar was devalued so long as it was.

At the end of September, two weeks after the London meeting of the Group of Ten, Connally met his adversaries again in Washington at the annual meeting of the International Monetary Fund. Talk among the 2,500 delegates was all about the threat of a world recession and possible countermeasures by the allies against the United States. In his speech at this meeting, Connally was only slightly more conciliatory than he had been in London. He hinted at some flexibility in America's gold position and indicated that the United States would lift the border tax on two conditions — that the allies float their currencies freely to establish their real values prior to a realignment and that they make "tangible progress toward dismantling specific barriers to trade over coming weeks."[90] The others refused to negotiate trade issues under the gun of the U.S. border tax and were committed to dirty floats to prevent too steep a revaluation of their currencies. The deadlock hardly displeased Connally, who continued to believe that the longer the crisis went on, the stronger would be the U.S. position.

The continuing stalemate emboldened Connally's critics in the administration. Arthur Burns, for one, was campaigning to restore as much of the old order as possible. Committed to multilateral cooperation and free trade, he wanted to devalue the dollar by raising its gold price, establish new fixed exchange rates, and then reopen the gold window, rescind the border tax,

---

[89] *Newsweek* (Dec. 20, 1971), 83.
[90] Text of Connally's speech in Treasury press release, Sept. 30, 1971, IMF Meeting file, SMOF: McCracken; *Manchester Guardian*, Oct. 1, 1971, 1.

and settle the remaining issues through normal negotiations. Fearing that Connally's tactics might precipitate a trade war, Burns kept a log of threatened allied retaliations, which he showed to Nixon and, with better effect, to Kissinger.[91] If the United States did not settle soon, Burns believed, a world recession would result. Though he had promised Nixon his loyalty at Camp David, Burns once again made himself persona non grata at the White House by taking his case against Connally to Congress. Burns told one committee, "In my judgment, those who feel time is on our side and that we can be relaxed about the import surcharge, I have grave doubts about such views. In my judgment time is on nobody's side. What we should try to do is return to a viable international order for the sake of our economy and for the sake of harmonious political relations with the rest of the world."[92] Reporters asked Burns who might hold the views he criticized. "Foreigners," he winked.[93] "Arthur unbearable," Nixon said. "Need to knock him again."[94]

Shultz too challenged Connally's performance but for reasons quite different from Burns. Burns wanted to restore Bretton Woods. Shultz wanted to accomplish its total destruction. Like his mentor Milton Friedman, Shultz would abandon gold entirely for a monetary regime of floating exchange rates, in which private buyers and sellers would daily establish the true value of currencies in markets free of government intervention.[95] In Shultz's too-romantic view, exchange rate changes in a floating world would be effected gradually and smoothly, eliminating the periodic crises that had afflicted Bretton Woods. And governments could at last pursue their domestic objectives free of the requirement that they defend their currencies at some fixed rate. Nixon, who had spoken often of his desire for an entirely new monetary system, was prepared to back floating if Connally backed it too. In Shultz's view, Connally was more interested in short-run achievements than in long-run reconstruction and was subject to the baleful influence of his undersecretary for monetary affairs, Paul Volcker,[96] who, like Burns, wanted to save Bretton Woods. In an effort to educate Connally

---

[91] Henry Kissinger, *White House Years* (1978), 957; Odell, *U.S. International Monetary Policy*, 280.

[92] "Economic Stabilization," Banking and Currency Committee, House hearings (1971), 467.

[93] *Wall Street Journal*, Nov. 2, 1971, 3.

[94] H-Notes, Oct. 3, 1971.

[95] E-Notes, Oct. 25, 1971; *Haldeman Diaries*, Aug. 23, 1971.

[96] *Haldeman Diaries*, Oct. 12, 1971.

on floating, Shultz invited him to his home one evening late in September for a one-on-one session with Friedman himself.[97]

Shultz made his bid to take control of the monetary issue on the eve of Connally's late-September speech before the International Monetary Fund. Offered a draft for comment, Shultz rewrote it to reflect his own views. As Volcker recalled, "He wanted to raise the offer of a transitional float into what could only be interpreted as a unilateral declaration by the United States that floating currencies should themselves be the basis for the new international monetary system, period." Volcker and Shultz argued the issue till early morning in a hotel suite and then presented Connally with rival drafts. Connally chose Volcker's, foreclosing for the time being a move to floating exchange rates.[98]

Meanwhile, Nixon moved to complete an important piece of unfinished business.[99] The bitter textile dispute with Japan had contributed significantly to the administration's nationalist mood in 1971 and to the harshness of Nixon's Japanese diplomacy. In the days just before August 15, blocked by Wilbur Mills from obtaining legislated textile quotas and by the Japanese government from negotiating acceptable voluntary quotas, Nixon had decided to impose quotas on his own authority by invoking the unfortunately named Trading with the Enemy Act of 1917. The sudden decision to announce the NEP had overtaken this initiative and prompted a temporary postponement. In September, learning that the administration again intended to go ahead with unilateral quotas, the Japanese trade minister crafted a scenario with Ambassador-at-Large David Kennedy that culminated in a memorandum of understanding on October 15, 1971. The Japanese agreed at last to accept voluntary quotas acceptable to Nixon. Though U.S. apparel manufacturers complained that these quotas still permitted too many Japanese imports, the industry would repay Nixon for his services by forking over $430,000 for his reelection campaign. The Japanese Textile Federation, by contrast, proclaimed October 15 as Humiliation Memorial Day and pledged to observe it for years to come. Almost immediately thereafter, for reasons having nothing to do with quotas, the Japanese textile industry went into drastic decline, its exports to the United States

---

[97] Milton Friedman to John Connally, Sept. 30, 1971, Economic Policy Division, OMB, NA.

[98] Volcker and Gyohten, *Changing Fortunes*, 82.

[99] The following account of textile negotiations follows I. M. Destler, Harukiro Fukui, Hideo Sato, *The Textile Wrangle* (1979), 291–314.

falling far below the quota limits that Nixon had extorted at so much cost to United States–Japanese relations.

In quest of bigger quarry than textiles, Connally pursued his export crusade despite increasing fears of a world recession. The U.S. border tax, which doubled the average effective tariff on half of U.S. imports (duty-free goods and goods under quota were exempt) hit select European industries hard. Europe's steel production sagged, and so did its capital goods sector. The Germans feared a 30 percent loss of exports to the United States in 1972,[100] and the European Economic Community estimated that the NEP would cost its member nations 300,000 jobs.[101] As the impasse dragged on and danger signals multiplied, there were increased attacks on Connally's "Texas brutality," not only by foreigners but by U.S. congressmen, academics, and the Eastern press.[102] Worried members of the administration pressed Volcker for some clue of Connally's intentions, but Volcker could give them none since not even he knew.[103]

At a meeting of Republican congressional leaders at the White House on November 16, 1971, Connally still seemed to be riding tall in the saddle. They're all saying that "if that Big Cowboy doesn't mend his ways, we're all going down the drain," Connally said. "Well, this cowboy knows that you can ride a good horse to death, and the world has been riding a good horse to death in the post-war years, and this has got to stop." The international economic crisis would not soon be settled, Connally warned. "They want us to remove the surcharge and raise the price of gold and then they'll talk to us. Well, that's not acceptable." Nixon agreed. If we caved in now and I were a Democrat, the president said, "I would give us hell." For a quarter century, Nixon continued, "the United States has not bargained hard for a better position in world trade, the goddamn State Department hasn't done the job. We're changing the rules of the game."[104]

By then Connally's position was already weakening. Nixon had said at the outset that he would stand by Connally as long as Connally's offensive did not undermine domestic prosperity or jeopardize Nixon's other foreign policy objectives. At first Henry Kissinger had kept his distance from the

---

[100] *Wall Street Journal*, Oct. 18, 1971, 1; *New York Times*, Oct. 25, 1971, 1, 53.

[101] *Newsweek* (Nov. 1, 1971), 69–72.

[102] This was phrase of Giovanni Agnelli, chairman of Fiat, quoted in *Business Week* (Nov. 20, 1971), 78.

[103] Volcker and Gyohten, *Changing Fortunes*, 83–84.

[104] Pat Buchanan for President's File, Nov. 16, 1971, Memo for President's file, POF.

NEP. "I had not expected to play a major role in international economics which — to put it mildly — had not been a central field of study for me," he wrote in his memoirs. "Only later did I learn that the key economic policy discussions are not technical but political."[105] Under Burns's tutelage, Kissinger grew increasingly concerned about the diplomatic consequences of Connally's nationalist offensive. "Set Kissinger against Burns," Nixon told Haldeman early in October. "They're playing anti-Connally game. Kissinger must stick four-square with Connally. Arthur wants to give away the store. Connally's standing firm. Arthur's playing like the State Department."[106] In time Kissinger became convinced that Burns was right and that he, Kissinger, would have to stop Connally. Confronting Nixon on November 11, 1971, Kissinger argued strongly for a quick settlement. Nixon countered that Kissinger should "drop the Burns line regarding return to the gold standard." Persisting, Kissinger said that Connally was "like all Texans and is just basically antiforeigner." Kissinger insisted that the United States state its terms to the allies and negotiate. Retreating, Nixon suggested that Kissinger visit Connally and see if he could "get him lined up."[107]

Nixon was also receiving warnings that Connally's policy could damage the domestic economy, whose health, he had said, was his highest priority. McCracken wrote Nixon on November 10 that the NEP "will have been massively successful if we now cash in . . . If we hold off indefinitely and the world drifts, there will be growing fears about an international disintegration, a process that could be expected to cast a pall over confidence." A pall over confidence! Nixon marked the salient passage of McCracken's memo and sent it along to Connally without comment.[108]

Connally might nevertheless have brazened it out except for the condition of the stock market, which had soared because of the NEP in August and then began sinking in October. At first the market's faltering performance seemed to be the fault of uncertainties surrounding Phase II. Then investors began blaming John Connally. Said one financial leader, "I think the market is saying something to Mr. Connally. The market is staging a 'peace demonstration' of its own. It wants peace on the international mon-

---

[105] Kissinger, *White House Years*, 950.

[106] H-Notes, Oct. 4, 1971.

[107] *Haldeman Diaries*, Nov. 11, 1971.

[108] McCracken for President, Nov. 10, 1971, President's Handwriting file, POF.

etary front."[109] On November 22, 1971, Bernard Lasker, head of the New York Stock Exchange and the man who had held Nixon's hand during the Cambodian crash, called the White House with a warning. With Europe descending into recession, Lasker said, "We cannot ride with the impasse which Connally keeps projecting." The longer it continued, "the worse off we will be . . . the political time clock is running against us."[110]

Pressured by Burns and Kissinger, worried about the stock market and a European recession, reluctant to meet Chinese and Russian leaders in the months ahead as leader of a fractured alliance, Nixon could no longer afford Connally's policy. On November 22, 1971, Nixon met Connally four separate times, with Burns, Kissinger, and Shultz variously in attendance.[111] Participants recalled that on that day Nixon signaled Connally to get the best deal he could in exchange for lifting the border tax, then settle.[112] Meanwhile, Kissinger was arranging a series of summits with NATO heads of state prior to Nixon's trips to Moscow and Beijing. For the first one, with President Georges Pompidou of France in the Azores in mid-December, Kissinger placed the monetary crisis on the agenda.[113] Pompidou had so far been the most determined opponent in Europe of Connally's demands. Heads of state, of course, meet not to discuss deadlocks but to resolve them.

Connally signaled the American retreat at the meeting of the Group of Ten on November 30 at a Renaissance palace overlooking Rome. The Americans opened by offering to rescind the border tax in return for an average 11 percent appreciation of other currencies in relation to the dollar — enough to produce an estimated $9 billion swing in the U.S. balance of payments rather than the $13 billion swing that Connally had previously said was nonnegotiable. In executive session, Giscard d' Estaing of France got to the point, asking what the U.S. contribution to realignment would be. Nudged by Connally, Volcker replied, "Well, suppose, just hypothetically, we were willing to discuss the price of gold. How would you respond if we increased the price by ten or fifteen percent?" Connally

---

[109] Sam Nakagama of Kidder, Peabody quoted in *New York Times*, Nov. 28, 1971, III, 1.

[110] Lasker's views contained in Chapin for Shultz, Nov. 22, 1971, Records of Director, OMB, NA.

[111] President's Daily Activities Calendar.

[112] O'Dell, *U.S. International Monetary Policy*, 283. O'Dell bases his account on participant interviews. Also Solomon, *International Monetary System*, 201.

[113] Kissinger, *White House Years*, 958–959.

interrupted. "All right, the issue has been raised," he said. "Let's assume ten percent. What will you people do?" The others were stunned.[114] The Americans had at last yielded on gold but instead of devaluing by 5 percent as expected, they were offering more dollar devaluation than the Europeans wanted, enough to choke on. With incomparable cheek, Connally had transformed the moment of defeat into an occasion to confound and embarrass his adversaries — "not economics but jujitsu," an Englishman called it. When the others recovered, the logjam broke. Discussion on currency realignment commenced, and the Europeans expressed a willingness to discuss trade issues. Connally listened for a while to tentative proposals on trade and then, as chair, abruptly recessed the meeting till December 17 in Washington, saying, "Any offers I heard that were construed as offers were ridiculous."[115] No settlement was possible in Rome in any case, because Nixon and Pompidou were waiting in the wings to garner the credit.

Though Nixon had signaled a retreat, he had not meant to signal a retreat on gold. Connally's concession on gold in Rome contradicted his firm direction, Nixon told members of his staff on December 2. Nixon conceded that the price of gold did not matter because the United States had ceased to convert dollars into gold anyway. "The real problem of devaluing is the Senate," he said, "and now everything hangs on this and we have to have Congressional authority [to devalue the dollar] so we give the political ball game away." Did Connally act under the pressure of the meeting in Rome? Nixon wondered. "What are we doing? What is our policy? Change in [the gold] price is now irretrievable. How do we make it an asset and market it through the Senate?"[116] Perhaps Connally had misunderstood Nixon's wishes. Perhaps he felt that to get a currency settlement, he had no choice except to make a concession on gold. Perhaps he thought he enjoyed more authority than Nixon intended to give him. Whatever the reason, it was done, and Nixon would have to live with it.

Connally spent the first two weeks of December attempting to extract trade concessions from the allies before Nixon met Pompidou. On December 11, U.S. negotiators presented a list of "short-term" trade demands to the European Economic Community in Brussels and the next day to the

[114] Volcker and Gyohten, *Changing Fortunes*, 86; Giscard d'Estaing quote, *Newsweek* (Dec. 13, 1971), 86.

[115] *Newsweek* (Dec. 13, 1971), 86.

[116] H-Notes, Dec. 12, 1971.

Japanese in Honolulu.[117] On December 14, Connally was still saying that the United States would not raise the dollar price of gold unless the others reduced barriers to U.S. exports. A day later the EEC rejected all but the most innocuous of Connally's proposals.[118] The Japanese proved no less resistant.[119] Connally's great mercantilist offensive was ending in a whimper.

Nixon met Pompidou in the Azores on December 13 and 14, 1971, to negotiate on money. Kissinger recalled, "It cannot be said that Nixon was clearly on top on the subject. He wanted a solution, not a discussion of exchange rates. If given truth serum, he would no doubt have revealed that he could not care less where in the new scale the various currencies were to be pegged."[120] More interested in the Washington Redskins, Nixon stayed up past 4:30 A.M. listening to them win a game on Armed Forces Radio.[121] Kissinger did much of the actual negotiating with Pompidou, a Rothschild's banker, while Connally remained close by as a brooding threat.[122] Before the trip, Connally had pressed Nixon to accept no change in the gold price without trade concessions, and he would not have been unhappy to see the summit fail.[123] But Nixon had grown tired of the whole business and was anxious to move on. The two presidents agreed that the United States would devalue the dollar by raising the price of gold for official transactions from $35 to $38 an ounce, a devaluation of 8.6 percent. The industrial nations would return to a system of fixed exchange rates, each nation buying and selling currencies to defend the new parities. As for the gold window, the United States would keep it closed for the time being. In fact, it would never be reopened. The United States having settled its currency differences with France, all that remained was for the two main surplus countries, Germany and Japan, to make a contribution to a settlement by revaluing the currencies upward.[124]

On December 17–18, the Group of Ten reconvened in an imitation Norman castle at the Smithsonian Institution in Washington to conclude the currency quarrel. Despite the Pompidou-Nixon meeting, success in the

---

[117] *Times* (London), Dec. 11, 1971, 19; *New York Times,* Dec. 13, 1971, 1.

[118] *Times* (London), Dec. 16, 1971, 4.

[119] *Time* (Dec. 27, 1971), 27; Angel, *Explaining Economic Policy Failure,* 245–252.

[120] Kissinger, *White House Years,* 961.

[121] *Haldeman Diaries,* Dec. 14, 1971.

[122] Kissinger, *White House Years,* 959.

[123] Connally for President, Dec. 10, 1971, President's Handwriting file, POF.

[124] Volcker and Gyohten, *Changing Fortunes,* 88; Solomon, *International Monetary System,* 204–205.

final stages was by no means assured, and negotiations proved difficult. Finally, on the afternoon of the second day, Japan consented to a total 16.9 percent appreciation of the yen against the dollar, and Germany to a 13.5 percent appreciation of the mark. Most of the other countries were little affected by the deals of the major antagonists but had to negotiate cross-rates, an acrimonious process requiring Connally's personal mediation. By the end of the day, it was all settled. Realigment was achieved. Connally pledged to seek congressional approval for raising the gold price of the dollar — readily obtained, as it turned out — and the United States agreed to rescind the border tax so resented by the others. Connally had tried until the last minute to extract some concessions on trade but made little progress. Volcker calculated that, excluding Canada, the trade-weighted depreciation of the dollar accomplished at the Smithsonian was less than 8 percent, that is, less than half the amount that he and Connally believed would be necessary to correct the overvalued dollar.[125] Nixon nonetheless appeared unannounced at the Smithsonian on Saturday night, December 18, 1971, to hail "the conclusion of the most significant monetary agreement in the history of the world." Volcker was heard to remark, "I hope it lasts three months."[126]

Nixon knew how to sell devaluation of the dollar to the country. "We've got to hit the 'more jobs for the United States' line," he told Connally on December 15. Connally agreed. "Devaluation has to be defined in terms of American goods being more competitive, so therefore there are more jobs in the United States," Connally said. "This is a means of keeping jobs at home."[127] Making this case to the press, Peter Peterson boasted that the depreciated dollar would create 700,000 new American jobs, enough to cut the current unemployment rate from 6 percent to 5.2 percent.[128] These mercantilist paeans to devaluation were foolish. Devaluation, however necessary, entailed serious economic costs, though Nixon and Connally never doubted the political benefits.

---

[125] Volcker and Gyohten, *Changing Fortunes*, 89; Solomon, *International Monetary System*, 206–209; *Haldeman Diaries*, Dec. 18, 1971. For Connally's account of his role at the Smithsonian, see excerpts of a 1981 TV interview he gave to a Japanese television program, reprinted in Angel, *Explaining Economic Failure*, 255–257.

[126] *Pub Paps RN 1971*, 1195–1196.

[127] *Haldeman Diaries*, Dec. 15, 1971.

[128] *Wall Street Journal*, Dec. 20, 1971, 15.

V

Nixon's New Economic Policy, with its mix of domestic and foreign measures, could be judged either as economics or as politics. As politics, the NEP worked. In the spring of 1971, Gallup had reported that in a three-man race with George Wallace, the Democratic front-runner Edmund Muskie led Nixon by two percentage points. Immediately after August 15, Nixon pulled ahead by six points, and in October, still riding the crest of the Nixon rally in the stock market, by eight. In November, when Nixon's lead was back down to three points, it was clear that the NEP alone would not reelect him, that more than the promise of a boom, he needed the boom itself. Nonetheless, as Nixon himself always believed, the NEP had made an indispensable contribution to his political rebound. By staging the NEP as spectacle, he had dispelled the gloom, changed the mood, and established the image he so much wanted of Nixon the leader. With a single stroke, he had deprived the Democrats of their best issue and allayed his greatest worry. Anything could happen in the year ahead, but the NEP had improved his chances immeasurably.

As economics, the NEP did not justify the administration's hype. Controls were not needed and lulled both the White House and the Fed into a false sense of security on prices, lowering resistance to risky expansionary policy. Tax cuts were ill-timed and hurt the permanent revenues. Taken as a whole, the program contributed only marginally to the forces that would propel the economy in 1972. A few days after Camp David, McCracken sent Nixon a memo estimating that the NEP would increase GNP by 1.3 percent in 1972, reducing unemployment by 350,000 jobs or only 0.4 percent. (McCracken omitted dollar depreciation from the exercise because it would have little impact on output for an estimated eighteen months.) Nearly half of McCracken's predicted gain would result from the intangible of confidence. Charles Colson found those numbers so disappointing that he pressured McCracken to produce better ones for his forthcoming congressional testimony.[129] Dutifully, McCracken told Congress that by his estimate the NEP would add 500,000 jobs.[130]

---

[129] Colson to Haldeman, Aug. 23, 1971, plus attachment, McCracken for President, Aug. 20, 1971, Alpha Name file: Charles Colson, SMOF: Haldeman.

[130] "The President's New Economic Program," Joint Economic Committee, 212 (McCracken testimony, Aug. 30).

On the international front, Connally deserved credit for breaking the monetary impasse that had plagued Bretton Woods during its dying days, but his strong-arm tactics undermined allied unity and trust, and his mercantilist premises were theoretically primitive. He failed to achieve a major reordering of trade arrangements and got less in the way of currency realignment than he wanted. The main consequence of the NEP was to take the United States off gold. Some conservatives regarded the abandonment of gold at Camp David as Nixon's great crime and would blame him for the decade of inflation that followed. In truth, the United States had long before declined to discipline its economy in defense of gold, and the dollar had de facto been inconvertible for years. Nixon and Connally did not kill the gold standard. The demand of voters in the Western democracies, especially in the United States, for expansive policies to promote full employment killed the gold standard. Nixon and Connally merely helped determine the time and manner of its demise.

After the international monetary crisis of 1971 was resolved, Nixon again lost interest in the whole subject. When the system came under renewed stress within months and the currency realignment negotiated at the Smithsonian began falling apart, he could not have cared less. On June 23, 1972, with the tape recorder running in the Oval Office, Haldeman interrupted an incriminating conversation on Watergate to brief Nixon on the latest crisis of the British pound. The resulting exchange provided the most revealing text extant on the political economy of Richard Nixon.[131]

> H: Did you get the report that the British floated the pound last night?
> P: No. I don't think so, they have?
> H: They did.
> P: That's devaluation?
> H: Yeah. Flanigan's got a report of it right here.
> P: I don't care about it.
> H: You want a rundown?
> P: No. I don't care. Nothing we can do about it.
> H: He argues it shows the wisdom of our refusal to consider convertibility until we get a new monetary system.

---

[131] Transcript of a Conversation, June 23, 1972, White House Tapes, Nixon Project, NA.

P: Good. I think he's right. It's too complicated for me to get into.

H: Burns expects a five percent devaluation against the dollar.

P: Yeah. O.K. Fine.

H: Burns is concerned about speculation about the lira.

P: Well, I don't give a shit about the lira.

H: That's the substance of that.

The conversation shifted to another subject, probably Nixon's recent announcement that he was considering suspension of quotas on imported meat to take the pressure off prices:

H: All our people are . . . they think it's great.

P: Well, ah. I hate to brag about it — there ain't a vote in it . . . only George Shultz and people like that think it's great. There's no votes in it, Bob.

# Chapter 7
# Election Year 1972

I

Entering 1972, despite the NEP, Nixon was hardly the runaway favorite. For three years he had been frustrated in his efforts to escape Vietnam, enact his programs, and make the economy hum. Gallup reported in January that Nixon's lead over Muskie in a three-man race was down to a single point.[1] "It will be another close election," one of Nixon's political strategists told *Newsweek*, "and if it were held today we'd just barely win."[2] But 1972 was the year everything seemed to break right for Richard Nixon. In November he would carry every state in the union except one, advance his goal of establishing a New Majority, and claim a mandate to change fundamentally the direction of the government.

It vastly helped Nixon that the year of the election coincided with his great foreign policy triumphs. The president's grand design was to move the Soviet Union toward détente by exploiting the Sino-Soviet rivalry.[3] In February 1972, he played the China card on a ten-day visit to the People's Republic, a brilliant stroke of triangular diplomacy that generated vivid televised images for the voters back home. As soon as the United States moved toward China, the Soviets hastened to invite Nixon to Moscow for a summit of their own, scheduled for late May 1972. Prospects for this summit dimmed on May 8, when Nixon responded to a North Vietnamese invasion of the South by stepping up B-52 attacks around Hanoi and mining Haiphong harbor.[4] In the past such acts of escalation would have triggered tremendous protests at home and placed relations with the Soviet

---

[1] *The Gallup Poll: Public Opinion 1972–1977* (vol. 1, 1978), 8.

[2] *Newsweek* (Jan. 10, 1972), 10.

[3] However self-serving, the best account of Nixon's diplomacy remains Henry Kissinger, *The White House Years* and *Years of Upheaval* (1982).

[4] *Pub Paps RN 1972*, 583–587.

Union in deep freeze. By reducing U.S. troops in South Vietnam from more than half a million in 1969 to less than 70,000 in 1972, Nixon had finally removed the war as a salient issue in American politics.[5] And the Soviets, anxious to counter the China ploy, warmly received Nixon in Moscow on May 28, 1972. Nixon returned home bearing a series of agreements, including one to limit strategic weapons, that would permit him to claim the peace issue in the campaign and to run as a statesman.

Meanwhile that spring the Democrats were self-destructing.[6] At the outset, Muskie was the man Nixon most feared. Presidential in bearing and Lincolnesque in appearance, Muskie could contest Nixon for the middle ground of American politics and appeal to those wavering Democrats whom Nixon most coveted. But Muskie never developed a message and was prone to temperamental outbursts, as he demonstrated to his misfortune in a tearful tirade against the slanders of the *Manchester Union Leader* during the first primary in New Hampshire.[7] Favored to win big in the Granite State, Muskie barely nosed out South Dakota Senator George McGovern. A week later, George Wallace, running against busing, won the Democratic primary in Florida, with Muskie finishing a distant fourth. Storming to the front now was McGovern, the 50-to-1 shot whose demands for immediate U.S. withdrawal from Vietnam and for redistribution of income had galvanized the left-wing of the party and inspired a cadre of youthful workers who moved from state to state organizing at the grassroots. When McGovern bested Wallace and Senator Hubert Humphrey in Wisconsin on April 4, he was on the way to the nomination, which he sewed up by a narrow victory over Humphrey in California early in June. Nixon could hardly believe his good fortune. Running against McGovern, he could claim the center and reap a harvest of blue-collar, Catholic, and white Southern votes for the New Majority.

George Wallace might have challenged Nixon for some of those votes, especially in the South. As a third-party candidate in 1968, Wallace had cost Nixon a near-sweep of the region, and if he did a reprise in '72 would likely do so again. On May 15, Arthur Bremer, a demented white man, shot

---

[5] Ibid., 550–554.
[6] For a narrative history of the campaign, Theodore White, *Making of the President 1972* (1973).
[7] *New York Times*, Feb. 27, 1972, 1.

Wallace as he campaigned in Maryland's Democratic primary. Bremer's bullet left Wallace permanently paralyzed and effectively ended the third-party threat that had tormented Nixon for so long.[8] In June Gallup showed Nixon outpointing McGovern in a two-man race by 53 percent to 34 percent.[9]

Nixon's good luck extended even to the economy. For three years, he had been plagued by disappointing economic performances — inflation in 1969, recession in 1970, sluggish recovery in 1971. When 1972 began, Nixon's advisers were not at all sure that there would be a boom, but there was. The one issue that the Democrats had counted on would belong to Nixon. In fact, Nixon was not nearly so lucky as it seemed. Errors of policy that year built up undetected excess demand that would explode in 1973, undermining Nixon politically as he confronted the mortal challenge of Watergate, another development of 1972 that would not affect the election but which would eventually undo its results.

## II

The boom had its origin in easy money. During 1972 M1 had grown by 6 percent and M2 at the extraordinary rate of 11 percent. A cautious public had been slow to spend its swelling money balances until late in the year but was spending freely as 1972 began. Housing emerged as the most dynamic sector. Rising interest rates had hurt housing in the late 1960s; lower interest rates and a backlog of demand sparked a building frenzy now. Housing starts in 1972 totaled 2.3 million, nearly a million more than in 1969 and the largest number in American history. Consumer expenditures lagged during the early months of the year and then took off too. Real GNP grew by 7.2 percent from December 1971 to December 1972. The unemployment rate, Nixon's personal economic barometer, hovered near 6 percent till June, then plunged to 5.5 percent, held there through the election,

---

[8] Dan T. Carter suggests the possibility that Nixon had earlier made a deal with Wallace that would keep the Justice Department from prosecuting corruption in Alabama involving Wallace's brother. In return, the governor would run in the Democratic primaries but not as a third-party candidate in November. Haldeman's diary indicates that the Nixon White House continued to take very seriously the possibility of Wallace's third-party candidacy into July. See Carter, *The Politics of Rage: George Corley Wallace, The Origins of the New Conservatism, and the Transformation of American Politics* (1995), chap. 12.

[9] *Gallup Poll*, 38.

and then plunged again to 5.1 percent in December. The benefits of the boom to Nixon that year were considerable; the costs came due later.[10]

The costs were a lot steeper than they should have been because policy-makers in 1972 misread the economy and gunned the motor when they should have applied the brakes. The mistakes were so glaring, at least in retrospect, that critics later charged bad faith. It became part of the Nixon folklore that the boom was just another example of Nixon's abuse of power, that he and his friend Arthur Burns had recklessly pumped up demand to win the election. Journalist Sanford Rose, in a 1974 *Fortune* article on the causes of resurgent inflation, reported that during a heated meeting of the Fed's Open Market Committee in 1972, Burns quelled a rebellion against easy money by departing in anger and returning to announce, "I have just talked to the White House." (No one present supported Rose's account.)[11] The Democratic chairman of a House subcommittee on monetary policy, Stephen Neal, said, "I'd be inclined to think" that Arthur Burns "tried to jack up the economy to get Richard Nixon reelected."[12] Later in the decade, the political scientist Edward R. Tufte charged that Nixon, practicing "deliberate concealment," had undertaken "the all-out stimulation of the economy for the 1972 reelection campaign" and thereby helped to cause "much of the inflation and economic distress of the 1970s."[13] The Princeton economist Alan Blinder, admitting that "motivation is not the sort of thing that can be established by econometrics," nevertheless suggested that the main cause of Nixon's policy of fiscal stimulation in 1972 was "proximity" to the election.[14]

Nixon was not above cynically overheating the economy in 1972 if that is what it would take to reelect him, but neither he nor his advisors thought they were overheating anything. Through the first half of the year, sluggish

---

[10] For money supply, *Federal Reserve Bulletin* (vol. 58, Apr. 1972), A17; for economic developments in early 1972, *Review of Economic and Financial Developments* (Mar. 24, 1972); housing statistics, CEA *Annual Report 1991*, 346; December to December calculated from CEA *Annual Report, 1975*, 250; unemployment rate, CEA *Annual Report 1972*, 223.

[11] Sanford Rose, "The Agony of the Federal Reserve," *Fortune* (vol. 40, July 1974), 91 ff., esp. 188. Rose's account finds no support in the minutes of the FOMC and was denied by several members. See *New York Times*, Aug. 18, 1974, III, 1, 5. Board member Arthur Brimmer also disputed Rose in an edited letter to *Fortune* (Aug. 1974), reprinted in an unpublished paper that Mr. Brimmer kindly furnished me.

[12] *New York Times*, July 11, 1976, III, 5.

[13] Edward R. Tufte, *Political Control of the Economy* (1978), 153–154.

[14] Alan S. Blinder, *Economic Policy and the Great Stagflation* (1979), 32.

recovery continued to seem the more likely problem. The cause of this mistake was the illusion of idle capacity. Flawed surveys of plant utilization showed excessive slack, and unemployment at 6 percent indicated too much unused labor.[15] Estimates at the time claimed that the economy was producing 3 percent less real GNP than it could. Pumping up demand, it followed, would put men and machines back to work without generating more inflation. Subsequent recalculation placed the gap between actual and potential GNP at only 1 percent, which is to say that the hypothesis of idle capacity was wrong.[16] "We all thought, 'We're a long way from full employment, we still have a lot of room for [expanding] the economy, and the inflation rate is low,' " Herbert Stein recalled. "We misinterpreted."[17] Though Nixon embraced expansive measures in 1972 with a zeal born of political self-interest, the mistaken belief in idle capacity would have produced rather similar policies even if there had been no election.

## III

On December 29, 1971, unconvinced by signs of a boom, Stein sent Nixon a memo that captured the anxious mood pervading the White House. "My great concern is that the economy is not going to rise fast enough in 1972 to cut the rate of unemployment very much," Stein said. Unemployment might drop to 5.2 percent by the third quarter of 1972, but then again it might hang around 6 percent. If the administration wished to avoid an unsatisfactory outcome, "we should be looking for ways to pump up the economy more rapidly." Because of wage and price controls, the danger of rekindling inflation appeard to be "relatively small." The issue, therefore, was not whether to stoke demand but how. A year before, Stein's preferred policy tool had been the money supply, but in 1971 monetary policy had proved to be a highly unreliable instrument. This time Stein preferred fiscal policy. For the rest of the fiscal year ending June 30, 1972 (FY 72), the federal goverment needed to spend a lot more money than currently planned, Stein said. This would mean running a full-employment deficit,

---

[15] For a discussion of inaccurate estimates of capacity, Lewis Beman, "Why Business Ran Out of Capacity," *Fortune* (May 1974), 261 ff.

[16] Blinder, *Economic Policy and the Great Stagflation*, 35. The 1 percent figure derived from Blinder and CEA *Annual Report 1978*, 84, Table 10.

[17] Erwin C. Hargrove and Samuel A. Morley, *The President and the Council of Economic Advisers* (1984), 396.

not by stealth, as with the NEP, but out in the open. The balanced full-employment budget, Stein observed, "was not handed down by Moses."[18]

Nixon agreed. Tired of waiting for monetary policy to produce, he too was ready by January 1972 to try fiscal measures. In practice, that meant pushing every department in the government to spend every cent it could through June. After that it would be too late to affect the election. At a meeting of his cabinet members on January 20, 1972, Nixon said — in Stein's paraphrase — "that whereas he had regularly in the past urged them to be economical in their expenditures he was now urging them to get out and spend. He recognized that this instruction would seem strange to them, as it did to him, but he passed on the assurance of his economists that it was the right thing to do."[19] Nixon added that it was not only "good for the country to spend it as fast as we can . . . [it] might help us politically, a thought that just occurred to me."[20] Thereafter, Nixon cracked the whip on the departments to raise federal spending by a total $1 billion per month for six months. In his January budget message, partly because of additional federal spending, he predicted a huge actual deficit of $38.8 billion for the fiscal year ending on June 30 and a full-employment deficit of $8 billion — "strong but necessary medicine," the president said, to combat unemployment.[21]

Running such a deficit would ordinarily embarrass a Republican president. Rather than apologize, Nixon decided "to make a virtue out of necessity."[22] "This is a political world," John Connally told doubting conservatives at the U.S. Chamber of Commerce, January 1972. "What position would we be in if we had a balanced budget with over five million persons unemployed?"[23] Testifying before Congress in February, Stein boasted of "the strongest program that any administration has ever put forward to deal with the problem of unemployment in this country." When Senator Proxmire challenged this statement, Stein flaunted the $38 billion deficit as proof. "I don't think you should belittle that," he said.[24] At the National

---

[18] Stein for President, Dec. 29, 1971, enclosure of Kehrili to Shultz, Ehrlichman, Peterson, Jan. 5, 1972, BE 5 file, WHCF.

[19] Herbert Stein, *Presidential Economics*, 2d rev. ed. (1988), 184.

[20] *Haldeman Diaries*, Jan. 20, 1972.

[21] *Pub Paps RN 1972*; for numbers, p. 84; for quote, p. 78.

[22] *Haldeman Diaries*, Jan. 20, 1972.

[23] Lester A. Sobel, ed., *Inflation and the Nixon Administration 1972–74* (vol. 2, 1973), 16; also reported in *New York Times*, Jan. 21, 1972, 1.

[24] "The 1972 Economic Report of the President," Joint Economic Committee, hearings (1972), 7, 19.

Press Club, Stein said, "There is no serious, coherent policy that is an alternative to the one the Administration has initiated."[25] Stein meant that the big deficit had stolen the Democrat's thunder. This was true. *Fortune* observed later, "It can be argued that what the country really needed in 1972 was a party out of power claiming that the party in power was being too loose with money. But the fact is that most Democratic economists, upset about a continuing high unemployment rate and persuaded that the economy still had plenty of room to expand, did nothing but egg the administration on."[26]

Assuming a substantial jolt from the budget, the administration publicly offered an optimistic forecast for the year ahead. Privately, the president's men remained doubtful.[27] "1972 may be one of those years that if it is good will be very, very good. But this has a well known corollary," Stein wrote late in January. The signs did not look very good to him. "Even the expansionary policy we have laid out produces no real boom," Stein said. The Fed was not printing enough money. Retail sales were poor. New orders for durables had declined, and even increased federal expenditures, now the main thrust of policy, were "problematical."[28]

As Stein indicated, the extra kick from fiscal policy was no sure thing. In fact, FY 72 turned out to be the year of the incredible shrinking deficit. Because of freak overwithholding, revenues ran much higher than the administration expected, while expenditures undershot the target.[29] As Stein explained, "most of the Cabinet members were no better at spending money than saving it."[30] That fact infuriated the president. In February Nixon insisted that key departments submit weekly reports describing their efforts "to stimulate the economy during that particular week."[31] In March, when Stein reported that the departments were not meeting their targets,

[25] Speech reprinted in *Cong Rec* (1972), 4262–4263.

[26] Carol J. Loomis, "The New Questions about the Economy," *Fortune* (Jan. 1974), 69 ff.

[27] Notes on the Economic Situation, Jan. 26, 1972, enclosure of Stein for President, Jan. 26, 1972, Troika file, SMOF: Solomon.

[28] "Notes on the Economic Situation," attached to Memo from Stein to President, Jan. 26, 1972, FI file, WHCF.

[29] In the Revenue Act of 1971 Congress enacted new withholding schedules that eliminated underwithholding for some taxpayers but also overwithheld taxes for 40 million one-earner families unless they claimed extra exemptions, which hardly any of them knew how to do. This and a stronger than expected economy meant that revenues exceeded January estimates by $10 billion.

[30] Stein, *Presidential Economics*, 184.

[31] Ehrlichman for Shultz, Feb. 15, 1972, FG 6-16, WHCF.

Nixon issued an order. "Get them off their duffs," he said.[32] A few days later, Nixon assigned Haldeman to help Shultz work the problem, "especially to kick Laird in the ass," he said, referring to the secretary of defense.[33] All to no avail. Spending from January to June rose not by the additional $6 billion that Nixon wanted but only by $2 billion. Instead of $38.8 billion, the actual deficit for FY 72 was $23.2 billion.[34] Nixon did not know it, but given the underlying strength of the economy, even this was too much.

With the deficit diminishing, the mood of the administration stayed somber through the winter and into the spring. Shultz said of the economy in February, "We've got a real problem."[35] Stein wrote Nixon in April that the administration might hit its targets, but "the danger is that we will be short, and we should be leaning to the side of more stimulus." "Right," Nixon commented in the margin.[36] Not until June did the clouds lift. The second-quarter GNP was looking "extraordinarily good," Stein admitted.[37] At the Quadriad meeting on June 21, Nixon exulted, "we *have* gotten the economy going."[38] On July 20, Stein said, "we have quite a story to tell."[39] Two days later, the *New York Times* told it under a two-column headline on page one: real GNP up in the second quarter at an annual rate of 8.9 percent; consumer prices for the month up by only 0.1 percent; unemployment down from 5.9 percent in May to 5.5 percent in June; real earnings of workers up 4 percent over the year before — the largest June-to-June increase ever recorded.[40] Stein told the press that these numbers were "the best combination of economic news to be released in one day in this decade." Spoofing Nixon's well-known penchant for hype, Stein added, "I will not say in the Christian era."[41] At the precise moment that Nixon had for so long hoped it would happen, the U.S. economy finally looked good.

One of the few economists who saw the volcanic possibilities of the expansion was Milton Friedman. Friedman admitted that he had recently

[32] Stein for President, Mar. 20, 1972, President's Handwriting file, POF.
[33] *Haldeman Diaries*, Mar. 23, 1972.
[34] *Pub Paps RN 1973*, 37.
[35] *Haldeman Diaries*, Feb. 10, 1972.
[36] Stein for President, Apr. 3, 1972, President's Handwriting file, POF.
[37] Ibid., June 20, 1972.
[38] Weinberger for President's file, June 21, 1972, Memos for President's file, POF.
[39] Stein for President, July 20, 1972, President's Handwriting file, POF.
[40] *New York Times*, July 22, 1972, 1.
[41] *Newsweek* (July 31, 1972), 51.

made forecasting mistakes, which, of course, he could explain after the fact. "We economists in recent years have done vast harm — to society at large and to our profession in particular — by claiming more than we can deliver," he said.[42] But Friedman never doubted that despite variable lags, the links between the money supply on the one hand and output and prices on the other were firm. In the spring of 1972, Friedman was back in the business of prophecy. "I believe," he wrote in May, "that we are now poised for a renewed acceleration of inflation." Friedman drew this conclusion not from the budget but from the money supply, and he blamed neither Nixon nor Congress but the Federal Reserve.[43]

## IV

"The failure of policy in 1972 to restrain monetary growth was a monumental blunder," the economist Phillip Cagan wrote later.[44] If so, the chief blunderer was Arthur Burns, who overrode the advocates of restraint within the Fed and in the teeth of a boom printed up money at historically rapid rates.[45] Of course, most right-thinking people outside the system favored easy money, and Burns was never more popular than when he provided it.

The Fed shared with the White House the illusion of idle capacity. At the meeting of the FOMC in January 1972, the system's senior economist, J. Charles Partee, said that he expected manufacturing capacity to reach only 77 percent by the end of the year. It followed, said Partee, that "it is far more preferable to err on the stimulative side in economic policy than not risk being stimulative enough." Burns agreed. Unless the money supply began to perform adequately — and for the moment it was sluggish — Burns would worry about the economy, and "he would also feel that there might be some validity in a charge that the System was not supporting the policies

---

[42] Friedman's paper to the American Economic Association in Dec. 1971, reported in *Wall Street Journal*, Jan. 10, 1972, 1; published in *American Economic Review Papers and Proceedings* (vol. 62, May 1972), 11–18.

[43] Friedman's column, *Newsweek* (May 22, 1972), 86.

[44] Phillip Cagan, *Persistent Inflation: Historical and Policy Essays* (1979), 172.

[45] On Burns's influence, James L. Pierce, "The Political Economy of Arthur Burns," *Journal of Finance* (vol. 34, May 1979), 485–496. Pierce, a senior staff member who attended FOMC meetings, wrote, "for all intents and purposes monetary policy was Burns. His colleagues on the Board and FOMC exerted little influence on monetary policy," p. 485.

of the Administration and Congress."[46] In February, Partee again noted the current "substantial amount of unused resources" and recommended "some spur to get the economy moving." The spur was a M1 target of 7 to 8 percent during the first quarter, enough to make up some of the recent shortfall in money and to provide a bracer for the economy to boot.[47] Actual M1 growth for the quarter reached an explosive 9.2 percent (annual rate).[48] By contrast, M1 had grown at an annual rate of 2.8 percent from 1920 to 1960 (excluding wars), 3.7 percent from 1962 to 1965, and 6 percent in 1971.[49]

Though M1 temporarily slowed down to 6.1 percent in the second quarter, Alfred Hayes, president of the Federal Reserve Bank of New York, expressed fear at the July meeting of the FOMC of a runaway boom. Burns brushed him off. According to the minutes, Burns said that he "personally wanted to enjoy the period—however brief it might prove to be—of relative tranquillity and marked achievement which monetary policy has experienced over the past half year."[50] Burns's enjoyment was no doubt enhanced by the goodwill that the Fed's recent performance was earning from the administration.[51] When the Fed resumed overshooting the target in July, Burns remained sanguine. He was "not afraid of prosperity, and he did not see an economic boom developing," he told the FOMC in August. If the Fed's economists were near the mark—"and he did not differ with them—extensive underutilization of resources would persist for at least another year."[52] Burns expressed no great alarm when the Fed, leaning against rising interest rates,[53] exceeded target in the third quarter, hitting 8.2 percent, and exceeded it again in the fourth quarter when M1 grew by 8.6 percent (annual rate).[54] In December, when Partee finally expressed concern for "the buildup of steam in the economic boiler" and wanted to slow money growth, Burns counseled against "concluding prematurely that

---

[46] FOMC minutes, Jan. 11, 1972, 8, 62.

[47] Ibid., Feb. 15, 1972, 24, 21.

[48] *Federal Reserve Bulletin* (vol. 59, Feb. 1973), 63.

[49] Milton Friedman, *Dollars and Deficits* (1968), 147.

[50] FOMC minutes, July 18, 1972, 25, 36.

[51] See Stein's comments in "Mid-Year Review," Joint Economic Committee, hearing (1972), 27.

[52] FOMC minutes, Aug. 15, 1972, 51.

[53] For critique of Fed's directives, William Poole, "Burnsian Monetary Policy: Eight Years of Progress," *Journal of Finance* (vol. 34, May 1979), 473–484, esp. 476–477.

[54] *Federal Reserve Bulletin* (Feb. 1973), 63.

a runaway boom was in process."[55] By then so much steam had built up and capacity was under so much strain that the boom had already slipped out of control.[56] Fortunately for Nixon, that fact became clear only after he was safely reelected.

V

Nixon's good luck extended to wage and price controls. Before the inevitable collapse, controls may appear to work. They appeared to work in 1972. It helped that Nixon had imposed controls when the economy was slack, and prices had stopped rising on their own. According to the GNP deflator, which is the broadest measure of price changes, inflation subsided from 4.9 percent in 1970 to 4.4 percent in the first half of 1971. Controls did not begin until August. Under controls prices performed even better. The inflation rate fell to 2.8 percent during the autumn of the freeze and then rose slightly in 1972 under Phase II to 3.2 percent.[57] Controls deserved some of the credit for declining inflation. Economists Otto Eckstein and Alan Blinder, the leading students of this period, independently concluded that, without controls, the rate of inflation would have been 1.2 percentage points higher by the end of 1972 than it was—a modest success, to be sure, but a success nonetheless.[58]

Controls did their work in unintended ways.[59] They had little impact on wages, which kept going up as if controls did not exist, and they restrained prices mainly indirectly. The basic Phase II regulation permitted businesses to raise prices by an amount equal to increased costs, plus the

---

[55] FOMC minutes, Dec. 19, 1972, 25, 31.

[56] Besides idle capacity, Burns had another reason to keep interest rates down in 1972. Considerable political pressure existed to control interest rates as part of the general controls program. Nixon had appointed Burns as chairman of the Committee on Interest and Dividends to monitor these areas. As chairman of the CID, Burns was supposed to keep interest rates down, while as chairman of the Fed he should have been keeping rates up. To protect the Fed politically, he might have acted more as CID chairman than as Fed chairman. Wyatt C. Wells, *Economist in an Uncertain World: Arthur Burns and the Federal Reserve, 1970–1978* (1994), 80–81, 99, 111–115.

[57] *Survey of Current Business* (June 1972), Table 19; (June 1973), Table 19.

[58] Otto Eckstein, *The Great Recession* (1978), 55. Alan S. Blinder, *Economic Policy and the Great Stagflation* (1979), 127. R. J. Gordon, "The Response of Wages and Prices to the First Two Years of Controls," *Brookings Papers on Economic Activity* (1973), finds that controls reduced the nonfarm price deflator by 2.3 percent during Phases I and II, 765–778, esp. 776.

[59] Conclusions on controls drawn from Blinder and Gordon.

usual markup. Before they could raise prices under this formula, the 1,500 largest firms in the country had to receive permission from the Price Commission. Noting that the price rule seemed simple to apply but was not, economist Arthur Okun said, "On the price side this thing is 99 percent Rube Goldberg. There is no clear definition of how to cost things out, no definition of productivity. What the price rules amount to is a test of competence for a corporation staff. There is enough elasticity for a good lawyer and accountant to get whatever a corporation wants from the Price Commission."[60] Price rules worked after a fashion, not because corporations literally applied them, but because the mere existence of rules created a "stabilization ethic." That ethic discouraged firms in tightening markets from raising prices as high as they might, even though costs were rising. In other words, controls worked by squeezing profits. Once controls were lifted, prices would inevitably snap back to restore depleted profits margins. Fortunately for Nixon that would not happen until after the election. During the campaign, with prices still temporarily restrained, controls lent point to the president's claim that he had cut inflation in half, though he was careful not to mention the controls that had contributed to this achievement.

In truth, the president and his chief White House advisers, George Shultz and Herbert Stein, despised controls. Nixon had imposed a price-wage freeze only to silence his critics and would have been happy afterward if controls had just gone away. Controls had proved so popular that in November 1971 Nixon had become the reluctant sponsor of Phase II, a comprehensive wage and price controls system complete with a Price Commission and Pay Board. These entities, Nixon hoped, would administer their powers under Phase II lightly and keep their interventions few. In January 1972 Stein, Shultz, and even Nixon each publicly stressed the temporary character of Phase II. That upset Jack Grayson, chairman of the Price Commission. If the public thought that controls would soon be gone, why obey them? Grayson turned to John Connally for help and got it.[61] As chair of the Cost of Living Council, which oversaw the whole program, Connally believed, first, that controls might work and, second, that since they were Nixon's controls, it was politically imperative that they did. In a speech at the end of January Connally said that "controls are the only game

---

[60] *New York Times*, Feb. 14, 1972, 1.
[61] J. Jackson Grayson, *Confessions of a Price Controller* (1974), 110–111.

in town" and would remain as long as they were needed.[62] That settled the matter for now. Concerning controls, Nixon told Haldeman, we "need to follow Connally's line." We "will have controls as long as we need them."[63]

The Price Commission took its responsibilities seriously even if the White House did not. The public expected the commission to save it from higher prices, and to the extent possible, it would try. It was rough going, especially at first. Following the freeze, which ended in November 1971, a large "bulge" in the price level was inevitable. Costs had accumulated during the freeze while prices stood still. As permitted under Phase II regulations, businesses quickly raised prices in a one-time effort to catch up with costs. At the same time, raw agricultural prices, which were entirely exempt from controls, were also rising rapidly. As a result, the February 1972 Consumer Price Index, published in March, showed prices rising at the alarming annual rate of 6 percent.[64] With Gallup reporting 55 percent of the public dissatisfied with controls, Phase II looked like it might back-fire on Nixon.[65] Arthur Okun remarked, "Before this, whenever rents went up, the tenant blamed his landlord. Now rents are still going up, but the tenants are blaming the President."[66]

Late in March, under mounting attack, the Price Commission consid-ered thoroughly revamping its regulations. One option was to junk existing regulations and start over. Another was to tighten existing regulations and extend them to agricultural products, as difficult as such products would be to control. The Price Commission circulated the possibilities among vari-ous administration officials, most of whom advised against change. But Grayson wanted to know what Nixon thought, so he went to see John Ehrlichman. Grayson warned Ehrlichman that unless food prices slowed down, labor would bust the 5.5 percent wage standard, and the game would be lost. "Is the White House ready to back us when we hold 'tough?'" Grayson wanted to know. Would the president "really want us to take whatever steps we felt necessary — even drastic ones — if we felt that the goal of two or three percent could not be achieved by the end of the year?" Ehrlichman replied that he did not know the president's views but would inform him of the conversation. "And it may be that he will want to get together and talk about it," Ehrlichman said. Grayson never heard from

---

[62] *Newsweek* (Jan. 31, 1972), 72.
[63] H-Notes, Jan. 25, 1972.
[64] Grayson, *Confessions*, 111–112.
[65] *Gallup Poll*, 6.
[66] *New York Times*, Feb. 14, 1972, 1.

Ehrlichman or from Nixon, who felt that the greater the distance between him and controls, the safer he would be.[67] The Price Commission was on its own.

At the commission's April 11 meeting to consider revamping its price rules, Grayson was sufficiently heartened by a favorable report on wholesale prices that he cast the deciding vote against tightening. He said that the commission should await developments.[68] Meanwhile, the critics were closing in. Controls were "a total farce," Senator Proxmire said.[69] Inflation "could be the sleeper issue that kicks Richard Nixon out of office," Senator Ribicoff said. Rising prices "may have outdistanced even busing as the big domestic political issue for 1972," *Newsweek* said.[70] Then on April 21 the government announced that consumer prices in March had risen by zero percent. On hearing the news, Grayson shouted with joy and quaffed several martinis in celebration. With "the Battle of the Bulge" over, the Price Commission's reputation instantly improved.[71]

But not necessarily in the White House. The Price Commission followed its advantage by strenthening enforcement, tightening some regulations, and even rolling back a few prices. The White House feared that the commission's tougher stance would antagonize its business constituents and cause them to retrench. "We did build a certain independence into the system," Stein said. "The Cost of Living Council has no control over these rules, and the Price Commission has shown no particular concern with our election."[72] Tension between the White House and the commission worsened in June when meat prices rose steeply. The Price Commission wrote the Cost of Living Council recommending the drastic step of controlling raw agricultural products, plus suspension of import quotas on meat. To force the administration's hand, the Price Commission leaked its letter to the press. On June 26, Nixon, who wanted the farm vote, suspended meat quotas but ruled out controls on farm products.[73] The episode confirmed

[67] Grayson, *Confessions*, 129–135, quotes p. 135. Grayson's account places this conversation in early April, but Grayson quotes Ehrlichman as saying that the President was in Moscow "right" now. Nixon went to Moscow late in May.
[68] Ibid., 136–137; Robert F. Lanzillotti, Mary T. Hamilton, R. Blaine Roberts, *Phase II in Review: The Price Commission Experience* (1975), 15.
[69] "Review of Phase II of the New Economic Program," Joint Economic Committee, hearings (1972), 47–49.
[70] *Newsweek* (April 10, 1972), 15.
[71] Grayson, *Confessions*, 138–139.
[72] Ibid., 140–147; Stein quote, 147.
[73] Ibid., 149–152; Lanzillotti et al., *Phase II*, 61–63.

the good reputation of the Price Commission with nearly everyone except those for whom the commission presumably worked. After that Nixon could hardly wait to get rid of it.

The Pay Board had an even more difficult existence, thanks to its built-in labor opposition. First the Board had given in to the coal miners by approving a 17 percent compensation increase, and then it caved in to the railroad signalmen. Said *Time* in January 1972, "the federal Pay Board seems well on its way to becoming the laughing stock of Phase II."[74] In defense of the Board's amiable but inept chairman, George Boldt, Shultz could only think to remark, "Just ask yourself, how would you like to be chairman of the Pay Board?"[75]

To attain respect, the Pay Board would have to face down a strong union. The opportunity came when the International Longshore and Warehouse Workers, representing the West Coast docks, won a strike with a 21 percent wage and benefits package grossly in violation of Pay Board standards. If the Board reduced the settlement "by as much as a penny," said the union's militant leader Harry Bridges, the union would resume the strike.[76] Thus, the dilemma of the Pay Board: avoid a showdown and lose all credibility, or pick up the gauntlet and risk a confrontation that could end with the U.S. Army taking over the docks.

George Meany, who had not personally attended a Pay Board meeting since November, was looking for an excuse to walk out. On March 10, 1972, at a breakfast at the White House hosted by the president, Meany "took great pains to point out the legitimacy of productivity as a justification for higher wages and here he had the Longshore in mind." Shultz responded that this was a matter for the Pay Board.[77] In fact, as Shultz knew, Nixon had already decided to take a stand against the unpopular Bridges, and if that meant a strike, he would break it.[78] On March 16, the Pay Board showed backbone at last by slicing the settlement of the dock workers from 21 percent to 16 percent.[79] Meany quit the Board in protest, taking with him all the other labor members except Frank Fitzsimmons,

[74] *Time* (Jan. 17, 1972), 20.

[75] *Newsweek* (Jan. 17, 1972), 62.

[76] Ibid. (Mar. 27, 1972), 83.

[77] Shultz for the President's file, Mar. 10, 1972, President's Meeting file, POF.

[78] Shultz for President, Mar. 7, 1972, President's Meeting file, POF.

[79] *New York Times*, Mar. 17, 1972, 1; *Newsweek* (Mar. 27, 1972), 83; Weber and Mitchell, *The Pay Board's Progress*, 182–191.

president of the independent Teamsters's union and a Nixon ally. Nixon remarked that "the only thing that bothers me about this is all those free breakfasts I gave the son of a bitch."[80] Nixon reconstituted the Pay Board by keeping all five public members, plus one member from the business contingent and Fitzsimmons from labor. Meany said he left the Board "to avoid any inference of complicity" in its decisions.[81] Since he did not leave to wreck controls, Phase II went on much as before.

Harry Bridges, meantime, gave no indication whether he would accept the Pay Board cut or fight it. Bridges was biding his time in hopes of forging an alliance with the International Longshoremen's Association (ILA), a separate union of dock workers on the East and Gulf coasts. In March 1972, the ILA ended a long dispute by accepting a contract providing first-year wage and benefit increases of 12 to 15 percent, depending on the port. If the Pay Board challenged this settlement too, the two unions might coordinate a strike that would paralyze the country. On May 8, 1972, the Pay Board voted to cut the ILA's first-year increase from 15 percent to 12 percent in some ports and 12 percent to 9 percent in others.[82] By coincidence, Nixon went on television that same day to announce that he had ordered the mining of Haiphong harbor to halt the flow of arms and supplies to North Vietnam. A hard-hat union friendly to Nixon, the ILA decided this was no time to fight the Pay Board. "Can you image us blockading all United States ports at the very moment the President is blockading North Vietnam?" one union official asked.[83] Rather than confront the Pay Board alone, Harry Bridges also capitulated. The Pay Board had won the big one. With no disputed contracts left on its docket and a light bargaining schedule ahead for the rest of 1972, the Board had not only survived, but it had also attained a measure of respect.

Despite the theatrics, the efforts of the Pay Board did not amount to much. True, first-year settlements in union contracts declined from 11.6 percent in 1971 to 7.3 percent in 1972.[84] But only 30 percent of nonfarm workers belonged to unions, and a mere 25 percent of those had got new contracts during Phase II. As one of the Pay Board's own economists concluded, "the short-run effects of influencing a portion of a minority of the

---

[80] *Haldeman Diaries*, Mar. 22, 1972.
[81] *Business Week* (Mar. 25, 1972), 25.
[82] Weber and Mitchell, *Pay Board's Progress*, 191–204.
[83] *New York Times*, May 14, 1972, IV, 2.
[84] Weber and Mitchell, *Pay Board's Progress*, 302.

labor force is likely to be lost in the general noise of aggregate economic data."[85] The best measure of wage behavior was compensation per man-hour in the private nonfarm economy. Showing hardly any effect of controls, compensation rose by 7.3 percent in 1970, 7.0 percent in 1971, and 6.9 percent in 1972.[86]

The major consequence of controls was the complacency they induced regarding inflation. Even among Nixon's advisers, who professed not to believe in them, controls encouraged the notion that inflation was in check and that the risks of expansion at a time of perceived excess capacity were few. Stein recalled, "Before we went into the controls, we argued many times that one of the great dangers of the controls was that they tempt you to an expansionist fiscal/monetary policy; that has been the universal history of controls. We fell into that trap again even though we said we never would."[87] Stein himself was guilty. Writing Nixon in December 1971, he had said, "We are all aware that price-wage controls can be a dangerous temptation to an excessive pumping up of demand. But still the controls . . . do make some room for expansive policy that would not otherwise be there."[88] It was the same at the Fed. Controls "had a profoundly expansionary impact on monetary policy," one of the system's economists wrote later.[89] Since he first voiced support for incomes policy in 1970, Burns had offered Nixon an implicit bargain. If Nixon would control prices, Burns would supply the money. In 1971 Nixon controlled prices, and in 1972 Burns supplied money by the bushel. The policy helped reelect the president but also assured the next cycle of boom and bust.

# VI

In the spring of 1972, as Nixon was getting ready for the campaign, John Connally went back to Texas. Nixon had recruited Connally in December

---

footnotes[85] Daniel J. B. Mitchell, "The Impact and Administration of Wage Controls," in John Kraft and R. Blaine Roberts, eds., *Wage and Price Controls: The U.S. Experiment* (1975), 36–67.

[86] *CEA Annual Report 1974*, 287. Some of these issues are discussed in Martin Estey, "Wage Stabilization Policy and the Nixon Administration," in Phillip Cagan et al., *A New Look at Inflation: Economic Policy in the Early 1970's* (1973), 107–123.

[87] Stein quote in Hargrove and Morley, *President and the Council of Economic Advisers*, 396; see also Herbert Stein, "Fiscal Policy: Reflections on the Past Decade," in William Fellner, ed., *AEI Studies in Contemporary Economic Problems* (1976), 76–78.

[88] Stein for President, Dec. 29, 1971, Memos for the President's file, SMOF: Solomon.

[89] Poole, "Burnsian Monetary Policy," 479.

1970 to take command of the economic issue and keep it from destroying him. Connally had done that, but after the Smithsonian agreement of December 1971, the drama had gone out of economic policy. All that mainly remained was routine business, for which Connally was ill-suited. Writing in his diary of Connally's recent visit to San Clemente after the new year, Haldeman noted, "the night they had dinner at the P's house, Connally told him he had spent his time in Texas going off on a horse, thinking through his future, and he had concluded that he had completed what he had come here for . . . and that he would be, therefore, leaving at the end of January." Nixon had to plead with Connally to stay on.[90]

As an enticement, Nixon considered making Connally not only his treasury secretary but the deputy president for international economic affairs. That proposal received a cool reception from certain precincts in the White House. Haldeman, Ehrlichman, and Shultz, talking among themselves on January 19, wondered how Connally, with "no staff and no time," could handle extra responsibilities and the Treasury too. They doubted that Connally as deputy president could enforce his authority on his fellow cabinet members and feared he would cut out the White House staff. "We are all Nixon men, not Connally men," Shultz said. The president needed his own people who knew what was going on and would look out for his interests. He, Shultz, had realized in a meeting the day before "how disconnected he has become from the P." The problem was that "Connally doesn't have the depth, breadth, or ultimate responsibility," Shultz observed. "Nixon is a much deeper, more subtle man than Connally; has values, Connally doesn't." Later in the day, Haldeman conveyed these views to Nixon, who decided that it was "not in Connally's interests to be out front on decision making . . . We need to take the heat off Connally on this and put it on the White House." In other words, Connally would not become deputy president after all. "What he really wants," Haldeman notes, "is Connally as an adviser, especially on the political input."[91]

Growing tension between Connally and the White House staff erupted on April 13, 1972, when someone contacted a treasury official before clearing it first with the secretary. Connally told Haldeman that "this was the last straw, he'd had it and he was through . . . that he feels there's clearly a conspiracy."[92] Connally cooled off enough a few days later to admit that his

---

[90] *Haldeman Diaries*, Jan. 19, 1972.
[91] Ibid.
[92] Ibid., Apr. 13, 1972.

problems with the staff were partly his own fault, but he did not change his mind about quitting. When Haldeman floated the name of George Shultz as his successor at the Treasury — undoubtedly at Nixon's instigation — Connally readily approved.[93]

Neither Nixon nor Connally intended Connally's departure to end their partnership. Nixon still talked of replacing Agnew with Connally on the ticket in 1972 — though opposition from Republican conservatives made this option highly unlikely — and he still considered Connally as the only man with the right stuff to succeed him in 1976. But how to do it? Nixon had a plan, or more precisely a wish. As Nixon explained to Haldeman in April, Connally would wait until after the Democratic convention in July and then form Democrats for Nixon. Following the November elections, the two of them would move to build a new political party, the Independent Conservative Party, "or something of that sort," that would include Southern and other conservative Democrats, along with middle "road to conservative Republicans." By structuring it right, Nixon said, "we could develop a new majority party. Under a new name. Get control of Congress without an election, simply by realignment, and make a truly historic change in the entire American political structure." The candidate of the new party in 1976 would be John Connally.[94]

On May 16, 1972, Nixon surprised Washington by announcing Connally's resignation from the Treasury. In June, Nixon sent Connally around the globe on a goodwill tour, and in August, Connally launched Democrats for Nixon. In September, as the campaign began, Nixon instructed Haldeman to "focus on Connally to the maximum possible" — part of Nixon's strategy to fashion a New Majority in contrast to a mere Republican majority.[95] One week in mid-September Connally did a five-minute nationwide television spot for the president, went to New York to announce a branch of Democrats for Nixon, delivered a campaign speech in Pittsburgh, and hosted a lavish roast beef and tortilla dinner for Nixon and 400 prominent Democrats at his ranch in Floresville, Texas.[96] Meanwhile, Nixon continued to rely on Connally for political advice and remained in close personal contact. That autumn the future of this unlikely pair could hardly have seemed brighter.

---

[93] Ibid., Apr. 18, 1972.
[94] Ibid., Apr. 22, 1972.
[95] Ibid., Sept. 20, 1972.
[96] *Wall Street Journal*, Sept. 15, 1972, 1; *Newsweek* (Oct. 2, 1972), 15–16.

"Big John Connally has put on an extraordinary performance," said his successor George Shultz.[97] Shultz, by contrast, lacked sizzle. Not an effective spokesman for administration policy, not an outstanding professional economist nor a political tactician, Shultz nonetheless enjoyed Nixon's confidence, first as secretary of labor and, since July 1970, as director of the Office of Management and Budget (OMB). Shultz was a superb manager and a team player, who had abdicated the role of Nixon's chief economic adviser to Connally in 1971 and stayed on loyally to execute policy he did not believe in. Now that the economy was no longer a pressing political problem, Nixon rewarded Shultz with Connally's job.

That job was made more difficult because the good Nixon who admired Shultz's integrity vied with the bad Nixon who hoped to corrupt it. During the fall campaign, John Dean, White House counsel, tried to pressure the Internal Revenue Service (IRS) into investigating the tax returns of McGovern staff members and supporters. Johnnie Walters, the IRS Commissioner, protested to his chief, the secretary of the treasury, George Shultz, who in effect told Walters to ignore Dean.[98] On September 15, 1972, Dean interrupted a conversation in the Oval Office about Watergate to warn that Shultz might complain " 'cause I made a request of Johnnie Walters." Nixon said, "I don't want George Shultz ever raising a question" about it and threatened to throw Shultz out of the office if he did. "He didn't get Secretary of the Treasury because he's got nice blue eyes . . . It was a goddamn favor to him to get that job." Nixon said that after the election, he would clean out the IRS and put in his own people, "The whole Goddamn bunch go out." And if Shultz would not do it, "he's out as Secretary of the Treasury. And that's the way it was going to be played."[99] Instead of getting rid of Shultz after the election, Nixon gave him the title of special assistant to the president for economic affairs, making him, as press secretary Ron Zeigler explained, "the focal point and the over-all coordinator of the entire economic decision-making process, both domestically and internationally."[100] In this position, wrote Herbert Stein, who was in a position

[97] *Newsweek* (May 29, 1972), 63.

[98] "Affidavit of Johnnie M. Walters in 'Presidential Campaign Activities of 1972: Senate Resolution 60,' " Select Committee on Presidential Campaign Activities, U.S. Senate, Executive Session, hearings (1974), 11680–11683.

[99] White House Tapes (Watergate Special Prosecutor Force File Segment), Transcript of Conversation, Sept. 15, 1972, Nixon Project. In this transcript, Nixon's remark that Shultz got this job as a favor is deleted ("researcher restricted"), but it is quoted in J. Anthony Lukas, *Nightmare: The Underside of the Nixon Years* (1976), 25–26.

[100] *New York Times*, Dec. 2, 1972, 1.

to know, Shultz "was as much a czar over economic policy as anyone has ever been in this country."[101]

Herbert Stein was the second member of Nixon's revamped Troika, having replaced Paul McCracken as chair of the Council of Economic Advisers on January 1, 1972. Stein brought Nixon important advantages, not least his devotion to Nixon's reelection, and he accepted with reasonably good grace the diminished role of the CEA in this administration and its subordination to George Shultz. A droll wit and taste for the limelight made Stein an effective public spokesmen for the administration's economic policies, though critics accused him of compromising the CEA's professional integrity by his partisanship. Attacking the Democrats for lack of new ideas in February 1972, Stein said, "It isn't good enough for the heroes of the New Politics to campaign against Herbert Hoover" or to rediscover the WPA or "palm off sincerity and platitudes as profundity."[102] In June, Stein attributed McGovern's welfare proposals to "the ferocious desire of the middle aged — and we might say middle class and Middle Western . . . to appeal to youth and the rest of the country which now idolizes the idea of youth."[103]

At a congressional hearing in July, Senator Proxmire admonished Stein for these speeches. "You are witty, you are literate, you are very good at this type of thing . . . But I just wonder if, having this remarkable and unusual knack of wit, you should use it in view of your present position." Stein admitted that "my language is sometimes more colorful than that used by many of my predecessors," and he promised that he would "try to be more sober in the future."[104] But Stein was irrepressible. In September, during a speech on meat prices, he claimed that he had just bought a four-pound chuck roast that cost forty-two cents less now than two weeks before. To provide visual emphasis, he pulled the roast from his briefcase and held it up triumphantly for the cameras.[105]

Caspar "Cap" Weinberger became the third member of the Troika by moving up from deputy director of OMB to director, replacing Shultz. A California politician who had been Governor Ronald Reagan's finance

[101] Stein, *Presidential Economics*, 145.
[102] Stein speech reprinted in *Cong Rec* (1972), 4262–4263.
[103] *New York Times*, June 18, 1972, 1.
[104] "The 1972 Midyear Review of the Economy," Joint Economic Committee, hearings (1972), 30–31.
[105] *Newsweek* (Sept. 18, 1972), 77.

chief in 1968 and 1969, Weinberger began his career in the Nixon administration in January 1970 as chairman of the Federal Trade Commission.[106] When Shultz took over the OMB six months later, he brought in Weinberger to oversee day-to-day operations while he concentrated on high policy at the White House. Weinberger had traditionally Republican views. "I know that there's hardly an economist these days who doesn't laugh when you talk about balancing budgets on some disciplined basis," said Cap the Knife, as he was known throughout the government for his budget-cutting prowess. "But there isn't a man in the bond market, the stock market or the international banking community who isn't inclined to see budget deficits as a sign of weakness and inflation."[107] Weinberger was the right budget chief for the dramatic shift in economic and political course that Nixon executed in mid-1972.

## VII

The whole point of Nixon's domestic presidency was to create a New Majority by taking the center and recruiting Democrats to his cause. The centrist Democrat whom he coveted remained symbolized by Ben Wattenberg's forty-seven-year-old housewife married to the blue-collar worker in suburban Dayton. Nixon's initial strategy to snare this voter had been to run as a conservative on the Social Issue and a moderate on the Economic Issue, mixing in a modest reform agenda. But the center was not some fixed point along the ideological spectrum; the center moved with the shifting sands of public sentiment. During the course of Nixon's first term, the center drifted ideologically to the right and not only on issues of culture. As Nixon saw it, no doubt correctly, the Dayton housewife had lost interest in reform and was turning conservative even on the Economic Issue. She had become disillusioned with big government, social engineering, and high taxes — in short, with the policies of the ultraliberal George McGovern. To recruit disaffected blue-collar, Catholic, and white southern Democrats to the New Majority, Nixon now veered sharply away from the moderation that had marked his early policies.

In June 1972, before the campaign began, Nixon instructed Haldeman "to turn off our people who want to move the P to the center or to the left

---

[106] Eleanora W. Schoenbaum, ed., *Profiles of an Era: The Nixon/Ford Years* (1979), 657–659.

[107] *Newsweek* (July 3, 1972), 60.

because of McGovern . . . He wants to carve out a clean-cut position on the right, away from McGovern."[108] Later in the year, again to Haldeman: "We've had enough social programs, forced integration, education, housing." Though Congress and the establishment "think that the country want this stuff," they were wrong. "The huge social programs have been tried. They don't work. People don't want more on welfare. They don't want to help the working poor, and our mood has to be harder on this, not softer . . . P feels . . . that the huge colossus of government is a mess. The people running it are incompetent and won't change, and the American people don't want to support it."[109]

Beginning in mid-1972, Nixon defined his new position through the budget. During the first half of the year, the emphasis had been on spending to revive a sluggish economy. Once it was too late for more expenditures to help in November, Nixon became the champion of frugality, the very antithesis of the spendthrift Democrat against whom he would run. From its earliest days, the administration had been expecting a budget crisis, the result of costly entitlements growing faster than revenues. At last, it appeared, the crisis was at hand. In its new mood, Nixon believed, the New Majority would support a defense of the budget by gutting the welfare state.

In May 1972, the administration's thesis of a coming budget crisis had received support from an unexpected source. The Brookings Institution, a haven for Democratic economists and recently considered for firebombing by Charles Colson,[110] published a study showing that, over the past decade, federal spending had accelerated, while taxes had been cut, squandering the historic surplus. Even if the government initiated no new programs, the budget would barely balance in FY 73 and swing heavily into deficit by FY 75. Locating the major cause of rising expenditures in Great Society programs, the study conceded that vast sums had been allocated in the 1960s to solve social problems without real knowledge of what to do. Nonetheless, the study called for continued efforts to achieve social justice and for higher taxes to fund them.[111]

The day after the *New York Times* ran a front-page story on the Brookings report, John Ehrlichman responded in a press conference that

---

[108] *Haldeman Diaries,* June 2, 1972.
[109] Ibid., Sept. 20, 1972.
[110] Lukas, *Nightmare,* 89–90.
[111] Charles L. Shultze et al., *Setting National Priorities: The 1973 Budget* (1972), chaps. 12, 13. Shultze had been budget director under LBJ.

launched Nixon's fiscal offensive. The way to balance the full-employment budget was not to raise taxes and spend more but to hold down taxes and spend less, Ehrlichman said. "The difficulty with the Brookings analysis is that it rejects the possibility of economies in the Federal Government. We do not think the alternative can be laid aside." Ehrlichman said that the administration had a list of 110 social programs that should neither be redesigned nor modified but simply dumped. The only example he offered was Model Cities, a Great Society program that most would agree deserved dumping.[112]

Nixon confirmed the administration's new direction for his lieutenants at the annual midyear budget review in the White House on June 26, 1972. "The President said firmly that there would be no new initiatives proposed by him in the 1974 budget," the minutes reported. "He also directed that we make major efforts after November to reduce farm expenditures . . . He said Great Society programs were well-intentioned, but they haven't accomplished their purpose and they need to be flushed. He mentioned Food Stamps in particular." Nixon directed another cut in federal employment and indicated he would liberally employ his veto power to block congressional overspending. The president said "that if we win, we will have a real chance, perhaps our only chance to change the direction of spending." The time "to take the heat" was 1973 because in 1974 "people would start telling him that he couldn't make reductions" because it was another election year.[113]

For the fiscal year beginning July 1972, Nixon drew a line in the sand. To balance the full-employment budget, expenditures could not exceed $246 billion. Because crossing that line would mean either an inflationary deficit or new taxes, defense of the budget became Nixon's highest domestic priority. Haldeman's diary for July 6, 1971: "The President considers that more important than all legislative proposals is to hold down the cost of living and avoid a tax increase . . . It's time to call a halt."[114]

There were limits to Nixon's reincarnation as a fiscal conservative. In 1971, he had proposed a modest 5 percent increase in social security benefits, which had good prospects of passage until Democrats campaigning in the 1972 primaries upped the bidding to 20 percent. Late in June, con-

[112] *New York Times*, May 26, 1972, 1.

[113] Weinberger for President's file, June 26, 1972, Memos for President's file, POF.

[114] *Haldeman Diary*, July 6, 1972.

gressional Democrats decided to short-circuit the legislative process by tacking social security amendments onto a bill to raise the ceiling of the national debt. The amendments increased social security benefits by 20 percent and authorized automatic future increases tied to the cost of living.[115] Higher benefits would be reflected in checks mailed in October 1972, but higher taxes to pay for them would not take effect till January 1973. As a result, the measure would push expenditures above Nixon's spending limit by $3.7 billion.[116] Though Nixon opposed the social security amendments as highly inflationary, Congress approved them anyway. Nixon had little choice but to sign. If he did not, the national debt would reach the legal limit, forcing the government to close down; Congress would override him anyway; and senior citizens would be furious. In October 1972, beneficiaries received bigger social security checks, along with a statement saying that the increase had been enacted by Congress, "and signed into law by Richard Nixon."[117]

The 1973 fiscal year had only just begun and already Nixon was losing the battle of the budget. On July 11, 1972, Weinberger delivered the bad news that Congress was exceeding Nixon's expenditure target by a total of $7.1 billion. Weinberger proposed a "Veto Strategy" to stop the bleeding.[118] Two weeks later, Nixon warned Congress that if it passed bills threatening his balanced full-employment budget, he would veto them. Proving he meant it, Nixon vetoed an appropriation bill for HEW and Labor that increased spending for a number of popular programs but exceeded Nixon's request by $1.8 billion.[119] "Good God!" said Senator Humphrey. "I thought President Nixon would sign this bill. I didn't believe that at least in this election year he would be so callous, so indifferent, and so foolish."[120]

In October, at the height of the campaign, Congress took up Nixon's proposal to impose a $250 billion expenditure ceiling for the current fiscal year. Appealing for passsage in a radio address on October 7, Nixon said, "I consider the battle against higher prices and higher taxes to be the major domestic issue of this Presidential campaign."[121] The House passed the

---

[115] *Congressional Quarterly Almanac* (vol. 27, 1972), 399–403.
[116] *Pub Paps RN 1972*, 713, 723–724.
[117] Tufte, *Political Control of the Economy*, 32.
[118] Weinberger for President, July 11, 1972, President's Handwriting file, POF.
[119] *Pub Paps RN 1972*, 776–777.
[120] *Wall Street Journal*, Sept. 11, 1972, 1.
[121] *Pub Paps RN 1972*, 964–967. Quote p. 965.

ceiling as Nixon wanted it, but in October the Senate decided to defend the power of the purse and killed it.[122] That night Nixon retaliated by vetoing the "staggering, budget-wrecking" Water Pollution Control Act, a veto that Congress overrode the next day, the last day of the session.[123] Nixon then proceeded to veto nine appropriation bills, which together exceeded his spending requests by $750 million.[124] Meanwhile, Shultz announced that Nixon did not really need Congressional approval to cut appropriated funds and would impound them when necessary to save his budget.[125] Reduced to counterpunching, McGovern declared that if Nixon were reelected, he was "going to veto us right back to where we were in 1932."[126] By then the majority of Americans had stopped paying any attention to McGovern.

## VIII

Three factors determine the choice of voters: party identification, candidates, and issues. Nixon's strategy in 1972 was to downplay parties. "Use the new American majority, not Republican majority," he instructed Haldeman. "Work for the election of Congressmen and Senators who will support the P, not who are Republicans."[127] "His basic point," Haldeman observed, "is that we've got to make clear that we have the clearest choice in a century on the issues and between the men."[128] By stressing issues and downplaying his Republican identity, Nixon sought to make it easier for centrist Democrats to join the New Majority. In this project, Nixon was fortunate in his opponent. "Contrary to some published reports," said John Mitchell, "the Committee for the Reelection of the President is not engaged in selecting the Democratic candidate."[129] This was not strictly true because one of the objectives of Nixon's team of dirty tricksters had been to discredit Muskie in the primaries and thereby facilitate the nomination of George McGovern. McGovern was the candidate Nixon wanted, and McGovern was the one he got.

---

[122] *New York Times*, Oct. 4, 1972, 27; Oct. 11, 1; Oct. 14, 1; Oct. 15, 1, 37; Oct. 18, 1.

[123] *Pub Paps RN 1972*, 990–993.

[124] Ibid., 1042–1045.

[125] *New York Times*, Oct. 19, 1972, 1.

[126] Ibid., Oct. 30, 1972, 1.

[127] *Haldeman Diaries*, Sept. 20, 1972.

[128] Ibid., July 17, 1972.

[129] *Time* (June 19, 1972), 14.

A prairie populist and preacher's son, McGovern won the nomination by rallying the left wing of his party. Moral revulsion against the Vietnam war had ignited his candidacy; commitment to reordering the nation's priorities sustained it. McGovern would get back the POWs and then unilaterally withdraw from Vietnam. He would slash defense spending and soak the rich to fund increased spending on agriculture, the environment, mass transportation, and education. He promised a job to anyone who wanted one and national health insurance for everybody.[130] He favored busing to dismantle dual school districts, supported amnesty for draft resisters, considered abortion a matter for the states, and opposed jail sentences for possession of small amounts of marijuana. Fatally for his chances, in January 1972, McGovern rather casually proposed a plan to reform welfare that would provide every man, woman, and child in the United States a Minimum Income Grant, which he suggested might be $1,000 per year.

The scheme worked this way: A family of four without any income would keep its entire $4,000; a family of four earning $8,000 would keep $2,000 and return $2,000. Families earning $12,000 would break even, while families with incomes above $12,000 would be taxed at progressively higher rates to obtain the estimated net $43 billion needed to fund the program.[131] (Median family income in 1972 was $11,000.) During the California primary, when Senator Humphrey charged that this plan would require an unmarried secretary earning $8,000 to pay $567 in additional taxes,[132] McGovern's welfare proposal became the most famous — and the most politically damaging — part of his campaign, convenient evidence to support Nixon's thesis that McGovern was not a Democrat at all but a dangerous radical outside the American mainstream.

Entering the summer fighting uphill on the issues, McGovern destroyed his candidacy by his selection of a running mate. Missouri Senator Tom Eagleton was not McGovern's first choice for vice president, but Eagleton seemed a good complement to McGovern on the ticket — Catholic, urban, on good terms with organized labor — and he got the nod on Thursday

---

[130] McGovern's testimony in "National Priorities: Next Five Years," Joint Economic Committee, hearings (1972), 325–367; David Ott et al., *Nixon, McGovern, and the Federal Budget* (Sept. 1973), publication of American Enterprise Institute.

[131] Ames speech reprinted in *Cong Rec* (1972), 11799–11801; for an inside account, Gordon L. Weil, *The Long Shot: George McGovern for President* (1973), chap. 3.

[132] White, *Making of the President 1972*, 128.

afternoon, July 14, 1972, the last full day of the Democratic convention. That night it took so long to nominate Eagleton that McGovern did not begin his acceptance speech, the most important of his career, until 2:48 Friday morning.[133] "From a conflict in Indochina which maims our ideals as well as our soldiers, come home, America," McGovern said as the people slept. "From military spending so wasteful it weakens the nation, come home America. From the waste of idle hands to the joy of useful labor, come home America . . . Come home to the belief we can seek a newer world."[134]

A week later, McGovern learned that Eagleton had been hospitalized three times since 1960 for mental illness. At a press conference in Custer, South Dakota, Sunday, July 24, with McGovern present, Eagleton responded to rumors by laying bare his medical history. McGovern said that even if he had known of this history at the convention, he would still have chosen Eagleton. On Wednesday McGovern declared he was "1000 percent for Tom Eagleton and [had] no intention of dropping him from the ticket." On Friday, as pressure mounted to remove Eagleton, McGovern buckled, and by Sunday Tom Eagleton was gone.[135] This sorry spectacle made McGovern appear both incompetent and indecisive, an impression that no amount of campaigning in succeeding months could erase. Some weeks later, when Gallup asked which of the candidates was more "sincere and believable," Nixon, incredibly, polled 59 percent to McGovern's 20 percent.[136]

Nixon made clear the purpose of his own campaign in his acceptance speech before the Republican national convention in Miami on August 23. "To those millions who have been driven out of their home in the Democratic party, we say come home. We say come home not to another party, but we say come home to the great principles we Americans believe in together . . . I ask you to join us as members of a new American majority bound together by our common ideas." In this speech and others that he and his surrogates would make in the weeks ahead, the point was to win Democrats by emphasizing the issues. McGovern would default on Vietnam, Nixon charged. His administration, by contrast, had withdrawn most

[133] *Newsweek* (July 24, 1972), 17.

[134] White, *Making of the President 1972*, 184–186; *Vital Speeches* (Aug. 1, 1972), 610–612.

[135] *New York Times*, July 26, 1972, 1; July 27, 1; July 29, 1; Aug. 1, 1; White, *Making of the President 1972*, chap. 8.

[136] *Gallup Poll*, 62.

U.S. troops, ended the draft, and nearly eliminated American casualties, all the while seeking peace with honor. McGovern was proposing programs that would add $144 billion to the budget, Nixon said, plucking a number out of the air. His administration would block inflation and prevent a tax increase by fighting federal spending. McGovern, said Nixon, "insults the intelligence of the American voters" by proposing to pay every person $1,000. His administration preferred incentives for people to "get off of welfare and to get to work." McGovern would wreck the national defense. Nixon promised "a defense second to none," with mutual rather than unilateral arms reductions. McGovern favored busing; Nixon, neighborhood schools.[137] McGovern was the candidate of "amnesty, acid, and abortion."[138] Nixon stood for old-fashioned American values, topped with gobs of patriotism symbolized by the America flags that he and all his top staffers except Kissinger conspicuously wore as pins on their lapels.[139] At the end of August, after the Eagleton fiasco and the Republican offensive on the issues, Gallup had Nixon outpointing McGovern 64 percent to 30 percent.[140]

On August 23, 1972, McGovern's chief issues man wrote him a memo advising a change of course. "Our primary and perhaps only chance to win will lie in reclaiming those millions of traditional Democrats who are now undecided or leaning to Nixon," Democrats who were "typically blue-collar, middle-minded," and socially conservative. This could be done as every Democrat since Roosevelt did it — by being for the little guy and against the fat cats.[141] A few days later, McGovern trimmed his message as well as his hair for the Society of Security Analysts, a Wall Street audience ill-disposed to anything he might have to say. Gone now was the $1,000 Minimum Income Grant and his vastly expensive national health insurance plan. To pay for his remaining program, McGovern would slice $30 billion from the defense budget over three years and close tax loopholes worth $22 billion. Tax reforms would hit the wealthy and the corporations, McGovern conceded, but "no American whose income comes from wages and salaries would pay one penny more in taxes than he does now."[142]

---

[137] *Pub Paps RN 1972*, 787–795.
[138] *Time* (June 19, 1973), 13.
[139] White, *Making of the President 1972*, 219.
[140] *Gallup Poll*, 55.
[141] White, *Making of the President 1972*, 217.
[142] *New York Times*, Aug. 30, 1972, 1; speech excerpted in the *Times*, 22.

Among fat cats hostile to these words were traditional Democratic donors. Middle America was not listening.

McGovern's efforts to reach traditional Democrats suffered from the opposition of the AFL-CIO to the ticket. At the beginning of the year, the federation declared that it would support any Democrat against Richard Nixon.[143] George Meany, after all, had been the most outspoken critic of the administration's controls program, had orchestrated the insulting reception that the president had received at the AFL-CIO convention in November 1971, and had walked out of the Pay Board in March 1972. Nixon's long courtship of Meany seemed doomed — until the unexpected rise of George McGovern, whose stand on the war, defense, and social issues Meany could not abide. Meany's dislike for McGovern, which was personal, stemmed from an episode in 1966 when McGovern had solemnly promised labor a vote on a crucial issue in the Senate and then did not deliver.[144] At the 1972 Democratic convention, Meany led a coalition of union leaders, big city bosses, and Southerners in a doomed effort to stop McGovern. A week after the convention, the AFL-CIO executive committee voted 27–3 to refrain from backing either candidate, though individual unions could make endorsements. It was the first time in its history that the federation declined to endorse the Democratic nominee.[145] In 1968, labor's heroic efforts had almost rescued Hubert Humphrey. In 1972, not a cent of the AFL-CIO's $6 million campaign fund would be available to George McGovern.[146]

Late in July, Meany joined Nixon, Shultz, and Secretary of State William Rogers for a private golf game at Burning Tree Country Club outside Washington. Paired with Meany, Nixon changed the handicaps on the back nine to make sure his team won and then retired to the porch for drinks and cigars. The talk was about politics. Meany dismissed McGovern as a double-dealer of little character and predicted that only twenty-seven of a hundred or so unions would endorse him. He himself would not vote for anybody, but his wife would vote for Nixon, Meany said. "Just so you won't get a swelled head, you ought to know that Mrs. Meany really hates McGovern."[147] Through the rest of the campaign, Meany stayed in touch

---

[143] Ibid., Jan. 26, 1972, 16.
[144] White, *Making of the President 1972*, 212.
[145] *New York Times*, July 20, 1972, 1.
[146] *Newsweek* (July 24, 1972), 36, 40.
[147] Shultz to Haldeman, Aug. 8, 1972, President's Meeting file, POF.

with Nixon via Shultz and freely gave advice on how the president should run his race.[148]

The Economic Issue, which Nixon had once feared would defeat him, played only a subordinate role in the 1972 campaign. If unemployment and inflation had remained problems, Nixon might indeed have been vulnerable. By the summer of 1972, the numbers were looking good enough for Nixon to hope that the issue had been neutralized, but he still did not consider the economy an asset in the campaign. Through July and August, Haldeman recorded Nixon's several observations on the subject. "The P made the point . . . that the economic issue is their ground not ours and we should not play to it." "The best he can do is avoid the negative as much as possible." "We will always be outbid, so we don't want them thinking about the economy on election day."[149] By late October, when Nixon finally left the White House for the campaign trail, the numbers looked so good that he told Haldeman, "The big issues are peace and pocketbook."[150] The economy hardly dominated his speeches, and he rarely mentioned the New Economic Policy and never controls, but he took credit for prosperity and ran on it hard.

Opening in upstate New York late in October, Nixon said the great goals were peace and jobs. The United States had the highest rate of growth in the world, he said, and the lowest inflation rate of any industrial power.[151] In Ohio he boasted that employment had increased "by a near-record 2½ million" during the past year, while the average worker enjoyed an increase in real spendable income equal to two extra weekly paychecks.[152] Speaking nationwide over radio on November 2, he said, "We are well on the way to achieving what America has not had since President Eisenhower lived here in the White House: prosperity with full employment, without inflation and without war."[153] Everywhere he emphasized his fight against McGovern's reckless spending proposals, which he claimed would mean inflation and a 50 percent increase in taxes. McGovern never found a way to counter these charges or turn the Economic Issue to his advantage.

---

[148] Ehrlichman for President, Aug. 25, 1972, President's Handwriting file, POF.
[149] *Haldeman Diaries*, July 6, 1972; July 31; Aug. 7.
[150] Ibid., Oct. 29, 1972.
[151] *Pub Paps RN 1972*, 1019.
[152] Ibid., 1059.
[153] Ibid., 1087.

On election day, November 7, 1972, Nixon scored a triumph beyond anything he could have imagined even six months before. Winning 60 percent of the popular votes, he lost only Massachusetts in the Electoral College. Though he polled well among all demographic groups except blacks, Nixon could take special satisfaction from the gains he made among the groups he courted hardest. Nixon swept the white South and carried nearly 60 percent of Catholic and working class voters.[154] Deemphasizing party and appealing to an increasingly conservative electorate on the issues, Nixon had forged not just a majority but, it appeared, a New Majority.

As Nixon understood, the significance of the Economic Issue in 1972 was that the Democrats had been unable to employ it against him. He could use the economy as an embellishment of his own record but not as the basis of his campaign. More important than the economy as an issue was the contribution of the boom to the mood of buoyancy and optimism that helped the incumbent in intangible but crucial ways. On December 2, 1972, Stein sent Nixon a memo reporting that real GNP was expected to rise 6.4 percent in 1972, "higher than any previous election year of the postwar period." Nixon wrote back, "Herb—This helped us win big."[155] Within weeks, the economy would become engulfed in its worst crisis since the Great Depression.

---

[154] Arthur H. Miller, Warren E. Miller, Alder S. Raine, Thad A. Brown, "A Majority Party in Disarray: Policy Polarization in the 1972 Election," *American Political Science Review* (vol. 70, Sept. 1976), 753–778. See also other articles in this issue offering differing but less persuasive views.

[155] Stein for President, Dec. 2, 1972, President's Handwriting file, POF.

## Chapter 8

# The Great Inflation

---

### I

When Nixon took the oath of office for the second time on January 20, 1973, he stood at the pinnacle of his career. The electorate had given him a resounding endorsement. The Paris Accords, officially concluded three days later, would extricate both his presidency and the nation from Vietnam. Preparations were proceeding for a June summit in the United States with Leonid Brezhnev, the next step toward détente. The economy seemed poised to achieve Nixon's goal of full employment without inflation. No one could then have foreseen that, by spring, Watergate and the economy would combine to drive him to the brink of ruin.

Nixon himself found little satisfaction in his landslide. "You'd think I'd be elated," he said. "Well, you're so drained emotionally at the end, you can't feel much. You'd think that just when the time comes, you'd have your greatest day. But there is this letdown."[1] Unable to shake his melancholy, Nixon spent the weeks after the campaign isolated in his various retreats, brooding not on how to heal the wounds of war and unify the country but how to punish his enemies and realize the ideological agenda of the second term. "Now I planned to give expression to the more conservative values and beliefs of the New Majority throughout the country," he wrote in his memoirs, "and use my power to put some teeth into my New American Revolution."[2]

Curiously, Nixon hesitated to combine his ideological offensive with practical moves toward party realignment, the preeminent goal in the first term. Having fought his last campaign, he had to face the fact that someone else would benefit from his creation of the New Majority. Perhaps

---

[1] *Time* (Jan. 22, 1973), 11.
[2] *RN: Memoirs*, 761.

Nixon thought that he had more time than he did to take the next steps. Perhaps when confronted with the challenge of moving from talk to action, he lost his nerve. Whatever the reason, by the time John Connally announced in May that he was a Republican, Watergate had already destroyed all their plans. Meanwhile, Nixon antagonized George Meany by appointing as his new secretary of labor Peter Brennan of the New York Building Trades, and he got at cross-purposes with Meany on issues of wage and price control. Watergate would soon drive Meany into final opposition and make labor unions once again Nixon's implacable foe. As for southern Democrats in Congress, a key component of a New Majority party, they were so offended by Nixon's imperial pretensions following the election that many of them went into opposition too. In the coming crisis of his presidency, when Nixon cast about for political allies, he would find but few.

Nixon's New American Revolution began in the executive branch of the government. Within hours of the election Nixon and Haldeman undertook a purge of the top 200 to 300 jobs in the departments and agencies, clearing out anyone suspected of being insufficiently loyal or an inadequate instrument of the president's will. Some of the new appointees moved directly from the White House to take over the bureaucracy; others were chosen to reflect the composition of the New Majority — Catholics, union officials, ethnics, southerners. Next, Nixon announced a radical reorganization of the government similar to one he had unsuccessfully asked Congress to approve in 1971 and that he now implemented on his own authority. Designed to consolidate and coordinate the existing departments, the plan created four super secretaries, who were lodged in the White House to tighten Nixon's grip.[3]

In his second inaugural, Nixon expressed the conservative purpose that this concentration of power would serve. "Let us remember that America was not built by government but by people; not by welfare, but by work; not by shirking responsibility but by seeking responsibility." Twelve years before to the day, John Kennedy had declared, "Ask not what your country can do for you; ask what you can do for your country." Nixon now offered

---

[3] Richard P. Nathan, *The Plot That Failed: Nixon and the Administrative Presidency* (1975), chap. 4; Frederic Malek, *Washington's Hidden Tragedy: The Failure to Make Government Work* (1978), 75–80; Stephen Hess, *Organizing the Presidency*, rev. ed. (1988), 126–128.

the Republican reply, "Let each of us ask — not just what government will do for me, but what can I do for myself?"[4] Or as Nixon restated the point in the privacy of his office, "Get off your ass and go to work."[5]

The instrument for effecting Nixon's conservative revolution was the budget. At a Cabinet meeting a few days after the Inauguration, Nixon explained the politics of the issue. "People are for spending," he said. The argument to use against spending "is that it's the only way to avoid inflation and higher taxes . . . You never debate the programs."[6] To achieve a balanced full-employment budget during the current fiscal year, Nixon was refusing to spend more than $12 billion in appropriated funds, an affront to its power so galling that Congress would soon debate whether impoundments warranted his impeachment.[7] Federal purchases of goods and services would actually decline in real terms that year, and expenditures would come in at $246 billion, Nixon's original target precisely.[8]

That was only the beginning. In February 1973, less than a month into his new term, Nixon submitted an extraordinary budget for FY 74, beginning on July 1. If expenditures were "unconstrained," Nixon explained, they would balloon to $283 billion, creating an estimated deficit of $30 billion. The only way to avoid inflation or higher taxes was to declare war on federal spending and balance the full-employment budget. That meant containing FY 74 expenditure to $269 billion. How to cut prospective spending from $283 billion to $269 billion? Not by slashing defense expenditures, which had fallen from 44 percent of the federal budget in 1969 to a projected 30 percent the following year. The entire burden of the administration's economy drive would fall on domestic programs, incidentally furthering the president's new conservative agenda.[9]

In the name of economy, the new budget aimed to starve the welfare state. The president proposed to terminate outright programs that had lost

---

[4] *Pub Paps RN 1973*, 12–15. Quotes, 14.

[5] E-Notes, Feb. 21, 1973.

[6] *Haldeman Diaries*, Jan 24, 1973.

[7] The administration claimed to have impounded $8.7 billion, but the Democrats convincingly argued that the actual figure was $12.2 billion. *New York Times*, Feb. 6, 1973, 1.

[8] *Pub Paps RN 1974*, 112.

[9] On 1974 budget, Nixon's budget message, *Pub Paps RN 1973*, 32–48; "The Budget of the United States Government for the Fiscal Year 1974," Committee on Appropriations, Senate hearings (1973); special budget issue, *National Journal* (vol. 5, Feb. 3, 1973); and Edward R. Fried, Alice M. Rivlin, Charles L. Schultze, and Nancy Teeters, *Setting National Priorities: The 1974 Budget* (1973).

their usefulness or never had any — urban renewal, aid to school districts impacted by federal installations, grants for hospital construction despite a national surplus of hospital beds. He repaid farmers for their votes in the election by cutting or terminating price supports, the Rural Electrification Administration, and payments to promote soil and water management on private farms. He invited charges of heartlessness by reducing vocational rehabilitation, subsidized milk for school children, and funding for mental health. He took special aim at the Great Society programs of the 1960s — "too often poorly conceived and hastily put together," he said — Model Cities, aid to school districts with high concentrations of disadvantaged children, job training programs, and subsidized housing for low-income families.[10] And he sought abolition of the Office of Economic Opportunity, the command post of Lyndon Johnson's War on Poverty, including dispersal of its programs into other agencies and abandonment of its nearly 1,000 local community action agencies. Not without reason, *Newsweek* called this budget "one of the most significant American political documents since the dawning of the New Deal."[11]

If the budget were no ordinary state paper, the Congress that received it was in no ordinary mood. By itself, the budget was a highly divisive document bound to antagonize powerful constituencies and congressional Democrats, who continued to control both houses despite Nixon's landslide. In the political atmosphere of 1973, Nixon's new budget appeared to be not merely an attempt to downsize government. It confirmed a deepening belief in a White House plot to subvert the Constitution and impose one-man rule. In the last of his many incarnations, Nixon appeared as "King Richard," anointed by the people in the election and freed of the checks and balances that had inhibited other presidents. This Nixon had undertaken the Christmas bombing of Hanoi without consultation with Congress or explanations to the public. He claimed executive privilege in ordering aides not to appear before congressional committees. He had impounded billions, used doubtful authority to impose executive reorganization, and abused the veto power.

Then came the budget, upon whose arrival at the Capitol, said the *New York Times*, "one could sense a skip in the city's political pulse. The new budget proposed so sweeping a challenge both to programs and to Congress

---

[10] *Pub Paps RN 1973*, 42.
[11] *Newsweek* (Feb. 12, 1973), 16.

that it provoked not just surprise but shock, awe and anger."[12] It was an anger that united southern Democrats and northern Democrats and gripped a not inconsiderable number of Republicans, many of whom resented Nixon's efforts to keep his recent campaign at arm's length from their party. Said Representative Wright Patman, a Texas Democrat, "I have been in Congress under seven presidents . . . and never during this 44-year period have we been closer to one-man rule."[13] Said Senator William Saxbe, an Ohio Republican, "Is there anything or anybody other than his own conscience that limits a President from any overt act? There's nobody that can touch him. No Security Council, no Joint Chiefs of Staff, no veto power, nothing."[14]

Nixon's challenge to the prerogatives of Congress aroused the deepest antagonism in the upper chamber, where North Carolina's avuncular Sam Ervin, a conservative Democrat who revered the Constitution, emerged as field general of the resistance. At the end of January 1973, Ervin opened hearings on his bill to empower Congress to rescind executive impoundments — legislation, Ervin said, that "raised the question of whether the Congress of the United States shall remain a viable institution."[15] Meanwhile, Congress moved to reenact appropriations that the president had either pocket-vetoed after the 1972 congressional session or that he had impounded. Everyone knew that the appropriations would pass and that Nixon would veto them. The question was whether the congressional opposition could muster the necessary two-thirds to override a veto.

The test came early in April 1973 when Nixon vetoed a generous appropriations bill for vocational rehabilitation.[16] Jubilant Democrats believed that the president had delivered them the perfect issue to dramatize his lack of compassion. On the day of the vote to override, senators thundered against Nixon for his cold-blooded economies, while throngs of handicapped people lobbied in the corridors. In the end, Nixon's appeal to Senate Republicans for party unity prevailed, and the vote to override fell four votes short. With the support of one-third plus one of either chamber, King Richard could have his way. "The president is in the driver's seat,"

---

[12] *New York Times*, Feb. 4, 1973, IV, 1.

[13] Ibid., Feb. 11, 1973, IV, 1.

[14] *Time* (Jan. 22, 1973), 12.

[15] "Impoundments of Appropriated Funds," Committee on Goverment Operations and Subcommittee on Separation of Powers of Judiciary Committee, U.S. Senate, joint hearings (1973), 1.

[16] *Pub Paps RN 1973*, 223–225.

said the despondent majority leader of the Senate, Mike Mansfield, "at least for the time being."[17]

Within days, Nixon's power vanished, and the New American Revolution, which had barely begun, was over. The public had paid scant attention to the burglary of the Democratic national headquarters at the Watergate apartment complex in June of 1972. But on March 23, 1973, Judge John Sirica released a letter from James McCord, one of the convicted burglars and former security coordinator of the Committee for the Re-Election of the President. McCord's letter alleged perjury, involvement of unnamed others, and political pressure to plead guilty for the Watergate crime. "The dam was cracking," Haldeman recalled.[18] Meeting with the president two days before, White House counsel John Dean had warned, "We have a cancer — within — close to the Presidency, that's growing. It's growing daily. It's compounding."[19] Himself steeped in the cover-up and facing imminent exposure, Dean went to federal prosecutors on April 8 and was soon spilling his guts. During the rest of the month, a flood of devastating revelations laid bare the dark underside of the Nixon presidency and implicated in crime the president's closest advisers, including Ehrlichman and Haldeman, who resigned from the government on April 30, 1973, to commence their losing fight to stay out of jail. As the bad news mounted, Nixon's standing in the polls fell from 65 percent approval in March to 45 percent in May.[20] Watergate was hardly the only reason why Nixon was in trouble. Gallup reported that while 16 percent of the public named Watergate as the most important problem facing the country, 62 percent named "the high cost of living," that is, inflation, the problem that Nixon had claimed only months before to have beaten.[21]

## II

As 1973 began, the Nixon White House believed its own rhetoric — that wise policy was guiding America to prosperity without inflation. No one in

---

[17] On battle to override, *Congressional Quarterly Weekly Reports* (vol. 31, Apr. 7, 1973), 795–796; also *New York Times*, Apr. 4, 1973, 1. The Mansfield quote appears in both accounts.

[18] There are a number of good accounts of Watergate, including J. Anthony Lukas, *Nightmare* (1976), and Stanley I. Kutler, *The Wars of Watergate* (1990). Haldeman quote in Kutler, 261.

[19] *The White House Transcripts* (edited by *New York Times*, 1973), 134.

[20] *The Gallup Poll: Public Opinion 1972–1977* (vol. 1, 1978), 101, 124.

[21] Ibid., 124.

or out of the government foresaw the approach of the cataclysm. The CEA's forecast for the year would, in retrospect, seem fantastic. Output would advance briskly through the first half of calendar 1973, the CEA said, then gently ease as full employment loomed into view. Inflation would fall from a 3.5 percent rate in 1972 to 2.5 percent in 1973[22] — a goal Herbert Stein called "inspiring but not incredible."[23] Few economists disagreed. "It's very rare that you can be as unqualifiedly bullish as you can now," said Alan Greenspan, a leading economic consultant.[24] Among the reasons why so many economists were so wrong was the lingering illusion of idle capacity. The Federal Reserve estimated that industry was operating at only 83 percent capacity during the first quarter of 1973, compared to the most recent high in 1966 of 92 percent.[25] The CEA estimated that the gap between actual and potential GNP during the last quarter of 1972 was $26 billion. The economy, it appeared, could expand further without reinflating prices.[26]

But there was no idle capacity. Instead, two years of exuberant fiscal and monetary policies were propelling the economy out of control. Real GNP, up at the annual rate of 8.1 percent during the last quarter of 1972, grew at an unsustainable 8.7 percent rate during the first quarter of 1973. Consumer spending exploded, especially for autos. Sales of new cars, which had been on a 9 million pace early in the record year of 1972, climbed to an annual average of more than 11 million in March 1973.[27] Aggregate demand was so strong that shortages developed in raw materials and the basic materials industries — notably chemicals, steel, paper, and copper — putting a crimp in the production of final goods and raising their costs.[28] Under controls, higher costs justified higher prices; thus, despite controls, prices rose. Though the boom peaked in the winter of 1973, the Great Inflation, which the boom helped to launch, had just begun.

Excess demand caused only an estimated one-half of the nation's inflation over the next two years. The other half derived from worldwide commodity shortages, beginning in early 1973 with food.[29] The effects of excess

---

[22] CEA Annual Report 1973, 82.
[23] New York Times, Jan. 7, 1973, III, 22.
[24] Ibid., III, 44.
[25] Federal Reserve Bulletin (Jan. 1974), A62.
[26] CEA Annual Report 1974, 64–65; Business Week (June 9, 1973), 76–77.
[27] Survey of Current Business (Apr. 1973); (Dec. 1973), Table 19.
[28] CEA Annual Report 1974, 63.
[29] Phillip Cagan, Persistent Inflation (1979), 180–184, and footnote 4, pp. 263–264.

demand on inflation built gradually through 1973. The effects of the food shortage hit with sudden and devastating force in the first quarter of the year. Driven by an astounding 30 percent increase (annual rate) in food prices, the Consumer Price Index rose that winter at a rate of 8.7 percent. It would run at 8.4 percent for the year, considerably more than twice the inflation rate of 1972. Confessed economist Walter Heller, "This was the year of infamy in inflationary forecasting."[30]

Nixon's critics blamed the price surge on his decision in early 1973 to loosen price and wage controls. "If not now, when?" Stein asked at the time. "If we agree with the proposition that the end of controls is both desirable and necessary, then they should be discarded before the system breaks down or before it becomes embalmed like the corpse of Lenin, as a permanent fixture of government policy."[31] Because the public was still addicted to controls, the administration dared not go cold turkey but opted instead for an intermediate step back to the free market. On January 11, 1973, a moment of inflation optimism, George Shultz announced the surprise replacement of Phase II by Phase III, which mainly retained existing regulations but dispensed with the bureaucracy. No longer would large firms have to await permission from the Price Commission to raise a price. The Price Commission, along with the Pay Board, was summarily abolished. Under the new rules, large firms could raise prices when they chose and provide justification after the fact in quarterly reports to the Cost of Living Council, which was retained. The system was not voluntary, Shultz emphasized, because the COLC could roll back unjustified increases. As for wages, the unions and the White House informally agreed to bury Phase II guidelines in favor of a case-by-case appraisal of new contracts.[32] The new director of the COLC was well-suited to handle this task. He was John Dunlop, former dean of Arts and Sciences at Harvard, friend of George Shultz, and a long-time labor mediator well-respected by the unions.

Nixon, who had an "intuition" that Phase III would be trouble, dele-

---

[30] *New York Times*, Dec. 29, 1973, 31.

[31] Ibid., May 1, 1974, 70.

[32] *Pub Paps RN 1973*, 9–11; also background statement and Executive Order 11695 reprinted in "Economic Stabilization Legislation — 1973," Committee on Banking and Currency, Senate hearings (1973), 52–63. Phase III softened price regulations somewhat. The number of years for determining the base for allowable profit margins was increased, and the limit abandoned altogether if a firm's average price increases did not exceed 1.5 percent. Price increases were also permitted "when necessary for efficient allocation of resources or to maintain adequate level of supply." See also Shultz for President, Jan. 8, 1973, BE-3 file, WHCF. On wage guideline, *New York Times*, Mar. 1, 1973, 55.

gated the task of announcing it to Shultz.[33] Incredulous journalists and irate Democrats immediately demanded to know why the administration was junking machinery that had worked so well. Self-regulation was no more than an euphemism for decontrol, they charged.[34] Shultz said the power to roll back prices was "the stick in the closet." Senator Proxmire said it was "a peashooter under the pillow."[35] Investors found the uncertainties of Phase II so unnerving that the day after its termination, and for no other reason, the stock market turned sharply downward.[36] When inflation took off shortly afterward, the critics claimed vindication. Said the *New York Times* in March 1973, "hasty abandonment of Phase II last January now appears to have been premature and ill-advised."[37] It was an unfair accusation. Agricultural prices were the initial source of resurgent inflation in 1973, and they had never been controlled, whatever the phase or freeze. Phase II or Phase III, it made no difference. Farm prices would have risen anyway.

## III

It took the conjunction of multiple misfortunes to produce the food supply shock of 1973, but the underlying cause was the policy of scarcity pursued by the Department of Agriculture since the Depression.[38] The world's leading grain producer, the United States routinely grew more grain than it consumed. To the rest of the world, U.S. grain reserves, especially wheat, were a buffer against bad harvests. To the Agriculture Department, ample grain reserves meant low prices for its lone constituent, the American farmer. In 1960, wheat stocks in the United States equaled 80 percent of world exports. Through the next decade, to reduce stocks and raise prices, the Department encouraged removal of one-sixth of the nation's cropland from production. By 1970, U.S. wheat stocks had fallen to 40 percent of world exports, as it happened, a dangerously low level.[39]

---

[33] E-Notes, Jan. 8, 1973.

[34] *Business Week* (Jan. 27, 1973), 18.

[35] "Economic Stabilization Legislation — 1973," Senate hearings, 18.

[36] *New York Times*, Jan. 13, 1973, 37; Jan. 21, III, 1; April 8, 1973, III, 15.

[37] Ibid., Mar. 25, 1973, III, 16.

[38] This account of the food shock of 1973 relies on Dale E. Hathaway, "Food Prices and Inflation," *Brookings Papers on Economic Activity* (No. 1, 1974), 65–107; D. Gale Johnson, *World Food Problems and Prospects* (1975), esp. chaps. 2, 3; John A. Schnittker, "The 1972–73 Food Price Spiral," *Brookings Papers on Economic Activity* (No. 2, 1973), 498–507; Staff Study of Joint Economic Committee, "The 1972–73 Food Price Spiral," printed in "The Cost of Living," Joint Economic Committee, hearings (1973), 103–110.

[39] Hathaway, "Food Prices and Inflation," 85, Table 6.

Nixon's quest for reelection squeezed food supplies further. During the 1968 campaign, Nixon had blamed the Democrats for low farm prices. With prices even lower in 1970, unhappy farmers had shown a disturbing tendency in that congressional election year to punish Republicans. Of the Democrat's net gain of nine seats in the House, seven had come at the expense of the GOP in predominantly farm districts.[40] Analyzing the 1970 returns for Nixon, Charles Colson wrote, "Republicans did badly in those states in which high parity price support has always been *the* issue (Nebraska, the Dakotas, Kansas, for example); witness the four contiguous House seats in which the farm issue beat us in . . . districts that we should have won, but for the farm issue. We had been warned of discontent in the Farm Belt but it was too late to counter it."[41]

Nixon's farm troubles got worse in 1971, mainly because of the price of corn. A corn blight had so ravaged the 1970 crop that even the Department of Agriculture became concerned about corn shortages. Fearing the blight's return, the Department increased its corn-production target for 1971 and reduced by half the number of acres that it would pay farmers to set aside (i.e., divert) from corn production. The corn blight did little damage in 1971, and yields exceeded all expectations. The resulting record harvest drove corn prices down from $1.42 a bushel in mid-1971 to $1.00 by November, barely enough to cover the costs of production.[42] Out in Greene County, Iowa, where surplus corn was overflowing storage bins, the Republican county chairman said that it was not fair, but farmers were blaming the Republicans. "If there isn't an evident improvement by next year, Mr. Nixon would lose the farm vote here and maybe the rest of the Midwest," this official warned.[43] Nixon agreed. Telling Ehrlichman in mid-October not to worry about wheat, the president said that "corn means everything — Illinois, Indiana, Ohio . . . Do the corn thing fast." Get the price up to $1.15, he instructed.[44]

As part of his farm offensive, Nixon decided to replace his ineffective agriculture secretary, Clifford Hardin, with someone who understood poli-

---

[40] J. S. Francis, Jr., National Educational Institute, "Farm Vote Patterns — 1970," Feb. 10, 1971, Ag file, WHCF.

[41] Colson for President, Nov. 6, 1970, Alpha Subject file: Campaign of 1970, President's Personal file.

[42] These developments discussed in "Nomination of Earl Lauer Butz," Committee on Agriculture and Forestry, Senate hearings (1971); and "Commodity Reserves and Wheat and Feed Grain Program," same Committee, hearing (1973).

[43] *New York Times*, Oct. 27, 1971, 20.

[44] E-Notes, Oct. 14, 1971.

tics. Submitting a list of candidates to the president on October 19, 1971, Frederic Malek, the administration's chief headhunter, wrote, "My evaluation assumes that while management and policy abilities are expected, the distinguishing basis for selection should be the next Secretary's impact on the 1972 Presidential election."[45] The man Nixon chose was Earl Butz, a colorful and abrasive professor of agricultural economics, who had served three years as assistant secretary of agriculture under Eisenhower, spent eight years as dean of agriculture at Purdue University, and unsuccessfully sought the Republican nomination for governor of Indiana in 1968. In their first meeting, November 1971, Nixon instructed Butz to reexamine the corn problem "not as an intellectual but as a politician."[46] It was an instruction that Butz would more than fulfill. Though Butz's connections to agribusinesses like Ralston-Purina nearly derailed his nomination in the Senate, he survived to become Nixon's bulldog for higher prices down on the farm.[47] By February 1972, Butz was claiming credit for getting the price of the remaining 1971 corn crop up to $1.20.

Even before Butz took over, the Department had responded to the corn surplus by resuming its normal policy of scarcity. In October 1971, the Department announced that it would seek to set aside 38 million acres of feed grains (mainly corn) in 1972, up from 18 million acres in 1971. For wheat, the set-aside was 20 million acres, also a substantial increase.[48] One result was that in the coming election year the government would provide cash payments of $4 billion for farmers participating in its various crop reduction and conservation programs, helping to raise farm income by 20 percent and to assure Nixon a bountiful harvest of farm votes in November.[49] Another result was that in 1972, with stocks already low relative to world export demand, U.S. grain production fell by 4 percent.

The timing could not have been worse. That year a plague of bad weather devastated harvests around the globe, from sub-Sahara Africa through India into China. Hardest hit was the Soviet Union, where snows needed to protect winter wheat did not fall, and searing drought damaged the spring wheat crop. Global wheat production had been increasing at an

---

[45] Malek for President, Oct. 19, 1971, (CF) FG-20, WHSF.

[46] E-Notes, Nov. 11, 1971.

[47] *New York Times*, Dec. 3, 1971, 24.

[48] Ibid., Oct. 19, 1971, 1.

[49] U.S. Department of Agriculture, *Agricultural Statistics* (1976), 518. Payouts were $3.1 billion in 1971; $3.95 billion in 1972. Corn farmers received almost all the increase.

average annual rate of 3 percent for a decade. In 1972, paced by a 4 percent decline in the United States and a decline of 8 percent in the Soviet Union, global wheat production fell 3 percent and 6 percent below expectation. At the same time, the world rice harvest also declined sharply, adding to the pressure on wheat. In total, world production of wheat, feed grains, and rice in the 1972–1973 crop year declined by more than 40 million tons. Because demand for these commodities is remarkably insensitive to price, the shortfall meant that prices would have to rise very high indeed to clear the market.[50]

By chance, 1972 was a year of El Niño, when warm water currents in the Pacific shifted to the fishing beds of Peru, killing the plankton on which anchovies feed. Anchovies had became a major source of high protein animal feed. Mainly as a result of the disappearing anchovy, fishmeal production declined from 14 million tons in 1970 to 2.5 million tons in 1972. Less fishmeal meant more pressure on shrinking supplies of feed grains, which in turn meant more inflation.[51]

United States grain reserves might have cushioned some of the domestic effects of the food shock in 1973 except for the "great grain robbery."[52] The robber was the Soviet Union. For some time, the Soviets had been importing sizable quantities of corn and other feed grains from countries other than the United States to increase meat production. The United States had lost out on this market beginning in 1963, when, at the insistence of the International Longshoremen's Association, President Kennedy required that 50 percent of any grain sales to the Soviet Union be transported on ships of the U.S. merchant marine, whose rates were 30 percent above world rates, too expensive for the Russians.[53] High diplomacy prompted a reconsideration of this obstacle to the grain trade. In June

---

[50] For Soviet decline, Schnittker, "The 1972–73 Food Price Spiral," 499; for U.S. wheat decline, USDA, *Agricultural Statistics* (1976), Table 1, p. 1; for rice production and decline in all three commodities, Hathaway, "Food Prices and Inflation," Table 5, p. 84. Metric tons converted to U.S. tons.

[51] Richard N. Cooper and Robert Z. Lawrence, "The 1972–75 Commodity Boom," *Brookings Papers on Economic Activity* (No. 3, 1975), 617–715, esp. footnote 689. (Metric tons converted to U.S. tons.)

[52] On Russian grain deal, Controller General's Report to Congress, "Russian Wheat Sales and Weakness in Agriculture's Management of Wheat Export Subsidy Program," July 9, 1973, reprinted in *Cong Rec* (1973), 23387–23389; and "Russian Grain Transactions," Committee on Government Operations, Senate hearings (1973).

[53] Marshall I. Goldman, *Detente and Dollars: Doing Business with the Soviets* (1975), 65–66 and chap. 7.

1971, as a payoff for a major Soviet concession in arms control talks, Nixon quietly terminated the 50 percent shipping requirement on grain shipped to communist countries. In November 1971, when Nixon was acutely worried about the price of corn, the Russians were ready to make a substantial corn purchase in the United States, except that the maritime unions still refused to load Soviet ships. Noting that the Russian sale could "raise price of mid-west corn," Nixon dispatched Charles Colson to negotiate a deal with the unions, which Colson did in early November. The Soviets immediately completed purchase of 3 million tons of corn and other feed grains worth $136 million.[54]

Beginning in February 1972, the U.S. agricultural attaché in Moscow sent a series of reports detailing significant weather damage to the Soviet wheat crop. Earl Butz himself viewed the damage on a tour of Soviet farms in April. By then neither Australia nor Canada had any wheat remaining for export, which left the United States as the only substantial supplier with stocks for sale. Agriculture officials remained blind to the disappearance of world reserves and thrilled that the Russians might help Nixon carry the farm vote in the approaching election by buying American grain. Soviet officials feigned indifference through the early spring.

At the Moscow summit in May 1972, Nixon and Brezhnev concluded agreements that paved the way for significant sales of U.S. grain. Toward the end of June, a Soviet delegation arrived secretly in Washington to talk trade, and on July 8 the United States announced that it would provide credits to finance $750 million in Soviet grain purchases over the next three years. Three days before, part of the Soviet delegation had departed Washington for clandestine meetings with American grain exporters. In a series of deals completed on August 9, the Soviets spent the entire $750 million credit, plus $500 million in hard currency to purchase 19 million tons of grain, including 12 million tons of wheat, fully one-quarter of the entire 1972 American wheat crop. Because the Russians operated early and in stealth, they bought at the bottom of the market.[55] United States agricultural officials, who apparently acceded to Soviet demands for secrecy, later claimed that they had no idea of the scope of Soviet intentions.

---

[54] Seymour Hersh, *The Price of Power* (1983), chap. 25; for Nixon quote, E-Notes, Oct. 28, 1971; Goldman, *Doing Business with the Soviets*, 196; Roger R. Porter, *The US–USSR Grain Agreement* (1984), chap. 2.

[55] See testimony of former USDA official Clarence D. Palmby, plus chronology of events in "Russian Grain Transactions," Government Operations, Senate hearing, 7–21; Goldman, *Doing Business with the Soviets*, 201–205.

Perhaps not. Without doubt, Butz and his colleagues in the Agriculture Department, not to mention Nixon, were initially delighted to unload U.S. grain reserves, raise grain prices for the American farmer, and boost the president's reelection prospects. To bare the shelves entirely, Butz announced mid-July 1972, in the midst of the gigantic Soviet purchase, that wheat set-asides for the 1973 crop would *increase* from 20 million to 25 million acres, approximately one-third of potential wheat acreage.[56]

This was the situation: drought abroad, depleted reserves at home, and U.S. crop restrictions ahead. Once the markets grasped what was happening, especially the staggering size of the Soviet purchase, prices began to rise rapidly. A bushel of wheat that traded for $1.46 early in July 1972, sold for $1.86 early in September and $2.52 early in December.[57] Feed grain prices rose by 40 percent.[58] By fall Democrats smelled a scandal, and Congress began investigating the Russian grain purchase, which had turned into a major political embarrassment for the administration. Nonetheless, in December, true to its religion of scarcity, the Department of Agriculture announced a corn set-aside for 1973 of 25 million acres.[59] By then, Earl Butz had ceased to be of any political use to Richard Nixon.

## IV

On January 8, 1973, the administration learned to its dismay that wholesale grain prices had risen by 21 percent in just one month.[60] George Shultz, now virtually Nixon's economic czar, decided that the time had come to take over control of agriculture policy. Shultz created the Food Committee of the Cost of Living Council and appointed himself chair. Over the opposition of the Agriculture Department, the Food Committee emptied out all the grain in government storage to relieve prices; reduced the corn set-aside program from 25 million to 11 million acres; and cut the set-aside for wheat, too late to affect the winter wheat crop already in the ground, but in time to expand spring wheat acreage by 25 percent.

Still, the White House did not yet fully comprehend the forces propel-

---

[56] Porter, *US–USSR Grain Agreement*, 18. Glenn L. Nelson, "Agricultural Developments," in John T. Dunlop and Kenneth J. Fedor, eds., *The Lessons of Wage and Price Controls — The Food Sector* (1977), 7–62; on wheat program, 27.

[57] On wheat prices, *New York Times,* July 4, 1972, 26; Sept. 2, 1972, 29; Dec. 6, 1972, 71.

[58] *Consumer Price Index*, Dec. 1972, 3.

[59] Nelson, "Agricultural Developments," 29.

[60] Memo from Stein for President, Jan. 8, 1973, President's Handwriting file, POF; *New York Times,* Jan. 10, 1973, 1.

ling food inflation. Its mistake was to take seriously the suspect forecasts of the Agriculture Department, which as late as February was still predicting food inflation of only 6 percent for the year.[61] (Food prices actually rose at the rate of 24 percent through the first three quarters.) On March 2, 1973, comforted by the department's inaccurate information and confident "that there is still a good deal of room for expansion," Stein assured Nixon that fears of inflation were "considerably exaggerated."[62] But Nixon was worried. The price of food was healing the breach between George Meany and the Democrats, united now in demanding that the administration do something about the rising price of hamburger and pork chops.[63] Nixon wondered whether some "gimmick" like a meat price freeze might appease labor. Stein tried to discourage the thought. A meat freeze would create shortages, Stein said, and besides, food prices would be coming down in the second quarter anyway.[64]

But on March 21, 1973, the government reported that the CPI for February had risen at a rate unseen since 1951.[65] Meat prices, soaring at a 75% annual rate, led the way.[66] Now even Stein buckled under the pressure for action. Because food prices would be coming down anyway, Stein rationalized in a memo to Shultz, a food freeze would do little harm. It might even do some good by silencing the "hysterical" reporting that was "heating up" inflationary psychology. But as Stein confessed, he offered this advice in bad conscience: "My constant concern is that we teach the country bad lessons about economic policy. But I guess that we have already done so much of this that we can hardly make the situation worse. If we don't put on food price control, all future economic problems will be ascribed to it. If we put on controls and there is a mess, maybe a lesson will be learned." Stein concluded by quoting Shultz a line from *Macbeth* (III, iv. 136):

> I am in blood
> Stepped in so far, that, should I wade no more,
> Returning were as tedious as go o'er.[67]

---

[61] Nelson, "Agricultural Developments," 48.

[62] Stein for President, Mar. 2, 1973, FI file, WHCF.

[63] *New York Times*, Feb. 23, 1973, 1; Mar. 1, 1973, 32.

[64] E-Notes, Mar. 9, 1973.

[65] *New York Times*, Mar. 22, 1973, 1.

[66] *Consumer Price Index*, Mar. 1973, 1–2.

[67] Stein for Shultz, Mar. 24, 1973, Agency file: Treasury Dept., 1972–1973, SMOF: Stein.

In a televised speech on March 29, 1973, Nixon took a step back to a controlled economy by announcing an immediate freeze on wholesale and retail prices of beef, pork, and lamb.[68] Prices were frozen at ceilings so high that they would likely have little effect except to reassure consumers. Meanwhile, consumers were taking things into their own hands. A nationwide, grassroots, week-long meat boycott that began April 1 temporarily reduced retail meat sales by one-half to two-thirds.[69] *Time* called it "the most successful boycott by women since *Lysistrata*."[70] Public anger so impressed Congress that one of its committees voted to roll back food prices all the way to May 1972.[71] Why 1972? Stein wondered. "Why not all the way back to the Garden of Eden?"[72] Consumer resistance persisted through the spring, helping to keep meat prices below the ceiling and rising at a 9.8 percent annual rate compared to 75 percent in the winter. That was the major reason why the CPI actually slowed a little in the second quarter.[73] Nevertheless, *Time* reported, inflation remained "Topic A."[74]

With good reason. In May 1973, White House optimism on prices took a body blow when buyers scouring world markets for scarce food began driving up wholesale prices at rates approaching hyperinflation. That month alone soybeans rose by 45 percent, wheat by 22 percent, and corn by 30 percent.[75] Rising wholesale prices guaranteed that consumer prices would soon follow. As commodity markets became frenzied, inflation fears grew, confidence lessened, the stock market tumbled, and the dollar declined in the rush to buy gold. In the Senate, William Proxmire, a leading Democratic spokesman on the economy, said that the administration's "paralysis" in the face of rocketing wholesale prices was "impossible to understand, justify, and defend."[76] The Democratic caucus unanimously adopted a resolution calling for another ninety-day freeze of prices and wages, with profits, dividends, and interest thrown in.[77]

---

[68] *Pub Paps RN 1973*, 235–236.

[69] *New York Times*, Apr. 1, 1973, III, 1.

[70] *Time* (Apr. 9, 1973), 11.

[71] *New York Times*, Apr. 4, 1973, 28.

[72] "Rollback to Zero," attached to a memo from Stein to Ehrlichman, Apr. 10, 1973, Ehrlichman Alpha file, Economy file, WHSF.

[73] *Consumer Price Index*, June 1973, 2–3.

[74] *Time* (Apr. 9, 1973), 94.

[75] *New York Times*, May 30, 1973, 51.

[76] Ibid., June 8, 1973, 51.

[77] Ibid., June 5, 1973, 11.

Nixon was sorely tempted. With Watergate by now eroding his capacity to govern, he was in desperate need of some quick fix to restore his leadership. A general price freeze had done that for him in August 1971 and might do it for him again. Nixon even brought John Connally back to the White House as a political consultant to help reenact their earlier triumph. This time Connally agreed with all the other of Nixon's advisers that a freeze would be a mistake.[78] It was one thing to freeze prices that were already falling and quite another to freeze prices that were rising. Stein in particular tried to save Nixon from himself. "The administration is in trouble because it is believed willing to do anything to win," Stein told Nixon. "In my opinion, the only good politics for the Administration is Spartan virtue. We must show our willingness to forego a dramatic and popular TV spectacular for the sake of what we believe to be good for the country."[79] Warning the president against trying a freeze again, Stein quoted the philosopher Heraclitus, who said, "You cannot step into the same river twice."[80] Nixon replied that you could if it were frozen.[81] In the entire record of Nixon's economic conversation, it was the only funny thing he ever said.

Nixon, who would not act alone to freeze prices, needed at least one adviser to tell him to go ahead, but all of them kept delivering the same message, which was "to fight for what we believe in."[82] Then, on June 6, 1973, Melvin Laird joined the White House staff for a short stint as Nixon's chief domestic adviser. A former Republican congressman and the secretary of defense during Nixon's first term, Laird agreed to lend the benefit of his long political experience to a sinking presidency. On June 11, in Italy reviewing the fleet, Laird studied a packet of papers on possible economic options, then cabled the White House endorsing a general price freeze. "Quite frankly," Laird said, "the political realities of the present situation outweigh the long-term, economic justification for milder action."[83]

That was all the encouragement that Nixon needed. Opting for an-

---

[78] Consensus of his advisers summarized in Stein for President, June 5, 1973, Policy Review file, SMOF: Stein. Connally first leaned toward the freeze, then changed his mind.

[79] Stein for President, May 26, 1973, BE 3 file, WHCF.

[80] Stein for President, Apr. 17, 1973, Agency File, Memos for President file, SMOF: Stein.

[81] Herbert Stein, *Presidential Economics* (1984), 186.

[82] Stein for President, June 5, 1973, Policy Review file, SMOF: Stein.

[83] Laird's memo attached to memo from Haig to President, June 11, 1973, President's Handwriting file, POF, WHSF; see also Laird's comment to *Business Week* (June 23, 1973), 97.

other television spectacular, the president announced Freeze II on June 13, 1973 — a sixty-day freeze that applied to prices but not wages and again exempted raw agricultural products, which were the main cause of the inflation problem.[84] Much to Nixon's disappointment, no great surge of acclaim ensued. Businessmen complained that the freeze applied to them but not to the unions.[85] The unions complained that Nixon had merely frozen prices, not rolled them back.[86] Shultz submitted his resignation, which Nixon rejected.[87] Connally returned to Texas,[88] and Milton Friedman pronounced the freeze "the worst mistake in American economic policy that has been made by an American president in the last 40 years."[89]

Freeze II was a disaster from the start — and for the predictable reason. Uncontrolled farm prices continued to rise, but processors, wholesalers, and retailers of food had to keep their prices frozen. The resulting squeeze first hit small firms with low inventories — flour millers, feed manufacturers, salad-oil refiners, meat packers, and broiler hatchers.[90] In all, 180 feed and food firms employing 8,000 people had to close down.[91] On the evening news of June 23, 1973, shocked viewers watched as workers at a hatchery in Joachim, Texas, drowned 43,000 baby chicks in barrels. Succinctly explaining the economics of the freeze, the manager said that since feed grain prices were rising and the price of broilers were frozen, "It's cheaper to drown 'em than to put 'em down and raise 'em."[92] The number of eggs set in incubators fell 8 percent below 1972 levels during the freeze, and cattle and hog growers who could afford it withheld animals from market in expectation of higher prices after the freeze.[93] By late June, the only story more damaging to the administration than Freeze II was the congressional testimony of John Dean implicating Richard Nixon in the Watergate cover-up.

On July 18, 1973, the thirty-fifth day of the sixty-day freeze, Nixon sounded the retreat. This time there was no television, and the tone of his

[84] *Pub Paps RN 1973*, 584–587.

[85] *Newsweek* (June 25, 1973), 18.

[86] *Time* (June 25, 1973), 23.

[87] *Washington Post*, Apr. 14, 1974, 1.

[88] *New York Times*, June 15, 1973, 1; *Wall Street Journal*, June 15, 1973, 1.

[89] Ibid., June 15, 1973, 16.

[90] Ibid., June 28, 1973, 1; June 29, 1973, 1.

[91] Nelson, "Agricultural Developments," 44.

[92] *New York Times*, June 25, 1973, 11; also, "The Price Freeze and its Effects on the Poultry Situation," Committee on Agriculture, House hearings (1973).

[93] Nelson, "Agricultural Developments," 46.

statement was somber, almost apologetic. Nixon conceded that "confidence in our management of our fiscal affairs is low, at home and abroad," and he could summon only enough optimism to offer, "we should not despair of our plight." Nothing he might say, after all, could disguise his purpose, which was to undo his own folly. First, the president addressed the problem of food. Unfreezing all food prices except beef, he permitted processors and distributors to pass on higher farm prices to customers immediately. Second, he unveiled the controls program for the rest of the economy once Freeze II ended on August 12. Phase IV, though somewhat stricter than Phase III, would again permit businesses to raise prices in response to higher costs. In truth, Phase IV might accurately have been called Phase Out. By now it was clear that controls had outlived their usefulness. Rather than free the economy all at once, igniting a huge one-time price explosion, the administration would stretch out decontrol during Phase IV a sector at a time until control authority expired in April 1974.[94] Shultz, for one, declined to assess the likelihood of success for this latest adventure in a controlled economy. "We have seen baby chicks drowned, pregnant sows and cows bearing next year's food slaughtered, and packing plants closed down," he said. "It is desirable to be a little humble."[95]

As soon as Nixon announced the early end of the food price freeze, food prices shot up to cover accumulating costs. Eggs rose fifteen cents a dozen, pork by twelve cents a pound. Just as the public had blamed Nixon for shortages resulting from the freeze, it blamed him now for the price consequences of ending the freeze. "In the first full week of Phase IV," *Time* reported, "each costly ring of the check-out cash register seemed to eat away at public patience with the Administration far more than the revelations of the Watergate scandal."[96] One shopper at a supermarket in Westchester County, New York, asked, "Why are they waiting to impeach Nixon?"[97]

The worst convulsions of the food supply shock of 1973 occurred in August. With U.S. wheat stocks down 50 percent from the previous year[98] and rumors flying of crop failures in Australia and Canada,[99] panic buyers of

---

[94] *Pub Paps RN 1973*, 647–653.
[95] *New York Times*, July 19, 1973, 25.
[96] *Time* (Aug. 6, 1973), 62.
[97] *New York Times*, July 29, 1973, III, 3.
[98] Nelson, "Agricultural Developments," 52.
[99] *Wall Street Journal*, Aug. 6, 1973, 1.

food and feed grains descended on the grain exchanges. Wheat, which had sold for $1.69 a bushel in July 1972, brought $3.07 at the end of July 1973. Then the markets lost touch with reality. Every day for two weeks frantic traders on the Chicago commodities exchange bid up the price of wheat to the twenty-cent limit within minutes of the opening bell. On August 6, for the first time in history, wheat hit $4.00. Next day, at $3.11, corn also set a record. When wheat reached $5.00 on August 15, pandemonium descended on the exchanges.[100] Though the fever broke on August 21, and commodity prices declined sharply, the effect of panic buying on U.S. consumer prices that month was spectacular. Herbert Stein had predicted that food inflation would slow during the last half of the year. In the single month of August 1973, food prices at retail climbed by 6 percent — or at a 72 percent annual rate. That, too, was a record.[101]

Meanwhile, Nixon became further ensnared in the controls he had created. In his July 18 speech on the controls program, he had singled out beef for special treatment, extending the freeze on beef prices into September as part of the strategy to keep inflation rising gradually. Extending the beef freeze provoked precisely the response that his advisers said would not happen. Cattle growers in large numbers decided they could make more money by waiting to market their animals after the freeze than by marketing them now. (They were wrong.) During the first week of August, cattlemen marketed one-quarter fewer cattle than the year before.[102] Shortages developed, 140 meat packers closed down, supermarket shoppers battled each other for steaks and hamburger,[103] and ordinarily honest merchants operated black markets in beef.[104] The stampede of the beef eaters subsided at the end of August, and the markets returned nearly to normal by the time the beef freeze ended two days early on September 10.[105] By then Nixon's economic leadership had been wholly discredited. Shultz and Stein had once consoled themselves that the freeze might finally temper the public's infatuation with controls. This was one of their predictions that actually came true. Freeze II was really "a great thing," Shultz decided

---

[100] *New York Times,* Aug. 12, 1973, IV, 5; Aug. 14, 43; Aug. 15, 47; Aug. 7, 1; Aug. 8, 47; Aug. 16, 51; Aug. 23, 52.

[101] *Consumer Price Index,* Aug. 1973, 1–2.

[102] *Time* (Aug. 13, 1973), 71; *New York Times,* Aug. 31, 1973, 1.

[103] *New York Times,* Aug. 5, 1973, IV, 5.

[104] Ibid., Aug. 12, 1973, 1.

[105] Ibid., Aug. 28, 1973, 45.

later. "It was so bad that even the most hardened advocates of freezes and controls could see that there were limitations on what you could accomplish by that means."[106]

## V

Yet another coincidence helped jack up food inflation in 1973. That year the dollar depreciated in world money markets, lowering the price of American exports, notably agricultural products. As foreign demand increased in response to lower prices, U.S. farm stocks dwindled, and food prices rose in the American market. Obvious in retrospect, this consequence of depreciation caught U.S. policymakers by surprise. Since the days of John Connally, the Nixon administration had regarded dollar depreciation as a blessing because depreciation increased exports and therefore created jobs. That was why Nixon had hailed the 8 percent trade-weighted depreciation of the dollar at the Smithsonian in December 1971 and why the administration would regard with initial complacency the depreciations of 1973. As the London Economist observed, "The United States continues to be one of the very few countries in which just about everyone of importance thinks that a devaluation is lovely."[107]

At the Smithsonian in 1971, the leading nations had attempted to stave off the final collapse of the Bretton Woods system by negotiating more realistic fixed exchange rates, but the odds against the survival of those rates had been long from the start. In 1972, foreigners held the vast sum of $150 billion in central banks, private banks, and corporate treasuries, far more dollars than they needed for trade, and dollars that were available for currency speculations beyond the capacity of central banks to manage.[108] Moreover, the United States rejected any responsibility for defending the Smithsonian parities, leaving that task to resentful foreign central bankers. Because it took time for markets to adjust to dollar devaluation,[109] the U.S. trade deficit actually worsened temporarily, increasing from $2.7 billion in 1971 to $6.9 billion in 1972 — "a shocking surprise" — that further eroded confidence in the dollar.[110]

---

[106] Washington Post, Apr. 14, 1974, 1.
[107] Quoted in the New York Times, Feb. 26, 1973, 45.
[108] CEA Annual Report 1974, 189.
[109] CEA Annual Report 1973, 115–116.
[110] Gottfried Haberler, "International Aspects of Inflation," in Phillip Cagan et al., A New Look at Inflation (1973), 79–105.

The house of cards built at the Smithsonian in December 1971 tottered uncertainly through 1972 and then collapsed early in 1973. Speculators began dumping lira for Swiss marks and then dollars for German marks. The Bundesbank responded gamely by buying dollars in defense of the Smithsonian parities.[111] Because U.S. officials privately favored another appreciation of the mark, they refused to defend the dollar and let the Smithsonian agreement go under. On February 7, 1973, Paul Volcker boarded a plane for a secret trip to foreign capitals, seeking a 20 percent devaluation of the dollar against the yen and a 10 percent devaluation against European currencies. The Europeans went along because Volcker's proposal provided them with an advantage over the Japanese in the American market. The Japanese went along because the United States insisted on it. (Actually, Japan chose to appreciate the yen by floating rather than committing to a new fixed parity.) On February 12, 1973, Volcker returned in triumph to Washington with essentially the new exchange rates he wanted.[112] Announcing the second devaluation of the dollar that night, George Shultz said, "there is no doubt that we have achieved a major improvement in the competitive position of American workers and American business."[113] Shultz had no intention of defending the new parities, any more than he had defended the old ones. As for the impact of devaluation on U.S. inflation, Arthur Burns himself assured the Federal Open Market Committee that it "would be quite small."[114] Applauded by both parties, the second devaluation of the dollar was one of the few popular acts of Nixon's second term.

"As far as I am concerned," Burns said, "this is the last devaluation of the dollar."[115] But the markets, which still believed the dollar was overvalued, decided otherwise. This time it did not take a year for the realignment to fall apart. It took two weeks. Speculators resumed dumping dollars, and European central banks resumed buying them — until March 1, 1973, when central bankers bought a huge $3.5 billion and then suspended official currency operations.[116]

---

[111] Haberler, "International Aspects of Inflation," 86; Robert Solomon, *The International Monetary System* (1982), 229–230; *CEA Annual Report 1974*, 184; *New York Times*, Feb. 4, 1973, III, 3; Feb. 9, 1973, 1, 45; Feb. 14, 1973, 1.

[112] Volcker and Gyohten, *Changing Fortunes*, 100–112; *New York Times*, Feb. 13, 1973, 1; *Wall Street Journal*, Feb. 14, 1973, 1.

[113] Excerpts from Shultz's statement reprinted in *IMF Survey* (Feb. 26, 1973), 56–58.

[114] FOMC minutes, Feb. 13, 1973, 8.

[115] *New York Times*, Feb. 21, 1973, 1.

[116] Solomon, *International Monetary System*, 231.

The international monetary system had arrived at a historic juncture. Meeting in Paris, the finance ministers of the European Community opposed yet another adjustment of fixed parities to depreciate the dollar, urging instead on March 8 that the United States join in defending existing exchange rates, for example, by raising U.S. interest rates.[117] In Paris for the crisis, Shultz politely declined.[118] Lacking other options, the Europeans joined with Shultz a week later in issuing a communiqué announcing rules for floating.[119] Instead of central bankers intervening to defend fixed parities, the value of a currency would ordinarily be established daily in private currency transactions on free currency markets. At the time, this regime was regarded as a temporary expedient, pending eventual agreement on a new international monetary system. Negotiations to create a new system proceeded at a leisurely pace during the coming months but got nowhere. The new system, it turned out, would be floating itself. It cannot be said that this result displeased either Stein or Shultz, who by now had become — in Stein's phrase — "religious floaters."[120] Freed of the necessity to defend fixed currency values, these two believed, nations could now pursue domestic economic objectives unhindered by external restraints.

Arthur Burns, who loathed floating, had pleaded unsuccessfully with Shultz in Paris to save the old order.[121] Burns regarded currency markets not as rational mechanisms for establishing currency values, as Shultz did, but as a collection of all-too-human traders subject to whim and panic.[122] After floating commenced, the two men disagreed on how to manage it. Shultz favored clean floating, meaning that governments should keep hands off and permit unfettered markets to set currency values. Burns favored dirty floating, meaning that governments should intervene in the markets when-

---

[117] EEC Finance Ministers joint views summarized in *IMF Survey* (March 12, 1973), 74–75.

[118] Volcker and Gyohten, *Changing Fortunes*, 112–113.

[119] The European Community agreed to a joint float, except for the pound and the lira, which were already floating independently. For text of communiqué, *IMF Survey* (Mar. 26, 1973), 88–89. For an interpretation of this episode, Sam I. Nakagama, "Recent Monetary Changes: An Assessment," *International Currency Review* (Mar.–Apr. 1973), 19–22.

[120] Stein interview in Erwin C. Hargrove and Samuel A. Morley, *The President and the Council of Economic Advisers: Interviews with CEA Chairmen* (1984), 402.

[121] Volcker and Gyohten, *Changing Fortunes*, 113; Burns also made his case at a meeting of the Quadriad with Nixon, Stein for President's file, Mar. 3, 1973, Memos for President's file, POF.

[122] For Burns's views of floating, *New York Times*, Mar. 8, 1973, 1.

ever currency trading went haywire. This disagreement between the ex-professors quickly transcended the merely academic.

For two months following the March agreement to float, calm reigned in the markets, but on May 7, 1973, following reports that inflation was worsening in the United States and that Nixon was resigning because of Watergate, whim and panic took over. Despite recent dramatic improvement in the U.S. trade balance — the belated result of devaluation — speculators again began fleeing dollars for stronger currencies.[123] During a lull in this flight at the end of the month, Shultz ventured that floating was working "very nicely."[124] The next day the Germans raised interest rates, and the dollar began a plunge into the monetary abyss.[125] Shultz, who believed the value of the dollar had been about right, called the free fall "a puzzling matter."[126] Not puzzled at all, French President Georges Pompidou declared, "We are witnessing the third devaluation of the dollar."[127]

On July 7, 1973, when the dollar found few buyers at any price, the currency markets faced a breakdown.[128] Two days later, leading central bankers in Basel called on the United States to intervene by buying back dollars with foreign currencies borrowed from central banks — a tactic called "swaps." Burns was more than willing to use swaps to conduct a substantial dirty float, but Shultz agreed to sully principle by mounting only a minor currency intervention conducted discreetly. As it turned out, that was enough. On July 10, the Fed announced an increase in its swap credit line, and the dollar immediately stabilized.[129] When the dollar began rising in August, the cause was not Shultz's dirty though cautious float; it was market fundamentals such as the restoration of the U.S. trade surplus and higher domestic interest rates. Shultz said all along that fundamentals would prevail, and they did.

The dollar depreciations of 1973 had nonetheless done damage. After

---

[123] *New York Times*, May 15, 1973, 62; May 20, IV, 4.

[124] Ibid., May 30, 1973, 58.

[125] Ibid., May 31, 1973, 59.

[126] Ibid., June 5, 1973, 1.

[127] Quoted in Solomon, *International Monetary System*, 336–337.

[128] FOMC minutes, July 9, 1973, 708, 735.

[129] *New York Times*, July 11, 1973, 1; FOMC minutes, July 17, 1973, 7–10. The Fed and Treasury jointly announced that the Fed had been intervening in the currency markets, *New York Times*, July 19, 1973, 49. In fact, in July the Fed spent only $270 million in foreign currencies to buy dollars. See Charles Coombs, *The Arena of International Finance* (1976), 232.

declining by a trade-weighted average of 8 percent in December 1971, the dollar fell another 10 percent during the first half of 1973.[130] The effects of devaluation were felt first in agricultural markets, where changes in currency values were instantaneously reflected in commodity prices. By lowering the price of U.S. agricultural exports, devaluation helped expand the volume of all U.S. exports by nearly one-third in 1973 over the previous year, exacerbate shortages in the domestic market, and fuel U.S. inflation.[131] If Shultz had acted decisively to defend the dollar in February or in May, he might have slowed the dollar's decline along with the U.S. inflation rate. Shultz had acted too late and too cautiously out of conviction and because, as Stein admitted later, the administration had "underestimated the effect of depreciation of the dollar on the inflation rate in the U.S."[132] From mid-1972 to mid-1973 U.S. consumer prices rose from a little more than 3 percent to 8 percent. An estimated two percentage points of this increase was the result of the direct and indirect effects of the depreciated dollar.[133]

As foreigners bought up cheap U.S. farm products, patriots began to demand aggressive measures in defense of the national interest. Soybeans emerged as a matter of particular concern. Rich in protein and oil, U.S. soybeans had become a major source of feed for the world's livestock industry as well as a staple rivaling rice in the Japanese diet. Though Nixon joked that "I don't even know what a soybean is," soybeans had become the nation's leading export product.[134] By the spring of 1973, with world wheat stocks low, fishmeal scarce, and the dollar falling, foreigners bought, or contracted to buy, vast quantities of U.S. soybeans, driving the price from $3.50 a bushel in 1972 to $12.00 in June 1973.[135] Responding to political pressure especially from the livestock industry, fifty-two members of the

---

[130] Testimony of Don Paarlberg, USDA Director of Agricultural Economics, in "U.S. and World Food Situation," Committee on Agriculture and Forestry, Senate hearings (1973), 39.

[131] USDA, *Agricultural Statistics 1976*, 569.

[132] Stein interview in Morley and Hargrove, *The President and the Council of Economic Advisers*, 402.

[133] Blinder, *Economic Policy and the Great Stagflation*, 29; on the effect of the dollar's depreciation on the U.S. price level and a survey of the literature, Marina v. N. Whitman, "International Interdependence and the U.S. Economy," in William Fellner, ed., *AEI Studies on Contemporary Economic Problems* (1976), 183–223, esp. 194–201.

[134] *Pub Paps RN 1973*, 751.

[135] *U.S. News and World Report*, July 30, 1973, 54.

House wrote Secretary Butz, demanding an embargo of soybean exports until the fall harvest.[136] On July 2, 1973, the administration took the extraordinary step of ordering exporters to limit soybean shipments abroad to 50 percent of commitments.[137] This partial embargo abrogated contracts, contradicted trade principles that the United States demanded others observe, infuriated soybean farmers, and deeply antagonized America's trade partners. The French accused the United States of "economic nationalism,"[138] and the Japanese added to their list of Nixon shocks the "Shoya Shokku."[139] To underscore the point that, in a pinch, it was every country for itself, the administration placed scrap metal under export controls, too. The connection between dollar depreciation, rising U.S. inflation, and the export embargoes dawned only slowly.

## VI

After the explosion of wholesale farm prices in August, food markets approached normalcy. By autumn, when farmers brought in record harvests, the food supply shock was over. Because reserves of agricultural commodities had been nearly exhausted and anxious buyers wanted to hedge against new shortages, demand for food still pressed hard against supply and food prices still rose, though at a sharply declining rate. The general inflation rate did not, however, slow down. Quarter by quarter, excess demand fueled by the mistaken expansionary policies of the recent past pushed up nonfood and nonenergy prices — from an annual rate of 2.5 percent during the winter to 6.8 percent in the fall. Meanwhile, it was Nixon's bad luck that an oil supply shock commenced just as the food supply shock was ending. The Great Inflation would only get worse.

As for the boom of 1972–1973, it had already ended. Real GNP, which had grown at an annualized rate of 8.8 percent during the first quarter of 1973, increased at a rate of only 1.4 percent during the last three quarters. As inflation cut into disposable income and the stock market declined,

---

[136] Letter reprinted in *Cong Rec* (1973), 18941–18942.

[137] USDA partial embargo explained in July 2 USDA press release, reprinted in "U.S. Export Control Policy," Committee on Agriculture and Forestry, Senate Report (Nov. 12, 1973), 39–42.

[138] Quoted in Stanley Nehmer, "Dilemmas of Export Control," *Nation's Business* (Nov. 1973), reprinted in *Cong Rec* (1973), 36127.

[139] *New York Times*, July 7, 1973, 27.

consumers grew cautious, spending less and saving more. At the same time, inflation caused the dollar value of GNP to rise, which meant that the economy needed more money merely to conduct the same volume of trans- actions. Money became tight; interest rates rose; and thrift institutions, hindered by government ceilings on the interest rates they could pay de- positors, stopped attracting deposits, curbing the availability of home mort- gage money. In June 1973, housing starts were running at the annual rate of 2.4 million; by December, at a mere 1.4 million. Only the desire of man- ufacturers, wholesalers, and retailers to rebuild inventories, which had been depleted during the boom, kept the economy out of recession. Over the last three quarters of 1973, final sales stagnated, but because business spending on inventories remained strong, GNP inched forward. Unem- ployment even declined as firms continued hoarding labor that had been scarce during the boom. Standing at 5 percent in January 1973, the unem- ployment rate fell to 4.6 percent in October. It would not get so low again till the end of the century. Low unemployment helped obscure the forces that had begun to flatten output.

At the beginning of 1973, the administration had predicted low infla- tion for the year ahead. It was the worst of the many bad forecasts that the administration made over the years. In September, Gallup asked the public to name the nation's number-one problem. Of those responding, 14 per- cent said Watergate and political corruption. Eighty-nine percent said "the high cost of living," the largest percentage ever to mention inflation in answer to that question since the poll began in 1935.[140] A month later, the Arab oil embargo would plunge the economy simultaneously into the worst inflation and the worst recession of the postwar period.

---

[140] *Gallup Poll (1972–1977)*, 186, 187.

# Chapter 9

# Oil Shock

## I

Like most other Americans, Nixon was slow to recognize the energy short-age that would darken his abbreviated second term. Get George Shultz out of energy, Nixon told Haldeman in March 1973. "It's escapist . . . Concen-trate on the big game," meaning inflation, trade, and labor.[1] Energy was already big game and would soon become the biggest. As Nixon spoke, the nation was emerging from a winter of scarce heating oil and preparing for a summer short of gasoline. Month by month, energy problems would worsen, until the Arab oil boycott in October 1973 turned energy into a full-fledged crisis, featuring panic, pessimism, gas lines, a plethora of conspiracy theories, accelerating inflation, and recession. Personally affect-ing the lives of virtually every citizen, the oil crisis was one of the most wrenching collective experiences of the American people in the post–World War II era. During his second term, Nixon had to endure not only the unanticipated traumas of Watergate and food shortages but an oil crisis that was a political disaster all by itself.

It was a disaster compounded by an irony. Nixon and his advisers had come to office philosophically disposed to reduce government regulation. Nonetheless, as Herbert Stein afterward confessed, "Probably more new regulation was imposed on the economy during the Nixon administration than in any other presidency since the New Deal" — regulations to clean up the environment, protect occupational health and safety, and assure the safety of consumer products.[2] Nixon entered the second term determined to reverse this trend. Instead, the energy crisis sank him deep into a quag-mire of new regulation, providing unwelcome but resounding confirmation of his belief that markets ordinarily set prices and allocate resources more sensibly than governments.

---

[1] H-Notes, Mar. 21, 1973.
[2] Herbert Stein, *Presidential Economics* (1988), 190.

241

Through most of the 1960s, oil markets were plagued by surpluses, even as energy consumption in the United States rose 50 percent during the decade.[3] By Nixon's time, demand began pushing against supply, and the era of energy abundance was over. Not that the world was running out of oil or other energy sources. It was not. Shortages developed because, for reasons wise and unwise, governments created them. The three main U.S. energy sources, accounting for 96 percent of U.S. supply in 1972, were coal, natural gas, and oil. Though supplies of these fuels were theoretically ample, political obstacles impeded access of each to the market.

America had so much coal that some experts said that coal could meet the nation's energy needs for 400 years, some said for 1,000, but coal had been suffering a long-term decline. In 1950, coal supplied 38 percent of the nation's energy needs; in 1972, 17 percent.[4] "There are only two things wrong with coal today," one authority remarked. "We can't mine it, and we can't burn it."[5] When it was mined, coal either injured the miners or blighted the landscape. When it was burned, it polluted the atmosphere with ash and sulfur. In 1964, New York became the first city to mandate limits on sulfur emissions, prompting the city's electric utilities to switch from coal to natural gas or low-sulfur oil. Other metropolitan areas soon followed New York's example.[6] If the nation's electrical utilities had used the same proportion of coal in their burners in 1972 as in the mid-1960s, they would have consumed 1.1 million fewer barrels of oil a day, more than all the petroleum imported daily that year from the Middle East.[7] Because oil was cheap, coal dirty, and the cleaning of coal to meet government standards costly and difficult, coal seemed doomed to further decline.

As coal lost ground, demand for natural gas expanded from 18 percent of total U.S. energy consumption in 1950 to 32 percent in 1972. Marketed in the early days mainly near points of production in the Southwest, natural gas reached homes and businesses nationwide after World War II through 900,000 miles of pipelines. The advantage of natural gas was that it was the cleanest of fuels. Its problem was a price too low to encourage

---

[3] Energy Information Administration, *Annual Energy Review 1989*, 11, Table 3.

[4] Richard H. K. Vietor, *Energy Policy in America Since 1945* (1984), 3. For figures on energy consumption 1950–1972, *Annual Energy Review 1989*, Table 3.

[5] S. David Freeman, quoted in the *New York Times*, Apr. 17, 1973, 26.

[6] Statement of Carl Bagge of the National Coal Commission in "Fuel and Energy Resources, 1972," Committee on Interior and Insular Affairs, House hearings (1972), 228–236.

[7] Joel Darmstadter and Hans H. Landsberg, "The Economic Background," in Raymond Vernon, ed., *The Oil Crisis* (1976), 13–37.

production. In 1954, the Supreme Court interpreted existing legislation to require the Federal Power Commission to regulate natural gas prices at the wellhead of 4,000 separate producers. The commission eventually adopted a rate-making formula so restrictive that the price of a thousand cubic feet of natural gas during the 1960s rose by only 2 cents; in real terms, it actually declined.[8] Given the artificially low price of natural gas, consumers had an incentive to increase consumption, and producers had a disincentive to find new supply. In 1968, for the first time in history, the industry found less gas than it produced, and the era of man-made natural gas shortages commenced.[9] In 1971, short supplies of natural gas forced the industry to cancel contracts approximating more than 1 percent of total U.S. production; in 1972, more than 3 percent.[10] Even as pressure for cleaner air was reducing the use of coal and high-sulfur oil, government regulation was inhibiting the supply of the most environmentally desirable alternative.

The nation's chief energy source was oil, which supplied 47 percent of the energy market in 1972. Surplus, not scarcity, had historically been this industry's problem. During the 1930s, the Texas Railroad Commission solved that problem by collaborating with similar bodies in other states to restrict the number of days a month oil wells could produce. In effect, state governments created a producer's cartel by curbing supplies to raise crude oil prices. When cheap foreign oil began flowing into the United States in the 1950s, mainly from Venezuela and Canada, the domestic cartel faced a challenge that only the federal government could meet. In 1959, at the behest of domestic oil producers and under cover of the doubtful rationale of national security, President Eisenhower imposed mandatory quotas on imported oil, that is, he limited the volume of foreign oil that could enter the American market.[11]

Under the import quota system, every oil refinery and petrochemical company in the country received a ticket to purchase a portion of allowable foreign oil, whether it intended to import any or not. Inland refiners who could not physically import oil traded their tickets to coastal refiners in

---

[8] Vietor, *Energy Policy*, chaps. 4, 7; Edward J. Mitchell, *U.S. Energy Policy: A Primer* (1974), chap. 4; see also Robert Stobaugh and Daniel Yergin, *Energy Future* (1979), chap. 3.

[9] Testimony of George Lawrence, American Gas Association, in "Fuel and Energy Resources," House hearings, 387–399.

[10] *New York Times*, Apr. 17, 1973, 26.

[11] On oil import quotas, Vietor, *Energy Policy*, esp. chaps. 2, 5, 6; Douglas R. Bohi and Milton Russell, *Limiting Oil Imports: An Economic Analysis* (1978); and E. Anthony Copp, *Regulating Competition in Oil: Government Intervention in the U.S. Refining Industry 1948–1975* (1976).

exchange for conveniently located domestic crude. Decaying over time, this system promoted a crazy-quilt of exceptions, arbitrary benefits, and market distortions.[12] As late as 1971, the combination of import quotas and domestic production controls was still operating to keep U.S. crude oil prices comfortably above the world price. Quotas that year restrained U.S. oil imports to 25% of consumption, and the Texas Railroad Commission reduced domestic crude oil production to 63% of capacity.[13] A year later, U.S. oil production began its irreversible decline, leaving American consumers increasingly dependent on foreign oil. That was no problem, so long as foreign governments refrained from interfering with oil exports, and the American government got rid of restrictions on oil imports. The oil was there if governments would let it flow.

During Nixon's first term, as energy shortages began to appear, a powerful environmental movement emerged to exacerbate the problem. Environmentalists forced the administration to halt oil operations in the Santa Barbara Channel in 1969, following an oil spill, and impeded oil exploration in the Outer Continental Shelf.[14] They fought the trans-Alaska pipeline to a standstill.[15] They blocked construction of new electric power plants, causing brownouts in some localities.[16] They stopped plans to build at least nine new East Coast oil refineries, which would have expanded the region's capacity by 50 percent and relieved its growing dependence on imported oil products.[17] They lobbied for amendments to the Clean Air Act in 1970, which prompted public utilities to hasten the switch from abundant high-sulfur coal to scare low-sulfur oil.[18] On their urging, auto-emission standards were imposed on car manufacturers, reducing fuel efficiency and adding an estimated 300,000 barrels a day to U.S. oil demand.[19] The air was much healthier to breathe, oil spills were less likely

---

[12] Allan T. Dewaree, "Our Crazy, Costly Life with Oil Quotas," *Fortune* (June 1969), 105 ff.

[13] DOE, 1980 *Annual Report to Congress* (vol. II: data), 49, Table 21.

[14] John C. Whitaker, *Striking a Balance: Environment and National Resource Policy in the Nixon–Ford Years* (1976), 264–275.

[15] Mary Clay Berry, *The Alaska Pipeline: The Politics of Oil and Native Land Claims* (1975).

[16] *New York Times*, Feb. 24, 1971, 12; Nov. 27, 1971, 17; Apr. 6, 1972, 107; Aug. 26, 1972, 1.

[17] "Decision to Suspend the Mandatory Oil Import Program," in Commission on the Organization of the Government for the Conduct of Foreign Policy (vol. 3, June 1975), 53.

[18] Whitaker, *Striking a Balance*, 95, 105.

[19] Barrels estimated by General George Lincoln of Office of Emergency Preparedness in "Oil and Gas Import Issues," Committee on Interior and Insular Affairs, Senate hearings (1973), 83.

to occur, and the Alaskan caribou got a reprieve, but energy supplies tightened, and dependence on foreign oil grew.

Though the public's interest in the energy problem flickered on and off, knowledgeable people in the government and the energy industry foresaw the coming shortage. Periodically, Nixon's advisers would propose policy options, but lacking the interest or the political will, the president declined to act. The administration began its ill-fated involvement with energy in 1969, when growing criticism of oil import quotas prompted Nixon to appoint a Cabinet task force to review them. Concern at the time was not with shortages but with the inefficiency of the ticket system, the bitter complaints of New England consumers thirsty for cheap imported oil, and the disappointing failure of quotas to encourage domestic exploration and development. Seeking a disinterested chairman, Nixon chose his secretary of labor, George Shultz. Shultz and the majority of his task force came down against quotas not because they feared scarcity but because quotas kept the price of domestic crude oil at $3.30 a barrel when the world price was $2.00 — at an estimated cost to U.S. consumers of $5 billion a year.

Taking deadly aim at the domestic oil cartel, Shultz proposed replacing quotas with a tariff. New England Congressmen cheered the tariff option. Independent Texas producers and their political allies fought to keep import quotas.[20] Caught in the cross fire, Nixon blamed Shultz's professional staff, whom he scorned as "a bunch of Harvard professors with a preconceived idea."[21] In December 1969, Haldeman summarized for his diary Nixon's thoughts on the quota problem. "Have to make some decisions, and can't win. If we do what we should, and what the task force recommends, we'd apparently end up losing at least a couple of Senate seats, including George Bush in Texas. Trying to figure a way to duck the whole thing and shift it to Congress."[22] By the time Shultz submitted his report to Nixon in February 1970, recommending an end of quotas, he knew it was dead.[23]

Soon after, Nixon had another chance to address the energy issue. In March 1970, with U.S. fuel supplies tightening and domestic oil production showing signs of leveling off, Paul McCracken of the CEA took charge

---

[20] Congressman George Bush to Shultz, Dec. 1, 1969, Records of the Secretary, DOL, RG 174, N.A.; Peter Flanigan, to Harlow, Zeigler, Shultz, Dec. 19, 1969, (CF) TA4/Oil, WFSF.

[21] E-Notes, Dec. 11, 1969.

[22] *The Haldeman Diaries*, Dec. 16, 1969.

[23] Cabinet Task Force on Oil Import Control, *The Oil Import Question* (Feb. 1970).

of an energy subcommitte of John Ehrlichman's Domestic Council. Mc-Cracken quickly concluded that the nation faced a serious shortage of fuels during the next five years. As McCracken saw it, the president had two choices. He could duck the tough issues or confront them. Seeking guidance from Nixon, McCracken presented him a list of politically explosive measures without which, McCracken said, "an action program of Presidential stature cannot be developed." The measures included deregulation of natural gas, termination of state restrictions on domestic crude oil production, reduction of limits on oil imports from Venezuela and Canada, and creation of a strategic reserve in case of emergencies.[24] Did the president want McCracken's subcommittee or perhaps some other high-level body to study these "political hot potatoes"? Nixon authorized a study but only on condition that it be conducted, he said, "in complete confidence. Don't stir up the political issue. If it can't be done without fanfare (which is probably not the case)," don't do it.[25]

A small group of Nixon's closest advisers did in fact form a group to study McCracken's options. Reporting to the president on April 21, 1971, the group yielded to his political priorities. Counseling against deregulating natural gas or liberalizing imports, the report said, "we conclude that the political risks of the above two measures are greater than the possible flak should energy shortages occur (brownouts and heating shortages) between now and the election."[26] The election was more than eighteen months away. In June 1971, Nixon sent Congress an energy message containing a list of palliatives. It disappeared without a trace.[27] In 1972, when energy shortages could no longer be ducked, Nixon again put off submitting a program until after the November election.[28]

## II

By 1972, energy was quickly graduating from a problem to a crisis. That year U.S. energy consumption increased by 5 percent. Domestic oil produc-

---

[24] McCracken for President, Feb. 16, 1971, UT, WHCF.

[25] John Whitaker for President (no date), President's Handwriting file, POF. Nixon's instructions written on this memo.

[26] Whitaker for President, Apr. 21, 1971, (CF) UT, WHSF.

[27] *Pub Paps RN 1971*, 703–714.

[28] Flanigan for Ehrlichman et al., July 7, 1972, (CF) UT, WHSF; Flanigan for President, July 11, 1972, (CF) UT, WHSF.

tion in the lower forty-eight stopped increasing, forcing the Texas Railroad
Commission to set allowable production at 100 percent.[29] And imported
oil grew to 29 percent of US consumption, with less originating in secure
Western Hemisphere sources and more in the Middle East.[30] Though Middle Eastern oil accounted for only 11 percent of U.S. consumption in 1972,
everyone knew that surplus capacity in that region would have to slake
most of the growing oil thirst in the industrial world, including the United
States.[31] Unfortunately, Arab producers had little surplus capacity at the
moment. Iraqi production declined following nationalization of the Iraq
Petroleum Company in June, and Libya had cut output in the name of
conservation.[32] With world supply temporarily tight and U.S. production
having peaked, U.S. refiners had to scour the globe for scarce low-sulfur
oil.[33] Nixon periodically relaxed oil import quotas that year but never
enough to keep up with spurting U.S. demand.[34] As the winter of 1972–
1973 approached, home-heating-oil stocks fell to dangerously low levels,
and fear of an energy crisis spread to the public at last.[35]

The home-heating-oil crisis owed something to the scarcity of crude
but more to the stupidities of price control. Nixon had initiated price
controls in August 1971 with Freeze I. August happens to be a month when
home-heating-oil prices are low and gasoline prices are high. Phase II of
price controls, which began in November 1971, established the base price
for gasoline and heating oil at their August 1971 level. In the fall, the price
of gasoline ordinarily declines and heating-oil prices rise, but because of
controls, heating-oil prices could not rise, depriving refiners of incentives
to produce heating oil in sufficient quantities. Thanks to ample stocks, the
nation escaped a heating-oil shortage during the winter of 1972, but with
stocks drawn down, luck might fail during the winter of 1973.[36] Theoretically, refiners could have sought a way out by asking the Price Commission

---

[29] *New York Times*, Mar. 17, 1972, 59.

[30] David Gisselquist, *Oil Prices and Trade Deficits* (1979), 61.

[31] DOE, *1980 Annual Report*, 55, Table 24.

[32] *Petroleum Intelligence Weekly*, Mar. 26, 1972, 5; Sept. 18, 1972, 7; DOE, *Annual Report
1980*, 79.

[33] *Petroleum Intelligence Weekly*, Nov. 6, 1972, 1.

[34] Ibid., May 15, 1972, 7; Sept. 25, 1973, 3.

[35] Ibid., Sept. 18, 1972, 3.

[36] William A. Johnson, "The Impact of Price Controls on the Oil Industry: How to
Worsen an Energy Crisis," in Gary Eppen, ed., *Energy: The Policy Issues* (1975), 99–121, esp.
100–103; *Petroleum Intelligence Weekly*, Sept. 18, 1972, 3.

for permission to raise the price of home heating oil on the incontestable grounds that the costs of producing it had risen. Because the oil industry was unpopular and New England Congressmen opposed any rise in this highly visible price, the Price Commission threatened hostile and lengthy hearings if the oil companies appealed for a price adjustment.[37] As a result, the price of home heating oil remained frozen into the next winter. The government could freeze the price, but only the companies could produce the fuel. On December 11, 1972, General George Lincoln of the Office of Emergency Preparedness pleaded with refiners to produce more heating oil regardless of price.[38] Refiners had already stepped up production, but not enough to meet demand.[39]

Matters improved on January 11, 1973, when the administration moved to Phase III of the controls program. No longer required to receive advance government permission for cost-justified price increases, oil refiners immediately raised the price of home heating oil by 8 percent and began producing it at top speed. Stocks were so low that if average temperatures that winter fell by five degrees, according to one expert, "your system is already breaking down. The outer reaches of your distribution system, like Maine, could have no fuel at all."[40] That winter the governors of Iowa and Nebraska imposed measures to conserve heating oil. Farmers in Kansas and Nebraska feared spoilage of late-harvested crops because fuel to dry them was running out. Amoco instructed its distributors to supply customers with only half-tanks of heating oil, and the city of Denver closed the schools for a few days in the absence of fuel to heat them.[41] In the end, stepped-up heating-oil production and a warm winter staved off the worse case, but there was a cost. By pushing production of heating oil so hard, refiners could not replenish stocks of gasoline in preparation for heavy summer demand.[42] Said the chairman of the Texas Railroad Commission,

---

[37] Charles R. Owens, "History of Petroleum Price Controls," in Office of Economic Stabilization, Dept. of Treasury, *Historical Working Papers on the Economic Stabilization Program* (1974), 1223–1339. On Price Commission, 1236–1237, 1248.

[38] Lincoln's appeal to National Petroleum Council, Dec. 11, 1972, reprinted in "Efficiency of Executive Agencies with Respect to the Petroleum Industry," Committee on Government Operations, Senate hearings (1973), 251–252.

[39] *Oil and Gas Journal* (Mar. 19, 1973), 27–30.

[40] *New York Times*, Feb. 1, 1973, 70.

[41] Ibid., Jan. 10, 1973, 40; Jan. 18, 1; *US News and World Report* (Feb. 5, 1973), 23–25.

[42] *Oil and Gas Journal* (March 19, 1973), 27–30.

"It appears that the petroleum industry has managed to get out of the frying pan and into the fire."[43]

## III

In 1973, months before the Arab oil boycott, energy issues moved to the top of the nation's agenda. Two in particular became political issues: rising oil prices and the plight of the independents in the oil industry. The public disliked any price increase but in particular disliked highly visible increases in gasoline and home heating oil. Congress, always sympathetic to small business, particularly favored independent oil firms in their struggle against the twenty or so vertically integrated major companies. The preference for low oil prices and competition in the oil industry translated into more controls and more regulations, which in the end hurt energy markets more than the temporary shortage itself.

As shortages drove up oil prices, the government had two options. It could permit oil prices to rise until the market cleared, ending the shortage, or it could resist the increase in oil prices, which would encourage consumption and aggravate the shortage. Committed to fighting inflation, the government opted to resist higher prices. Oil refiners had irritated the government in January 1973 by raising the price of home heating oil. Conceding that the price rise was permissible under Phase III, the Cost of Living Council decided to punish the big oil companies anyway, incidentally demonstrating to a skeptical public that there really was a stick in the closet.[44] On March 6, 1973, the COLC took the extraordinary step of issuing Special Rule #1, slapping mandatory price controls back on the oil industry, or more specifically on the twenty-four major companies presumed to control 95 percent of industry sales. Essentially, the rule froze the prices of the big companies. The consequence was to take a bad situation and make it worse.[45]

The COLC was wrong to believe that the top twenty-four firms con-

---

[43] *New York Times*, Feb. 16, 1973, 49.

[44] "Talking Points Re Reassertion of Mandatory Controls," Feb. 21, 1973, Records of Deputy Diretor of COLC (James McLane), Economic Stabilization Program, RG 433, NA.

[45] Special Rule #1 permitted the majors to raise product prices up to 1.5 percent. After that, the companies would have to request permission of the COLC to raise prices again, permission that everybody understood the COLC would be loathe to grant. Prices quickly moved to the allowable 1.5 percent limit and then became effectively frozen.

trolled the oil industry. Special Rule #1 in effect created two classes of oil firms: the twenty-four major companies that were under the rule, and all the rest, which were not. The special rule did not cover independent producers of crude oil, the hundred or so independent refiners of oil products, or the hundreds of thousands of product distributors, including gas stations. Though independent oil producers and refiners theoretically remained under Phase III controls, they pretty much set prices as they wished. Most product distributors had been exempt from all price controls since the small business exemption of May 1972.[46] In all, 15 percent of refinery production, 40 percent of crude oil production, and nearly all oil distributors were exempt from Special Rule #1, which could not and did not control oil prices. During the second quarter of 1973, when the special rule was fully effective, gasoline prices rose at an annual rate of 26 percent and heating oil prices by 16 percent, exceeding by far the price increases of the previous quarter.[47]

The special rule was not only ineffective in slowing oil inflation; it had the unfortunate effect of imperiling supply. The major companies bought substantial quantities of imported oil, which was exempt from price control. While the price of the oil they were importing was rising, the prices of the products the majors refined were effectively frozen. Unable to pass on higher crude oil prices, the big twenty-four had an incentive to divert foreign crude to their refineries abroad or not to import at all. On May 31, 1971, the president of Shell Oil company wrote a leading government official to report that in view of rising world prices, his company had just declined to purchase two cargoes of foreign crude. "We believe that the time has come to permit the pass through of the increased cost of foreign crude to product prices," he said.[48] By then, the COLC itself was reconsidering Special Rule #1.

That spring, while the administration tried to control the prices of the major oil companies, Congress took up the cause of the independents. Liberals cast the independents as heroes in a drama of enterprise, valiant underdogs fighting to save America from monopoly. Big Oil, by contrast, considered the independents little more than parasites, a not altogether

---

[46] Owens, "History of Petroleum Price Controls," 1244.

[47] *Consumer Price Index for June 1973*, 12.

[48] H. Bridges to Simon, May 31, 1973, Oil Phase IV 1973, Drawer 15, file 38, Simon papers, Lafayette College.

inaccurate view. During the 1960s, the major companies, plagued by surplus production, had dumped surplus gasoline at cut-rate prices on independent distributors, permitting this sector of the industry to flourish. Independent service stations, supplied by the majors with cheap gas, undersold
the branded gasolines of the major's own affiliates by two to six cents a
gallon. By the spring of 1973, the days of the gasoline surplus were over.
The majors needed all their gas for the 180,000 stations they owned or fran-
chised. Forty thousand independent stations, therefore, faced a squeeze. By
June 1973, for want of gas, an estimated 2,000 independent stations closed,
and thousands of others curtailed hours or limited sales.[49] Independent
distributors turned to Congress for rescue.

So, meanwhile, did independent refiners. Though the largest independents could find crude themselves, many small firms, especially in the
Midwest, had trouble locating supplies. These refiners existed mainly because of a quirk in the oil import quota system. Under that system, small
refiners obtained a disproportionate number of import tickets, a subsidy
essential for the survival of these mainly inefficient firms. Lacking capacity
to import foreign oil themselves, inland refiners had exchanged their
tickets with coastal refiners for domestic crude on advantageous terms.
Coastal refiners profited by getting oil at the lower world price, and inland
independents got oil that helped keep them running. By the beginning of
1973, the world oil price had risen to the level of the domestic price, and
the value of import tickets fell to zero. The majors stopped exchanging
domestic crude for import tickets, and small refiners began hurting. As
early as February 1973, a survey of forty-six independent refinery companies, approximately half of all the independent firms in the industry,
reported 795,000 barrels of crude oil on hand for an operating capacity of
1.1 million.[50] Only Congress, it appeared, could force the majors to share

---

[49] "The Gasoline Shortage: A National Perspective," Background Paper by the Congressional Research Service, Senate Committee on Interior and Insular Affairs (June 19,
1973), 54–66. See also "Preliminary Federal Trade Commission Staff Report and Its Investigation of the Petroleum Industry," Committee Print, Senate Committee on Interior Affairs
(1973); and "Department of Treasury Staff Analysis of Federal Trade Commission Staff
Report and It's Investigation of the Petroleum Industry," July 2, 1973, Committee Print, same
committee, esp. 56–64.

[50] Statement of Edwin Dyer, Independent Refiners Association of America, in "Fuel
Shortages," Committee on Interior and Insular Affairs, Senate hearings (1973), 180–212; for
survey of independent refiners, same hearing 205–206; see also "The Gasoline and Fuel Oil
Shortage," Joint Economic Committee, hearings (1973), 208–214.

their oil with independent competitors, whose demise the majors would hardly regret.

Many industry critics considered Nixon an unindicted co-conspirator in the crimes of Big Oil. In truth, the president's own views on the energy problem were not all that different from those of the majors. He favored policies to promote production rather than conservation, was indifferent to the independents, and believed, as he said, that "environmentalists will have to move aside."[51] When an adviser suggested that relaxing federal clean-air standards might increase respiratory disease and lung cancer, Nixon snapped, "I don't believe that. When I was young, people didn't get lung cancer. They got TB from being cold and almost freezing to death."[52] In his eagerly awaited energy message, finally transmitted to Congress on April 18, 1973, the president endorsed a list of proposals long advocated by the industry — partial deregulation of natural gas, delay of clean air standards, construction of the Alaska pipeline, more reliance on nuclear power, and increased efforts to find offshore oil. Because imported crude oil no longer undersold domestic crude, the president also ended at last the mandatory import quota program.[53] The message served to confirm the view that Nixon was in bed with the oil companies. As if on cue, Exxon praised the message for emphasizing the role of the private sector.[54] Senator James Abourezk, by contrast, accused the administration of fostering collusion among the majors "to manipulate shortages for their own advantage, to drive out what little competition remains, to force already high prices upward, and to increase their real profit far beyond the limits allowed for other industries."[55]

To save the independents from Big Oil, leading Congressmen came to the remarkable conclusion that the government should take over the allocation of scarce supplies from the industry. Only then would endangered independent service stations get enough gasoline and independent refiners get enough crude. On April 30, 1972, Nixon signed legislation that granted him discretionary authority to allocate crude oil supplies only. Unsatisfied, friends of the independents introduced separate legislation to force the president to allocate supplies for the whole industry. In hopes of forestalling

---

[51] Cabinet Meeting Notes, Dec. 5, 1973, Memos for President's file, POF.
[52] Quoted in *Newsweek* (Nov. 5, 1973), 89.
[53] *Pub Paps RN 1973*, 302–319.
[54] *Platt's Oilgram*, Apr. 19, 1973, 1.
[55] *Cong Rec* (1973), 17952–17953.

mandatory allocation, the administration announced voluntary allocations in May, a solution ultimately undercut by spotty compliance.[56] In June, the Senate passed mandatory allocation legislation and sent it to the House, where it bogged down in committee until fall. Step by step the administration was sinking deeper into the quagmire.

The COLC did its part. On June 13, 1973, Nixon ended Phase III by imposing Freeze II, a sixty-day general freeze that applied to all prices, including all oil prices. Using the interlude to rethink oil price controls, the COLC's energy desk, which contained no economists and little oil expertise, decided to abandon the failed Special Rule #1 and impose mandatory price controls on the entire oil industry—from producers of crude oil through refiners to the gas station on the corner.[57] Begun September 7, 1973, Phase IV of oil controls did its worst damage in the effort to control crude oil prices. The COLC set a ceiling price for domestic crude at an average $4.25 a barrel, approximately $1.00 below the world price. At that price, what was the incentive for domestic producers to hunt for new oil or pump it? To solve this problem, the COLC exempted from price controls so-called new oil, that is, oil pumped from a lease above 1972 production levels and oil pumped from new leases. Now there were two prices for oil— "old" oil at the controlled prices and "new" and imported oil at the market price. Refiners fortunate enough to have access to cheaper "old" oil enjoyed a tremendous cost advantage over refiners that did not. The same refined products could now sell for widely different prices in the same market. The COLC had originally intended to raise the price of old oil gradually to the world level. But in December 1973, when the COLC raised the crude oil price to $5.25 to narrow the rapidly widening gap with foreign oil, the public outcry was so great that the government dared not raise the controlled price again. The two-tier oil price, which later became multi-tiered, would last till 1981. Efforts of regulators in intervening years to make the system work succeeded only in multiplying its inanity.[58]

Short-term Phase IV price controls on retail distributors got the administration in the most trouble. Nixon himself was to blame. In his June

---

[56] *New York Times*, May 11, 1973, 23; also, *Oil and Gas Journal* (May 21, 1973), 72–73; on failure of voluntary allocation, exchange of letters between Simon and Senator Thomas J. McIntyre, reprinted in *Cong Rec* (1973), 28894–28895; *New York Times*, June 19, 1973, 62; *Oil and Gas Journal* (June 18, 1973), 47–48.

[57] Stein, *Presidential Economics*, 191–192.

[58] Vietor, *Energy Policy*, chap. 10.

speech announcing Freeze II, Nixon promised that Phase IV would stabilize "the price of gasoline at your service station."[59] The COLC obliged the president with a rule freezing the retail prices of gasoline, home heating oil, and diesel fuel — 70 percent of all refined oil products. Thus, under Phase IV, refiners could raise prices for cost reasons but the prices that retailers could charge were frozen. A lid on retail prices, the COLC theorized, would place backward pressure to force price restraint on some of the largest corporations in the world.[60] Immediately after Phase IV took effect, some of these corporations raised gasoline prices by one cent a gallon, an increase that the gas stations had to swallow. Outraged retailers staged scattered pump-ins and shutdowns, most effectively in San Francisco, where thousands of stations closed for three days. To still the clamor Nixon ordered the COLC to cut through the red tape and undo the damage that he himself had thoughtlessly inflicted on the nation's gasoline distributors.[61]

By early autumn 1973, the energy problem, which Nixon had labeled escapist in March, had become a national obsession. World petroleum supplies were tight, U.S. crude oil production had leveled off, natural gas companies were canceling contracts, brownouts of electric power had occurred, and price controls were breeding chaos. The oil industry had barely avoided gas lines that summer by maximizing gasoline production, with the result that stocks of heating oil were once again at rock bottom by the fall. Assistant Interior Secretary Stephen Wakefield warned that in the absence of conservation measures, serious dislocations could hardly be avoided. "I am talking about men without jobs, homes without heat, children without schools," he said.[62] On October 2, 1973, Nixon used his discretionary authority to impose mandatory allocations on home heating oil and propane gas with the intention of assuring each dealer some supply.[63] Congress meanwhile was moving closer to passing mandatory allocation legislation for the entire industry. "Almost no one in the administration favors a mandatory program except for political pressures," Nixon's advisers informed him.[64] If a mandatory allocation bill passed, Nixon would no doubt

---

[59] *Pub Paps RN 1973*, 584–587.

[60] *New York Times*, Sept. 7, 1973, 1; Sept. 8, 1973, 1; Sept. 11, 1973, 30.

[61] Ibid., Sept. 25, 1973, 1; Sept. 27, IV, 6; *Business Week* (Sept. 29, 1973), 53–54; Owens, "History of Petroleum Price Controls," 1285–1288.

[62] Quoted in "Energy II: Immediate Prospects," *National Journal* (Oct. 10, 1973), 1508.

[63] *Pub Paps RN 1973*, 851–852; *Wall Street Journal*, Oct. 3, 1973, 2.

[64] John Love and Roy Ash to President, Sept. 15, 1973, EPO file, SMOF: Love.

veto it. But on October 23, 1973, the Arab oil states imposed an oil boycott against the United States, raising the energy crisis to a new level and initiating another self-defeating spasm of regulation.

## IV

The United States remained the world's leading producer of crude oil, but its surplus capacity was gone. Because imports would now have to satisfy increases in U.S. demand, the United States faced a future dependent on the vast reserves of Middle Eastern oil. In 1972, 29 percent of U.S. oil supplies had come from foreign sources, with Middle Eastern oil accounting for 11 percent of imports. In 1973, 35 percent of U.S. oil came from foreign sources, with Middle Eastern oil accounting for 18 percent.[65] As long as the international oil companies controlled the flow of oil from the Middle East, the West was safe. During the Nixon years, the balance of power swung from the oil companies to oil countries more or less allied in the Organization of Petroleum Exporting Countries (OPEC).

OPEC began in 1960 at a meeting in Baghdad of five nations then producing more than 80 percent of the world's exported oil: Iraq, Iran, Saudi Arabia, and Venezuela.[66] Soon joined by others, these states hoped to combat the price-cutting tendencies of the multinational corporations operating oil concessions in their territories. The lower the price of oil, the less each barrel yielded to the countries in royalties and taxes. Because the world market was glutted with oil through the 1960s, OPEC had little leverage to force higher prices on the companies. The multinationals therefore kept control, especially the largest among them, the so-called Seven Sisters: Exxon, Standard Oil of California (Socal), Texaco, Mobil, Gulf, British Petroleum, and Shell.

The man who first exploited OPEC's possibilities was Colonel Mu'ammar al-Gadhafi, leader of a coup that installed a radical government in Libya on September 1, 1969. Gadhafi wanted higher prices for Libyan oil. There were actually two oil prices in countries like Libya, where the multinationals operated oil concessions. One was the market price established by buyers and sellers. The other was the so-called posted price, a fictional price negotiated by the companies and host governments for the purpose of

---

[65] DOE, Energy Information Administration, *1980 Annual Report*, 49, Table 21.

[66] On OPEC's origins and history, Daniel Yergin, *The Prize: The Epic Quest for Oil, Money, and Power* (1991), chaps. 26, 28, esp. 519–563.

calculating royalties and tax payments per barrel. In addition to a 12.5 percent royalty on the posted price, host governments levied a 50 percent tax on "profits." Profits were calculated by subtracting the cost of producing a barrel plus the royalty payment from the posted price. The higher the posted price, the larger the 50 percent take of the countries. Because the companies had to pay royalties and taxes from revenues received from market prices, higher posted prices meant lower revenues for the companies — unless the market price rose too, which was no sure thing in times of glut. In January 1970, when there was still plenty of oil, Gadhafi demanded that the twenty-one oil companies operating in Libya raise the posted price of Libyan crude by forty cents a barrel. The companies, of course, refused.[67]

Gadhafi's strategy was to conquer by dividing the Seven Sisters from the independent companies pumping oil in Libya. The Seven Sisters resented the independents for having elbowed their way into Libya and then worsening the glut by reckless production. Gadhafi singled out the largest of the independents, Occidental Petroleum, based in California and headed by legendary deal-maker Armand Hammer. In May and June 1970, to enforce his demand that Occidental raise the posted price, Gadhafi cut the company's production from 800,000 to 500,000 barrels a day. Totally dependent on Libyan oil for its European refineries, as the majors were not, Occidental had either to find alternative supplies or yield to the Libyans. On July 10, 1970, Hammer met in New York with Kenneth Jamison, chairman of Exxon, seeking to buy at cost the crude Occidental needed so it could resist Gadhafi. Regarding Occidental as a competitor, Jamison declined. This was the West's first great mistake. On September 2, 1971, Hammer shocked the industry by agreeing to an increase of thirty cents in the posted price of crude he pumped in Libya, cutting Occidental's estimated profit margin in half. Within weeks the other companies had no choice except to cave in too. Shell alone resisted and got kicked out of the country for its defiance. Though small, the Libyan price increase signaled a massive shift of oil power from the companies to the countries.[68]

Libya's jealous OPEC partners immediately began making demands of

---

[67] On the Libyan episode, Steven A. Schneider, *The Oil Price Revolution* (1983), 135–148; John M. Blair, *The Control of Oil* (1976), chap. 9.

[68] "Multinational Oil Corporations and United States Foreign Policy," Foreign Relations Committee, Senate Report (Jan. 1975), 123–124; for estimate of posted price rise on profit, *New York Times*, Sept. 23, 1971, 7. The *Times* article referred to the effect of posted price increase on Marathon Oil's profits. I assume a similar effect on Occidental's profits.

their own. A committee of Persian Gulf states — Iran, Saudi Arabia, Kuwait, Iraq, Abu Dhabi, Qatar — formed in December 1970 with the purpose
of negotiating higher posted prices for their crude. On January 2, 1971,
Gadhafi overleaped everyone else by issuing an ultimatum for a second
increase, this one of fifty cents per barrel. Confronted by challenges on two
fronts, the companies saw a trap. If they settled on one price in the Persian
Gulf, Libya would insist on still higher prices, leaving the companies vulnerable to an escalating spiral of demands. The companies decided to bury
their differences and form a united front on behalf of a single comprehensive price negotiation with all the Middle East exporting nations.[69] Meeting in New York on January 13, 1971, representatives of 15 multinational
companies agreed that this time, if Gadhafi cut the production of any one
of them, the others would replace the loss at cost. The chief executives of
the Seven Sisters, along with their famous lawyer John J. McCloy, then met
in Washington with Secretary of State William Rogers and Undersecretary
John Irwin III to seek the support of the U.S. government for the coming
showdown. With Nixon's approval, Rogers dispatched Irwin to Tehran to
reconnoiter.[70]

Irwin met with the Shah of Iran on January 17, 1971. Like Gadhafi, the
Shah adamantly opposed a single negotiation, saying it would only play
into the hands of Libya. If the companies were prepared to conduct two
separate negotiations, the Shah promised a five-year agreement, which the
Gulf states would honor regardless of what the Libyans did. Reassured,
Irwin told the Shah that the U.S. government would not intervene in the
price negotiations and then cabled the State Department to recommend
that the companies be "encouraged to negotiate with the Gulf countries
separately." Without waiting for the companies's negotiators, due to arrive
two days later, Irwin departed Iran. On January 19, 1971, the U.S. ambassador in Tehran, Douglas MacArthur II, advised the negotiators "in the
strongest terms" to accept separate negotiations with the Gulf countries
and settle.[71] Undercut by their own government, the companies accepted
separate negotiations. This was their second great mistake. In a private

---

[69] Testimony of John Irwin II in "Multinational Corporations and United States Foreign
Policy," Part 5, Foreign Relations Committee, Senate hearings (1974), 145–150.
[70] "Multinational Corporations," Senate hearings, 60–61, 147–149; "Multinational Oil
Corporations," Senate Report, 126–130.
[71] "Multinational Oil Corporations," Senate Report, 131. MacArthur's account of the
Shah-Irwin conversations and his advice to the companies summarized in Exhibit 4, "Multinational Corporations," Senate hearings, Part 6, 63–65.

conference with Saudi Oil Minister Zaki Yamani, one company official asked whether the companies should credit the Shah's promise of five years of stable prices. Yamani's reply was resolutely noncommittal.[72]

The talks in Tehran featured breakdowns, deadlines, and threats of shutdown. On February 14, 1972, the Gulf states got what they wanted — an increase in posted prices from $1.80 a barrel to $2.18, with a schedule of small annual increases over the next five years.[73] Negotiations moved next to the Libyan capital of Tripoli. For market reasons, everyone knew that the Libyans would get higher prices than the Gulf, but the extent of the Libyan bonanza, announced April 2, 1971, nonetheless jolted the oil world. Posted prices for Libyan oil rose from $2.55 to $3.45 — a price also good for five years, the Libyans promised.[74] Soon afterward OPEC governments began demanding ownership of part of the oil produced by the companies, and Iraq and Libya moved to nationalize some companies outright.[75]

In 1973, with world oil supplies very tight, OPEC reopened the issue of oil prices. "We are in a position to dictate prices," said Sheik Yamani, "and we are going to be very rich."[76] After obtaining a 12 percent increase in posted prices in June, OPEC moved in August to dispense with the Tehran and Tripoli agreements altogether. Oil markets had changed drastically over the past few years. Now the market price of oil actually exceeded posted prices, which meant that the companies were garnering most of the benefits of price escalation. To rectify the wrongs of Tehran and Tripoli, OPEC summoned the companies to a meeting in Vienna, scheduled for October 8, 1973.[77] The promise of five years of price stability had lasted two and a half years.

A commodity as precious as oil could affect not only the economic but political relations among nations. As far as the Arabs were concerned, the

---

[72] "Multinational Corporations," Senate hearings, Part 6, 70–71.

[73] Mohammed E. Ahrari, *The Dynamics of Oil Diplomacy: Conflict and Consensus* (1980), 172–177. The Tehran agreement also increased the tax on oil profits from 50 percent to 55 percent.

[74] Ahrari, *Dynamics of Oil Diplomacy*, 180–181; also, "Chronology of Libyan Oil Negotiations, 1970–1971," Senate Committee on Foreign Relations, Committee Print (1974), 13–16.

[75] Participation Negotiations Chronology in "Multinational Corporations," Part V, 229–230; Ahrari, *Dynamics of Oil Diplomacy*, 302–316.

[76] *New York Times*, Apr. 16, 1973, 1.

[77] Ahrari, *Dynamics of Oil Diplomacy*, 223–233; *New York Times*, Aug. 24, 1973, 1, Sept. 17, 1973, 1.

political issue that counted was Israel. Among moderate and radical Arab states alike, the conviction grew that if it wanted Arab oil, America would have to abandon unconditional support of Israel. In April 1973, Sheik Yamani told Secretary Rogers that an increase in Saudi production would hinge on a settlement of the Arab-Israeli conflict on terms favorable to the Arabs.[78] In May, King Faisal sent a warning to Washington through the directors of Aramco, the consortium of American oil companies operating in Saudi Arabia. Unless the United States took urgent steps to change its Middle Eastern policy, the king said, his government would be unable to preserve American business interests in the kingdom and "you will lose everything."[79] That month Iraq, Kuwait, Algeria, and Libya imposed a symbolic one-hour shut down of their oil fields to protest the Middle East policy of the United States.[80]

Washington resented the sheiks and colonels for their insolence. "I must say they swagger these days," George Shultz said. "I don't appreciate it particularly."[81] At his press conference on September 5, 1973, Nixon was asked how he was meeting Arab threats "to use oil as a club." On the one hand, Nixon replied, the United States had little influence on radical oil states like Libya. On the other, "Oil without a market, as Mr. Mossadeq learned many, many years ago, does not do a country much good." (Mossadeq was the unfortunate prime minister of Iran whose attempt to nationalize the Anglo-Iranian Oil Company in 1953 failed because the major companies refused to buy his oil.) Responsible Arabs will see, Nixon said, "that if they continue to up the price, if they continue to expropriate, if they expropriate without fair compensation, the inevitable result is that they will lose their markets, and other sources will be developed."[82] Astounded by these remarks, the New York Times asked, "Could it really be that the President of the United States has not grasped the predominant fact of life in the energy picture over the coming decade, that the problem is not whether oil will find a market, but whether markets will find oil?"[83]

In a follow-up question at the same press conference, a reporter asked

[78] New York Times, Apr. 22, 1973, IV, 2.
[79] "Multinational Oil Companies," Senate Report 142; "Multinational Companies," Senate hearings, Part 7, 504.
[80] Lester A. Sobel, ed., Energy Crisis: 1969–73 (vol. 1, 1974), 178–179.
[81] New York Times, Sept. 8, 1973, 47.
[82] Pub Paps RN 1973, 735–736.
[83] New York Times, Oct. 7, 1973, III, 1.

whether the Arab oil weapon might induce the United States to moderate
its support of Israel. Nixon replied, "We are not pro-Israel, and we are not
pro-Arab, and we are not any more pro-Arab because they have oil and
Israel hasn't. We are pro-peace, and it is in the interest of the whole area for
us to get those negotiations off dead center."[84] But it was precisely because
negotiations were so unpromising that Egyptian president Anwar el-Sādāt
sent troops across the Suez Canal into the Israeli-occupied Sinai peninsula
on October 6, 1973, Yom Kippur, to commence the fourth Arab-Israeli war.
The purpose of Sādāt's attack and the simultaneous assault by Syria on the
Golan Heights was to initiate a chain of events that would culminate in a
negotiated return of Arab territories seized by Israel in 1967.[85] Eleven Arab
countries immediately announced that they would use the oil weapon
against any country that came to Israel's defense.[86]

President Nixon and Secretary of State Henry Kissinger conceived the
latest Middle East war as a struggle between the United States and Israel on
one side and Arab states armed by the Soviets on the other. If Israel won,
Kissinger reasoned, the Arabs would see at last that the only way to achieve
their objectives was in cooperation with the United States. Kissinger expected Israeli military power quickly to reestablish the status quo, after
which fruitful negotiations could at last commence. On October 9, Israel
informed the United States that it had suffered devastating losses in the
effort to recover Suez and that unless the United States shipped military
supplies immediately, the situation would be desperate.[87] The United
States heeded this plea. After Israeli commercial aircraft and chartered
planes proved inadequate to carry out a military resupply, Kissinger informed Israel on October 13 that the United States would undertake a
massive airlift exclusively with its own cargo planes. "What will be your
posture when the Arabs start screaming oil at you?" the British ambassador
asked Kissinger. "Defiance," Kissinger replied.[88] A day later, fortunes in the
Sinai shifted again. Israel won a great tank battle in the desert and then
followed up by crossing the Suez to begin destruction of Soviet-made
surface-to-air missiles, Egypt's only shield against aerial attack.

[84] Pub Paps RN 1973, 742.
[85] Anwar el-Sādāt, In Search of Identity (1978), chap. 9; for military developments, Peter
Allen, The Yom Kippur War (1982).
[86] William C. Lane, "Mandatory Petroleum Prices and Allocation Regulations" (American Petroleum Institute, 1989), 30.
[87] Kissinger, Years of Upheaval, chap. XI.
[88] Ibid., 520.

Meantime, on October 8, two days after the war began, the Persian Gulf states and the oil companies kept their appointment in Vienna to discuss oil prices. Negotiations broke down immediately. On October 12, the four presidents of the major companies owning Aramco wrote Nixon warning that increased military aid to Israel would provoke a cutback in Saudi oil.[89] On October 16, the Gulf states unilaterally raised the posted price of crude from $3.00 to $5.11, and a day later played the oil card. The Arab states pledged to reduce production 5 percent a month until Israel abandoned the occupied territories.[90] Unimpressed, Nixon sent Congress a $2.2 billion emergency aid package to pay for the resupply of Israel. In apparent retaliation, on October 20, 1973, the Saudis at last took the fateful step so long feared. They augmented the production cutback with a total embargo on oil exports to the United States and also the Netherlands, another country deemed too friendly to Israel.[91] The other Arab states followed the Saudi lead, with the exception of Iraq, which damned the embargo as insufficiently radical but would not forego the opportunity to make a killing. Iran, of course, was not an Arab state and kept pumping.

These were traumatic days for the American people. Within hours of the Saudi embargo announcement, Nixon plunged his presidency into its greatest crisis by firing Watergate Special Prosecutor Archibald Cox in an effort to keep recordings of his White House conversation from the inquiring ear of the federal courts. Rather than carry out Nixon's order to dismiss Cox, Attorney General Elliot Richardson and the Deputy Attorney General William Ruckelshaus resigned.[92] The so-called Saturday Night Massacre prompted the House Judiciary Committee on October 23 to open hearings on Nixon's possible impeachment. A day later, while Kissinger was in tense discussions on the Middle East with the Soviet ambassador, Nixon phoned him to say, "They are doing it because of their desire to kill the president."[93]

On October 24, the Middle East situation took a serious turn. Soviet Premier Leonid Brezhnev sent the United States a message that Kissinger described as "one of the most serious challenges to an American President

---

[89] Memo from J. K. Jamison et al. for President, Oct. 12, 1974, reprinted in "Multinational Corporations," Senate hearings, Part 7, 546–547.

[90] "Multinational Oil Corporations," Senate report, 144–145; *New York Times*, Oct. 18, 1973, 1.

[91] Kissinger, *Years of Upheaval*, 873; *New York Times*, Oct. 21, 1973, 28.

[92] Stanley I. Kulter, *The Wars of Watergate* (1990), 406–407.

[93] Kissinger, *Years of Upheaval*, 581.

by a Soviet leader." Join us in sending troops to rescue endangered Egypt, Brezhnev seemed to say, or we will send troops ourselves.[94] Late that night, while Nixon slept unconsulted, Kissinger and Defense Secretary James Schlesinger sent the Soviets a signal by putting the United States on nuclear alert.[95] The Soviets, who did not intend to move into Egypt unilaterally anyway, stayed out.[96] In the end, intense American diplomatic pressures prevented Israel from finishing Egypt "with a knockout blow," preserving Kissinger's hope for U.S. mediation. On October 27, 1973, a U.N. cease-fire took hold, and the war was over, but the oil embargo continued.

## V

At first there was no panic. After all, oil tankers loaded with Middle Eastern oil were on the high seas, and it would take four to six weeks for the embargo to interrupt supplies. Besides, no one knew for sure how deep the embargo would bite. It was Nixon who finally sounded the alarm. In a televised address on November 7, 1973, two weeks after the Arabs had imposed the embargo, the president proclaimed "a very stark fact: We are heading into the most acute energy shortage since World War II." To underscore his sense of urgency, the president announced a dramatic program to combat the shortage and, incidentally, restore his flagging leadership. He ordered industrial plants to halt conversions from coal to oil, reduced air travel 10 percent, and asked Americans to lower thermostats by six degrees. From Congress he requested authority to impose emergency measures to save energy: year-round daylight savings time, relaxed environmental standards, lower highway speed limits. For an inspirational climax, the president announced Project Independence, a massive national effort, he said, as ambitious as the Manhattan Project or Project Apollo, to achieve total energy self-sufficiency by 1980. ("It's a pipe dream," one expert remarked.) Putting aside his prepared text, chin up, Nixon closed "on a personal note." Observing that Watergate had raised concerns about his integrity and that some publishers had called for his resignation, he said, "I have no intention whatever of walking away from this job I was elected to do."[97]

---

[94] Ibid., 583.

[95] *New York Times*, Nov. 25, 1973, IV, 3; Kissinger, *Years of Upheaval*, 585–588.

[96] Victor Israelyan, *Inside the Kremlin during the Yom Kippur War* (1995), chap. 7.

[97] *Pub Paps RN 1973*, 916–922; for pipe dream quote, *National Journal* (Nov. 11, 1973), 1730.

Congress responded by rushing to pass laws before the Christmas recess. The Alaskan pipeline finally won approval, as did year-long daylight savings and a 55-mile-per-hour speed limit. It took the Senate only a week to pass emergency legislation ceding Nixon the vast authority he had requested to curb other nonessential energy use. (The bill never became law because Nixon vetoed it in February rather than accept an amendment to roll back the price of domestic crude oil.) And on November 14, Congress finally passed the Emergency Petroleum Allocation Act, requiring the president to take over from the oil companies the power to allocate crude oil and refined products.[98] Given the rising hysteria, Nixon had no choice except to sign.

Oil supplies were tight in December, though less tight than the government predicted or the public perceived. Good cheer that Christmas was also in short supply. Airlines and auto companies announced layoffs, and schools closed early.[99] New England power plants reduced voltage; truck drivers blocked highways to protest the price of diesel fuel;[100] and most gas stations observed Nixon's request to close down from 9:00 P.M. Saturday to midnight Sunday, stranding some motorists.[101] Homes and businesses usually ablaze with Christmas lights stood darkened. Nixon flew to San Clemente for the holiday on a commercial jet to save fuel.[102] On Christmas Eve, the Persian oil ministers sent seasons greetings by announcing a price increase of Gulf crude from $5.11 to $11.65, making a total increase of 470 percent since January. Said the Shah of Iran, "The industrial world would have to realize that the era of their terrific progress and even more terrific income and wealth based on cheap oil is finished. They will have to find new sources of energy, tighten their belts. If you want to live as well as now, you'll have to work for it."[103]

Before Nixon could implement a program for the embargo, he would first have to impose order on the bureacratic chaos that had plagued energy policy throughout 1973. At the beginning of the year, John Ehrlichman had bid to take over energy policy, but Ehrlichman was gone by April. In February, Deputy Treasury Secretary William Simon assumed the chair of

---

[98] For a summary of energy legislation rushed through Congress, *Congressional Quarterly Weekly Report* (Dec. 29, 1973), 3432.

[99] *Newsweek* (Dec. 10, 1973), 91.

[100] *Time* (Dec. 3, 1973), 22–38; *New York Times*, Dec. 5, 1; Dec. 9, 1973, III, 1.

[101] *New York Times*, Dec. 10, 1973, 1.

[102] *RN: Memoirs* (1978), 985.

[103] *New York Times*, Dec. 24, 1974, 1.

the Oil Policy Committee, a body that oversaw imports and now aspired to coordinate energy policy throughout the government. In June, Roy Ash of Office of Management and Budget persuaded Nixon to take oil policy away from Simon by creating an Energy Policy Office in the White House. Nixon appointed Governor John Love of Colorado to head the new office and then ignored him. On December 4, 1973, Love was out and Simon was back, this time as director of the brand-new Federal Energy Office, which Nixon created by executive order.[104] Nixon told his Cabinet that Simon would have "absolute authority" in oil, the kind of authority, he said, that Hitler had given Albert Speer to produce armaments in the Third Reich.[105]

A successful Wall Street bond dealer when Shultz brought him into the Treasury as the number-two man in January 1973, William Simon was a thin, intense, hard-driving conservative with strong free-market views, but he was also ambitious to succeed Shultz as secretary and not above dispensing special favors to congressmen or trimming his convictions to win the prize.[106] So it was that Simon, the free-market ideologue, embraced with unseemly zeal his chance to wield power over the oil industry and become a hero of the embargo. Simon had spent hours every day taking a cram course on energy after he took over the Oil Policy Committee early in the year, and he set a frenetic pace now that he was energy czar. In a matter of weeks Simon fashioned an agency out of bits and pieces of the existing bureaucracy; formulated crucial policies in an atmosphere of panic; tried in his many speeches to convince the public that the shortage had not been contrived by greedy oil companies; and answered the summons of congressional committees for his testimony, which by his count he rendered 102 times in five months, an average of one appearance for every working day. On one occasion, the House Ways and Means Committee refused to let Simon tend to a bloody gash on his forehead, suffered in an accident, until he completed six hours of grueling testimony.[107] The remarkable fact about William Simon was that, despite his disastrous tenure as director of the Federal Energy Office, he actually did become secretary of the treasury.

---

[104] For history of administration's effort to organize for energy, Neil De Marchi, "Energy Policy under Nixon: Mainly Putting Out Fires," in Craufurd D. Goodwin, ed., *Energy Policy in Perspective: Today's Problems, Yesterday's Solutions* (1981), 395–473; *National Journal* (Dec. 8, 1973), 1830–1838.

[105] William E. Simon, *A Time for Truth* (1978), 47.

[106] Marchi, "Energy Policy under Nixon," 451, 455 (including fn 133).

[107] Simon, *Time for Truth*, 61–62.

In Simon's view, the dimensions of the crisis facing the country fully justified the new law mandating allocation of crude and refined oil supplies. Before departing the government, Governor Love had predicted a shortage of 3.5 million barrels a day during the first quarter of 1973. Simon scaled that estimate back to a still substantial 2.7 million barrels — or 13 percent of demand.[108] The first task was to establish priorities for the allocation of what was left. The government decided first, to meet fully the current needs of the Defense Department and essential civilian services; second, to save jobs by keeping industry and commerce adequately supplied; third, to tilt refinery production toward heating oil to warm homes; and finally, to do "everything we can to curtail gasoline production and consumption as a way of increasing the availabilities of other refined products."[109] In short, the nation's 80 million cars, guzzlers of nearly half of every barrel of oil, would have to bear the brunt of the shortage in the form of a 15 percent cutback in gasoline consumption.

Through late November and early December the president's advisers engaged in a fascinating debate on how to manage a gasoline shortage.[110] Offering the classical solution, the CEA favored letting gasoline prices rise until the market cleared, eliminating the shortage. Politically, this option was viable only if the price did not rise very far. Simon guessed that gas price in a free market would rise from forty-six to seventy-five cents a gallon. A Brookings Institution study said eighty cents. A staff study in the government went as high as $1.51, and the *Wall Street Journal* claimed that many intelligent people apparently believed that "gasoline is the only commodity in history with an elasticity of zero."[111] Milton Friedman, a classical economist if there ever was one, estimated that the embargo would cut oil supplies by 10 percent, raising prices by only 20 percent.[112]

---

[108] See Simon's testimony, "Current Energy Shortages Series: The Federal Energy Office," Part 5, Government Operations Committee, Senate hearings (1974), 605.

[109] John Hill to Charles Owens, Nov. 20, 1973, Econ. Stab. Programs file, Records of Deputy Director, COLC, RG 432.

[110] Energy Emergency Action Group: Tab III — Gasoline Options, Nov. 30, 1973, (CF) UT, WHSF; John Love for President, Nov. 27, 1973, same file; Stein to Love et al., Nov. 29, 1973, Energy file, SMOF: Stein.

[111] For Simon and Brookings estimate, as well as the quote, see *Wall Street Journal* article reprinted in "Oversight — Mandatory Petroleum Allocation Programs," Committee on Interior and Insular Affairs, Senate hearings (1974), 189–190; for the $1.51 estimate, Energy Emergency Action Group: Tab III — Gasoline Options, 7.

[112] Friedman's column in *Newsweek* (Nov. 19, 1973), 130.

For gasoline, this would mean a market-clearing price of approximately fifty-five cents. As it happened, the real world provided an actual laboratory to test the conflicting estimates. Canada's eastern provinces, totally dependent on scarce imported crude, imposed no price controls during the Arab cutback. The price cleared at fifty-nine cents a U.S. gallon, not very high, and there were no gas lines in Canada. Neither were there gas lines in Germany, which also elected to ration gas by the market.[113]

There was another way to raise gasoline prices besides letting the market clear, one that would not swell the profits of the hated oil companies. If the government raised gasoline prices by levying a tax on the sale of gasoline, say thirty cents a gallon, gasoline demand would fall an estimated million barrels a day, with the government rather than the companies reaping the revenue benefits.[114] On reading reports that Shultz favored a gas tax, Friedman wrote to chide him for his violation of market logic. A tax would dampen demand, Friedman said, but it would also deny the oil companies the higher profits that would provide the incentive to look for more oil. "I realize that you are fully aware of these arguments, so hesitate somewhat to repeat them," Friedman said. "However, the whole atmosphere is so poisoned with irrational views, so hysterical and lacking in perspective that it may do no harm to reiterate them."[115]

The third alternative for handling the gasoline shortage was coupon rationing, which the Senate came within eight votes of approving late in November. Nixon had loathed rationing since his brief tour with the Office of Price Administration during World War II, rationing tires. Under the rationing option, the government would issue each motorist coupons for the purchase of, say, ten gallons a week, thereby controlling demand, reducing pressure on prices, and preventing gas lines. Coupon rationing was clearly superior to the free-market option, Paul Samuelson wrote in the *New York Times*. "Letting the market price be bid up to whatever level is needed is the traditional capitalistic way of meeting shortages," he said. "The Irish potato famine was handled in this fashion . . . As a classical economist of the day would say, 'Why speak of a food crisis? There is no crisis. There is simply a need for a higher price to ration the excess demand

---

[113] *Wall Street Journal* article reprinted in "Oversight — Mandatory Allocation Program."

[114] Stein and Shultz et al., Nov. 7, 1973, Interstaff Communication, Nixon-Stein file, SMOF: Haig; Stein and Love et al., Energy file, SMOF: Stein; and *Congressional Quarterly Weekly Report* (Dec. 1, 1973), 3139–3141.

[115] Friedman to Shultz, Nov. 16, 1973 (no file info.), SMOF: Stein.

down to the scarce supply, to coax out higher supplies in the future.' "[116] Coupons could not cure a shortage, but they could reduce its irritations and assure equity of suffering.

In the end, the administration rejected each of these options — the market because of the inflationary consequences of higher gasoline prices; a gas tax because the public would hate it; and coupons because of the attendant bureaucracy, though the White House did order the Bureau of Printing and Engraving to print 10 to 15 billion coupons just in case. As Samuelson warned, the only other option was "congestion rationing, the most inefficient form of all." Said Samuelson, "If we have to spend enough time waiting in lines . . . that will in the end chop down the demand to the Procrustean bed of reduced supply." And wait in line is precisely what the public had to do.

For millions of Americans that winter, gas lines were the oil crisis. Ordinarily sensible people acted in peculiar ways when their cars were at stake. In New York City during the last days of 1973, even before there was an actual shortage, the mere fear of a shortage led to gas lines as motorists sought to top off. Others, seeing the lines, joined them to get gas before the pumps went dry.[117] When real shortages hit and gas lines spread and lengthened, especially during February 1974, civility was a leading casualty. "In the past month," the *New York Times* reported, "people in metropolitan areas have become increasingly suspicious and angry, insecure, devious, often violent and seldom resigned, all because of the lack of gasoline."[118] In Miami, a driver of a Cadillac, enraged by his failure to break into a gas line, tried to run over an attendant.[119] On Jerome Avenue in the Bronx, cars rammed through oil drums to get gas at a station trying to close.[120] In Gary, Indiana, a customer who cut into line shot and killed a station owner who refused him service.[121] "These people are like animals foraging for food," a harried Amoco dealer said. "If you can't sell them gas, they'll threaten to beat you up, wreck your station, and run over you with a car."[122] The panic

---

[116] Paul Samuelson, "The Great Hunger," *New York Times*, Dec. 3, 1973, 39.

[117] Richard B. Mancke, *Squeaking By: U.S. Energy Policy Since the Embargo* (1976), 23; *New York Times*, Dec. 28, 1973, 1.

[118] *New York Times*, Feb. 8, 1974, 15.

[119] *Newsweek* (Feb. 18, 1974), 21.

[120] *New York Times*, Feb. 2, 1974, 1.

[121] *Washington Post*, Feb. 21, 1973, A5.

[122] *Time* (Feb. 18, 1974), 35.

fed on itself. Drivers idling six-cylinder engines in a gas line a mile long burned up 150 gallons every hour.[123] People who once drove tanks half-full joined lines to top off, shifting inventory from pumps to gas tanks. "Gasoline fever," *Time* reported, had gripped America.[124]

The Arabs had something to do with the gas lines, of course, but the efforts of the U.S. government to counter the shortage hurt much more, especially the effort of Simon's Federal Energy Office (FEO) to implement the Emergency Petroleum Allocation Act of November 1973. The purpose of that act was to protect independent segments of the oil industry and oil consumers by assuring equitable distribution of scarce supplies. FEO's allocation regulations said that oil-refining companies should first meet the priority gasoline needs of the states they served (public transportation, emergency services, farmers) and then distribute the remainder proportionately to the same wholesalers and retailers they had supplied in the same month of 1972. Congress chose 1972 as the base period in the belief that independent marketers had received a fair share of gasoline supplies that year. In fact, during the early months of 1972, the market share of the independents was less than at any time in 1973. The choice of the base, therefore, penalized rather than benefited independent marketers.[125]

Simon's allocation regulations compounded the damage. After meeting the priority needs of the states in February 1974, the companies had average remaining gasoline supplies equal to 84 percent of the gas they had distributed to marketers in February 1972. With this gas each company had to supply the same distributors it supplied in 1972, but many of these gas stations no longer existed. Since 1972, major companies — including Gulf, Phillips, and British Petroleum — had consolidated marketing operations by closing thousands of filling stations, especially in the South and the Midwest. Stations that had opened or expanded to fill the resulting gap after 1972 had to receive special dispensation from the FEO to get supplies. Some lucky refiners had gasoline supplies in excess of the industry average, which benefited the gas stations in states they happened to serve. Other refiners — for example, East Coast companies dependent on foreign oil — had less than the national average of gasoline supply, leaving stations in

---

[123] *New York Times*, Feb. 8, 1974, 15.

[124] *Time* (Feb. 18, 1974), 35.

[125] Staff Report to Federal Trade Commission, "An Evaluation of the Mandatory Petroleum Allocation Program, January 15–February 28, 1974" (Mar. 15, 1974), A33–34, reprinted as Appendix, "Oversight–Mandatory Allocation Program," Senate hearings.

their states starved for gas. Cities on the Gulf Coast or near western Canada had little problem getting gas; regions of the East Coast suffered gas lines up to two miles long. Wyoming received 122 percent of its gasoline needs and Louisiana 109 percent. Vermont and New Hampshire trailed the nation with 63 percent each.[126] One FEO official was forced to admit, "The only thing that will save the situation is if companies do the regulating themselves."[127]

As his critics charged at the time, Simon had undertaken to allocate oil supplies on the basis of a false premise, namely, that the oil shortage was severe. At the beginning of January 1974, the Federal Energy Office forecast that oil supplies in February would fall 14 percent below demand.[128] But FEO overstated demand and understated supply. FEO defined demand as "unconstrained" demand, meaning the demand for oil that would have existed if there had been no embargo and no price increase. These were facts not to be ignored but reckoned with. FEO's demand projections assumed real growth in GNP of 2.5 percent in 1974. But partly because of higher oil prices, the economy plunged into recession during the first quarter, curbing demand for oil products by an estimated 3 to 4 percent. Higher prices also induced consumers to cut demand an additional 2 to 3 percent, and the embargo was responsible for voluntary oil conservation of maybe 1 or 2 percent.[129] Conservatively estimated, these effects knocked something like 7 percent off FEO's unconstrained demand estimate, reducing estimated demand from 20.9 million barrels per day in February to, say, 19.6 million. Even within FEO itself, the concept of unconstrained demand had its critics. One member of the agency's staff, Eric Zausner, wrote a colleague in March to congratulate him for finally acknowledging "that price and conservation effects will reduce demand. This is important since there are a hell of a lot of people, both inside FEO and outside, who have wondered about our inability, or apparent unwillingness, to recognize demand elasticities. Frankly, I think our past practice of comparing everything to

---

[126] Federal Trade Commission, "An Evaluation", 98–103; Mancke, *Squeaking By*, 29–33, including Table 2.4 with state-by-state allocation of need figures.

[127] *Newsweek* (Feb. 25, 1973), 76.

[128] Federal Energy Office, "National Supply and Demand 1974" (Jan. 2, 1974), 8, reprinted in "Current Analysis of Petroleum Supplies for First Quarter 1974," Committee on Interior and Insular Affairs, Committee Print (1974).

[129] George L. Perry, "The United States," in Edward R. Fried and Charles L. Schultze, eds. *Higher Oil Prices and the World Economy: The Adjustment Problem* (1975), 71–104; for estimates of the effects of the recession, higher prices, and conservation on oil demand, 87–88.

an unconstrained demand estimate has caused FEO to lose considerable credibility."[130]

FEO's supply calculations were likewise off the mark. Arab oil production fell during the embargo, to be sure — from 20.1 million barrels per day in September 1973 to 15.0 million in November.[131] On December 25, the day after they doubled oil prices, the Arabs announced a 10 percent increase in oil production to reward consumer nations, other than the United States, for tilting to the Arab position.[132] In January, production climbed back to 17.6 million barrels a day. Despite the total Arab embargo of the United States, a rise in Arab production, indeed a rise in oil exports anywhere, meant more oil for America, thanks to the crisis management of the multinational companies.

The Seven Sisters managed the world's supply of exported oil during the embargo — or at least the 75 percent of internationally traded oil that they produced. Operating on the transnational principle of equal suffering, the multinationals tried to distribute the shortage evenly among the United States, Japan, and Western Europe. In particular, the companies delivered Arab oil ordinarily destined for the United States elsewhere but diverted non-Arab oil to the United States as replacement. The Arabs winked at this partial subversion of the embargo because, as Sheik Yamani said, "We just cannot afford to damage the U.S. economy."[133] As a result of the shell game that the companies played with oil tankers, the United States imported 470,000 more barrels a day of crude and refined oil in February than the FEO had expected.[134]

In sum, for February 1974, the FEO had predicted demand at 20.9 million barrels per day and supply at 18.0 million barrels, leaving a shortage of 2.9 million, but in that month actual demand approximated 19.6 million barrels and supply 18.5 million barrels, leaving a shortage of only 1.1 million barrels. Even this gap between supply and demand might have been eliminated except for the most egregious of all FEO's regulations — the so-called buy/sell rule.

---

[130] Eric Zausner to P. L. Essley, Jr., Mar. 19, 1974, Box 2504, Collection 1410, FEO/FEA papers, DOE Archives.

[131] For this and next paragraph, Federal Energy Agency, "US Oil Companies and the Arab Embargo" (1975); Robert B. Stobaugh, "The Oil Companies in Crisis," in Vernon, *The Oil Crisis*, 179–202.

[132] *New York Times*, Dec. 26, 1973, 1; Dec. 27, 1973, 26.

[133] *Newsweek* (Dec. 24, 1973), 109.

[134] For estimates, FEO, National Petroleum Supply and Demand 1974 (Jan. 2, 1974); for actual imports, Federal Energy Administration, *Monthly Energy Review* (Dec. 1974), 6, 8.

The Emergency Energy Allocation Act intended independent refiners to get their fair share of crude oil supplies. As a result, beginning on February 1, 1974, refiners with more than an average supply of crude had to share it with refiners having less than the average. The buy/sell rule was intended to compel the Goliaths of the industry to sell to David. That did not happen. As the Federal Trade Commission reported, "Seven of the largest refiners (ARCO, Texaco, Sohio, Ashland, Union, Sun, and Marathon) were entitled to purchase a total of nearly 17 million barrels or 30 percent of the total to be exchanged" during the first quarter. No less absurd, nineteen refiners, each with a capacity of only 30,000 barrels a day, "were slated to sell 1.5 million barrels of crude."[135] But the most harmful effect of buy/sell was the disincentive it provided to imports.

If surplus refiners had to sell crude oil to deficit refiners, what price should they charge? There were, after all, two crude oil prices — "old" oil at $5.25 and "new" oil at the world price of approximately $11.00. Assuming that a surplus company had equal stocks of both, the average price of its crude oil would be, say, $7.50. Under the rules, this company would have to resell its surplus crude to deficit companies at the $7.50 price. Why would a surplus company import oil at $11.00 for resale at $7.50 — a $3.50 loss? And why would a deficit company import oil at $11.00 when it could be bought for $7.50 under buy/sell?[136] As one student of the episode observed, "This regulation thus had the perverse effect of encouraging both crude-short and crude-rich refiners to cut back their oil imports during precisely those

---

[135] Federal Trade Commission, "An Evaluation of the Mandatory Petroleum Allocation Program," A118.

[136] Federal Trade Commission, "An Evaluation of the Mandatory Petroleum Allocation Program," A142–146; Paul W. MacAvoy, *Energy Policy: An Economic Analysis* (1983), 57–58; William C. Lane, "The Mandatory Petroleum Price and Allocation Regulations," 39–43. Mancke, *Squeaking By*, notes that FEO regulations permitted crude-rich firms to recover losses from forced sales under buy/sell by raising the price of their refined products. He concludes that imports "did not decline appreciably" because of buy/sell. But Mancke uses the weekly import statistics in the *Oil and Gas Journal* instead of the more commonly cited import statistics of the Bureau of Mines. In all likelihood, Mancke overstates oil imports in February. Moreover, on page 166, footnote 18, he says that the import decline that did occur was partly due "to the discrimination caused by the interrefinery reallocation regulations" — i.e., buy/sell — undercutting his argument. In its report, "An Evaluation of the Mandatory Petroleum Allocation Program," the Federal Trade Commission commented, "the mathematical operation of the crude buy/sell program and product sales price formula, coupled with candid interviews, convinced the task force" that buy/sell was discouraging imports. "Unfortunately, the extent is unknown," the report said, suggesting, however, that buy/sell was the reason for the continuing drop in imports even after the embargo had become fully effective, p. A187.

months when the . . . embargo was most effective."[137] When Simon's chief economist, William Johnson, polled a sample of oil companies on the causes for declining crude oil imports, "at least eight of them" reported that because of buy/sell, they had canceled substantial shipments of foreign crude.[138] "They said 'the hell with it,'" reported one official in touch with a major that had decided to stop importing altogether. "'It's not worth it.'"[139] Johnson estimated that buy/sell was reducing imports of crude oil by 1 million barrels a day, approximately equal to the actual shortage that month.[140] Simon got the point. Asking Congress to change the allocation law, Simon said that buy/sell served "to defeat the very purpose of the program."[141] By the time Congress changed the law, the embargo was over.

Simon's highly publicized claims of critical oil shortages requiring dramatic federal action failed to persuade, among others, the White House. At first, Roy Ash, who had moved from Litton Industries to take over the Office of Management and Budget after the 1972 election, bought Simon's view of a serious shortage.[142] But in mid-December two OMB economists sent Ash a memo revising the estimated shortage downward to only 1 million barrels a day, citing slower than anticipated economic growth, the dampening effect on oil demand of higher oil prices, and a leaky embargo. A shortage so small did not require "strong intervention measures," these analysts warned, especially not the allocation plans FEO was then preparing.[143] From then on, Ash missed no opportunity to undercut Simon with Nixon, not least because Ash saw Simon as a rival in the struggle for power amid the ruins of Nixon's presidency.

In mid-January 1974, Ash sent Nixon a copy of an article in the *Economist*, predicting that misguided government policies and higher prices would produce an oil glut in a few years. "We certainly should continue the pressures for energy conservation, and Bill Simon should continue to cry

---

[137] Mancke, *Squeaking By*, 34.

[138] William A. Johnson to William Simon and John Sawhill, Jan. 25, 1974, FEO-Exports-Imports of Energy 1974 file, Drawer 13, file 30, Simon papers.

[139] *New York Times*, Feb. 22, 1974, 1.

[140] For Johnson's estimate, *Oil and Gas Journal* (Mar. 4, 1974), 25.

[141] *Washington Post*, Feb. 23, 1974, 7.

[142] Ash to Al Haig, Nov. 14, 1973, Ash: SMOF. Ash said, "Whether we like it or not, we must temporarily inject the government into the private sector in ways reserved only for emergencies."

[143] Jack W. Carlson and Terrence R. Colvin for the Director, Dec. 14, 1973, SMOF: Ash. Troika 2, which prepared forecasts for the Troika and included Carlson, took the same view, with little effect. Fellner, Fiedler, and Carlson for Shultz, Ash, and Stein, Jan. 5, 1973, CEA-Troika Memos—Troika 1974 file, SMOF: Stein.

shortage," Ash said. "But I would suggest that we avoid longer-term commitments based on panic, that you personally avoid magnifying the crisis, and that particularly we avoid meddling with the private sector in ways which interfere with its abilities to produce." Commending Adam Smith's *The Wealth of Nations* to the president, Ash concluded, "Just as a physician whose first rule is 'primum non nocere — first at least do not harm,' we should, in our governmental policies, have the same concern for the economy."[144] Early in February 1974, Ash wrote Nixon again on the energy crisis, estimating the shortage for 1974 at only 5 to 7 percent. "The conservation actions and demand reductions in response to higher prices have quite likely already offset this supply shortage," he said. Ash advised against predicting "vast shortages which will not materialize, and that we change from a crisis mode of operation to a more thoughtful problem-solving role." Underlining these words for Alexander Haig, Nixon wrote, "Al — absolutely right."[145]

The Ash-Simon disagreement assumed the status of a feud on February 12, 1974, when Ash publicly said that the oil crisis was "manageable, it's one-time and it's short-term."[146] The next day on NBC's "Today Show" Simon replied, "Maybe I should ask him to keep his cotton-pickin' hands off energy policy."[147] (Simon borrowed the phrase from Shultz who had recently used it in a different turf war with Melvin Laird.) Nixon chose sides on February 19 when he told Simon to end gas lines by drawing down gasoline inventories. Simon, who had been hoarding gas for fear of worse shortages later, complied by releasing too little to make much difference.[148] On February 22, 1974, at a meeting with his advisers, including both Simon and Ash, Nixon emphasized the importance of ending the gas-line problem promptly. According to the minutes, "The President directed Simon to be generous in authorizing the drawdown of gasoline inventories. He recognized the risk this would create for the future and accepted the risk."[149] The next day Simon increased gasoline allocations for twenty-six oil-short states.[150] By the beginning of March, thanks to increased alloca-

---

[144] Ash for President, Jan. 16, 1974, Ash memos for President's file, SMOF: Ash.

[145] Ibid., Feb. 7, 1974, attached to Bruce Kehrli to Ash, Feb. 11, 1974, President's Handwriting file, POF. The date is not on the copy in this file but is handwritten on the copy in Stein's file.

[146] *New York Times*, Feb. 13, 1974, 29.

[147] Ibid., Feb. 14, 1974, 29.

[148] Ibid., Feb. 20, 1974, 1.

[149] Stein, Memo for the President's file (meeting of Feb. 22, 1974), Mar. 11, 1974, Memos for President's file, POF.

[150] *New York Times*, Feb. 24, 1974, 38.

tions, gasoline fever finally broke, and the gas lines, which the government had created, disappeared.

The embargo soon ended too. At the outset, the Arabs had threatened to maintain the embargo until Israel withdrew from the occupied territories. In December 1973, Egypt's Sādāt indicated that it might be enough if the United States, through even-handed mediation, helped arrange a military disengagement of the belligerents along the Suez Canal, which Kissinger did in January 17, 1974. Nixon dared briefly hope that he might electrify the nation in his State of the Union Message by announcing the end of the embargo, but the Saudis had the oil, not Sādāt, and the Saudis hesitated for fear of alienating the radical Arab states. Kissinger broke the impasse by threatening the Arabs with delay in his mediation of military disengagement on the Golan Heights. "The shoe was on the other foot: They, not we, had to find a way to end the embargo," Kissinger wrote in his memoirs.[151] Though the embargo persisted for several more weeks, everybody, except maybe the FEO, knew it would soon be over. Most Arab governments finally canceled the embargo at a meeting in Tripoli on March 18, 1974.[152] By May, when Kissinger effected military disengagement on the Golan Heights, U.S. oil imports had risen by more than 1 million barrels a day above February levels.

In June 1974, Jack Carlson of Roy Ash's staff wrote him a memo recalling "our debate with FEO concerning the impact that higher product prices and slower growth in incomes would have on the reduction in the demand for oil products." Citing an independent study that confirmed the OMB view, Carlson wrote, "Next time we have a shortage problem, in oil or elsewhere, the first thing we should do is review how well the economy works without government intervention. By the way, . . . all oil products should be in ample supply this summer . . . Under these conditions, controls can result only in distortions."[153] Unfortunately, though supplies would indeed be ample, controls would last for years. "I think of our failure to deregulate [oil], as one of the great mistakes," Stein said later. "We somehow muddled through the crisis but we left ourselves with a terribly inefficient, cumbersome system for the future."[154] Not long after President

---

[151] Kissinger, *Years of Upheaval*, 891–895.

[152] *New York Times*, Mar. 18, 1974, 1.

[153] Carlson for Ash, June 20, 1974, Economic Policy Division file, OMB, RG 51.

[154] Stein Interview in Erwin C. Hargrove and Samuel A. Morley, eds., *The President and the Council of Economic Advisers* (1984), 403, 404.

Ronald Reagan finally got rid of controls, spaceship earth would once again be glutted with oil.

Watergate would have finished Nixon anyway, but the oil crisis did not help. The administration's confusions before the embargo and its bumbling performance afterward confirmed doubts that Nixon could govern any longer. Nixon also suffered from the popular belief that he was the servant of the oil industry, a belief reinforced in January 1974 with the revelation that $5 million of the $60 million raised for his 1972 campaign was oil money.[155] These contributions, said Congressman Les Aspin, make clear why "the Administration's attitude has been so consistently anticonsumer and pro big oil."[156] "Impeach Nixxon," declared one slogan that suggested the reciprocal relation of the energy crisis and Watergate in facilitating the president's fall.[157]

The sharp run-up in world prices did Nixon even more political damage than the embargo or Simon's regulations, because of the impact of oil prices on the larger economy. It had always been an article of Nixon's faith that the economy makes or breaks presidents. Higher oil prices helped raise the inflation rate from 8.4 percent during 1973 to 12.1 percent in 1974. Higher oil prices also depressed aggregate demand, contributing to what contemporaries would call the Great Recession, whose approach Nixon's advisers did not see and whose severity their policies exacerbated.

---

[155] *Washington Post*, Jan. 2, 1974, 1.

[156] *New York Times*, Jan. 2, 1974, 31.

[157] Anthony Sampson, *The Seven Sisters: The Great Oil Companies and the World They Shaped* (1975), 209.

# Chapter 10

# The Great Recession

## I

Nixon spent the first days of 1974 isolated under gloomy skies in the Western White House at San Clemente. Only two aides saw him regularly: Alexander Haig, who had assumed Haldeman's duties as manager of the government; and Ron Zeigler, the thirty-four-year-old White House press secretary, who had once been an ad man for J. Walter Thompson and was now the president's lone confidant. Henry Kissinger flew in for four days to discuss the Middle East but saw Nixon only twice. Office of Management and Budget director Roy Ash came for a weekend to discuss the budget and saw him not at all.[1] The president, it appeared, was too depressed to conduct the nation's business. A year ago, in the wake of his reelection, Nixon had plotted the punishment of his enemies. Now, because of Watergate, his enemies were punishing him. Twelve of Nixon's former aides or their assistants had been convicted of Watergate-related crimes. Six others were under indictment, with more to follow.[2] Even as he brooded in seclusion, the noose of Watergate tightened round him. *Time* proclaimed his implacable pursuer, Judge John Sirica, as Man of the Year. The Internal Revenue Service announced resumption of the investigation into his income tax returns. The usual denunciations greeted news that he would defy a Senate Watergate subpoena of hundreds of his taped conversations. A panel of experts was preparing to report that a critical eighteen and a half minutes of one tape had intentionally been erased, and forty zealous staffers were sifting through mounds of evidence for the House committee preparing to consider his impeachment.[3] With his Gallup poll rating down to 29 percent and Republicans losing heart, chances of surviving the committee's inquiry looked increasingly bleak.[4]

---

[1] *Time* (Jan. 21, 1974), 12–13; *Newsweek* (Jan. 21, 1974), 19.

[2] Ibid., (Jan. 7, 1974), 9–10.

[3] Ibid., (Jan. 21, 1974), 14.

[4] *Gallup Poll* (vol. 1, 1978), 226.

Back in Washington in mid-January 1974, his spirits recovered, Nixon was ready to embark on his last campaign. "But this time, instead of campaigning for a political office," he recalled, "I would be campaigning for my political life."[5] That meant that he must once again appear to be the president. But the smooth-running machinery of the first term had by now fallen into disrepair. Nixon's absorption in Watergate and Haldeman's departure had left the administration drifting and leaderless. Haig tried to keep things together but lacked the authority. Nowhere was the resulting vacuum more apparent than in the realm of economic policy, where Nixon's subordinates engaged in an unseemly competition for power.

After the 1972 election, Nixon had designated Treasury Secretary George Shultz as assistant to the president for economic affairs and let him run the economy. For a time, Shultz's brilliant ad hoc management kept the system in effective operation. Describing his methods, Herbert Stein recalled, "Shultz always operated through a committee system, and he was the most wonderful manager of a committee you can imagine because he brought everyone into the act, made sure that everybody had an opportunity to say his piece, did not dominate the discussion, but always made sure we came to a conclusion."[6] Working sixteen hours a day, Shultz tended the domestic economy, oversaw international monetary matters, chaired the COLC, supervised East-West trade and agricultural policy, and continued to serve as Nixon's liaison with labor. It was a killing job, made more so in 1973 by disappointment. Shultz was so distressed by Nixon's decision in June to impose Freeze II that he tried to resign. Watergate, meanwhile, slowly eroded his morale.

In November 1973, two weeks after the Saturday Night Massacre, Shultz wrote Nixon to advise an entirely new Watergate defense. "Spirits within the Administration are at a low because no counterattack has been launched and the President is being battered and drained day after day by new charges of wrongdoing," Shultz wrote. Officials who wanted to speak up for the president "have been reluctant to do so because they simply do not have the facts . . . They are afraid that the rug will be pulled out from under them by new charges under the next day's headlines." Shultz proposed full disclosure of all the facts — the "good and the bad" — so that a

---

[5] *RN: Memoirs* (1978), 972.

[6] Stein interview in Hargrove and Morely, eds., *The President and the Council of Economic Advisers* (1984), 370.

beefed-up defense team could make the case for Nixon with confidence.[7] It apparently did not occur to the ever-loyal Shultz that the reason why Nixon might be sitting on the evidence was that he was guilty.

By 1974 Shultz — "the best of all the Nixon men" in the words of William Safire — was weary.[8] The constant partisan sniping at the administration's economic policies, seldom helpful and often unfair, added to the strain. At a hearing in February 1974, Senator Proxmire attacked the administration for lack of economic leadership. Shultz stunned the room by banging on the table and venting his pent-up anger. "I do not see why you just keep saying, saying, saying something that is not true," Shultz said. "In the stampede for action, action, do something . . . , you find yourself doing the wrong thing." Accusations of Proxmire's kind were "gross misinterpretations and I'm frankly tired of it."[9] By the time Shultz announced his intention on March 14, 1974, to leave the government in May, no one in Washington was surprised. Shultz had stayed as long as he did only to avoid the appearance of deserting a sinking presidency.[10] "It leaves a gaping void," said Herbert Stein, who was himself making plans to join the faculty of the University of Virginia. Shultz "has been as near to an indispensable man on the domestic side as any man can be."[11] Stein foresaw the consequence. "There will be," he said, "a kind of shuffling around and a grabbing for authority and influence."[12]

"Somebody has to be the straw boss," Shultz said.[13] The main contender to succeed Shultz as the administration's economic czar was Roy Ash, the big campaign contributor and systems analyst, who had been president of Litton Industries and chairman of the President's Advisory Council on Executive Reorganization before Nixon brought him on board in November 1972 to head OMB. Though Nixon respected Ash, Congress never liked him. Under his leadership, Litton Industries had come to epitomize everything that was wrong with the military-industrial complex. In 1970, it was Ash who walked the halls of Washington to obtain for Litton lucrative naval contracts to build ships. When Litton botched the job, it

---

[7] Shultz for President, Nov. 5, 1973, President's Handwriting file, POF.
[8] *New York Times*, Sept. 17, 1973, 33.
[9] Ibid., Feb. 14, 1974, 41.
[10] Ibid., Feb. 22, 1974, 41.
[11] *Wall Street Journal*, Mar. 15, 1974, 3.
[12] Ibid., Apr. 4, 1974, 1.
[13] Ibid., May 6, 1974, 3.

was Ash who billed the Navy for hundreds of millions in disputed cost overruns to stave off Litton's collapse.[14] Key Congressmen objected to the appointment of Ash to OMB because it seemed hardly appropriate for one who had supped in this fashion at the public trough to become its guardian, especially since decisions at OMB could affect Litton's claims against the Navy.[15] It did not help Ash either that, once in office, he became identified with Nixon's policy of executive impoundments or that he was more com-fortable with flow charts than with people. One White House insider de-scribed a meeting with Ash as akin to "sitting in a room with some chilled liver."[16]

Ash was a management expert who did not know how to manage. Shultz led because he had mastered his own ambition and could subordi-nate personal conviction for the sake of an effective consensus. Ash's ambi-tion was so intense that he turned rivals into victims. Toward the end of Shultz's tenure, Ash found a symbolic way to demonstrate his growing clout with the president and to knock Shultz himself down a peg or two. Shultz had submitted a request to OMB for an increase in the Treasury's annual budget. Twice Ash rejected his full request, and twice Shultz appealed to the president. Though finally the sum at issue amounted to less than $40 million, Nixon signaled the imminence of a new order when early in January 1974 he upheld Ash.[17] The day after Shultz announced in March 1974 that he would soon resign, Ash wrote Nixon positioning himself to inherit Shultz's policy role.[18]

Ash saw his main rival for dominance as William Simon, one reason Ash seized on Simon's mistakes during the energy crisis to promote himself with the president. Nixon was no admirer of Simon either, but now that Shultz was leaving, he had little choice except to appoint Simon as treasury

---

[14] *New Republic* (Jan. 20, 1973), 5–7; Richard J. Whalen, "Welfare Capitalism," *News-week* (Feb. 19, 1973), 11–12; Gerald R. Rosen, "The Growing Power of Roy Ash," *Dun's* (May 1974), 67 ff.; Les Aspin, "The Litton Ship Fiasco," *Nation* (Dec. 11, 1972), 581–584.

[15] Congress retaliated against the Ash appointment by requiring Senate confirmation of OMB directors, including the incumbent. Ash was not safe until May 23, 1973, when the House failed to override Nixon's veto of the bill. *Congressional Quarterly Weekly Report,* various issues, May and June 1973.

[16] Quoted in John Herbers, "The Other Presidency," *New York Times Magazine* (Mar. 3, 1974), 17.

[17] Ash for President, Dec. 13, 1973, Ash Memos for President's file, SMOF: Ash; Ash for President, Jan. 4, 1974, President's Handwriting file, POF.

[18] Ash for President, Mar. 15, 1974, Ash Memos for President's file, SMOF: Ash.

secretary. Simon was, after all, Shultz's own choice and a favorite of the Congress that might soon try Nixon for high crimes and misdemeanors. Though Nixon took his time making the appointment, Simon assumed that he would be taking over both the treasury and Shultz's role as economic straw boss. Ash had other ideas.

Early in April 1974, flying back with Nixon from Key Biscayne on Air Force One, Ash wrote the description for Simon's job. Simon would be secretary of the treasury only. He would not chair the 8:00 A.M. White House meeting of economic officials, as Shultz had done, and would be barred entirely from Haig's 8:30 A.M. meeting of the White House staff. On the plane that night, Nixon apparently agreed that the boss would be Ash himself. The next day Ash leaked choice details of these arrangements to the press, guaranteeing Simon's undying enmity. "Bill and I didn't get along too well," Ash recalled, understating the matter.[19]

Before Simon's appointment to the treasury, Ash became worried that Simon might use the Troika as a base from which to contend for authority. Writing Haig, Ash cited history to show that more often than not, someone other than the secretary of the treasury had chaired the Troika. Soon Ash was maneuvering to downgrade the Troika or eliminate it altogether.[20] Meanwhile, on April 14, 1974, with "all the pageantry of a White House laundry pickup," the deputy press secretary announced at his regular 11:00 A.M. briefing that Nixon would appoint Simon as treasury secretary. Neither Nixon nor Simon was present.[21] Simon scored one against Ash, however, by retrieving for himself the chairmanship of the Troika. "I still have some concern," Ash complained to Haig, "about the apparent attempt (internally and externally) to portray the Troika . . . as the key economic policy mechanism."[22] When Haig, no doubt exasperated, told Ash that the agreement on Air Force One was now "inoperative," Ash hinted at resigning.[23] On May 20, 1974, with nothing really settled, Ash attempted to force the issue by writing Haig to propose the appointment of an assistant to the president for economic policy, with a staff, an office in the West Wing, and

---

[19] Oral History Interview, Roy Ash, Jan. 13, 1988, Nixon Project. Ash does not say Nixon approved him for straw boss on their trip, but that is the clear inference of Ash's subsequent memos to Haig; New York Times, Apr. 3, 1974, 1.

[20] Ash to Haig. Apr. 8, 1974, Ash Chrono file, SMOF: Ash; Ash to Haig, Apr. 11, 1974.

[21] Time (Apr. 29, 1974), 91; New York Times, Apr. 18, 1974, 1. Quote from Time.

[22] Ash to Haig, Apr. 18, 1974, Ash Chrono file, SMOF: Ash.

[23] Ibid., May 14, 1974, Ash Chrono file, SMOF: Ash.

authority to coordinate economic policy throughout the government. This assistant would chair the 8:00 A.M. economic meeting. The Troika would go.[24] Ash was too modest to suggest who the assistant might be.

By now the Ash-Simon feud had become something of a scandal, and Nixon could not afford another scandal. On May 25, the White House suddenly announced the appointment of Kenneth Rush as counselor to the president for economic policy.[25] Rush had been one of Nixon's teachers in law school at Duke and then went on to Union Carbide, where he rose to be president of the company. "Ken Rush," Nixon said on one of the White House tapes. "He's a fine lawyer, utterly clean."[26] Nixon had appointed Rush ambassador to West Germany, deputy secretary of defense, and deputy secretary of state. Why he appointed him to head his fractious crew of economic officials was not entirely clear. Described as a "non-irritating non-economist," Rush would not attempt to fill Shultz's role as czar.[27] His job was to mediate between Ash and Simon and keep the peace between them. But Rush was not the solution either. As Stein said later, Rush "was then in competition with these other two people, Simon and Ash, and . . . he didn't have the standing in the field."[28]

Disorder, therefore, characterized the organization of economic policy during Nixon's last months. A team so divided by conflicting ambitions seemed bound to divide on policy too, and occasionally it did. Remarkably, the group shared a common analysis of the nation's economic problems and favored rather similar remedies. It is even likely that had there been no Watergate and perfect harmony, policy would have been just as it was. The important question, therefore, was not who made the policy but whether it was the right one.

## II

Nixon's economists never had a harder task than to frame policy for the year 1974. Shultz and Stein, who had been along for the ride from the beginning, had wrestled with inflation and recession, seen the administration adopt and reject different fiscal and monetary policies, agonized along with

[24] Ibid., May 20, 1974, Ash Chrono file, SMOF: Ash.
[25] *Pub Paps RN 1974*, 452–456.
[26] *New York Times*, May 28, 1974, 57.
[27] Ibid., May 25, 1974, 1.
[28] Stein interview in Kenneth W. Thompson, ed., *The Nixon Presidency* (1987), 173.

the president on the political implications of his decisions. Looking back, they were filled with regret for past error. They realized that the administration had prematurely abandoned steady-as-you-go in 1971. They knew that the consequences had been the mistake of controls and the disaster of overexpansive fiscal and monetary policies. With one last chance to steer a proper course and under the very shadow of Watergate, Nixon's men and even Nixon himself were now determined to pursue sound policy regardless of politics. There was something heroic in this posture and something sad, since the policy ultimately chosen was the wrong one.

In January 1974, as the administration was putting the finishing touches on the forecast and the game plan, conditions could hardly have been more bleak. Gas lines were snaking through the streets of cities. Auto sales were plunging. Unemployment had risen from 4.8 percent to 5.2 percent in a month, the largest one-month increase in four years.[29] The stock market was in the midst of a crash as severe as the one that began in 1929; and housing had slumped. According to Gallup, only 7 percent of the public expected prosperity in January 1974, compared to 40 percent in January 1973.[30] One reason for declining consumer confidence was Watergate. If Congress wanted to revive the economy, MIT economist Franco Modigliani testified, it must impeach Nixon, a matter he deemed "of great urgency."[31]

The administration leaned slightly toward economic optimism. Rising oil prices would cut into consumer spending only temporarily, the CEA reasoned, and healthy business investment, plus a rebound in housing, might prevent real trouble. But the president's economists were wracked by more than the usual doubts. They knew that they might be wrong, that the economy could crash. On January 20, 1974, the eve of final decisions, Stein wrote Nixon describing the "excruciating question of policy" that the administration was now facing. "Should we now turn to pumping up the economy . . . and increase the risk that inflation doesn't slow down?" Stein asked. "Or should we stick with a 'steady' policy, risking a longer slowdown, . . . [but] cutting the rate of inflation?" Stein concluded, "The reason the question is excruciating is that six months from now we will probably wish we had taken the anti-depression role and three years from now we will probably wish we had taken the anti-inflation role."[32]

---

[29] *New York Times*, Feb. 2, 1974, 1.

[30] Ibid., Jan. 3, 1974, 35; *Gallup Poll* (vol. 1, 1978), 225.

[31] "The 1974 Economic Report of the President," Joint Economic Committee, hearings (1974), 648.

[32] Stein for President, Jan. 20, 1974, (CF) FI file, WHSF.

The next day, at a meeting of the Troika, Nixon himself had to make the choice between Stein's two options — to be "the Puritanical enemy of inflation" or the "champion of the fight against worldwide depression." In the past Nixon would run any risk to reduce the threat of a recession, and he had good reasons to avoid one now. A congressional election loomed in November, and hard times would cancel any chance he himself had for a political comeback. Nonetheless, Nixon shared the preference of his advisers for caution. Perhaps in his weakened state he lacked the will to resist them. Perhaps he so regretted the past mistakes of his economic management that he was determined for once to do the right thing. Whatever the reason, he told the Troika, "we should not make a decision to pump up the economy at this time," and we should postpone proposals to stimulate the economy "until there is more evidence of need for them." Nixon concluded by reflecting "on the difficulty which everybody shares, including his advisers, in foretelling what is going to happen. He indicated his strong preference for a steady policy which would pay off best in the long run even though it might miss certain opportunities for political advantage in the short run."[33]

The administration's forecast that year was only slightly more optimistic than the consensus. Real output would fall during the winter, flatten during the next two quarters, then turn up in the fall. For the year, real output would increase 1 percent, and unemployment would average 5.5 percent. Inflation would keep rising at the current rate of 8.5 percent for a few more months and then gradually subside to 5 percent, the underlying rate. In short, the economy would dodge a recession, unemployment would rise only a little, and the rate of inflation would fall back to something resembling normalcy.[34] A strong believer in confidence, Nixon tried to pump it up in his State of the Union message. "There will be no recession in the United States of America," the president stated flatly.[35] Telling a reporter that the president was right, Stein muttered under his breath, "But we're sure gonna have the littlest boom you ever saw."[36]

---

[33] Stein for President's file, Jan. 21, 1974, Memos for President's file, POF.

[34] On the forecast, *CEA Annual Report 1974*, 21–35; Stein's testimony in "The 1974 Economic Report of the President," 2–45; for price expectations, which were not spelled out in the Annual Report, T3 to T2, March 31, 1974, CEA-Troika Memos file, SMOF: Stein. Using the GNP deflator, Troika 2 forecast inflation falling from 8.2 percent in the first quarter to 5.3 percent in the second.

[35] *Pub Paps RN 1974*, 48.

[36] *New York Times*, Feb. 14, 1974, 41.

Persuaded that recession was not the problem, the administration made inflation the target. It followed that fiscal and monetary policy should remain essentially neutral, neither pumping up demand nor squeezing it, but letting the forces already at work foster a moderate recovery while inflation subsided. The budget should run approximately the same small full-employment surplus that it ran in 1973, and the money supply should grow by 5.5 percent, approximately the same rate as the year before.[37] In other words, in its last days the administration took a sentimental journey back to steady-as-you-go. Correct in 1971, it was a mistake for 1974.

Democratic economists differed from the Republicans only slightly. Democrats predicted a recession or said that one had already begun, but their dispute with the administration on the point was mainly semantic. They preferred a dose of stimulus to steady-as-you-go, but not a dose large enough to make much difference.[38] As Arthur Okun would confess, practically everybody was wrong that year, "whether Keynesians or monetarists, builders of large econometric models, devotees of leading indicators, or gazers into crystal balls."[39] Whatever their school or party, economists simply lacked the conceptual tools to comprehend the contractionary forces now at work. For a generation they had analyzed the economy in terms of aggregate demand. Push the demand peddle, and output would expand; hit the brakes, and it would slow down. But the primary force destabilizing the economy in 1974 was not demand. It was supply.

First had come the shortage in food supply, now oil. As consumers bid up the price of these scarce commodities, the general inflation rate climbed into double figures. But this was an inflation unlike those of the recent past. Inflations caused by excess demand initially increase output. Inflations caused by supply shocks initially contract it. Failure to appreciate the recessionary consequences of the supply shocks led to the errors of 1974. If Nixon had foreseen how deeply the food shock, the oil shock, and the decontrol of prices in April 1974, which acted like a supply shock, would

[37] The policy was described in *CEA Annual Report 1974*, chap. 2; and in Stein's testimony in "The 1974 Economic Report of the President." Though the Council actually set the monetary target in terms of M2 (8 percent), James Tobin explained that this translated into a M1 of 5.6 percent. James Tobin, "Monetary Policy in 1974 and Beyond," *Brookings Papers on Economic Activity* (no. 1, 1974), 218–232, esp. 219.

[38] See testimony of Okun and Tobin in "The 1974 Economic Report of the President," 584–589, 691–695.

[39] Arthur Okun, "A Postmortem of the 1974 Recession," *Brookings Papers on Economic Activity* (no. 1, 1975), 207–221.

cut into demand, he would have certainly chosen to pump it up. By making the fight against inflation the object of policy, Nixon helped bring on the Great Recession.

## III

To be sure, inflation in 1974 far exceeded the administration's expectation. Instead of stabilizing at 8.5 percent and then declining, consumer price inflation increased from the end of 1973 through the end of 1974 by a truly extraordinary 12 percent. Assuming an underlying inflation rate of 5 percent, the economist Robert J. Gordon accounted for the additional 7 percent inflation this way: 2 percent from excess demand generated during the boom, 1 percent from the lingering food shock, 2 percent from the oil shock, and 2 percent from the shock of decontrolling prices.[40] Price shocks not only caused inflation to escalate; they caused output to decline beginning in the first quarter and to go into free fall in the fourth. Because its impact was concentrated in so short a time, the oil shock did the most damage.

Because of the oil shortage, the economy suffered simultaneous inflation and recession. Energy prices in the United States rose at the astronomical annual rate of 72 percent in the winter quarter of 1974 — the principal reason why the quarterly CPI rose at the rate of 14 percent, a U.S. peacetime record.[41] As a result of higher oil prices, consumers spent nearly $40 billion more on energy in 1974 and less on most everything else, in particular autos, depressing output. The beneficiaries of increased expenditures for oil were oil countries and oil companies, which were slow to spend their additional income, worsening the contraction. As auto and other energy-related firms laid off workers, income and aggregate demand fell further,

---

[40] Robert J. Gordon, "Postwar Macroeconomics: The Evolution of Events and Ideas," in Martin Feldstein, ed., *The American Economy in Transition* (1980), 101–162; see 151.

[41] *Consumer Price Index*, March 1974. Estimates of the effects of the energy shock on the inflation rate varied widely. Two different econometric models reported by George Perry estimated that oil price inflation contributed 1.7 percent to the GNP deflator (1973:4–1975:1) in one case, 3.3 percent in the other. Perry's own model placed the contribution at 3.55 percent (1973:4–1974:4) for the consumption deflator. Perry, "The United States," 90, 96–97. Blinder computed "the implied direct effect of energy prices on the overall level of the deflator for personal consumption expenditures" in 1974 at under 2 percent. Blinder, *Economic Policy and the Great Stagflation*, 85. Eckstein's model estimated the price impact of higher oil prices on the implicit deflator at approximately 3 percent. I follow Gordon's estimate in "Postwar Macroeconomics," *Economic Policy and the Great Stagflation*, 85.

and the U.S. economy found itself caught in a downward spiral. During the first quarter of 1974, real GNP fell at an annual rate of 3.9 percent.[42]

Nonetheless, as the second quarter began, the administration continued to believe there would be no recession. It had reasons. After the oil embargo ended in March, businessmen decided that inflation was more likely than recession. Corporations increased their raw material inventories to beat higher prices later, spent more on plant and equipment, and continued to hoard labor. True, consumer spending was still falling, and real GNP that spring would continue to decline, but prosperity seemed to be right around the corner. Writing Nixon in April, the CEA said that "after mid-year the economy will be expanding at approximately a normal pace." With oil and food prices tapering off, the Council said, general inflation would soon slow down, too.[43] Economists outside the government agreed.

Energy prices did decelerate, as the administration said they would — from 72 percent in the first quarter, to 20 percent in the second, 6 percent in the third, and 0 percent in the fourth quarter[44] — but the effects of the oil shock lingered. Higher energy prices raised fuel costs for businesses, forcing up the prices they charged. Rising prices cut into the income of workers, prompting demands for catch-up wage settlements. These effects of the oil shock gradually percolated through the economy, driving the price level long after the shock had ended and further contracting output. Indeed the oil shock by itself was responsible for approximately half the decline in real output that occurred in 1974 and 1975.[45] In his extensive study of this episode, Otto Eckstein concluded, "The energy crisis was the single largest cause of the Great Recession."[46]

As soon as the embargo lifted, the oil shortage ended. It was Nixon's bad luck that almost immediately another shock began, one whose full effects would also go unrecognized until it was over. That was the shock of decontrol.

---

[42] For a brief overview, Arthur M. Okun, "A Postmortem of the 1974 Recession," 207–221. See also, CEA Annual Report 1975, chap. 2; Blinder, Economic Policy and the Great Stagflation (1979), 37; Perry, "The United States," 88–95.

[43] Gary L. Seevers for President, Apr. 17, 1974, (CF) BE 5-4, WHSF. For real GNP, Wyatt C. Wells, Economist in an Uncertain World: Arthur Burns and the Federal Reserve, 1970–78 (1994), Appendix 2, 259.

[44] Inflation rates for Consumer Price Index compiled with assistance of Guillermo Rabiela.

[45] Blinder, Economic Policy and the Great Stagflation, 86; Eckstein, The Great Recession, 117.

[46] Eckstein, The Great Recession, 124.

## IV

At the beginning of 1974, the administration faced a hard decision on price and wage controls. The Economic Stabilization Act, which authorized controls, was due to expire on April 30. As Shultz said, controls were like Vietnam. "Once the troops are in, it's hard to get them out."[47] The administration had in fact adopted a strategy on controls much like the strategy of Vietnamization. After Phase IV began in August 1973, John Dunlop, director of the COLC, gradually withdrew from controls sector by sector — first fertilizers, then cement, furniture, rubber. The point was to avoid a sudden one-time price explosion. On occasion Dunlop extracted from an industry a promise of good price behavior in exchange for early decontrol. In the most publicized of these agreements, Dunlop granted automakers release from controls in December 1973 in return for a pledge to hold the price line on 1974 models through the next year, barring the unforeseen.[48] As late as February 1974, 57 percent of the items on the Wholesale Price Index still remained under price control regulations.[49]

Though the White House despised controls, Congress was expected to extend them. Rather than incur the political costs of opposing any extension of controls, the administration proposed limited legislation that would continue controls on petroleum and health care only and retain the COLC as no more than a watchdog to monitor sensitive prices. In this form, said Senator Proxmire, the COLC would have "about the force of a butterfly's hiccup."[50] Who, for example, would enforce Dunlop's decontrol agreements? In March 1974 a Senate committee rejected the administration bill 15 to 0.[51]

By then the mood of Congress had shifted against controls in any form, mainly because business and labor united to kill them. Business had originally backed controls to help restrain wages. Now 90 percent of the membership of the National Association of Manufacturers opposed controls.[52] Explaining the reason, the *Wall Street Journal* observed, "They murder

[47] *Boston Globe*, Feb. 4, 1974, 1.

[48] Dunlop testimony, "Oversight on Economic Stabilization," Banking, Housing and Urban Affairs, Senate hearings (1974), 445–507; *New York Times*, Dec. 16, 1973, IV, 2; quote, *New York Times*, May 9, 1974, 1.

[49] "Oversight on Economic Stabilization," Senate hearings, 456.

[50] Shultz's testimony, "Oversight on Economic Stabilization," Senate hearings, 413–444; Proxmire's remark, 433.

[51] *Congressional Quarterly Weekly Reports* (Mar. 30, 1974), 843.

[52] "Oversight on Economic Stabilization," Senate hearings, 321.

profits."[53] By contrast, George Meany of the AFL-CIO charged that, regardless of the freeze or phase, Nixon had never given labor a fair shake.[54] Meany's strong stand helped swing liberal Democrats, otherwise the natural constituency for controls, against them. With a glance at the soaring CPI, Democratic Senator Alan Cranston of California remarked, "Things can't get much worse under the free market."[55] He was wrong about that.

In the White House, John Dunlop of the COLC was the only one disposed to controls and worried about their threatened demise. A labor economist unencumbered by classical theory, Dunlop was willing to use the power of the federal government in ways that Stein, Shultz, and Nixon would rather not. But Shultz and Stein were preparing to depart, and Nixon had lost his grip. Exploiting the absence of a strong hand, Dunlop set out on his own to save as much of controls as he could. First, Dunlop lobbied hard for the administration's bill.[56] Neither Stein nor Shultz helped him. Next he went beyond the administration's position by calling for continued controls on construction and authority to enforce his decontrol agreements with industry.[57] Congress ignored him. Two weeks later, warning that decontrol would unleash "suppressed inflation," Dunlop repudiated the administration's rosy forecast on prices. "I don't want to be associated in any way with predictions for the second half of the year," he said.[58]

Despite Dunlop's impassioned pleas, Congress let controls lapse on April 30, 1974.[59] Within days, the Ford Motor Co. thumbed its nose at John Dunlop by repudiating its December agreement and raising prices on 1974 models by an average of $110 a car.[60] Except for Dunlop, the White House was unconcerned. Deceleration of food and oil prices, Stein told Nixon, would likely offset any price increases resulting from decontrol.[61] A modest "bulge," perhaps, but no explosion.[62] The administration was still forecasting an inflation rate down to 5.5 percent by the end of the year.

---

[53] Wall Street Journal, Mar. 4, 1974, 1.
[54] "Economic Stabilization Act — 1974," Banking, Housing, and Urban Affairs, Senate hearings (1974), 256–267.
[55] New York Times, Mar. 31, 1974, III, 1.
[56] Ibid., Mar. 27, 1974, 25.
[57] Ibid., Mar. 28, 1974, 46.
[58] Dunlop testimony, "Oversight on Economic Stabilization," Senate hearings, 445–507; New York Times, Dec. 16, 1973, IV, 2; quote, New York Times, May 9, 1974, 64.
[59] New York Times, Apr. 28, 1974, 1; Apr. 28, 1974, IV, 3; May 2, 1974, 1; May 10, 1974, 47.
[60] Ibid., May 9, 1974, 64.
[61] Stein for President, Apr. 11, 1974, Agency Files, Memo for the President file, SMOF: Stein.
[62] Wall Street Journal, Mar. 28, 1974, 1.

Decontrol caused the inflation rate to take off again. Free of the stabilization ethic that had disciplined price behavior under controls, corporations rushed to raise prices to restore profit margins. Subsequent studies indicated that prices snapped back even higher than they would have if there had been no controls.[63] The resulting one-time burst of nonfood, nonenergy prices was not a supply shock but acted like one, a "surrogate supply shock," in the phrase of economist Alan Blinder.[64] Nonfood, nonenergy prices, which had risen by only 6.3 percent (annual rate) under controls during the first quarter of 1974, accelerated to 14.2 percent in the second and 15.1 percent in the third, before slowing to a 9.7 percent rate in the fourth.[65] Therefore, during the very quarters when food and energy prices were subsiding, decontrol caused other prices to rise substantially, keeping the inflation rate in double digits. For the year, nonfood, nonenergy prices contributed an additional two percentage points to the CPI, with the by now familiar contractionary consequences for demand.[66] The problem was not that prices were decontrolled. Decontrol was long overdue. The problem was the failure to foresee the effects of higher prices on output and to counteract these effects with expansive policy. At least for Nixon, price controls, the economic mistake he most regretted, were now behind him.

## V

Steady-as-you-go ironically exacerbated the destabilizing consequences of the food, oil, and decontrol shocks. At the beginning of the year, the administration had laid out a neutral policy intended to permit inflation to subside. When the various shocks propelled inflation unexpectedly upward, one consequence was to transform apparently neutral fiscal and monetary policies into instruments of recession. Steady-as-you-go successfully prevented policy from making inflation worse, but few in or out of the

---

[63] Blinder believes that once controls ended, firms moved to reestablish the pattern of relative prices distorted by controls. Since prices were rigid downward, some prices had to rise higher than they otherwise would to reestablish the normal price hierarchy. Blinder's econometric exercise finds that the price level was "ultimately about 1% higher on account of controls." Blinder, *Economic Policy and the Great Stagflation*, 114–116, 128.

[64] Blinder, *Economic Policy and the Great Stagflation*, 266.

[65] Inflation rates compiled from Consumer Price Index.

[66] Gordon, "Postwar Macroeconomics," 115; Blinder concluded, "during the year from February 1974 to February 1975, the termination of controls added 2.6 percentage points to the inflation rate." Blinder, *Economic Policy and the Great Stagflation*, 128.

administration would have accepted the resulting cost in unemployment, if they had known it in advance.

The administration's fiscal policy kept tax rates where they were and expenditures under restraint. The result, the administration believed, would be a small full-employment surplus in calendar 1974 of approximately the same size as in 1973. Accelerating inflation had the unexpected consequence of shifting fiscal policy from neutral to sharply restrictive. Inflation raised money income so rapidly that taxpayers were forced into higher brackets, increasing federal revenues far beyond expectation. As a result, the full-employment surplus, targeted at a modest $6 billion in calendar 1974, actually climbed to $25.4 billion. This huge swing in the surplus, the essence of unsteadiness, placed a substantial fiscal drag on demand at precisely the wrong time.[67]

The administration did not know it was the wrong time. "There's a very, very low likelihood of a recession," Roy Ash said in the spring, even as the GNP was declining for the second consecutive quarter.[68] Indeed, in the very midst of recession and swelling revenues, the administration lifted the banner of austerity and fought congressional efforts to overspend the president's budget. Inflation, the White House continued to believe, was the main threat facing the nation. Accused of expediency and cynicism, Nixon and his men sought a measure of redemption for Watergate by preaching harsh economic truths and summoning the people to virtue. They called their new faith "the old-time religion."[69]

The tent preachers of the revival confessed their own sins, Stein especially testifying to his regret that the administration had abandoned steady-as-you-go back in 1971.[70] They pointed the finger of blame as well at the people themselves because the people demanded the benefits of government but shirked the costs.[71] In this view, sacrifice alone offered the hope of economic salvation. Recovery, Nixon said, would require "harsh medicine — budgetary restraint, no tax cut, tight money," as it happened, the worst possible prescription for what really ailed the economy. "I wish I could tell you there is a way out of the present inflation without such

---

[67] CEA Annual Report 1974, 29–31. For full-employment surpluses and deficits, I use revised figures in CEA Annual Report 1976, 55.

[68] *New York Times*, Apr. 10, 1974, 51.

[69] *Wall Street Journal*, July 19, 1973, 1, 18.

[70] *New York Times*, July 20, 1974, 36.

[71] Ibid., July 10, 1974, 1.

measures," the president said, "but there is not."[72] If austerity proved to be good politics, it would be because the people agreed with the administration, not because the administration curried favor with the people.

The administration knew, of course, that neither past monetary and fiscal policies nor a profligate public was entirely to blame for the current inflation. Supply shocks in food and oil had played their role too. "My devotion to the old-time religion is not so great as to make me believe that M1 or the full-employment budget deficit determines the amount of rainfall in the Russian wheat lands, the location of Peruvian anchovies or the decisions of the oil cartel," Stein said. Once the supply shocks faded, he believed, prices would drift back toward the underlying inflation rate — if policymakers let them. The point of steady-as-you-go was to avoid reaccelerating prices later and to begin draining away the inflationary residue now. Said Stein, "while Providence may average out the wheat and the anchovies and the oil, there seems to be no Providence to average out our fiscal and monetary policies and to prevent persistent sins and errors there. That we shall have to do for ourselves."[73]

Fundamentalists in the revival even challenged the orthodoxy of the full-employment budget. Shultz had persuaded Nixon to adopt this budget as the administration's chief conceptual tool for fiscal policy back in 1970. In May 1974, Shultz was gone, and William Simon was secretary of the treasury. At a congressional hearing, Simon was asked whether he intended to use the full-employment budget as his fiscal guide. Simon replied, "No, sir."[74] An old-fashioned conservative, Simon believed that the only budget that mattered was the actual budget and that, regardless of circumstances, actual budget deficits were inflationary. In February 1974, Nixon had submitted a budget for the fiscal year beginning July 1 that projected a full-employment surplus of $8 billion but an actual deficit of $10 billion. From the day Simon took over the Treasury in May, his goal was to get rid of this deficit by slashing $10 billion from expenditures.[75] Given the recession, that was folly.

In this, as in so many other matters, Roy Ash resisted William Simon.

[72] *Pub Paps RN 1974*, 455.

[73] Remarks before the International Monetary Conference, June 6, 1974, President's Handwriting file, POF.

[74] "Long-Term Economic Growth," Joint Economic Committee, hearings (1974), 347.

[75] Simon's views summarized in Stein for President, May 6, 1974, (CF) BE 5, WHSF. Simon detailed where cuts could be made in Simon to Rush, July 8, 1974, SMOF: Rush.

Ash knew that Nixon would reject cuts in defense; that Congress would reject cuts in domestic programs; and that, given the economic uncertainties, this was not the time to cut federal spending anyway.[76] Very quickly the intramural squabble over the deficit broke into public view. Speaking in Cleveland, Ash stated that the budget had already been cut to the bone. "Simply baying at the moon won't do the job," Ash said.[77] Simon retorted, "We have to get back to the old-time religion of spending what we take in in this country . . . I don't consider this baying at the moon."[78] Stein, taking up middle ground, called for a $5 billion expenditure cut — more than Ash wanted but less than Simon. Stein called this "yipping at the moon."[79] It was in the midst of this dispute that Nixon brought in Kenneth Rush.

The debate tilted a bit in Simon's favor when fifty-four mainly conservative senators from both parties sent Nixon a letter on June 19, 1974, demanding expenditure cuts to balance the budget in FY 75.[80] Nixon needed these senators if he was going to survive a trial on impeachment charges in the Senate. At a Quadriad meeting of June 24, the president approved cosmetic budget cuts of $5 billion, along with "an innocuous" presidential announcement of the decision.[81] There was not much the administration could really do about the deficit except to oppose the $6 billion tax cut that congressional Democrats had been promoting since spring and to veto overgenerous appropriations, which Nixon became more reluctant to do as his position deteriorated.[82] Nevertheless, till the last day, the old-time religion remained the foundation of Nixon's fiscal policy.

## VI

A religious revival of sorts was also underway at the Fed. Reminding Stein of an Old Testament prophet, Burns told the graduating class of Illinois College in May that America had become a nation "of impulse shoppers, of

[76] Ash views summarized in Stein for President, May 6, 1974. In June, Ash wrote Nixon summarizing budget prospects for FY 75: "Therefore the deficit would probably be $5-10 billion. This would be within the range of good fiscal policy." Ash for President, June 18, 1974, attached to Ash for President, June 19, 1974, Ash Memos for President's File, SMOF: Ash.
[77] Wall Street Journal, May 13, 1974, 2.
[78] New York Times, May 28, 1974, 55.
[79] Time (June 10, 1974), 73.
[80] Letter from fifty-four Senators to President, June 19, 1974, (CF) FI, WHSF.
[81] Stein for President, June 21, 1974, (CF) FI, WHSF; for Nixon's announcement, Pub Paps RN 1974, 544–545.
[82] Business Week (Aug. 3, 1974), 15.

gadget buyers," of undisciplined citizens who had come "to depend less and less on their own initiative and more and more on the government." The result was budget deficits and inflation, "the most dangerous ailment of our time." Said Burns, "I do not exaggerate in saying that the ultimate consequence of inflation could well be a significant decline of economic and political freedom of the American people."[83] In the battle against inflation Burns was finally ready to stand and deliver. "Because weak governments could not cope with the problem of inflation," he told the FOMC, "the task had become the inevitable responsibility of central banks."[84]

The Fed agreed with the White House, as the new year began, that there would be no recession in 1974. Inflation was the problem. Indeed, Burns endorsed the policy of "moderate restraint" favored by the administration, setting the target for M1 growth at 5.25 percent and intending to hold it steady, like the good monetarist that Milton Friedman had always hoped he would be.[85]

If Burns had heeded Friedman during Nixon's first term, the economy would have been better off. In 1974 monetarism did not work. High inflation was the reason, as economists James Tobin and Franco Modigliani understood at the time. If, as predicted, GNP in current dollars rose in 1974 by 8 percent mainly because of inflation, the public would need a lot more money to conduct the same volume of transactions. But money growth at a steady 5.5 percent rate would not keep pace with 8 percent growth in dollar GNP. In other words, M1 only appeared to be growing steadily; money relative to GNP was actually declining and had been declining since early 1973. Burns thought he was following a neutral monetary policy that would promote economic stability. In fact, reduction of the real money supply could only mean rising interest rates and falling output.[86] This view of monetary policy attracted little attention until the wholly unanticipated credit crunch that gripped the economy in the spring of 1974.

When business turned bullish after the end of the oil embargo, corpora-

---

[83] Burns, "The Menace of Inflation," May 26, 1974, Inflation — White Paper file, SMOF: Stein.

[84] FOMC minutes, Mar. 19, 1974, 139.

[85] Ibid., 153.

[86] Franco Modigliani, "The 1974 Report of the President's Council of Economic Advisers: A Critique of Past and Prospective Policies," *The American Economic Review* (Sept. 1974), 544–557, esp. pp. 554–556; James Tobin, "Monetary Policy and Beyond," *Brookings Papers on Economic Activity* (no. 1, 1974), 219–232; Franco Modigliani and Lucas Papademos, "Targets for Monetary Policy in the Coming Year," *Brookings Papers on Economic Activity* (no. 1, 1975), 141–163.

tions began borrowing to buy up new materials and to expand plant and equipment. Because money was a lot tighter than Burns believed, the pressure for new business loans sent interest rates climbing very steeply very fast—the prime rate rising from 8.75 percent in early March to 10.25 percent in April. To meet the demand of corporate customers for more credit, the banks had to sell CDs at rates of return so high that weaker banks might have trouble turning them over. Scarce credit, rising rates, and shaky banks created severe tension in financial markets.[87] On April 22, 1974, Burns responded with a news conference to address the "veritable explosion of business loans." The message he delivered was mixed. The Fed would stick to the path of supplying money at a "moderate" rate, Burns said, but would also respect its "obligation of being a lender of last resort." In other words, if a bank got in trouble, the Fed would bail it out. "There need be no fear of a credit crunch," Burns said.[88]

On May 10, 1974, the Franklin National Bank, the nation's twentieth largest, signaled that it was in trouble by canceling its quarterly dividend, the first time a major bank had skipped a dividend since the 1930s. On Wall Street, rumors spread that if the Franklin failed, another half dozen banks would go down too, with potentially dreadful consequences for the whole economy. On Monday, May 12, the Fed quelled the incipient panic by announcing that it would extend the necessary loans to bail out the Franklin.[89] Burns himself was so shaken by the episode that he briefly relaxed the pressure on money.[90] By July he was back on course. That month the prime rate climbed to 12 percent, the highest in history.[91]

High interest rates took their usual high toll on housing. At the beginning of the year, when interest rates sagged and deposits were flowing into thrift institutions, mortgage funds became plentiful, and housing held its own. In the spring, when market interest rates rose above the ceiling that thrifts were permitted to pay, deposits flowed out, and housing starts plummeted. Running at an annual rate of 1.6 million in January, housing starts

---

[87] *New York Times*, Apr. 7, 1974, III, 1; May 5, III, 1; *Business Week* (May 11, 1974), 34; (May 18, 1974), 19.

[88] Excerpts from Burns's press conference in *U.S. News and World Report* (May 6, 1974), 70.

[89] *Business Week* (May 18, 1974), 22–23; Burns's efforts also to assist Real Estate Investment Trusts, cattle feeders, airlines, and electrical utilities are discussed in Wells, *Economist in an Uncertain World*, 139–144.

[90] FOMC minutes, May 21, 1974, 48–49.

[91] *New York Times*, July 4, 1974, 25.

fell below 900,000 in December. This decline, the most pronounced since World War II, was one of the main reasons for the severity of the recession and an unintended consequence of keeping money growth apparently steady but declining in real terms.[92]

The reputation of monetarism declined too in 1974. The policy of keeping money growing close to target proved inappropriate for supply shocks and contributed to the recessionary debacle. Arthur Okun found the performance of his monetarist colleagues puzzling. "If M1 had been growing at a zero rate with inflation at 4 percent, monetarists would generally have been very bearish about real GNP. It is not clear why 6 percent M1 growth and 10 percent inflation did not make them equivalently bearish."[93] In 1974, like everyone else, monetarists were fogged in by novel circumstances and blinded to what was happening.

When interest rates turned down again in August, the cause was not easier money but loss of business confidence, with a consequent shrinking of loan demand. Burns by now realized that the economy had fallen into a recession, but he regarded it as mild and still considered inflation the greater danger. At the August meeting of the Fed's Open Market Committee, the Fed's chief staff economist finally recognized that negative real money growth had been stifling the economy.[94] Burns paid the warning no heed. Stubbornly, he held to the policy of restraint through the fall and into the winter, though money growth fell short of the target and output was plunging. Herbert Stein stated the general view in the spring of 1975 when he said that the Fed was "squeezing the economy to death."[95]

What should policy have been in 1974? Policymakers had not expected recession and therefore geared policy to slow inflation. If they could have foretold the future, they would have primed the pump to cushion the crash. As Stein said later, "Of course, we did not at all foresee that the unemployment rate was going to rise to 9%. If we had foreseen that, we would probably have backed off some."[96] That is, policymakers would have tried to accommodate the price effects of supply shocks instead of resisting them. If the Fed had ignored monetarist prescriptions and attempted to steady short-term interest rates instead of the money supply, M1 would have

---

[92] CEA *Annual Report 1975*, 41, 295.
[93] Okun, "A Postmortem on the 1974 Recession," 220.
[94] FOMC minutes, Aug. 20, 1974, 17.
[95] Stein quoted in Wells, *Economist in an Uncertain World*, 150.
[96] Hargrove and Morley, *President and the Council of Economic Advisers*, 401.

grown by an estimated 11 percent from mid-1973 to mid-1974, approximately twice the actual rate.[97] One study concluded that if the government had added a $20 billion tax cut early in 1974 to a policy of holding down short-term rates, the resulting stimulus might have restored normal growth by the middle quarters of 1974 and "have avoided any decline in GNP thereafter."[98] The cost in inflation would have been an eventual price level perhaps 6 percent higher than the actual case.[99] In other words, to counter the effects of a supply shock, the correct formula was a one-time spike in the money supply equal to a one-time spike in prices, with a tax cut thrown in. To escape or moderate the Great Recession, most economists would have been willing to pay the price in higher inflation.

But not all economists. A minority argued that if policy had accommodated the supply shocks by pumping up demand, inflation would have been worse than the economic models at the time estimated, and unemployment would have been only temporarily reduced. Business and labor would conclude from the effort to accommodate that the government would never accept recessions and cast aside all restraint in setting prices and demanding wages. In the wake of the accelerating inflation bound to follow, the public would demand countermeasures to slow prices, initiating another recession. The real choice, then, as one economist put it, "is not between inflation and unemployment but between unemployment now and unemployment later."[100] Maybe so. The only thing known for certain is that the actual policy followed—steady-as-you-go—facilitated the Great Recession.

## VII

Because of Watergate, Nixon would not be around when the bottom fell out of the economy. The battle for the survival of his presidency shifted decisively against him on April 30, 1974, when he responded after a fashion to

---

[97] Eckstein, *Great Recession*, 81–87.

[98] George Perry, "Policy Alternatives for 1974," *Brookings Papers on Economic Activity* (no. 1, 1975), 222–245; quote, 234. Perry's conclusion here is more optimistic than his own model, whose results he calls "too gloomy."

[99] Blinder, *Economic Policy and the Great Recession*, 192–193. Blinder's inflation estimate is based on a case not quite the same as Eckstein's but is close enough to make his price calculation appropriate here.

[100] For discussion of this point, William Poole, "Monetary Policy during the Recession," *Brookings Papers on Economic Activity* (no. 1, 1975), 123–139, quote 125; and Blinder, *Economic Policy and the Great Stagflation*, 104–105.

a subpoena from the House Judiciary Committee by releasing 2,000 heavily edited pages of transcribed Watergate tapes. On television the night before, Nixon said that though the words might be ambiguous, the transcripts would nonetheless prove him innocent of the charge that he had participated in the Watergate cover-up.[101] But lawyers found in the transcripts evidence of indictable offenses, while the public recoiled from the image they conveyed of a president "foul-mouthed, conniving, amoral."[102] Instead of burying Watergate as Nixon hoped, the transcripts destroyed the remnants of his authority. Senate Republican leader Hugh Scott denounced the president's conversations as "deplorable . . . shabby." House Republican leader John Rhodes, long a staunch Nixonian, said that among the options Nixon must now consider was his resignation.[103]

In June 1974, while his defense team fought off efforts of the House Judiciary Committee and the special prosecutor to obtain more of his taped conversations, Nixon sought escape and vindication abroad. In Egypt at midmonth President Sādāt greeted Nixon effusively, and 300,000 cheered as the two leaders rode in an open car along a seven-mile route to Cairo.[104] On Nixon's return to Washington, Charles Colson further implicated him in crime by stating in court that he, Colson, had attempted to ruin Daniel Ellsberg, leaker of the Pentagon Papers, on orders of the president.[105] At the end of June, Nixon took flight to Moscow for a summit with Brezhnev, who gave him a warm reception and toasted "the cardinal turn" in United States–USSR relations since Nixon's first visit in 1972.[106] Two weeks later, back in Washington, Nixon absorbed more punishing blows. The Judiciary Committee exposed distortions in the White House version of the transcribed tapes released in April. The Senate Watergate Committee charged that Nixon's friend Bebe Rebozo had funneled laundered campaign contributions for Nixon's personal use, including purchase of a pair of platinum-and-diamond earrings that the president gave Mrs. Nixon on her birthday. And a jury convicted John Ehrlichman for his role in the burglary of the office of Ellsberg's psychiatrist.[107] Standing deathwatch at the White House,

---

[101] *Pub Paps RN 1974*, 389–397.
[102] *Time* (May 20, 1974), 15.
[103] Ibid., 24–25.
[104] Ibid., (June 24, 1974), 14.
[105] *New York Times*, June 22, 1974, 1.
[106] *Newsweek* (July 8, 1974), 18–25.
[107] Ibid., (July 22, 1974), 14–18, 48; and various issues of *New York Times*. See also Bob Woodward and Carl Bernstein, *The Final Days* (1976), chaps. 18, 20.

reporters portrayed a president paralyzed by Watergate and no longer capable of governing.

In fact, with no more foreign trips scheduled, Nixon sought refuge from Watergate by holding meetings on the economy. Amid the bad political news of the second week of July, he met with top advisers to reaffirm his tough line on congressional spending,[108] presided over a cabinet meeting devoted entirely to the subject of inflation, and spent two and a half hours with twenty-five business leaders and economists to discuss economic issues.[109] One businessman said afterward, "I went away with a sense that there is still a government."[110] It was more of the same through the rest of the month. On July 16, John Doar, chief counsel for the House Judiciary Committee, presented his draft articles of impeachment. Three days later in San Clemente, Nixon met with Kenneth Rush and Herbert Stein to discuss whether the time had come for the Fed to ease.[111] On July 23, three key Southern conservatives killed Nixon's chances in the Judiciary Committee by announcing that they would vote to impeach him.[112] That same day Nixon conferred with thirty-two business leaders, economists, and labor chieftains in still another meeting on economic conditions.[113] On July 24, the Supreme Court dismissed Nixon's claim of executive privilege and ordered him to turn over sixty-four of his taped conversations to Judge Sirica. A day later, Nixon traveled to a Los Angeles hotel to deliver a nationally televised speech on the economy. Outside, picketers carried signs reading, "Jail to the Chief."[114]

Nixon's Los Angeles speech, his last economic testament, was a declaration of steadiness. Inflation was the basic problem confronting America, he said. It's main cause had been the willingness of governments to permit demand for goods and services to exceed their supply. Exceptional circumstances had recently added to the problem: the decline in worldwide grain production, the oil crisis, the industrialized nations all booming at once. These pressures were abating, but their aftereffects would keep prices rising

---

[108] Stein for President's File, July 15, 1974, Memos for President's File, POF.

[109] Notes of cabinet meeting, July 11, 1974, Memos for President's file, POF.

[110] *New York Times*, July 12, 1974, 47.

[111] Stein for President's Files, Aug. 10, 1974, Agency Files — Memos for President, SMOF: Stein (Minutes of Meeting, July 19, 1974).

[112] *RN: Memoirs*, 1050.

[113] *Newsweek* (Aug. 5, 1974), 50.

[114] *New York Times*, July 26, 1974, 1.

for some time. Confronted now with continued inflation on the one hand and slackening output on the other, voices were demanding "some swift spectacular action" — price controls, pump priming, wringing out the economy. Instead, Nixon went on, the administration would hew to the course of cutting federal expenditures, and the Fed would keep on the course of moderate money growth, though interest rates were rising. "The key to fighting inflation, therefore, is steadiness," he said. "The steadiness that accepts the need for hard decisions, for occasional unpleasant statistics and even a measure of sacrifice in the short run in order to ensure stable growth without inflation for the long run, the steadiness that stands fixed against the clamor to take dramatic action just to create an appearance of action, and the kind of steadiness that rejects demagoguery, that rejects gimmickry, and that gives the enormous creative forces of the marketplace in America a chance to work."[115]

These brave words expressed implicit regret for the opportunity lost in the first term and described a policy that, with the best of intentions, was deepening the recession in the second. Of the possibility of recession, Nixon in Los Angeles said nothing. Phoning from retirement to praise the speech, which faithfully reflected the advice he had given for years, George Shultz encouraged the president to "hang in."[116]

Late in July, the Judiciary Committee voted three articles of impeachment, two by large bipartisan majorities. Busy listening to the tapes that the Supreme Court had ordered him to produce for Judge Sirica, Nixon canceled his Quadriad meeting on August 1. On August 5, the White House made public the transcript of a conversation held six days after the Watergate burglary in which Nixon conspired with Haldeman to cover up the crime by using the CIA to call off the investigation of the FBI. That conversation, which finished Richard Nixon, incidentally contained his remark that he didn't "give a shit about the lira," and his dismissal of a recent economic initiative with the words, "There ain't a vote in it."[117] This accidental glimpse into Nixon's political economy confirmed the belief of his critics in its cynicism at a moment when it was not cynical at all.[118]

Nixon informed the nation of his intention to resign in a prime-time

---

[115] *Pub Paps RN 1974*, 606–614.
[116] Steve Bull for President, July 26, 1974, (CF) SP3-213, WHSF.
[117] Transcript reprinted in *New York Times*, Aug. 7, 1974, 47.
[118] See Leonard Silk's commentary in *New York Times*, Aug. 7, 1974, 47.

address on August 8, 1974. He said that quitting was "abhorrent to every instinct in my body" but that he no longer had enough support in Congress to justify prolonging the struggle and immobilizing the government. Reviewing his accomplishments in office, he listed ending the Vietnam war, the opening to China, improved relations with the Arab world, arms agreements with the Soviets, and progress in moving superpower relations from confrontation to cooperation. He boasted of no domestic accomplishment and said of the economy only that "we must press on" toward a goal "we are striving so hard right now to achieve, prosperity without inflation."[119] He did not say that the nation was much further from attaining that goal now than when he first proclaimed it five and a half years before.

## VIII

If there was any consolation for Nixon in his exile, it was that when the crash came, Gerald Ford was president. On the issue of inflation, Ford was a Republican fundamentalist. Speaking as vice president to the New York Economic Club in May 1974, Ford said, "We all have our pet whipping boy when it comes to inflation, but the real culprit today, as it has been, is excessive demand. Double-digit inflation is the result of double-digit increases in money supply and double-digit budget deficits."[120] On August 11, in his first speech as president, Ford labeled inflation "public enemy number one," pledged to reduce federal spending, and accepted the suggestion of the Senate that he convene an economic summit "to develop a unified plan of action to restore stability and prosperity to America."[121]

On September 9, 1974, the first in a series of nine economic summits leading up to the main event took place in the White House. Twenty-seven top academic and business economists joined administration officials, including Ford, to discuss the economy. Many of the big names of the day were there: Friedman, Samuelson, Galbraith, Heller, Okun, Eckstein, McCracken, Richard Cooper of Yale, Herbert Stein of the University of Virginia, and George Shultz of the Bechtel Corporation. It was, in its way, a remarkable meeting. Standing on the edge of the cliff, none there saw the abyss. Output would remain flat or perhaps decline a little during the next

[119] *Pub Paps RN 1974*, 626–629; quote, 629.
[120] *Newsweek* (Aug. 19, 1974), 64.
[121] *Pub Paps Gerald Ford 1974*, 6–13.

year, they said, and unemployment would rise, though not as high as 6.5 percent. Few supported the administration's devotion to the old-time religion of budget cutting, however, and practically every independent economist present wanted Burns to loosen the money supply.[122]

Neither this meeting nor the main economic summit, which passed uneventfully on September 23, had any effect on Ford's thinking. On October 8 he asked Congress for a $5 billion tax *increase* to help balance the budget and unintentionally provoked much mirth by calling on citizens to enlist in a volunteer mobilization against inflation by signing a form in the next day's newspaper and displaying lapel buttons bearing the letters WIN, Whip Inflation Now.[123]

A few weeks later, the economy cratered. In the last quarter of 1974, real GNP declined at an annual rate of 7.7 percent, and in the first quarter of 1975 at a rate of 10 percent. Business spending, which had been supporting the economy, collapsed. Consumer spending, flat through most of the 1974, fell sharply. More than 2.5 million workers lost their jobs from October 1974 through March 1975, and the unemployment rate rose to the near-depression level of 8.7 percent in May.[124] In the entire post–World War II era, only the recession of 1981–1982 would rival this one.

Recognizing at last that recession, not inflation, was really the nation's number-one economic problem, Ford abandoned his proposal to raise taxes and in January 1975 called for Congress to enact a tax cut of $16 billion.[125] Congress approved a $23 billion cut in March, too late to affect the downturn but in time to assist the recovery.[126] Meanwhile, the supply shocks having passed, the inflation rate fell from 12 percent in 1974 to 6 percent in the winter of 1975, close to the underlying rate.[127] In the spring the economy began its slow recovery, so slow that at the end of 1976, unemploy-

---

[122] The Economists Conference on Inflation: Report (vol. 1), Sept. 9, 1974. See especially Okun's summary, 3–5.

[123] *Pub Paps Ford 1974*, 228–238.

[124] *CEA Annual Report 1975*, chap. 2; U.S. Dept. of Commerce, *Survey of Current Business* (Jan. 1975), 1–20; (Apr. 1975), 1; (May, 1975), S-14; Okun, "Postmortem or 1974 Recession," 207–221. Real growth statistics from Wells, *Economist in an Uncertain World* (Appendix 2), 259.

[125] *Pub Paps Ford 1975*, 37–38.

[126] Blinder, *Economic Policy and the Great Stagflation*, 150–152, 155–167.

[127] Wells, *Economist in an Uncertain World* (Appendix 2), 259. For the year, Consumer Price Index rose 7.0 percent.

ment still stood at 7.8 percent, and output continued to lag far behind the economy's productive capacity.[128] The Great Recession was the low point on the roller coaster ride of booms and busts that began in 1969 and lasted into the early 1980s. It was a ride for which Nixon's inconsistent and ill-considered policies deserved no small amount of blame.

---

[128] Blinder, *Economic Policy and the Great Stagflation*, 4.

# CONCLUSION

Nixon took office at the end of the postwar golden age of the American economy. Abroad, the nation had provided creative leadership in an alliance cemented by liberal trade and monetary arrangements. At home, rapid economic growth had spawned unprecedented affluence. Confidence in the ideas of economists was soaring in the mid-1960s, and the business cycle seemed a relic of history. But by 1969, storm warnings were rapidly gathering. With Europe and Japan challenging the nation's commercial supremacy, free trade and Bretton Woods had come under attack. Vietnam and the Great Society were generating budget deficits and excessive money growth, destabilizing the economy. Long-term economic growth would soon slow to a crawl. The business cycle was back, and economists had not only lost the confidence of the public, they had lost confidence in themselves.

The new administration was blind to the coming era of hard times. Looking ahead in 1970 to the next five years and presumably beyond, the Council of Economic Advisers extrapolated from the past to imagine a lush future. But instead of growing at an average annual rate of 2.8 percent, as the CEA expected, productivity slumped to an annual average of 1.1 percent from 1973 through 1979 and remained low for years thereafter.[1] The result would be glacial improvement in living standards and deteriorating public services.[2]

The one economic problem that the first set of Nixon's advisers recognized was inflation. It was not a problem that seemed particularly vexing. Deflate the economy gradually, the president's economists believed, and you could reduce inflation at a politically acceptable cost. Of course, only the president could decide if the political costs were worth it. And the president was skeptical from the start.

Nixon had no firm convictions on economic policy except that pros-

---

[1] CEA Annual Report 1970, 78.
[2] Edward F. Denison, *Trends in American Economic Growth, 1929–1982* (1985), 3; Jeffrey Maddrick, *The End of Affluence* (1995).

perity was essential for winning elections and the necessary precondition for creating the New Majority. Politics, therefore, was the one constant of his policy during the first term. When gradualism cost more in unemployment than his advisers expected and he lost the Congressional election of 1970, Nixon brought in John Connally to rid him of its burden. Together, these two shameless opportunists initiated the New Economic Policy, violating every tenet of the president's past belief but retrieving for him the Economic Issue before the 1972 campaign. By the president's calculus, the political benefits were worth the economic costs. Nixon's economic views, therefore, might be characterized by the phrase *après moi le deluge*.

Politics explained much about the economic policies of Richard Nixon, but it did not explain everything. Nixon retained George Shultz and Herbert Stein as advisers for the duration of his presidency, respected them both, and more often than not took their advice. Shultz and Stein were economists, not politicians, conscientious public servants who made mistakes but tried to do the right thing. Given the stakes, it is a wonder that Nixon adopted their policy of gradualism at the beginning and then stayed with it as long as he did. Of course, if he had been more patient, gradualism eventually would have worked. By the time Nixon abandoned it, nearly everybody in the country except Milton Friedman and George Shultz were urging price and wage restraints along with more expansive policy. Among those succumbing to these temptations were some of the president's key advisers. In the spring of 1971, McCracken suggested wage and price controls; Stein recommended a switch to expansion; and Arthur Burns was urging both. None of these men was unmindful of the political implications of their advice, but each also had the good of the economy at heart. Nixon's political requirements and right policy seemed not in conflict but conveniently to coincide in the New Economic Policy.

To explain economic failure in the Nixon administration, lack of knowledge weighs at least as much as political calculation. Because federal spending accounted for approximately 20 percent of Gross Domestic Product, the government had no choice. It had to have an economic policy. The problem was that economists did not know enough to make economic policy. Stein said later, "Many economists have the view that the economists know the answers; they come into Washington with a little briefcase in which they can look up the answer to any question and if the right answers are not given by the government, it's because something nasty called politics has intruded. That is not the situation at all. Our experience really confirmed how little economists know."[3] Economic officials lacked even good information. Preliminary data on the money supply, business investment, and GNP were unreliable. Estimates of capacity utilization were wildly off the mark. Agricultural statistics were a scandal. Even if the administration had better information, the numberless variables assured that correct forecasts would mainly result from accident. In fact, every one of the administration's annual forecasts was wrong. Because policy hinged on the forecast, the consequences were hardly trivial.

The administration found itself handicapped not only by uncertain information but by inherited assumptions of doubtful utility. The most harmful of these was the definition of full employment. Beginning in the Kennedy administration, economists rather casually assumed that 4 percent unemployment was consistent with stable prices. By 1970, this clearly was no longer so. The recent influx of teenagers and women into the labor force — groups with higher unemployment rates than adult white males — had raised the noninflationary unemployment rate to the vicinity of 5 percent, but the administration began by assuming it could stabilize the economy at 4 percent, establishing an unrealistic standard for successs and dooming gradualism. After his service was over, Stein came to believe that tying policy to some rate of unemployment had been a mistake. "If we look back at it now," Stein said, "not only Nixon but McCracken and I were excessively obsessed with the unemployment problem, and that's probably true of everybody who grew up in the 1930s. We never shook that off."[4] If GNP were growing at an appropriate rate, Stein concluded, accept the accompanying rate of unemployment.[5]

Whatever the target, the principal means for achieving it were fiscal and monetary policies. Here Nixon's economists were done in by the poverty of economic theory. As they well knew, no one could any longer offer a persuasive account of how fiscal policy worked or even if it did, but of course the administration had to have a fiscal policy. Over time it had several. In 1969, the goal of policy was a budget surplus in normal times; in 1970, a balanced full-employment budget; in 1971, a covert full-employment deficit; in 1972, an open full-employment deficit; in 1973, a

[3] Stein interview in Erwin S. Hargrove and Samuel A. Morley, eds., *The President and the Council of Economic Advisers* (1984), 364.

[4] Hargrove and Morley, *President and the Council of Economic Advisers*, 366.

[5] Herbert Stein, "Fiscal Policy: Reflections on the Past Decade," in William Fellner, ed., *AEI Studies on Contemporary Economic Problems* (1976), 82.

balanced full-employment budget once again; and in 1974, at least for William Simon, a balanced actual budget. Conceding defeat in the long quest for a fiscal rule, Herbert Stein wrote a colleague in the spring of 1974, "The Administration is now without any generally-agreed view of the principles by which budget policy should be guided, and relies on ad hoc decisions heavily weighted by what are believed to be political or psychological considerations."[6] At the time, the administration was engaged in a misguided effort to contain federal expenditures amid a sharp decline in output. Nothing better illustrated Stein's point, which was that, after more than five years, the administration was fiscally lost.

Monetary policy suffered its own confusions. William McChesney Martin slammed on the brakes in mid-1969, bringing on a recession. Arthur Burns resumed money growth at a reasonable pace in 1970 and then shifted money into high gear during the first half of 1971. Pointing to easy money, Friedman predicted a rapid recovery from the 1970 recession. When recovery advanced only slowly, monetarism lost authority. After Nixon imposed price controls in August 1971, the Fed committed one of the great blunders of its history in 1972 by printing up money at reckless rates. Urged on by the rogue monetarist in the White House, Burns turned the Fed into the very engine of inflation he dreaded. If policymakers had shown more patience, the brisk recovery that Friedman expected would almost certainly have happened without additional stimulus and in time to reelect Nixon, and much of the ensuing pain would have thereby been avoided. But as subsequent events showed, Friedman was not always the answer either. Burns did precisely what monetarists would have him do through most of 1974, refusing to lean against a steep rise in interest rates by printing more money. The result was the Great Recession. Monetarism limped out of these years in no better shape than Keynesianism.

Consistency also eluded the administration in foreign economic policy. Nixon became interested in America's relative decline in the world economy only after Peter Peterson and especially John Connally apprised him of the domestic implications, economic and political. Facing stiff foreign competition, a trade deficit, and speculative attacks on the overvalued dollar, Connally declared war on the rest of the trading world in August 1971. The point was to create jobs for Americans and recruit the unions for the New Majority by vastly expanding U.S. exports. Connally's atavistic

---

[6] Stein for Rush, June 10, 1974, (CF) BE 4 file, WHSF.

mercantilism produced one real accomplishment. He brought the dollar closer to its real value through devaluation and hastened the end of a Bretton Woods system that had become dysfunctional. Though Connally's commercial offensive appealed to Nixon's intuitive nationalism, the president finally rejected the risks in November 1971 and called it off. Thereafter George Shultz resumed normal diplomacy, seeking to promote freer trade through multilateral negotiations. Shultz did force the rest of the trading world to accept floating exchange rates in March 1973. The results, Shultz expected, would be to liberate domestic policy from international constraints and promote the smooth adjustment of currencies. Volatile swings in the dollar's value during the first months of the new regime demonstrated the limits of this theory too.

While the Nixon administration did not acquit itself particularly well in economic matters, the Democrats would probably have done little better. The country would have avoided Connally's mercantilist adventures, and Bretton Woods would not have died in quite the brutal manner it did. The country might even have avoided the absurdities of mandatory price-wage controls, because the Democrats would have resorted to some kind of voluntary guideposts in 1970 and been without an irresponsible opposition demanding stronger measures later. But the Democrats and their economists were no less limited than the Republicans by lack of knowledge, faulty assumptions, and flawed theories. If anything, they might have pumped up the economy even more in 1971–1972 and taken it on a bumpier ride. During the supply shock episode of 1973–1974, the policy proposals of the Democrats were only marginally better than Nixon's actual policies and would have failed to prevent the Great Recession. As for the nation's deteriorating global position and slowing economic growth, the Democrats had no answers either. It is even possible that the economy would have looked much as it did in mid-1974 no matter who was in power. Since Nixon happened to be in the White House, the failures belonged to him.

The economic events of Nixon's presidency had enduring historical consequences. In the late 1960s, still living under the shadow of the Depression, the public feared unemployment above all and relied on activist government to prevent business cycles and improve living standards. Nixon's mismanagement demonstrated the dangers of activism and exposed the inadequacies of the usual tools of policy. Indeed, government error significantly contributed to both the Great Inflation and the Great Recession of 1973–1975, genuine traumas that fundamentally reordered the economic hopes and fears of the American people. Inflation replaced unemployment as the chief economic terror. Boom and bust undermined faith in activist policy. The business system rather than government now seemed the source of prosperity, and the health of business became a matter of growing public solicitude. The poor economic performance of the Nixon years and the economic anxieties that resulted fed a growing mood of conservatism that culminated but did not end with the election of Ronald Reagon in 1980. Tight money, disciplined domestic expenditures, and pro-market pro-business policies became the new economic orthodoxy. The final irony of Nixon's political economy was this: The conservative economic policies that he so abruptly embraced in his shortened second term would eventually triumph in no small measure because of the manifest failure of his own stewardship.

# INDEX